Benjamin L. Farjeion

Joshua Marvel

Benjamin L. Farjeion

Joshua Marvel

ISBN/EAN: 9783337733100

Printed in Europe, USA, Canada, Australia, Japan

Cover: Foto ©ninafisch / pixelio.de

More available books at **www.hansebooks.com**

JOSHUA MARVEL.

BY

B. L. FARJEON,

AUTHOR OF "GRIF."

NEW YORK:
HARPER & BROTHERS, PUBLISHERS,
FRANKLIN SQUARE.
1872.

JOSHUA MARVEL.

CHAPTER I.

CONCERNING CERTAIN FAMILY CONVERSATIONS AND THEIR RESULT.

IN the parish of Stepney, in the county of Middlesex, there lived, amidst the hundreds of thousands of human bees who throng that overcrowded locality, a family composed of four persons — mother, father, and two children, boy and girl — who owned the surprising name of Marvel. They had lived in their hive for goodness knows how many years. The father's father had lived there and died there; the father had been married from there; and the children had been born there. The bees in the locality, who elbowed each other and trod upon each other's toes, were poor and common bees, and did not make much honey. Some of them made just enough to live upon; and a good many of them, now and then, ran a little short. The consequence was, that they could not store any honey for a rainy day, and were compelled to labor and toil right through the year, in cold weather and in warm weather, in sunshine and in rain. In which respect they were worse off than other bees we know of that work in the summer and make themselves cosey in the winter.

The bees in the neighborhood being common and poor, it was natural that the neighborhood itself should partake of the character of its inhabitants. But, common and poor as it was, it was not too common nor too poor for love to dwell in it. Love did reside there; not only in the hive of the Marvels, but in hundreds of other hives, tenanted by the humblest of humble bees.

George Marvel had married for love; and, lest the reader should suppose that the contract was one-sided, it may be as well to mention that George Marvel's wife had also married for love. They fell in love in the usual way, and they married in the usual way; and, happy and satisfied with each other, they did not mar their enjoyment of the then present by thinking of the sharp stones which, from the very circumstances of their position, were pretty sure to dot the road of their future lives. There are many such simple couples in the world who believe that the future is carpeted with velvet grass, with the sun always shining upon it, and who find themselves all too soon stumbling over a dark and rocky thoroughfare.

It was not long before the Marvels came to the end of *their* little bit of carpet sunshine; yet, when they got upon the sharp stones, they contrived by industry and management to keep their feet. George Marvel was a wood-turner by trade, and earned on an average about thirty-two shillings a week. What with a little new furniture now and then, and a little harmless enjoyment now and then, and a few articles of necessary clothing now and then, and the usual breakfasts, dinners, and teas, with a little bit of supper now and then, the thirty-two shillings a week were pretty well and pretty fully employed. So well and so fully were those weekly shillings employed, that it was often a very puzzling matter to solve that problem which millions of human atoms are studying at this present moment, and which consists in endeavoring to make both ends meet. That they did contrive, however, to make both ends meet (not, of course, without the tugging and stretching always employed in the process), was satisfactorily demonstrated by the fact that the family were respected and esteemed by their neighbors, and that they owed no man a shilling. Not even the baker; for they sent for their loaves, and paid for them across the counter. By that

5

they almost always received an extra piece to make up weight; and such extra pieces are of importance in a family. Not even the butcher; for Mrs. Marvel did her own marketing, and found it far cheaper to select her own joints, which you may be sure never had too much bone in them. Not even the cat's-meat man; for the farthing a day laid out with that tradesman was faithfully paid in presence of the carroty-haired cat (who ever heard of a cat with auburn hair?) who sat the while with eager appetite, looking with hungry eyes at the skewer upon which hung her modicum of the flesh of horse.

Mrs. Marvel was a pale but not sad woman, who had no ambition in life worthy of being called one, save the ambition of making both ends meet, and of being able, although Stepney was not liable to floods, to keep the heads of her family above water. But, because Mrs. Marvel had no ambition, that was no reason why Mr. Marvel should not have any. Not that he could have defined precisely what it was if he had been asked; but that the constant difficulties which cropped up in the constant attempt to solve the problem (which has something perpetual in its nature) of making both ends meet, made him fretful. This fretfulness had found vent in speech day after day for many years; so that Joshua Marvel, the wood-turner's heir, had from his infancy upwards been in the habit of hearing what a miserable thing it was to be poor, and what a miserable thing it was to be cooped up, as George Marvel expressed it, and what a miserable thing it was to live until one's hair turned gray without ever having had a start in the world. It is not to be wondered at, therefore, that Joshua Marvel had gathered slowly in his mind the determination not to be a wood-turner all his life, but to start in the world for himself, and try to be something better; never for one moment thinking there was the most remote possibility of his ever being any thing worse. When, in the course of certain family discussions and conversations, this determination became known, it did not receive discouragement from the head of the family, although the tender-hearted mother cried by the hour together, and could not for the life of her see why Joshua should not be satisfied to do as his father had done before him.

"And what is that, mother?" Mr. Marvel would ask. "What have I done before him? I've been wood-turning all my life before him — that's what I've been doing; and I shall go on wood-turning, I suppose, till my dying day, when I can't wood-turn any more. Why, it might be yesterday that I started as a boy to learn wood-turning. The first day I used the lathe I dreamed that I had cut my thumb off; and I woke up with a curious sensation in my jaw which has haunted me ever since like a ghost. That was before I knew you, mother. And now it is to-day, and I'm wood-turning still; and — How many white hairs did you pull out of my head last night, Sarah?"

"Fourteen," replied Sarah; "and you owe me a farthing."

"Fourteen," said Mr. Marvel, quietly repudiating the liability, which arose from an existing arrangement that Sarah should have a farthing for every dozen white hairs she pulled out of his head; "and next week it will be forty, perhaps; and the week after four hundred."

"White hairs will come, father," said Mrs. Marvel; "we must all get 'em when we're old enough."

"I'm not old enough," grumbled Mr. Marvel.

"And I don't see, father," continued Mrs. Marvel, "what the fourteen white hairs Sarah pulled out of your head has to do with Joshua."

"Of course you don't see, mother," said Mr. Marvel, who had a contempt for a woman's argument; "you're not supposed to see, being a woman; but I do see; and what I say is, wood-turning brings on white hairs quicker than any thing else."

"Grandfather was a wood-turner," remarked Mrs. Marvel, "and he didn't have white hairs until he was quite old."

"Well, he was lucky — that's all I can say; but, for all that, Josh isn't going to be a wood-turner, unless he's set his mind upon it."

"I won't be a wood-turner, father," said Joshua.

"All right, Josh," said Mr. Marvel; "you sha'n't."

From this it will be seen that the voice maternal was weak and impotent when opposed to the voice paternal. But Mrs. Marvel, although by no means a strong-minded woman, had a will of her own, and a quiet unobtrusive way of working which often achieved a victory without inflicting humiliation. She did not like the idea of her boy leading an idle life; she had an intuitive conviction that Joshua would come to no good if he had nothing to do. She argued the matter with her good man, and never introduced the subject at an improper time. The consequence was, that her first moves were crowned with success.

"If Joshua won't be a wood-turner, father," she said.

"Which he won't," asserted her husband.

"Which he won't, as you say," Mrs. Marvel replied, like a sensible woman. "If he won't be a wood-turner, he must be something. Now he must be something, father — mustn't he?"

This being spoken in the form of a question, left the decision with Mr. Marvel; and he said, as if the remark originated with himself, —

"Yes; he must be something."

And with that admission Mrs. Marvel rested content for a little while; but not for long. She soon returned to the attack; and asked her husband what Joshua should be. Now this puzzled Mr. Marvel; and he could not see any way out of the difficulty, except by remarking that the boy would make up his mind one of these fine days. But "these fine days" — in which people, especially boys, make up their minds — are remarkably like angels' visits; and the calendar of our lives often comes to an end without one of them being marked upon the record. To all outward appearance, this was likely to be the case with Joshua; and the task of making up his mind seemed to be so tardy in its accomplishment, that George Marvel himself began to grow perplexed as to the future groove of his son and heir; for Joshua kept himself mentally very much to himself. Vague wishes and desires he had; but they had not yet shaped themselves in his mind — which was most likely the reason why they had not found expression.

Meanwhile Mrs. Marvel was not idle. She saw her husband's perplexity, and rejoiced at it. Her great desire was to see Joshua settled down to a trade, whether it were wood-turning or any other. Wood-turning she would have preferred; but, failing that, some other trade which would fix him at home; for with that keen perception which mothers only possess with regard to their children — a perception which springs from the maternal intellect alone, and which is born of a mother's watchful anxious love — she felt that her son's desires, unknown even to himself, might possibly lead him to be a wanderer from her world, the parish of Stepney, in which she was content to live and die. In that beehive she had been born; in that beehive she had experienced calm happiness and wholesome trouble; and in that beehive she wished to close her eyes; and to see her children's faces smiling upon her, when her time came to say good-by to the world of which she knew so little. With all a woman's cunning, with all a woman's love, she devoted herself to the task of weaning the mind of her favorite child from the restless aspirations which might drive him from her side.

"Until Joshua makes up his mind what he is going to be, father," she said one night at candle-time, "it's a pity he should remain idle. Idleness isn't a good thing for a boy."

"Idleness isn't a good thing for boy or man," said Mr. Marvel, converting his wife's remark into an original expression of opinion by the addition of the last two words. "But I don't see what we are to do, mother."

"Suppose I get him a situation — as an errand-boy, perhaps — until he makes up his mind."

"I'm agreeable," said Mr. Marvel, "if Josh is."

But Josh was not agreeable. Many a fruitless journey did Mrs. Marvel make, trudging here and trudging there; and many an application did she answer in person to written announcements in shop-windows of "Errand-boy wanted." Joshua would not accept any of the situations she obtained for him. She got him one at a watchmaker's; no, he would not go to a watchmaker's: at a saddler's; no, he would not go to a saddler's: at a bootmaker's, at a tailor's; no, nor that, nor that. Still she persevered, appearing to gain fresh courage from every rebuff. As for Joshua, he was beginning to grow wearied of her assiduity. He was resolved not to go to any trade, but being of a very affectionate nature he desired to please his mother, and at the same time to convince her that it was of no use for her to worry him any longer. So he set her, what he considered to be an impossible task; he told her that he was determined not to go anywhere except to a printing-office. He felt assured that she would never be able to get him within the sacred precincts of such an establishment. And even if she did, there was something more noble, something more distinguished and grander, in printing than in bootmaking, or tailoring, or watchmaking, or wood-turning. There was a fascinating mystery about it; he had seen watchmakers, and tailors, and cobblers working, but he had never seen the inside of a printing-office. Neither had any of his boy-friends. He had been told, too, that there was an act of parliament which allowed printers to wear swords in the streets. That was a fine thing. How all the neighbors would stare when they saw him walking through the narrow streets of Stepney with a sword at his side! Joshua had some sense of humor; and he chuckled to himself at the impossible task he had set his mother.

He was therefore considerably astonished one day, when Mrs. Marvel told him she had obtained a situation for him as errand-boy in a newspaper-office. Did ever a woman fail, except from physical or mental prostration, in the accomplishment of a certain thing upon which she has set her mind?

And if, in working for the accomplishment of the desired result, she brings to her aid an unselfish, unwearying love, *then* did ever a woman fail? At all events Mrs. Marvel did not. After much labor, fortune befriended her; and she heard that an errand-boy was wanted at a certain printing-office where a weekly newspaper was printed. Thither she hurried, and soon found herself in a small dark office, in which the master sat.

He treated her in the most off-hand manner. Yes, he wanted an errand-boy. Was he sharp, intelligent, willing? Oh, her son! Very well. Let him come to-morrow. Wages, four shillings a week. Time, from eight to eight. An hour to dinner, half an hour to tea. Good-morning.

Thus the matter was settled, and Joshua engaged. Mrs. Marvel went home rejoicing.

With fear and trembling, a little pleased and a good deal dismayed, Joshua made his way the next morning to the printing-office. Groping along a dark passage he came to a door on which the word "Office" was dimly discernible. The freshness of youthful paint had departed from the word; the letters were faded, and they appeared to be waiting to be quite rubbed out with a kind of jaded resignation. In response to the sharply-uttered "Come in!" Joshua opened the door, and entered the room. The person he saw before him had such a dissipated appearance, that any stranger would have been warranted in coming to the conclusion that he had not been in bed for a fortnight. The room was full of papers, very dusty and very dirty; and looked as if, from the day it was built, it had not found time to wash itself. Scarcely raising his eyes from a long slip of paper, upon which he was making a number of complicated marks, the occupant of the room said,—

"It's of no use bothering me. I sha'n't have any copy ready for half an hour. Hallo! Who are you?"

"The new errand-boy, sir," said Joshua, humbly.

"Oh, very well! Take this proof up stairs and sweep the composing-room; then come down and clean the street-door plate. Cut along! Look sharp!"

Looking as sharp as he could, Joshua walked up stairs, and found himself in the composing-room of the establishment. A number of men and boys, decorated with aprons with large bibs, were playing a mysterious game with hundreds and thousands of small pieces of lead, which they clicked with marvellous rapidity, but without any apparent meaning, against an instrument they held in their hands. He looked in vain for the swords which he had heard printers were allowed to wear, and he was covered with confusion at finding himself in the midst of so large an assemblage, who one and all appeared as if they were playing on a number of pianos without any tune in them. Going up to a youth whose head, covered with a profusion of red hair, looked as if it were in a blaze, Joshua asked to whom he should give the proof. "To Snooks," was the prompt reply. For which piece of information he received a slap on the side of his head from some person in authority; who, taking the proof from Joshua, directed him to sweep up the room. While performing this task he surveyed the scene before him. There were sixteen men and four boys at work. All the men had the same dissipated look that he had observed upon the countenance of the master. Their faces, otherwise, were very clean; but the tips of the right-hand fore-finger and thumb of each were black with dirt, caused by the types which they picked up with those extremities from the boxes before them. Not a word was spoken, except what appeared to have reference to the business, and the conversation proceeded somewhat in this wise. One of the workmen, walking to a slab of iron placed in the middle of the room, took therefrom a sheet of manuscript, and looking at it negligently, shouted,—

"Number three!"

Another voice at the end of the room cried out,—

"Awful Collision!"

Joshua stopped in the midst of his sweeping, and waited for the shock. But as none came, he proceeded with his work, and thought that the second speaker was crazy. In the mean time the dialogue continued.

Speaker number one: "End a break."

Speaker number two: "All right," with a growl.

Speaker number one: "What type?"

Speaker number two, with another growl: "Minion."

At the word "minion," which Joshua considered was a term expressive of any thing but respect, he expected speaker number one would walk up to speaker number two, and punch his head. Instead of which the insulted individual went into his corner again, and re-commenced playing his tuneless piano in the meekest possible manner. The overseer then going to a part of the room where long rows of type were placed in detached pieces, asked,—

"How long will this Dreadful Suicide be before it's finished?"

"Done in five minutes, sir," was the reply, in a cheerful voice.

"Who's on the Inquest?" asked the overseer.

"I am, sir."

"Be quick and get it finished; you've been long enough over it. Now, then, how long is this Chancery Court to remain open?"

"Close it up in two minutes, sir."

And Joshua gazed with a kind of wonder at the individual who spoke, as if it were as easy to close the Court of Chancery as to close his hand.

It was the day on which the paper was sent to press; the publishing hour was three o'clock in the afternoon; and as the work was behindhand, everybody was very busy. In the centre of the room was a large iron slab, and at one time the hammering and beating on this slab were terrific. Two or three excited individuals, with mallets and iron sticks in their hands, advanced towards the type, which was laid upon the slab, with the apparent intention of smashing it to pieces. They commenced to do this with such extraordinary earnestness, that Joshua was on the point of rushing down stairs to the master to inform him that his property was being wantonly destroyed; but as the other workmen appeared to regard the proceeding as quite a matter of course, Joshua checked himself and thought it would perhaps be as well for him to say nothing about it. The overseer also continued to issue his strange orders; and during a slight cessation in the hammering, he peremptorily ordered the workman to "lock up that Escaped Lunatic, and be quick about it." At another time he gave directions to lay the Female in Disguise on the stone (meaning the iron slab), to unlock the Old Bailey, and to correct the Chancellor's Budget. Joshua grew perfectly bewildered. The information that there was an Escaped Lunatic in the room did not so much astonish as alarm him; but as to the Female in Disguise he could not identify her, and he waited in amazement to see what disguise she wore and where she would be brought from; at the same time entertaining the idea that to lay any female upon a stone was a decidedly improper proceeding. While in this state of mental perplexity, the overseer cried out,—

"Now, then, who has the Female in Disguise in hand?"

"I have, sir," a voice replied.

"Bring it here, then," ordered the overseer, "and finish the corrections on the stone."

"All right, sir."

Joshua started and looked round to catch a sight of the female; in his agitation he stumbled against a workman who held a column of type in his arms. The type fell to the ground, and was smashed into thousands of pieces. In an instant the whole office was in confusion.

"You've done it this time, youngster," the workman said in dismay, looking at the scattered type on the floor.

Joshua did not exactly know what it was he had done, but felt that it must be something very bad. He soon received practical proof of the extent of the mischief, for the master, rushing into the room, kicked him down stairs, and told him to go about his business. Which Joshua did in a state of much bewilderment.

Thus all the good intentions of Mrs. Marvel were frustrated. Joshua declared he would not take another situation, and his father sided with him and encouraged him. It must be confessed that Mr. Marvel continued to have his perplexities about Joshua's career, but to have openly admitted them would have been handing the victory to his wife. So he kept them to himself, and thus maintained his supremacy as master of the house. Many of his neighbors were henpecked, and he used to laugh at them. It would not have done to have given them the chance to laugh at him. Therefore, as time progressed, Mrs. Marvel's protests were less and less frequently made, and Joshua's determination not to be a wood-turner gathering strength month after month, it soon came to be recognized as quite a settled thing that he was to start in life for himself, and was not to do as his father had done before him. Pending his decision, Joshua continued to lead an idle life. But he was by no means viciously inclined; and much of his time was spent in the cultivation of two innocent amusements, both of which served him in good stead in the singular future which was in store for him. One of these amusements was a passion for music. He knew nothing of musical notation, and played entirely by ear; yet he managed to extract sweet melody from a second-hand accordion, of which, after long and patient saving of half pence and pence, he had become the happy purchaser. The other of his tastes grew out of a boyish love. How he acquired it will be recounted in the following chapters.

CHAPTER II.

SHOWING HOW A PASSION FOR PUNCH AND JUDY MAY LEAD TO DISASTROUS CONSEQUENCES.

THERE are few boys in the world who are without their boy-friends whom they worship, or by whom they are worshipped, with a love far surpassing in its unselfishness the love of maturer years. The memory of times that are gone is too often blurred by waves of sorrowful circumstance. Our lives are like old pictures; the canvas grows wrinkled, and the accumulated dust of years lies heavy upon figures that once were bright and fair. But neither dust nor wrinkles can obliterate the memory of the love we bore to the boy-friend with whom we used to wander in fields that were greener, beneath skies that were bluer, than fields and skies are now.

Cannot you and I remember the time when we used to stroll into the country with our boy-friend, and, with arms thrown lovingly around each other's neck, indulge in day-dreams not the less sweet because they were never to be realized? And how, when we had built our castles, and were looking at them in the clouds, with our hearts filled with joyful fancies, we wandered in silence down the shady lane, sweet with the scent of the flowering May that shut us out from view on either side; and across the field with its luxuriant grass up to our ankles with everywhere the daisy peeping out to watch us as we passed; and over the heath where the golden gorse was blushing with joy; and down the narrow path to the well which shrunk from public observation at the bottom of a flight of cool stone steps, hewn out by the monks of a cloister which should have been hard by, but wasn't, having been destroyed in a bloody battle which took place once upon a time?

Not many such experiences as these did Joshua and his boy-friend enjoy; for our Damon's Pythias, whose proper name was Daniel Taylor, was lame, with both his legs so badly broken that, had he lived unto the age of Methuselah and been fed upon the fat of the land, those props of his body would have been as useless to him all through his long life as if they had been blades of the tenderest grass.

The Taylors had three children: Susan, Ellen, and Daniel. Ellen and Daniel were twins, and when they were born Susan was ten years old. The worldly circumstances of the Taylors were no better than those of their neighbors; indeed, if any thing, they were a little worse than those of many around them. The parents, therefore, could not afford to keep a nurse-girl, and it was fortunate for them that they had provided one in the person of their elder daughter, and had allowed her to grow to a suitable age before they ventured to bring other children into the world. Fortunate as it was for the parents, it was most unfortunate for Daniel; for before he and his other half were born, Susan Taylor had contracted a passion almost insane in its intensity, to which her only brother was doomed to be a victim. That passion was a love for the British drama, as represented in Punch and Judy. All Susan's ambitions and yearnings were centred in the show; and it was not to be supposed that she would allow so small a matter as twins to interfere with her absorbing passion. How the liking for Punch and Judy had grown with her years and strengthened with her strength, it is not necessary here to trace. The fact remains, and is sufficient for the tragedy of poor Daniel's life. Squeezed to their sister's breast, Daniel and Ellen were condemned to take long journeys after Punch and Judy, and to be nursed at street-corners by a girl who had eyes and mind for nothing but the *dramatis personæ* of that time-honored play. In her scrambles after the show she often wandered a long way from home, and tore her dress, and jammed her bonnet, and muddied her stockings, and knocked her boots out at the toes, and got herself generally into a disreputable condition. But in presence of the glories of Punch and Judy, which were to her ever fresh and ever bright, such discomforts sank into absolute insignificance. All paltry considerations were forgotten in the absorbing interest with which she watched the extraordinary career of the hero of the drama. She was insensible to the cuffs and remarks of the acting-manager who went round for contributions, which the on-lookers were solicited to drop into a tin plate or a greasy cap. He naturally resented Susan's presence at the exhibition, for she had never been known to contribute the smallest piece of copper towards the expenses. But neither his cuffs nor his resentful language had any effect upon Susan, who, in her utter disregard of all adverse circumstances, proved herself to be an ardent and conscientious admirer of the British drama. As a consequence of her peregrinations, she often found herself in strange neighborhoods, and did not know her way home. The anxiety she caused her mother, who was naturally proud of her twins, almost maddened that poor woman. She used to run about the neighborhood of Stepney, wringing her hands and declaring that her twins were kidnapped. At first the neighbors were in the habit of sympathizing with her, and of making anxious inquiries of one another concerning the children; but when, after some months of such uneventful excitement, they found that Susan and her twins were always brought home in good condition as regarded their limbs — although in a very disgraceful condition as regarded their personal appearance: but dirt counted for nothing in such a case of excited expectation —

their ardor cooled, and they withheld their sympathy from the distressed mother. Indeed, they looked upon themselves in the light of injured individuals, because something really calamitous had not happened to the children. At length Susan became such a nuisance — not only at home, but at many police-stations, where she was popularly known as "that dirty girl again, with the twins"—that the mother was recommended to lock her up. Despairing of being able to cure her daughter of her Punch-and-Judy mania by any other means, the mother locked her up with her infant charges in a room on the first floor.

That was a sad thing for poor Daniel. Susan very naturally sulked at being locked up, and at being deprived of her favorite amusement. Life had no joy for her without Punch and Judy. With Punch and Judy, existence was blissful; without Punch and Judy, existence was a blank. Regarding the twins as the cause of her imprisonment, she vented her spleen upon the unfortunate couple, and was spiteful enough to leave traces of yellow soap in their eyes when she washed them; and when they cried because of the smart, and rubbed their eyelids with their little fists to get rid of the unwelcome particles, she smacked them on the tenderest parts of their persons, and made them cry the more. But they were not destined to endure this kind of torture for more than a couple of days.

On the third day of their imprisonment, Susan was sitting moodily on the floor, sulking as usual, and biting her lips and fretting, when suddenly the well-beloved "too-to-too-a-too" of the Punch-and-Judy showman came floating through the window. Wild with delight, she snatched up the twins, and, rushing to the window, bent her body forward, and looked out. Yes; there it was—there was the show! Preparations were being made for the drama; the green curtain was down, the crowd was collecting, and the acting manager was already taking a critical survey of the persons who loitered, and was mentally marking down those who would not be allowed to stroll or slink away without being solicited for a fee. The front of the stage was not turned towards the window out of which Susan was looking; and she could only see part of the show. That was a terrible disappointment to her; and her suffering was really very great when she found that the gallows upon which Punch was to be hanged was erected just in that corner of the stage of which she could not obtain a glimpse. She stamped her foot upon the floor excitedly; and, bending her body still more forward in her eagerness, poor Daniel slipped out of her arms on to the pavement. For a moment Susan was so bewildered that she could not realize what had occurred; but, when she heard the sharp cry of agony to which Daniel gave utterance, and when she saw the crowd of people rushing with frightened faces towards the spot where the little fellow was lying, she ran into a corner of the room with the other child in her arms, and throwing her frock over her head, cowered down with her face to the wall, and began to cry. But little notice was taken of her. Daniel was picked up and carried into the house. He was not killed; but his two legs were badly broken, and were destined never to be of any use to him. So, as he had to depend upon artificial legs for support, Daniel began to learn the use of crutches almost before he had begun to learn to toddle.

The love that existed between Joshua and Daniel sprang out of an innocent flirtation which was indulged in by Joshua Marvel and Ellen Taylor. The amatory youngsters exchanged vows when they were quite little things, and pledged themselves not to marry any one else: "no, not for the wide, wide world!" Innocent kisses, broken pieces of crockery with which they played at dinners and shops on back-window sills, and the building of grottoes when the oyster-season came round, were the material bonds which united the youthful loves of Joshua and Ellen.

In due time Joshua was introduced to the family; not exactly as the accepted suitor of the little damsel, but in a surreptitious sneaking manner, which older suitors would have considered undignified. Such a mean position did he for sometime occupy in the house of his affianced, that on several occasions when Mr. Taylor came home drunk, Joshua was locked up in the coal-cellar, lest he should meet the eye of the tipsy parent, who, when he was in his cups, did not possess the most amiable disposition in the world. From that coal-cellar Joshua would emerge low-spirited and grimy, and in a despondent mood; but sundry marks of affection from Ellen, the effects of which were afterwards visible in black patches on her nose and cheeks and cherry lips, invariably restored him to cheerfulness. Such a courtship was not dignified; but Joshua and Ellen were perfectly satisfied; and so was Dan, who thoroughly approved of his twin-sister's choice of a sweetheart.

As the children grew in years, the ties that united Ellen and Joshua were weakened; while those that united the boys were strengthened, until a very perfect and unselfish love was established between them. Both the lads were in the same condition as regarded their time. Joshua had his on his hands because he had not made up his mind what he was going to be; and Daniel had his on his hands because he had broken his legs. Each had his particular fancy. Joshua's was music; Dan's was birds.

Condemned to a sedentary life from the nature of his affliction, and not able to run about as other boys did — for when his sister had let him fall from her arms out of the window the breaking of his legs was not the only injury he had received — Dan turned his attention to a couple of canaries which were part of his parents' household gods. In course of time the birds grew to be very fond of him; and he trained them to do such pretty tricks, and was himself of so gentle and amiable a disposition, that good-natured neighbors made him occasional presents of birds — such as a linnet, or a lark, or a pair of bullfinches — until he had gathered around him a small collection of feathered younglings. With these companions his life was as happy as life could be. He did not mope or fret because his legs were useless, and because he was compelled to use crutches; on the contrary, he absolutely loved his wooden props, as if they were bone of his bone and flesh of his flesh.

"You are right not to be a wood-turner Jo," said Dan, when his friend related to him the substance of the family discussions. "If my legs were like yours, I wouldn't be."

Dan called his friend "Jo." It was not quite right for Joshua, he said, but it sounded pretty. And so it did, especially from his lips.

"I wish your legs *were* like mine, Dan," said Joshua.

"It's of no use wishing," replied Dan. "You know what mother says; it takes all sorts to make a world."

"Sound legs and broken legs — eh, Dan?"

"Yes," answered Dan merrily; "and long ones and short ones, and thick ones and thin ones. Besides, if I had the strongest and biggest legs in the world, I don't think I should be happier than I am."

"But wouldn't you like to be a hero — the same as I am going to be?" asked Joshua.

"We can't all be heroes. You go and fight with lions; I will stop and play with birds. I couldn't tame lions; but I *can* tame birds." Which he could, and did.

Dan was fond of speaking about lions because his name was Daniel; and many and many a time had he and Joshua read the wonderful story of Daniel in the lions' den. Joshua did not know much of the Bible until Dan introduced it to him, and read to him in his thin sweet voice the marvellous romances in that Book of books.

"There was a hero for you!" exclaimed Joshua admiringly, referring to the biblical Daniel. "I wonder what made him so brave."

"Because he was doing what he knew to be right," replied Dan.

"I dare say," was the acquiescent rejoinder.

"And because he was not afraid to speak the truth even to Belshazzar; and because, above all, he believed in God. So God delivered him."

"All because he was doing right," said Joshua.

"All because he was doing right," repeated Dan. "I'm not a bit brave; that is because I am lame, perhaps. If I was thrown into a lions' den I should die of fear — I am sure I should; but if I was thrown into a birds' cage, full of strange birds, I would soon make friends with them; they would come and eat out of my hand in no time."

Dan, indeed, was wonderfully learned about birds and their habits, and possessed a singular power over them. He could train them to any thing almost. And bear this in mind; he used no cruel means in his training of them. What he taught them he taught them by kindness; and they were subservient to him from love, and not from fear. The nature of the affliction which condemned him to a sedentary life, sharpened and concentrated his mental faculties, and endued him with a surprising patience. If it had been otherwise, he could never have trained the birds so thoroughly. Never mind what they were — blackbirds, linnets, larks, bullfinches, canaries — they were one and all his willing slaves, and, in the course of time, performed the tasks he set them with their best ability. Give Dan any one of these birds, and in a few weeks it would hop upon his finger, dance at his whistle, come at his call, fall dead upon the table, and jump up again at a given signal as lively as a cricket. He made little carts for them to draw, little swords for them to carry, little ladders for them to climb up, little guns for them to fire off, little houses for them to go in at the doors of and come out of the chimneys of. It was a sight worth seeing to watch them go through their performances; to see the dead bird lie on its back on the table, and watch cunningly out of a corner of its left eye for the signal which allowed it to come to life again; to see the family birds, after indulging in a little sensible conversation on the doorstep, go into the house, the door of which closed with a spring directly they got on the inside of it, and then presently to see their heads pop out of the chimneys, as if their owners were wondering what sort of weather it was; to see the first villain of the company hop upon the cart in which the pop-gun was fixed, and hop upon a slip of wood which in some mysterious manner acted upon the gun, and caused it to go off — and then to see the desperado watch for dreadful consequences which never followed; to see that cold-blooded and desperate bird jump briskly down, as if it were not disappointed, and place its neck in a ring in the shafts, and hop away to another battle-field; to see the two military birds march up and down in front of the house, holding little wooden swords in their beaks, as who should say to an advancing foe, "Approach if you dare, and meet your doom!" to see the climbing-bird hop up the steps of the ladder, and then hop down again triumphantly, as if it had performed a feat of which bird-kind might be proud; and to know that the birds enjoyed the fun and delighted in it; were pleasant things to see and know, and could do no one any harm. Of course there were hitches in the performances; occasionally the birds were dull or obstinate; but, as a rule, they were tractable and obedient; and if they did sometimes bungle their tricks they might very well be excused, for they were but feeble creatures after all.

So Dan passed his time innocently, and loved his pets, and his pets loved him. Joshua grew to love them too. He learned all their pretty little vocal tricks, and could imitate the different languages of the birds in such a wonderful manner that they would stop and listen to his warbling, and would answer it with similar joyful notes of their own. And when Dan and he were in a merry mood — which was not seldom — they and the birds would join in a concert which was almost as good, and quite as enjoyable, as the scraping of fiddles and the playing of flutes. Sometimes, in the evening, Joshua would play soft music upon his second-hand accordion; and directly he sounded the first note the birds would hop upon the table and stand in a line, with their heads inclined on one side, listening to Joshua's simple melodies with the gravity of connoisseurs, and would not flutter a feather of their little wings for fear they should disturb the harmony of sound.

CHAPTER III.

LIFE AND DEATH OF GOLDEN CLOUD.

THERE was one canary which they had christened Golden Cloud. It was one of the two canaries that Dan had first trained; and for this and other reasons Golden Cloud was a special favorite with the lads. Dan used to declare that Golden Cloud literally understood every word he spoke to it. And it really appeared as if Dan were right in so declaring and so believing; it was certainly a fact that Golden Cloud was a bird of superior intelligence. The other birds were of that opinion, or they would not have accepted its leadership. When they marched, Golden Cloud was at the head of them — and very proud it appeared to be of its position; when the performances took place, Golden Cloud was the first to commence; if any thing *very* responsible and *very* particular were to be done, Golden Cloud was intrusted with it; and if any new bird was refractory, it devolved upon Golden Cloud to assist Dan to bring that bird to its senses. The birds did not entertain a particle of envy towards Golden Cloud because it had attained an eminence more distinguished than their own; and this fact was as apparent, as it must have been astonishing, to any reflective human being who enjoyed the happy privilege of being present now and then at the performances of Dan's clever troupe. Even when old age crept upon it — it was in the prime of life when Dan first took it in hand — the same respect was paid to the sagamore of the company. Its sight grew filmed, its legs grew scaly, its feathers grew ragged. What matter? Had it not been kind and gentle to them when in its prime? Should they not be kind and gentle to it now that Time was striking it down? And was it not, even in its decrepitude, the wise bird of them all?

Notwithstanding that it grew more and more shaky every hour almost, the old sense of duty was strong in the heart of Golden Cloud; and it strove to take part in the performances to the last. Golden Cloud had evidently learned the lesson, that to try always to do one's duty is the sweetest thing in life. In that respect it was wiser than many human beings, who should have been wiser than it. It was a melancholy sight, yet a comical one, withal, to see Golden Cloud lift a sword with its beak, and try to hold it there, and hop with it at the head of the company. It staggered here and there, and, being almost blind, sometimes hit an inoffensive bird across the beak, which caused a momentary confusion; but every thing was set right as quickly as could be. The other birds bore with Golden Cloud's infirmities, and made its labors light for it. Even the tomtit — that saucy, beautiful rascal, with its crown of Cambridge blue, who had been the most refractory bird that Golden Cloud ever had to deal with, who *would* turn heels over head in the midst of a serious lesson, and who *would* hop and twist about and agitate its staid companions with its restless tricks — even the tomtit, whose greatest delight was to steal things and break things, but whose spirit had been subdued and tamed by Golden Cloud's firmness, assisted the veteran in its old age, and did not make game of it.

One evening Joshua came round to Dan's room rather later than usual, and found Dan in tears.

"What is the matter, Dan?" asked Joshua.

Dan did not reply.

"Do your legs hurt you, Dan?" asked Joshua tenderly.

Dan formed a "No" with his lips, but uttered no sound.

Joshua thought it best not to tease his friend with any more questions. He saw that Dan was suffering from a grief which he would presently unbosom. He took his accordion on his knee, and began to play very softly. As he played, a canary in a mourning-cloak came out of the toy-house; another canary in a mourning-cloak followed; then a bullfinch, and another bullfinch; then the tomtit and the linnets; and then the blackbirds; all in little black cloaks which Ellen Taylor's nimble fingers had made for them that day out of a piece of the lining of an old frock. At the sight of the first canary, with its black cloak on, Joshua was filled with astonishment; but when bird after bird followed, and ranged themselves solemnly in a line before him, and when he missed the presence of one familiar friend, he solved the riddle of their strange appearance; the birds were in mourning for the death of Golden Cloud.

They seemed to know it, too; they seemed to know that they had lost a friend, and that they were about to pay the last tribute of respect to their once guide and master. The bullfinches, their crimson breasts hidden by their cloaks, looked, with their black masks of faces, like negro birds in mourning; the amiable linnets, unobtrusive and shy as they generally were, were still more quiet and sad than usual; even the daring blackbirds were subdued — with the exception of one who, in the midst of a silent interval, struck up "Polly, put the kettle on," in its shrill whistle, but, observing the eyes of the tomtit fixed upon it with an air of reproach, stopped in sudden remorse, with the "kettle" sticking in its throat.

Dan had made a white shroud for Golden Cloud; and it was both quaint and mournful to see it as it lay in its coffin — Dan's money-box — surrounded by the mourners in their black cloaks. They stood quite still, with their cunning little heads all inclined one way, as if they were waiting for news concerning their dead leader from the world beyond the present.

Joshua, with a glance of sorrow at the coffin, said, —

"Your money-box, Dan!"

"I wish I could have buried it in a flower-pot, Jo," replied Dan, suppressing a sob.

"Why didn't you?"

"Mother said father would be angry," —

Here the blackbird — perceiving that the tomtit was no longer observing it, and inwardly fretting that it should have been pulled up short in the midst of its favorite song; also feeling awkward, doubtless, with a kettle in its throat — piped out, with amazing rapidity and shrillness, "Polly, put the kettle on; we'll all have tea."

The blue feathers in the tomtit's tail quivered with indignation, and its white-tipped wings fluttered reprovingly. Moral force was evidently quite thrown away upon such a blackbird as that; so the tomtit bestowed upon the recreant a sharp dig with its iron beak, and the blackbird bore the punishment with meekness; merely giving vent, in response, to a wonderful imitation of the crowing of an extremely weak cock, who led a discontented life in a neighboring back-yard. After which it relapsed into silence.

Dan, who had stopped his speech to observe this passage between the birds, repeated, —

"Mother said father would be angry; he knows how many flower-pots we have. So I used my money-box."

"But you would rather have a flower-pot, Dan?"

"I should have liked a flower-pot above all things; it seems more natural for a bird. Something might grow out of it; something that Golden Cloud would like to know is above it, if it was only a blade of grass."

Joshua ran out of Dan's room, and returned in a very few minutes with a flower-pot with mignonette growing in it. He was almost breathless with excitement.

"It is mine, Dan," he said, "and it is yours. I bought it with my own money; and it shall be Golden Cloud's coffin."

"Kiss me, Jo," said Dan.

Joshua kissed him, and then carefully lifted the flower-roots from the pot, and placed Golden Cloud in the soft mould beneath. A few tears fell from Dan's eyes into the flower-pot coffin, as he looked for the last time upon the form of his pet canary. Then Joshua replaced the flower-roots, and arranged the earth, and Golden Cloud was ready for burial.

"Play something, Jo," said Dan.

Joshua took his accordion in his hands, and played a slow solemn march; and the birds, directed by Dan, hopped gravely round the flower-pot, the tomtit keeping its eye sternly fixed upon the rebellious blackbird, expressing in the look an unmistakable determination to put an instant stop to the slightest exhibition of indecency.

"I don't know where to bury it," said Dan, when the ceremony was completed. "Ellen has been trying to pick out a flagstone in the yard, but she made her fingers bleed, and then couldn't move it. And if it *was* buried there, the stone would have to be trodden down, and the flowers in the coffin couldn't grow."

"There's that little bit of garden in *our* yard," said Joshua. "I can bury it there, if you don't mind. I can put the flower-pot in so that the mignonette will grow out of it quite nicely. It isn't very far, Dan," continued Joshua, divining Dan's wish that Golden Cloud should be buried near him; "only five yards off, and it is the best place we know of."

Dan assenting, Joshua took the flower-pot, and buried it in what he called his garden; which was an estate of such magnificent proportions that he could have covered it with his jacket. He was proud of it notwithstanding, and considered it a grand property. A boundary of oyster-shells defined the limits of the estate, and served as a warning to trespassing feet. In the centre of this garden Golden Cloud was buried. When Joshua returned to Dan's room, the mourning-cloaks were taken off the birds — who seemed very glad to get rid of them — and they were sent to bed.

Dan was allowed to sit up an hour longer than usual that night, and he and Joshua occupied those precious minutes in confidential conversation. First they spoke of Golden Cloud, and then of Joshua's prospects.

"You haven't made up your mind yet what you are going to be, Jo," said Dan.

"I haven't made up my mind," replied Joshua, "but I have an idea. I don't want you to ask me what it is. I will tell you soon — in a few weeks perhaps."

"Where have you been to-day? You were late."

"I went to the waterside."

"To the river?"

"To the river."

"To the river that runs to the sea," said Dan musingly, with a dash of regret in his voice. "What a wonderful sight it must be to see the sea, as we read of it! Would you like to see it, Jo?"

"Dearly, Dan!"

"And to be on it?"

"Dearly, Dan!"

Dan looked at Joshua sadly. There was an eager longing in Joshua's eyes, and an eager longing in the parting of his lips, as he sat with hands clasped upon his knee.

"I can see a great many things that I have never seen," said Dan; "see them with my mind, I mean. I can see gardens and fields and trees, almost as they are. I can fancy myself lying in fields with the grass waving about me. I can fancy myself in a forest with the great trees spreading out their great limbs, and I can see the branches bowing to each other as the wind sweeps by them. I can see a little stream running down a hill, and hiding itself in a valley. I can even see a river — but all rivers must be muddy, I think; not bright, like the streams. But I can't see the sea, Jo. It is too big — too wonderful!"

Rapt in the contemplation of the subject, Dan and Joshua were silent for a little while.

"Ships on the top of water-mountains," resumed Dan presently, "then down in a valley like, with curling waves above them. That is what I have read; but I can't see it. 'Robinson Crusoe' is behind you, Jo."

Joshua opened the book — it was a favorite one with the lads, as with what lads is it not? — and skimmed down the pages as he turned them over.

"'A raging wave, mountain-like, came rolling astern of us,'" he said.

"That is the shipwreck," said Dan, looking over Joshua's shoulder. "Then here, farther down: 'I saw the sea come after me as high as a great hill, and as furious as an enemy.' Think of that! Here picture."

The lads looked for the thousandth time at the rough wood-cut, in which Robinson was depicted casting a look of terror over his shoulder at the curling waves, ten times as tall as himself; his arms were extended, and he was supposed to be running away from the waves; although, according to the picture, nothing short of a miracle could save him.

"Look!" said Joshua, turning a few pages back and reading, 'yonder lies a dreadful monster on the side of that hillock, fast asleep.'"

"'I looked where he pointed,'" read Dan — it was a favorite custom with them to read each a few lines at a time — "'and saw a dreadful monster indeed, for it was a terrible great lion that lay on the side of the shore, under the shade of a piece of the hill that hung as it were a little over him. Xury, says I, you shall go on shore, and kill him.'"

"Could you kill a lion, Jo?" asked Dan, breaking off in his reading.

"I don't know," said Joshua, considering and feeling very doubtful of his capability.

Dan resumed the reading:—

"'I took our biggest gun, which was almost musket-bore, and loaded it with a good charge of powder and with two slugs, and laid it down; then I loaded another gun with two bullets; and the third (for we had three pieces), I loaded with five smaller bullets.'"

"No, I couldn't kill a lion," said Joshua, in a tone of disappointed conviction; "for I can't fire off a gun. But that occurred nearly two hundred years ago, Dan. I don't suppose there are as many lions now as there used to be."

"And ships are different, too, to what they were then, Jo," said Dan, closing the book. "Stronger and better built. I dare say if it had been a very strong ship that Robinson Crusoe went out in, he wouldn't have been wrecked."

"I am glad he was, though; if he hadn't been, we shouldn't have been able to read about him. It is beautiful, isn't it?"

"Beautiful to read," replied Dan. "But he was dreadfully miserable sometimes; for twenty-four years and more he had no one to speak to. It appears strange to me that he didn't forget how to speak the English language, and that he didn't go mad. Now, Jo, supposing it was you! Do you think, if you had no one to speak to for twenty years, that you would be able to speak as well as you do now? Don't you think you would stammer over a word sometimes, and lose the sense of it?"

Dan asked these questions so earnestly, that Joshua laughed, and said,—

"Upon my word, I don't know, Dan."

But the time was to come when the memory of Dan's questions came to Joshua's mind with a deep and solemn significance.

"He had his parrot certainly," continued Dan; "but what used he to say to it? 'Robin, Robin, Robin Crusoe! Poor Robin Crusoe! How came you here? Where have you been, Robin?' That wasn't much to say, and to be always saying; and I am sure that if he kept on saying it for so many years, he must have entirely forgotten what the meaning of it was. You try it,—say a word, or two or three words, for a hundred times. You will begin to wonder what it means before you come to the end."

"But he had his Bible; and you know what a comfort that was to him."

"Perhaps that was the reason he didn't go mad. I dare say, too, that some qualities in him were strengthened and came to his aid because he was so strangely situated. What qualities now, Jo?"

"I don't understand you, Dan."

"I *do* say things sometimes you don't understand at first, don't I, Jo?"

Joshua nodded good-humoredly.

"I am often puzzled myself to know what I mean. Leaving Robinson Crusoe alone, and speaking of qualities, Jo, take me for an instance. I am a cripple, and shall never be able to go about. And do you know, Jo, that my mind is stronger than it would have been if I were not helpless? I can see things."

"Can you see any thing now, Dan?"

"Yes."

"What?"

"I can see something that will separate you and me, Jo."

"Forever, Dan?"

"No, not forever; we shall be together sometimes, and then you can tell me all sorts of things that I shall never be able to see myself."

"Don't you think your legs will ever get strong?" asked Joshua.

"Never, Jo; they get worse and worse. And I feel, too, so weak, that I am afraid I shall not have strength to use my crutches much longer. Every thing about me — my limbs, and joints, and every thing — gets weaker and weaker every day. If it wasn't for my body, I should be all right. My mind is right. I can talk and think as well as if my body were strong. Stupid bits of flesh and bone!" he exclaimed, looking at his limbs, and good-humoredly scolding them. "Why don't you fly away and leave me?"

At this point of the conversation Mrs. Taylor called out that it was time for Dan to go to bed, so the lads parted. That night Joshua dreamed that he killed a lion; and Dan dreamed that Golden Cloud came out of the flower-pot, and it wasn't dead, but only pretending.

Dan had good reason for speaking in the way he did of his body, for it distressed him very much. Soon after the death of Golden Cloud, he grew so weak and ill that he was confined to his bed. But his mind scarcely seemed to be affected by his bodily ills, and his cheerfulness never deserted him. He had his dear winged companions brought to his bedroom, and they hopped about his bed as contentedly as could be. And there he played with them and took delight in them; and, as he hearkened to their chirruppings, and looked at their pretty forms, a sweet pleasure was in his eyes, a sweet pleasure was in his heart. And this pleasure was enhanced by the presence of Joshua, who spent a great deal of time with his sick friend.

The tender love that existed between the lads was undefiled by a single selfish act or thought. They were one in sympathy and sentiment. Joshua was Dan's almost only companion during his illness. Dan's mother tended him and gave him his physic, which could not do him any good, the doctor said; but Mrs. Taylor's household duties and responsibilities occupied nearly the whole of her time; she could not afford to keep a servant, and she had all the kitchen-work to do. Ellen — Dan's twin-sister and Joshua's quondam sweetheart — was often in the room; but, young as she was, she was already being employed about the house assisting her mother. She scrubbed the floors and washed the clothes; and, although she was so little that she had to stand on a chair in the tiny yard to hang the clothes on the line, she was as proud of her work, and took as much pleasure in it, as if she were a grown woman, who had been properly brought up. Notwithstanding the onerous nature of her duties, she managed to spend half an hour now and again with Josh and Dan, and would sit quite still listening to the conversation. Her presence in the room was pleasing to the boy-friends, for Ellen was as modest and tidy a little girl as could be met with in a day's walk.

Susan, Dan's unfortunate nursemaid, was a young woman now. But she had a horror of the sick-room. She entertained a secret conviction that she was a murderess, and really had some sort of an idea that if Daniel died she would be taken up and hanged. She was as fascinated as ever with Punch and Judy; but the fascination had something horrible in it. Often when she was standing looking at the show — and she was more welcome to the showman than she used to be, for now she sometimes gave him a penny — she would begin to tremble when the hangman came on the scene with his gallows, and would then fairly run away in a fright. Ever since she had let Daniel slip from her arms out of the window, there had been growing in her mind a fear that something dreadful was following her; and a dozen times a day she would throw a startled look behind her, as if to assure herself that there was nothing horrible there. She had been sufficiently punished for her carelessness. For a good many weeks after it occurred, bad little boys and girls in the neighborhood used to call after her, "Ah-h-h! Who killed her little brother? Ah-h-h!" If she ran, they ran after her, and hooted her with the dreadful accusation. It took different forms. Now it was, "Ah-h-h-h! Who killed her little brother? Ah-h-h!" And now it was, "Ah-h-h! Who'll be hung for killing her little brother? Ah-h-h-h!" Such an effect did this cruel punishment have upon her, that she would wake up in terror in the middle of the night with all her fevered pulses quivering to the cry, "Ah-h-h-h! Who'll be hung for killing her little brother? Ah-h-h-h!" But time, which cures all things, relieved her. The bad boys and girls grew tired of saying the same thing over and over again. A new excitement claimed their attention, and poor Susan was allowed to walk unmolested through the streets. But the effect remained in the terror-flashes that would spring in her eyes, and in the agonized looks of fear that she would throw behind her every now and again, without any apparent cause. These feelings had such a powerful effect upon her, that she never entered Dan's room unless she were compelled to do so; and once, when Dan sent for her and asked her to forgive him for being naughty when he was a baby, she was so affected that she did nothing but shed remorseful tears for a week afterwards.

One day, when Dan was playing with the birds, and no other person but he and Joshua was in the room, he said, —

"Do you think the birds know that I am so weak and ill, Jo, dear?"

"Sometimes I think they do, Dan," answered Joshua.

"Dear little things! You haven't any idea how weak I really am. But I am strong enough for something."

"What, Dan?"

"If you don't ask any questions, I sha'n't tell you any stories," replied Dan gayly. "Lend me your penknife."

Joshua gave Dan his penknife, and when he came the next day Dan was cutting strips of wood from one of his crutches.

"O Dan!" exclaimed Joshua, bursting into tears.

Dan looked at Joshua, and smiled.

"O you cry-baby!" he said. But he said it in a voice of exquisite tenderness; and he drew Joshua's head on to the pillow, and he laid his own beside it, and he kissed Joshua's lips.

"I shall not want my crutches any more," he whispered in Joshua's ear as thus they lay; "that is all. It isn't as bad as you think."

"You are not going to die, Dan?" asked Joshua in a trembling voice.

"I don't think I am — yet. It is only because I am almost certain — I feel it, Jo — that I shall be a helpless cripple all my life, and that I shall not be able to move about, even with the help of crutches."

"Poor dear Dan!" said Joshua, checking his sobs with difficulty.

"Poor Dan! Not at all! I can read, I can think, and I can love you, Jo, all the same. I have made up my mind what I am going to do. I shall live in you. You are my friend, and strong as you are, you can't love me more than I love you. And even if I was to die, dear"—

"Don't say that, Dan; I can't bear to think of it."

"Why? It isn't dreadful. If I was to die, we should still be friends — we should still love each other. Don't you love Golden Cloud?"

Joshua whispered "Yes."

"But Golden Cloud is not here. Yet you love him. And so do I, more than I did when pet was alive. I don't quite know how it is with birds, but I do know how it is with us. If you was here, Jo, and I was there, we should meet again."

"Amen, Dan!"

"And it is nice to believe and know — as you and I believe and know — that if we were parted, we should come together again by and by; and that perhaps the dear little birds would be with us there as they are here, and that we should love them as we love them now. They are so pretty and harmless that I think God will let them come. Besides, what would the trees do without them?"

"What do you mean, Dan, by saying that you are going to live in me?"

"It is a curious fancy, Jo, but I have thought of it a good deal, and I want you to think of it too. I want to be with you, although I shall not be able to move. You are going to be a hero, and are going to see strange sights perhaps. I can see farther than you can; and I know the meaning of your going down to the riverside, as you have done a good many times lately. I know what you will make up your mind to be, although I sha'n't say until you tell me yourself. Well, Jo, I want you to fancy, if I don't know what is happening to you — if you are in any strange place, and are seeing wonderful things — I want you to fancy, 'Dan is here with me, although I cannot see him.' Will you do that, Jo, dear?"

"Yes; wherever I am, and whatever I shall see, I will think, 'Dan is here with me, although I cannot see him.'"

"That is friendship. This isn't," said Dan, holding up a finger; "this is only a little bit of flesh. If it is anywhere about us, it is here;" and he took Joshua's fingers, and pressed them to his heart. Then, after a pause of a few moments, he said, "So don't cry any more because I am cutting up my crutches; I am making some new things for the birds."

They had a concert after that; and the blackbird whistled "Polly, put the kettle on," to its heart's content; and the tomtit performed certain difficult acrobatic tricks in token of approval.

Dan recovered so far from his sickness as to be able to leave his bed. But it almost appeared as if he was right in saying that he should not want his crutches. He had not sufficient strength in his shoulders to use them. He had to be lifted in and out of bed, and sometimes could not even wash and dress himself. Ellen Taylor was his nurse, and a dear good nurse she proved herself to be. A cross word never passed her lips. She devoted herself to the service of her helpless brother with a very perfect love; and her nature was so beautiful in its gentleness and tenderness that those qualities found expression in her face, and made that beautiful also. Dan had yielded to Joshua's entreaties not to destroy his crutches. "You might be able to use them some day," Joshua would say. To which Dan would reply by asking gayly if Joshua had ever heard of a miracle in Stepney. However, he kept his crutches, and Joshua was satisfied. In course of time Joshua began to train a few birds at his own house, and now and then Dan's parents would allow Dan to be carried to Joshua's house, and to stop there for a few days. When that occurred, Dan and Joshua slept together, and would tell stories to each other long after the candle had been blown out — stories of which Joshua was almost always the hero. Joshua had one great difficulty to overcome when he first introduced the birds into his house; that difficulty was the yellow-haired cat, of which mention has already been made. With the usual amiability of her species, the domestic tigress, directly she set eyes upon the birds, determined to make a meal of them, and it required all Joshua's vigilance to prevent the slaughter of the innocents. But he was patient, and firm, and kind, and he so conquered the tigerish propensities of the cat towards the birds, that in a few weeks she began to tolerate them, and in a few weeks more to play with them and to allow them to play with her, and gradually grew so cordial with them that it might have been supposed she had kittened them by mistake.

CHAPTER IV.

IN WHICH DAN GETS WILD NOTIONS INTO HIS HEAD, AND MAKES SOME VERY BOYISH EXPERIMENTS.

IF every farthing of the allowance of pocket-money which Joshua and Dan received from their respective parents had been carefully saved up, it would not have amounted to a very large sum in the course of the year. Insignificant, however, as was the allowance, it sufficed for their small wants, and was made to yield good interest in the way of social enjoyment. The lads did not keep separate accounts. What was Joshua's was Dan's, and what was Dan's was Joshua's. As there were no secret clasps in their minds concealing something which the other was not to share and enjoy, so there was no secret clasp in their money-box which debarred either from spending that which, strictly speaking, belonged to his friend. Dan was the treasurer; the treasury was the money-box which was to have been Golden Cloud's coffin. Dan's allowance was two pence a week, which was often in arrears in consequence of his father being too fond of public-houses; Joshua's allowance was four pence a week, which he received very regularly. But each of their allowances was supplemented by contributions from independent sources. The motives which prompted these contributions were of a very different nature; as the following will explain:—

"Something more for the money-box, Dan," said Joshua, producing a four-penny piece, and dropping it into the box.

"From the same party, Jo?" asked Dan.

"From the same jolly old party, Dan. From the Old Sailor."

"Is he nice?"

"The Old Sailor? You should see him, that's all."

"You have been down to the waterside again, then?"

"Yes. Tuck-tuck-joey!" This latter to the linnet, who came out to have a peep at Joshua, and who, directly it heard the greeting, responded with the sweetest peal of music that mortal ever listened to. When the linnet had finished its song the obtrusive and greedy blackbird, determined not to be outdone, and quite ignoring the fact that it had had a very good supper, ordered Polly to put the kettle on, in its most piercing notes.

"Did you go on the river, Jo?" asked Dan.

"Yes. In a boat. Rowing. The Old Sailor says I am getting along famously."

"I *should* like to see the Old Sailor."

"I wish you could; but he is such a strange old fellow! He doesn't care for the land. When I tell mother what I am making up my mind to be — what I shall have *made* up mind then to be — I will coax him to come to our house. I want him to talk to mother about the sea, for she is sure to cry and fret, and although the Old Sailor doesn't think that women are as good as men, he thinks mothers are better."

Dan laughed a pleasant little laugh.

"That is queer," he said.

"He knows all about you, and he asks me every day, 'How is Dan?'"

"I am glad of that — very glad."

"So am I. I have told him all about the birds, and how they love you. You would never guess what he said to-day about you."

"Something very bad, I dare say," said Dan, knowing very well, all the time, that it was something good, or Joshua would not tell him.

"Something *very* bad. He said, 'He must be a fine little chap' — meaning you, Dan — 'or the birds wouldn't love him.'"

"Has he been all over the world, Jo?"

"All over the world; and O Dan, he has seen *such* places!"

"I tell you what we will do," said Dan. "To-morrow you shall buy a couple of young bullfinches, and you shall find out some tune the Old Sailor is fond of, and I will teach the bullfinches to whistle it. Then you shall give the birds to the Old Sailor, and say they are a present from me and you."

"That will be prime! He will be so pleased!"

"Have you ever heard him sing, Jo?"

"Yes," answered Joshua, laughing; "I have heard him sing, —

'Which is the properest day to drink,
    Saturday, Sunday, Monday?
Each is the properest day, I think —
    Why should I name but one day?
Tell me but yours, I'll mention my day,
    Let us but fix on some day —
Tuesday, Wednesday, Thursday, Friday,
    Saturday, Sunday, or Monday.'"

"I don't think that would do," said Dan, echoing Joshua's laugh.

"Here's another," said Joshua, and he played a prelude to "Poor Tom Bowling," and sang the first verse, —

'Here a sheer hulk lies poor Tom Bowling,
    The darling of our crew;
No more he'll hear the tempest howling,
    For death has broached him too.
His form was of the manliest beauty,
    His heart was kind and soft,
Faithful below Tom did his duty,
    But now he's gone aloft,
    But now he's gone aloft.'"

Joshua sang the words with much tender feeling, but Dan shook his head.

"The birds would never be able to get the spirit of the song into them," he said, "and the tune is nothing without that. Never mind — we'll teach them something, and then the Old Sailor shall have them."

"And I shall tell him they are a present from you alone."

"No," said Dan energetically; "that

would spoil it all. They are from you and me together. Can't you guess the reason why?"

"I believe I can," replied Joshua, after a little consideration. "The Old Sailor likes me, and you want him to like you because of me, not because of yourself alone; you want him to like me more because of you—as I am sure he will when he knows you."

"That's it. I want him to know that we love each other, and that we shall always love each other, whether we are together or separated. I want everybody who likes you, Jo, to like me."

Joshua laid his hand upon Dan's, which rested on the table, and Dan placed his other hand upon Joshua's playfully. Their hands were growing to be very unlike. Dan's hand, as it grew, became more delicate, while Joshua's grew stronger and more muscular. Dan laughed another pleasant laugh as he remarked the difference between them. "That is a proper kind of hand for a hero," he said. And then, in a more serious voice, "Joshua, do you know I think we can see each other's thoughts." And so, indeed, it appeared as if they could.

The next day the bullfinches were bought, and Dan began to train them. They were a pair of very young birds, not a dozen days old, and the air Dan fixed upon to teach them first was "Rule, Britannia."

So much for Joshua's supplemental contributions to the general fund. Now for Dan's.

"Another sixpence in a piece of paper, Jo!"

"That makes eighteen pence this month, Dan. Poor Susan!"

"Poor Susan!" echoed Dan.

Susan was very much to be pitied. Looking upon herself as her brother's destroyer, she endeavored, by offerings of sixpences as often as she could afford them, to atone for the crime—for so she now regarded it—by which she had made him a helpless cripple. These sixpences were not given openly; they were laid, as it were, upon the sacrificial altar in secret. Sometimes the altar was one of Ellen's shoes, and Ellen, when she dressed herself, would feel something sticking in her heel, and discover it to be a sixpence tightly screwed up in a piece of paper, with the words, "For Dan; from Susan," written on it; sometimes the altar was one of Dan's pocket-handkerchiefs, and the sixpence was tied up in a knot; sometimes it was a bag of bird-seed; sometimes Dan's cap. She was so imbued with a sense of guilt, that she trembled when she met Dan's eye. He was as kind and gentle to her, when he had the opportunity, as he was to all around him; and divining her secret remorse, he tried by every means in his power to lessen it. But the feeling, that, if Dan died, she was a murderess, was too deeply implanted in her to be ever removed. She lived in constant fear. She was afraid of the dark, and could not sleep without a rush-light near her bedside. Often in the night, on occasions when Dan was weaker than usual, she would creep down stairs, and listen at his bedroom-door to catch the sound of his breathing. If she did not hear it at first, the ghostly echo of the old terrible cry, "Ah-h-h-h! who killed her little brother? Ah-h-h-h!" filled the staircase and the passage with dreadful shadows; shadows that seemed to thicken and gather about her as if possessed with a desire to stifle her—and she would press her hands tightly upon her eyes so that she should not see them. Then perhaps she would open Dan's door quietly, and hearing him breathe, ever so softly, would creep up stairs again, a little more composed; always closing her door quickly, to prevent the shadows on the stairs from coming into her room.

The supplemental contributions from Susan and the Old Sailor were very acceptable to Dan and Joshua, who were both fond of reading. What was not spent in birds' food was spent in books. They subscribed to two magazines, the "Penny Magazine" and the "Mirror," which came out weekly; the subscription was a serious one for them, and made a great hole in their pocket-money: it swallowed up three pence per week. The addition of a new book to their modest library was one of the proudest events in their quiet lives. "New" books is not a strictly correct phrase, for the collection consisted of second-hand volumes, picked up almost at random at old-book stalls. Although their library was a small one, not numbering in its palmiest days more than fifty volumes, it was wonderfully miscellaneous. Now it was a book of travels that Joshua bought; now a book of poems; now an odd volume of a magazine; now a book on natural history; now a speculative book which neither of the boys could understand — not at all a weak reason in favor of its being purchased. Over these books the boys would pore night after night, and extract such marrow from them as best suited their humor. The conversations which arose out of their readings were worth listening to; Dan's observations, especially, were very quaint and original, and gave evidence, not only of good taste, but of the possession of reflective powers of a high order.

An old book on dreams which Joshua

bought for a song, as the saying is, proved especially attractive to Dan. The proper title of the book was the "Philosophy of Dreams," an ambitious sub-title — the "Triumph of Mind over Matter" — being affixed. Dan read and re-read this book with avidity. In it the writer contended that a person could so command and control his mental forces, as to train himself to dream of events which were actually taking place at a distance from him, at the precise moment they occurred. Space, said the author, was of the smallest consequence. There was one thing, however, that was absolutely necessary — that a perfect sympathy should exist between the dreamer and the person or persons of whom he was dreaming. It was a wildly-speculative book taken at its best, and contained much irrelevant and ridiculous matter; but it was just the kind of book to attract such a lad as Dan, and it set him thinking. "Perfect sympathy! Such a sympathy," he thought, "as exists between me and Jo;" and he proceeded to read with greater eagerness. The author, in support of his theory, dragged in nearly all the sciences; and drew largely upon that of phrenology. He explained where certain organs lay, such as wonder, veneration, benevolence, destructiveness, and proceeded somewhat in the following fashion: Say that a person is sleeping, and that he is not disturbed by any special powerful emotion, arising probably from strong anxiety connected with his worldly circumstances. His mind must be at rest, and his sleep be calm and peaceful. Under these circumstances, if a certain organ, say the organ of veneration, be gently pressed, the sleeper will presently dream a dream, in which the sentiment of veneration will be the quality most prominently brought into play. And so with wonder, and benevolence, and combativeness, and other qualities. Having stated this very distinctly, the writer proceeded, as if the mere statement were sufficient proof of its incontestability: say that between the sleeper and the operator a strong and earnest sympathy existed; the operator, selecting in his mind some person with whom they are both acquainted, brings his power of will to bear upon the sleeper. (Here the writer interpolated that the experiment would fail if the organs of concentrativeness and firmness were not more than ordinarily large in the operator.) With his mind firmly fixed upon the one object, he wills that the sleeper shall dream of their mutual acquaintance; and as he wills it, with all the intensity he can exercise, he gently manipulates the sleeper's organ of tune — which, by the way, the author stated he believed was the only one of the purely intellectual faculties which could be pressed into service. The sleeper will then dream of the selected person, and his sense of melody and the harmony of sound will be gratified. Then, in a decidedly vague manner, as if he had got himself in a tangle from which he did not know how to extricate himself, the author argued that what one person could do to another, he could do also to himself, and that the effect produced upon another person by physical manipulation may be produced upon one's self by a strong concentration of will. During our waking moments he said, the affective faculties of our mind are brought into play. Thus, we see and wonder; thus, we see and venerate; thus, we see and pity. These faculties or sentiments are excited and make themselves felt without any effort on our part. If, then, circumstances, which previously did not affect us, can thus act upon us without the exercise of voluntary effort to produce sensation; if circumstances, in which we had no reason to feel the slightest active interest, can cause us to venerate, to pity, to wonder — broadly, to rejoice and to suffer — why should we not be able, by the aid of a powerful sympathy and an earnest desire, to bring into reasoning action the faculties which are thus excited by uninteresting and independent circumstances?

Thus far the author: unconscious that he had fallen into the serious error of confounding the affective with the intellectual faculties, and not appearing to understand that, whereas an affective faculty can be brought into conscious action by independent circumstances, an intellectual faculty requires a direct mental effort before it is excited. His essay was not convincing. He wandered off at tangents; laid down a theory, and, proceeding to establish it, so entangled himself that he lost its connecting threads; and had evidently been unable to properly think out a subject which is not entirely unworthy of consideration. However, he had written his book, and it got into Dan's hands and into Dan's head. Joshua did not understand it a bit, and said so; and when he asked Dan to explain it, Dan could scarcely fit words to what was in his mind.

"Although I cannot explain it very clearly, I can understand it," said Dan. "He means to say that a person can see with his mental sight" —

"That is, with his eyes shut," interrupted Joshua jocularly.

"Certainly, with his eyes shut," said Dan very decidedly. "Our eyes are shut when we dream, yet we see things." Joshua became serious immediately; the answer was a convincing one. "And that proves that we have two senses of sight — one in the eyes, the other in the mind. Haven't you seen rings, and circles, and clouds when you are in bed at night, and before you go to sleep? I can press my face on the pillow and say — not out loud, and yet I say it and can hear it — which shows that all our senses are double." (In his eagerness to explain what he could scarcely comprehend, Dan was in danger of falling into the same error as the author of the "Triumph of Mind over Matter" had fallen into, that of flying off at tangents: it was with difficulty he could keep to his subject.) "Well, Jo, I press my head into the pillow, and say, 'I will see rings,' and presently I see a little ball, black, perhaps, and it grows and grows into rings — like what you see when you throw a stone in the water — larger and larger, all the different colors of the rainbow; and then, when they have grown so large as to appear to have lost themselves in space — just like the rings in the water, Jo — another little ball shapes itself in the dark, and gradually becomes visible, and then the rings come and grow and disappear as the others did. When I have seen enough, I say — not out loud again, Jo, but silently as I did before — 'I don't want to see any more,' and they don't come again. What I can do with rings, I can do with clouds. I say, 'I will see clouds,' and they come, all colors of blue, from white-blue to black-blue; sometimes I see sunsets."

"I have seen them too, Dan," said Joshua; "I have seen skies with stars in them, just as I have seen them with my eyes wide open."

"Now, if we can do this," continued Dan, "why cannot we do more?"

"We can't do what he says in this book," said Joshua, drumming with his fingers on the "Philosophy of Dreams."

"I don't know. Why should he write all that unless he knew something? There is no harm in trying, at all events. Let me see. Here is a chart of a head, Jo turning to a diagram in the book. "Where is combativeness? Oh! here, at the back of the head, behind the ear. Can you feel it, Jo? Is it a large bump? No; you are going too high up, I am sure. Now you are too much in the middle. Ah! that's the place, I think."

These last sentences referred to Joshua's attempt to find Dan's organ of combativeness.

"I don't feel any thing particular, Dan," he said.

"But you feel something, don't you, Jo?" asked Dan anxiously. "There *is* a bump there, isn't there?"

"A very little one," answered Joshua, earnestly manipulating Dan's head, and pressing the bump. "Do you feel spiteful?"

"No," said Dan, laughing.

"There's a bump twice as large just above your fighting one."

"What is that bump?" said Dan, examining the diagram again. "Ah! that must be adhesiveness."

"I don't know what that means."

"Give me the dictionary;" and Dan with eager fingers turned over the pages of an old Walker's Dictionary. "'Adhesive — sticking, tenacious,'" he read. "That is, that I stick to a thing, as I mean to do to this. Now I'll tell you what we'll do, Jo. I shall sleep at your house to-morrow night, and when I am asleep, you shall press my organ of combativeness — put your fingers on it — yes, there; and when I wake I will tell you what I have dreamed of."

"All right," said Joshua, removing his fingers.

"You will be able to find the place again?"

"Yes, Dan."

"And you will be sure to keep awake?"

"Sure, Dan."

The following night, Joshua waited very patiently until Dan was asleep. He had to wait a long time; for Dan, in consequence of his anxiety, was longer than usual getting to sleep. Once or twice Joshua thought that his friend was in the Land of Nod, and he commenced operations, but he was interrupted by Dan saying drowsily, "I am not asleep yet, Jo." At length Dan really went off, and then Joshua, very quietly and with great care, felt for Dan's organ of combativeness, and pressed it. Joshua looked at his sleeping friend with anxiety. "Perhaps he will bit out at me," he thought. But Dan lay perfectly still, and Joshua, after waiting and watching in vain for some indication of the nature of Dan's sleeping fancies, began to feel very sleepy himself, and went to bed. In the morning, when they were both awake, Joshua asked what Dan had dreamed of.

"I can't remember," said Dan, rubbing his eyes.

"I pressed your combativeness for a long time, Dan," said Joshua; "and I pressed it so hard that I was almost afraid you would hit out."

"I didn't, did I?"

"No; you were as still as a mouse."

"I dreamed of something, though," said Dan, considering. "Oh, I remember! I dreamed of you, Jo; you were standing on a big ship, with a big telescope in your hand. You had no cap on, and your hair was all flying about."

"Were there any sailors on the ship?"

"A good many."

"Did you quarrel with any of them?"

"I didn't dream of myself at all."

"Did any of the sailors quarrel with me?"

"There wasn't any quarrelling, Jo, that I can remember."

"So you see," said Joshua, "that it is all fudge."

"I don't see that at all. Now I think of it, it isn't likely that I should dream of quarrelling with any one or fighting with any one when I was dreaming of you, Jo."

"Or perhaps you haven't any combativeness, Dan."

"Perhaps I haven't. It wouldn't be of much use to me if I had, for I shouldn't know how to fight."

"Or perhaps your combativeness is so small that it won't act," said Joshua sportively.

"Don't joke about it, Jo," said Dan. "You don't know how serious I am, and how disappointed I feel at its being a failure. Will you try it again to-night?"

Joshua, seeing that Dan was very much in earnest, readily promised; and the experiment was repeated that night, with the same result. After that the subject dropped for a time.

But if Dan's organ of adhesiveness — which, phrenologically, means affection, friendship, attachment — was large, it was scarcely more powerful than his organ of concentrativeness. His love for Joshua was perfect. He knew that Joshua's choice of a pursuit would separate him from his friend. When he said to Joshua, "I shall live in you, Jo," the words conveyed the expression of no light feeling, but of a deep earnest longing and desire to be always with his friend — to be always with him, although oceans divided them. If no misfortune had befallen him, if his limbs had been sound and his body strong, Dan would have been intellectually superior to boys in the same station of life as himself. Debarred as he was from their amusements, their anxieties, and their general ways of life, he was thrown, as it were, upon his intellect for consolation. It brought him, by the blessing of God, such consolation that his misfortune might have been construed into a thing to be coveted. There is good in every thing.

All Dan's sympathies were with Joshua. Dan admired him for his determination, for his desire to be better than his fellows. It was Dan who first declared that Joshua was to be a hero; and Joshua accepted Dan's dictum with complacency. It threw a halo of romance around his determination not to be a wood-turner, and not to do as his father had done before him. The reader, from these remarks, or the incidents that follow, may now or presently understand why the wildly-vague essay on the "Philosophy of Dreams; or the Triumph of Mind over Matter," took Dan's mind prisoner and so infatuated him.

Referring to the book again, after the failure of the experiments upon his organ of combativeness, Dan found a few simple directions by which the reader could test, in a minor degree, the power of the mind over the sleeping body. One of the most simple was this: A person, before he goes to sleep, must resolutely make up his mind to wake at a certain hour in the morning. He must say to himself, "I want to wake at five o'clock — at five o'clock — at five o'clock; I *will* awake at five o'clock — I will — I will — I will!" and continue to repeat the words and the determination over and over again until he fell asleep, with the resolve firmly fixed in his mind. If you do this, said the writer, you will awake at five o'clock. Dan tried this experiment the same night — and failed. He repeated it the following night, and the night following that, with the same result. His sleep was disturbed, but that was all. But on the fourth night matters were different. Five o'clock was the hour Dan fixed upon, and nothing was more certain than that on the fourth night Dan woke up at the precise moment. There were two churches in the immediate neighborhood, and, as he woke, Dan heard the first church-bell toll the hour. One, two, three, four, five. Each stroke of the bell was followed by a dismal hum of woful tribulation. Then the other church-bell struck the hour, and each stroke of that was followed by a cheerful ring, bright and crisp and clear. Dan smiled and hugged himself, and went to sleep again, cherishing wild hopes which he dared not confess even to himself. He tried the experiment on the following night, fixing on a different time, half-past three. Undaunted by that and many other failures, he tried again and again, until one night he awoke when it was dark. He waited anxiously to hear the clocks strike. It seemed to be a very long half-hour, but the church-bell struck at last. One, two, three, four. With a droning sound at the end of each stroke, as if a myriad bees, imprisoned in a cell, were giving vent to a long-sustained and simultaneous groan of entreaty to be set free; or as if the bell were wailing for the hour that was dead. Then the joyous church-bell struck One, two, three, four. A wedding-peal in each stroke; sparkling, although invisible, like stars in a clear sky on a frosty night.

Dan went to sleep, almost perfectly happy.

He repeated his experiment every night, until he had a very nearly perfect command over sleep as far as regarded time, and could wake almost at any hour he desired. Then he took a forward step. While playing with his birds he said, "To-night I will dream of you." But the thought intervened that he had often dreamed of the birds, and that to dream of them that night would not be very remarkable. So he said, "No, I will not dream of the birds that are living; I will dream of Golden Cloud." It was a long time now since Golden Cloud had been buried, but Dan had never forgotten his pet. When he went to bed he said, "I will dream of Golden Cloud — a pleasant dream." And he dwelt upon his wish, and expressed it in words, again and again. That night he dreamed of Golden Cloud, and of its pretty tricks; of its growing old and shaky; of its death and burial. Then he saw something that he had never seen before. He saw it lying quite contented and happy at the bottom of its flower-pot coffin, and when he chirruped to it, it chirruped in return.

He told his dream to Joshua.

"I have dreamed of Golden Cloud a good many times," said Joshua.

"But I made up my mind especially to dream of Golden Cloud," said Dan, "and I dreamed of it the same night. At other times, my dreaming of it was not premeditated. It came in the usual way of dreams."

"What do you want me to believe from all this, Dan?"

"That, as the author of that book says, you can dream of any thing you wish. I scarcely dare believe that I shall be able to dream of what I shall most desire, by and by. By and by, Jo," he repeatedly sadly, "when you and me are parted."

Joshua threw his arms around Dan's neck.

"And you are doing all this, dear Dan, because you want to dream of me?"

"And because I want to be with you, Jo, and to see things that you see, and never, never to be parted from you." The wistful tears ran down Dan's cheek as he said these words.

"It would be very wonderful," said Joshua; "almost too wonderful. And I shall think, 'Dan is here with me, although I cannot see him.'"

"Listen again to what he says, Jo," said Dan, opening the "Triumph of Mind over Matter." "A person can so command and control his mental forces as to train himself to dream of events that are actually taking place at a distance from him, at the precise moment they occur."

"And that is what you want to do when I am away, Dan."

"That is what I want to do when you are away, dear Jo."

"I am positive you can't do it."

"Why? I dreamed of Golden Cloud when I wanted to."

"I can understand that. But how did you dream of Golden Cloud, Dan? You dreamed of him as if he was alive"—

"At first I did; but afterwards I saw him in the flower-pot, dead."

"And Golden Cloud chirruped to you?"

"Yes, Jo."

"Think again, Dan. Golden Cloud was dead, and Golden Cloud chirruped to you!"

"Yes, Jo," faltered Dan, beginning to understand the drift of Joshua's remarks.

"That is not dreaming of things as they are, Dan," said Joshua gently, taking Dan's hand and patting it. "If you could dream of Golden Cloud as he is now, you would see nothing of him but a few bones — feathers and flesh all turned to clay. Not a chirrup in him, Dan dear, not a chirrup!"

Dan covered his eyes with his hand, and the tears came through his fingers, But he soon recovered himself.

"You are right, Jo," he said: "yet I'm not quite wrong. The man who wrote that book knew things, depend upon it. He was not a fool. I was, to think I could do such wonders in so short a time."

Dan showed, in the last sentence, that he did not intend to relinquish his desire. He said nothing more about it, however, and in a few minutes the pair of bullfinches were on the table in a little cage, whistling, "Rule, Britannia," the high notes of which one of the birds took with consummate ease.

CHAPTER V.

JOSHUA MAKES UP HIS MIND TO GO TO SEA.

WHO was the Old Sailor?

Simply an old sailor. Having been a very young sailor indeed once upon a time, a great many years ago now, when, quite a little boy, he ran away from home and went to sea out of sheer love for blue water. In those times many boys did just the same thing, but that kind of boyish romance has been gradually dying away, and is now almost dead. Steam has washed off a great deal of its bright coloring. The taste of the salt spray grew so sweet to the young sailor's mouth, and the sight of the ocean —

the waters of which were not always blue, as he had imagined — grew so dear to his eyes, that every thing else became as naught to him. And so, faithful to his first love, he had grown from a young sailor to an old sailor. At the present time he was living in a rusty coal-barge, moored near the Tower stairs; and, although he could see land and houses on the other side of the water, there was a curl in his great nostrils as if he were smelling the sweet salt spray of the sea, and a staring look in his great blue eyes, as if the grand ocean were before him instead of a dirty river. He was a short thick-set man, and his face was deeply indented with small-pox; indeed, so marked were the impressions which that disease had left upon him, that his face looked for all the world like a conglomeration of miniature salt-cellars. His name was Praiseworthy Meddler. The sea was his world — the land was of no importance whatever. Not only was the land of no importance in his eyes, but it was a place to be despised, and the people who inhabited it were an inferior race. From him did Joshua Marvel learn of the glories and the wonders of the ocean, and from him came Joshua's inspiration to be a sailor.

For Joshua had settled upon the road which was to lead him to fame and fortune. By the time that he had made up his mind what was to be his future walk in life, most other lads in the parish of Stepney of the same age and condition as himself were already at work at different businesses, and had already commenced mounting that ladder which led almost always to an average of something less than thirty-two shillings a week for the natural term of their lives. Although, up to this period of his life, Joshua's career had been a profitless one, as far as earning money was concerned, his time had not been thrown away. The tastes he had acquired were innocent and good, and were destined to bear good fruit in the future. The boyish friendship he had formed was of incalculable value to him; for it was undoubtedly due, in a great measure, to that association that Joshua was kept from contact with bad companions. He had not yet given evidence of the possession of decided character, except what might be gathered from a certain quiet determination of will inherited from his mother, but stronger in him than in her because of his sex, and from a certain unswerving affection for any thing he loved. A phrenologist, examining his head, would probably have found that the organs of firmness and adhesiveness predominated over all his other faculties; and for the rest, something very much as follows. (Let it be understood that no attempt is here being made to give a perfect analysis of Joshua's faculties, but that mention is only being made of those organs which may help to explain, if they be remembered by the reader, and if there be any truth in phrenology, certain circumstances connected with Joshua's career, the consequences of which may have been varied in another man.) Well, then, adhesiveness and firmness very large; the first of which will account for his strong attachment for Dan, and the second for his determination, notwithstanding his mother's efforts, not to take to wood-turning nor any other trade, but to start in life for himself. Inhabitiveness very small; and as inhabitiveness means a tendency to dwell in one place, the want of that faculty will account for his desire to roam. All his moral and religious faculties — such as benevolence, wonder, veneration, and conscientiousness — were large; what are understood as the semi-intellectual sentiments — constructiveness, imitation and mirthfulness — he possessed only in a moderate degree; but one, ideality, was largely developed. Four of his intellectual faculties — individuality, language, eventuality, and time — call for especial notice: they were all very small, the smallest of them being eventuality, the especial function of which is a memory of events. Mention being made that his organs of color and tune were large, this brief analysis of Joshua's phrenological development is completed.

For the purpose of fitting himself for his future career, Joshua had lately spent a great deal of his time at the waterside, and in the course of a few months' experience in boats and barges on the River Thames, had made himself perfectly familiar with all the dangers of the sea. Praiseworthy Meddler had a great deal to do with Joshua's resolve. His attention had been directed to the quiet well-behaved lad, who came down so often to the waterside, and who sat gazing, with unformed thoughts, upon the river. Not upon the other side of it, where tumble-down wharves and melancholy walls were, but along the course of it, as far as its winding form would allow him to do so. Then his imagination followed the river, and gave it pleasanter banks and broader, until he could scarcely see any banks at all, so wide had the river grown; then he followed it farther still, until it merged into an ocean of waters, in which were crowded all the wonders he had read of in books of travel and adventure : wastes of sea, calm and grand in sunlight and in moonlight; fire following the ship at night, fire in the waters, as if millions of fire-fish had rushed up from the depths to oppose the wooden monster which ploughed them through; shoals of porpoises, sharks, whales, and all the wondrous breathing life in the mighty waters; curling waves lifting up the ship, which afterwards glides down into the valleys: blood moons, and such a wealth of stars in the heavens, and such feather-fringed azure clouds as made the heart beat to think of them; storms, too — dark waters seething and hissing, thunder awfully pealing, lightning flashes cutting the heavens open, and darting into the sea and cutting that with keen blades of light, then all darker than it was before: all these pictures came to Joshua's mind as, with eager eyes and clasped hands, he sat gazing at the dirty river. He held his breath as the storm-pictures came, but there was no terror in them; bright or dark, every thing he saw was tinged with the romance of youthful imagining. Praiseworthy Meddler spoke first to Joshua, divined his wish, encouraged it, told the lad stories of his own experience, and told them with such heartiness and enthusiasm, and made such a light matter of shipwreck and such like despondencies, that Joshua's aspirations grew and grew until he could no longer keep them to himself. And, of course, to whom should he first unbosom himself in plain terms but to his more than brother, Dan?

He disclosed his intentions in this manner: he was playing and singing 'Tom Bowling,' the words of which he had learned from old Praiseworthy. He sang the song through to the end, and Dan repeated the last two lines, —

"For though his body's under hatches,
His soul is gone aloft."

"*My* body has been under hatches to-day, Dan," said Joshua, "although I wasn't in the same condition as poor Tom Bowling. I dare say," with a furtive look at Dan, "that I shall often be under hatches."

"Ah!" said Dan. He knew what was coming.

"The Old Sailor has been telling me such stories, Dan! What do you think? He was taken by a pirate-ship once, and served with them for three months."

"As a pirate?"

"Yes; he has been a pirate. Isn't that glorious? It was an awful thing, though; the ship he was in — a merchantman — saw the pirate-ship giving chase. They tried to get away, but the pirates had a ship twice as good as theirs, and soon overhauled them. Then the grappling-irons were thrown, and the pirates swarmed into the merchantman, and there was a terrible fight. Those who were not killed were taken on board the pirate-ship, the Old Sailor among the rest. There were three women with them, and O Dan! would you believe it? — those devils, the pirates, killed them every one, men and women too, and threw them overboard — killed every one of them but the Old Sailor."

"How was it that he was saved, Jo?"

"That is a thing he never could make out, he says. It turned him sick to see the pirates slashing away with their cutlasses, but when they came to the women he was almost mad. He was bound to a mast by a strong rope, and when he saw a woman's face turned to him and looking at him imploringly, although her eyes were almost blinded by blood" —

"Oh!" cried Dan with a shudder, as if he could see the dreadful picture.

"It was a woman who had had a kind word for every one on the merchant-ship — a lady she was, and everybody loved her," continued Joshua, with kindling eyes and clinched fists. "When the Old Sailor saw her looking at him, he gave a yell, and actually broke the rope that bound him. But a dozen pirates had him down on the deck the next moment. He fought with them, and called out to them, 'Kill me, you devils!' You should hear the Old Sailor tell the story, Dan! 'Kill me, you devils!' he cried out, and he grappled with them, and hurt some of them. You may guess that they were too many for him. They bound him in such a zig-zag of ropes — round his neck and legs and back and arms — that he couldn't move, and they kicked him into a corner. There he lay, with his eyes shut, and heard the shrieks of his poor companions, and the splashes in the water as their bodies were thrown overboard. After that there was a great silence. 'Now it is my turn,' he said to himself, and he bit his tongue, so that he should not scream out. But it wasn't his turn; some of the pirates came about him, and talked in a lingo he couldn't understand, and when he thought they were going to slash at him, they went away, and left him lying on the deck alive! He lay there all night, dozing now and then, and, waking up in awful fright; for every time he dozed, he fancied that he heard the screams of the poor people who had been killed, and that he saw the bloody face of the poor lady he had tried to save. They didn't give him any thing to eat or drink all night; all they gave him was kicks. 'Then,' said the Old Sailor, 'they're going to starve me!' If he could have moved, he would have thrown himself into the sea, but he was too securely tied. Well, in the morning, the captain, who could speak a little English, came and ordered that the ropes should be loosened. 'Now's my time,' said the Old Sailor, and he felt quite glad, Dan, he says; and he says, too, that he felt as if he could have died happy if they had given him a chew of tobacco. 'Open your eyes, pig of an Englishman!' cried the captain, for the Old Sailor kept his eyes shut all the time. 'I sha'n't, pig of the devil!' roared the Old Sailor; but, without meaning it, he did open his eyes. 'Look here, pig,' said the captain, 'you are a strong man, and you ought to be a good sailor.' 'I'd show you what sort of a sailor I am, if you would cut these infernal'"—

"O Jo!" said Dan, with a warning finger to his lips.

"That is what the Old Sailor said, Dan," continued Joshua. "'I'd show you what sort of a sailor I am, if you would cut these — you know what — ropes, and give me a cutlass or a marlin-spike!' But the captain only laughed at him; and said, 'Now, pig, listen. You will either do one of two things. You will either be one of us'— 'Turn pirate!' cried the Old Sailor; 'no, I'll be — you know what, Dan — if I do!' 'Very well, pig,' said the captain; 'refuse, and you shall be cut to pieces, finger by finger, and every limb of you. I give you an hour, pig, to think of it.' The Old Sailor says that, if he had had a bit of tobacco, he would have chosen to be killed, even in that dreadful manner, rather than consent to join them. He never in all his life longed so for a thing as he longed then for a quid, as he calls it. It made him mad to see the dark devils chewing their tobacco as they worked. 'Anyhow,' he thought, 'I may as well live as be killed. I shall get a chance of escape one day.' So when the hour was up, and the captain came, the Old Sailor told him that he would oblige them by not being chopped into mince-meat, if they would give him a chew of tobacco. They gave it to him, and unbound him; and that is the way he became a pirate."

"And how did he get away, Jo?" asked Dan.

"That is wonderful, too," continued Joshua. "He was with them for three months, and saw strange things and bad things, but never took part in them. They tried to force him to do as they did, but he wouldn't. And he made himself so useful to them, and worked so hard, that it wasn't to their interest to get rid of him."

"I think the Old Sailor must be a little bit of a hero, Jo," interrupted Dan.

Joshua laughed heartily at this. "You will not say so when you see him."

"Why? I suppose he is ugly."

Joshua raised his hand expressively.

"And weather-beaten, and all that"—

"And knows," said Joshua, still laughing, "'Which is the properest day to drink, Saturday, Sunday, Monday?'"

"Still he may be a hero — not like you, Jo, because you will be handsome."

"Do you think so?"

If by some strange chance a picture of Joshua, as he was to be one day, had presented itself to the lads, how they would have wondered and marvelled as to what could have been the youth of such a man as they saw before them! Look at Joshua now, as he is sitting by Dan's side. A handsome open-faced lad, full of kindly feeling, and with the reflex of a generous loving nature beaming in his eyes. Honest face, bright eyes, laughing mouth that could be serious, strong limbs, head covered with curls — a beautiful picture of happy boyhood. But no more surprising miracle could have occurred to Dan than to see Joshua, as he saw him then, sitting by his side, and then to see the shadow of what was to come.

"Do you think so?" and Joshua laughingly repeated the question.

"Do I think so" said Dan, gazing with pride at his friend. "O Mr. Vanity! as if you didn't know!"

Joshua, laughing more than ever, protested that he had never given it a thought, and promised that he would take a good long look at himself in the glass that very night. At the rate the lads were going on, it appeared as if the Old Sailor's story would never be completed, and so Daniel said, to put a stop to Joshua's nonsense.

"It is all your fault, Dan," said Joshua, "because you *will* interrupt. Well, when the Old Sailor had been in the ship for three months, it was attacked by a cruiser which had been hunting it down for a long time. All the pirates were taken — the Old Sailor and all — and sold as slaves at Algiers. They wouldn't believe his story about his not being a pirate, and he was sold for a slave with the rest of them. He worked in chains in the fields for a good many weeks — he doesn't remember how many — until Lord Exmouth bombarded the forts, and put a stop to Christian slavery. And that is the Old Sailor's pirate-story."

"And now to return to what we were saying before you commenced," said Dan. Joshua placed his hands at the back of his head, and interlacing his fingers, looked seriously at Dan, and drew a long breath: "You have something to tell me, Jo."

"I have," said Joshua. "I have made up my mind what I am going to be. You can guess if you like."

"I have no need to guess, Jo, dear; I know, I have seen it all along."

"What is it, then?"

"You are going to sea," said Dan, striving to speak in a cheerful voice, but failing.

"Yes, I shall go to sea;" and Joshua drew another long breath. "How did you find it out, Dan the Wise?"

"How did I find it out, Jo the Simple? Haven't I seen it in your eyes for ever so long? Haven't you been telling me so every day? It might escape others' notice, but not mine."

"I told the Old Sailor to-day, and he clapped me on the back, and said I was a brave fellow. But he knew it all along, too, he said. And he took me into his cabin — such a cabin, Dan — and poured out a tiny glass of rum, and made me drink it. My throat was on fire for an hour afterwards."

"Have you told mother and father?"

"No."

"Tell them at once, Jo. Go home now, and tell them. I want to be left alone to think of it. O Jo! and I am going to lose you!"

Dan had tried hard to control himself, but he now burst into a passion of weeping; and it is a fact, notwithstanding that they were both big boys, that their heads the next moment were so close together that Dan's tears rolled down both their faces. Joshua's heart was as full as Dan's, and he ran out of the room more to lessen Dan's grief than his own.

Thus it fell out that in the evening, when the members of the Marvel family, variously occupied, were sitting at the kitchen fire, Joshua said suddenly to his relatives, —

"I should like to go to sea."

George Marvel was smoking a long claypipe; Mrs. Marvel was darning a pair of worsted stockings, in which scarcely a vestige of their original structure was left; and Sarah Marvel was busily engaged in a writing-lesson, in the execution of which she was materially assisted by her tongue, which, hanging its full length out of her mouth, was making occasional excursions to the corners of her lips. George Marvel took the pipe from his lips and looked at the fire meditatively; Mrs. Marvel burst into tears, and let the worsted stocking, with the needle sticking in it, drop into her lap; and Sarah Marvel, casting a doubtful look at her writing-lesson, every letter in which appeared to be possessed with a peculiar species of drunkenness, removed her eyes to her brother's face, upon which she gazed with wonder and admiration. So engrossed was she in the contemplation, that she put the inky part of the pen into her mouth, and sucked at it in sheer absence of mind.

"Don't cry, mother," said George Marvel. "What was that you said, Josh?"

"I should like to go to sea, father."

"Ah!" ejaculated Mr. Marvel thoughtfully, looking steadily into the fire.

Joshua was also looking into the fire, and he saw in it, as plain as plain could be, a fiery ship, full-rigged, with fiery ropes and fiery sails, and saw himself, Joshua Marvel, standing on the poop, dressed in gold-laced coat and gold-laced cocked-hat, with a telescope in his hand. For Joshua, without the slightest idea as to how it was all to come about, had made up his mind that he was to be a captain, dressed as Nelson was in a picture which was one of Praiseworthy Meddler's prize possessions, and which occupied the place of honor in the Old Sailor's cabin. While this vision was before Joshua Mrs. Marvel continued to cry, but in a more subdued manner.

"And so you want to be sailor, Josh?" queried Mr. Marvel.

"Yes. A sailor first, and then a captain."

The intermediate grades were of too small importance to be considered.

"I am sure, Josh," said Mrs. Marvel, crying all the while, "I don't see what you want to go away for. Why don't you make up your mind even now to apprentice yourself to father's trade and be contented? You might get a little shop of your own in time, if you worked very hard, and it would be pleasant for all of us."

"You be quiet, mother," said Mr. Marvel. "What do women know about these things? I'm Joshua's father, I believe "—

"Yes, George, I believe you are," sobbed Mrs. Marvel.

"And, as Joshua's father, I tell you again, once and for all, that he's not going to be a wood-turner. Here's the old subject come up again with a vengeance! I wish a woman's clothes were like a woman's ideas; then they would never wear out. A woodturner! A pretty thing a wood-turner is! I've been a wood-turner all my life, and what better off am I for it?"

"I am sure, father, we have been very happy,' said Mrs. Marvel.

"I am not saying any thing about that." observed Mr. Marvel, expressing in his voice a very small regard for domestic happiness, although, in reality, no man better appreciated it. "What I say is, I've been a wood-turner all my life; and what I ask is, what better off am I, or you, or any of us, for it? If Josh likes to be a wood-turner, he can; I have nothing to say against it, except that he's been a precious long time making up his mind. And if he likes to be a sailor, he can; I have nothing to say against that. I'm Joshua's father, and, as Joshua's father, I say if Josh likes to make a start in life for himself as a sailor, let him. If I was Josh, I would do the same myself."

"Thank you, father," said Joshua.

"And, mother, if you only heard what Mr. Praiseworthy Meddler says of the sea, you would think very differently; I know you would."

But Mrs. Marvel shook her head and would not be comforted.

"My father was a wood-turner," said Mr. Marvel, "and he made me a wood-turner. He never asked me whether I would or I wouldn't, and I didn't have a choice. If he had have asked me, perhaps we shouldn't have gone on pinching and pinching all our lives. Now Joshua's different; he's got his choice: never forget, Josh, that it was your father who gave you the world to pick from — and I think he's acting sensibly, as I should have done if *my* father had given me the chance. But he didn't, and it's too late for a man with his head full of white hairs to commence life all over again."

And Mr. Marvel fell to smoking his pipe again, and studying the fire.

"I've never seen the sea myself," he presently resumed; "but I've read of it, and heard talk of it. There are better lands across the seas than Stepney, for a youngster like Josh. There are lots of chances, too; and who knows what may happen?"

"That's where it is, father," whimpered Mrs. Marvel; "we don't know what might happen. Suppose Josh is shipwrecked; what would you say then? You'd lie awake night after night, father — you know you would — and wish he had been a wood-turner. I've never seen the sea, and I never want to; I've been happy enough without it. It's like flying in the face of Providence. And what's to become of us when we are old, if Josh can't take care of us?"

"Just so, mother. Listen to me, and be sensible. Suppose Josh becomes a wood-turner; he can't expect to do better than his father has done. I am not a bad workman myself; and though Josh might make as good, I don't think he'd make a better. Now what I say again is — and it's wonderful what a many times a man has to say a thing before he can drive it into a woman's head, if she ain't willing — although I'm a good workman, what better off am I for it? And what better off would Josh be for it, when he gets to be as old as I am? We've commenced to lay by a good many times — haven't we, Maggie? — but we never could keep on with it. First a bit of sickness took it; then a bit of furniture that we couldn't do without took it; then a rise in bread and meat took it; and then a bit of something else took it. You've been a good woman to me, Maggie, and you've pinched all you could for twenty years; and what has come of all your pinching? There's that old teapot you used to lay by in. It's at the back of the cupboard now, and it hasn't had a shilling in it for I don't know when's the time. It would be full of dust, mother, only you don't like dust; and a good job too. But it ain't your fault that it isn't full of something better; and it ain't my fault. It's all because I've been a wood-turner all my days. And the upshot of it is, that we're not a bit better off now than we were twenty years ago. We're worse off; for we've spent twenty good years and got nothing for them."

"We've got Josh and Sarah," Mrs. Marvel ventured to say. The simple woman actually regarded those possessions as of inestimable value — but that is the way of a great many foolish mothers.

Her husband did not heed the remark. He took another pull at his pipe, but drew no smoke from it. His pipe was out; but in his earnestness he puffed away at nothing, and continued, —

"Who is to take care of us, you want to know, when we grow old, if Josh don't. When Josh grows up, Josh will get married, naturally."

"So shall I, father," interrupted Sarah, who was listening with the deepest interest to the conversation.

"Perhaps, Sarah," said Mr. Marvel a little dubiously. "Girls ain't like boys; they can't pick and choose. Josh will get married, naturally; and Josh will have children, naturally. Perhaps he'll have two; perhaps he'll have six."

"Mrs. Pigeon's got thirteen," remarked Sarah vivaciously.

"Be quiet, Sarah. Where did you learn manners? Now if Josh has six children, and, being a wood-turner, doesn't do any better as a wood-turner than his father has done — and he's a presumptuous young beggar if he thinks he's going to do better than me —"

"I don't think so, father," said Joshua.

"Never mind. And he's a presumptuous young beggar if he thinks he's going to do better than me," Mr. Marvel repeated; he relished the roll of the words — " what's to become of us then? Josh, if he's a wood-turner with six children, can't be expected to keep his old father and mother. He will have enough to do as it is. But if Josh strikes out for himself, who knows what may happen? He may do this, or he may do that; and then we shall be all right."

There was not the shadow of a doubt that in that house the gray mare was the worse horse, in defiance of the old adage.

"And as to Joshua's being shipwrecked,"

continued Mr. Marvel, "you know as well as I do, mother, that it would be enough to break my heart. But I don't believe there's more danger on the sea than on the land. There was Bill Brackett run over yesterday by a brewer's dray, and three of his ribs broken. You don't get run over by a brewer's dray at sea. And what occurred to William Small a month ago? He was walking along as quiet and inoffensive as could be, when a brick from a scaffold fell upon his head, and knocked every bit of sense clean out of him. They don't build brick houses on the sea. Why, it might have happened to me, or you, or Josh!"

"Or me, father," cried Sarah, not at all pleased at being deprived of the chance of being knocked on the head by a brick.

"Or you, Sarah. So, mother, don't let us have any more talk about shipwrecks."

"But if Josh does get shipwrecked, father," persisted Mrs. Marvel, "remember that I warned you beforehand."

"But Josh is not going to get shipwrecked," exclaimed Mr. Marvel, slightly raising his voice, determined not to tolerate domestic insubordination; "therefore, hold your tongue, and say nothing more about it."

There was one privilege for the possession of which Mr. Marvel had fought many a hard battle in the early days of his married life, and which he now believed he possessed by right of conquest; that was the privilege of having the last word. To all outward appearance Mrs. Marvel respected this privilege; but in reality she set it at defiance. It was a deceptive victory that he had gained; for if he had the last audible word, Mrs. Marvel had the last inaudible one. Woman is a long-suffering creature; she endures much with patience and resignation; but to yield the last word to a man is a sacrifice too great for her to make. There are, no doubt, instances of such sacrifice; but they are very rare. Many precious oblations had Mrs. Marvel made in the course of her married life; but she had not sacrificed the last word upon the domestic altar. True, it was always whispered inly, under her breath; but it was hers nevertheless; and she exulted in it. When a woman cannot get what she wants by hook, she gets it by crook, depend upon it. For twenty years had the Marvels lived together man and wife; and during all that time Mr. Marvel had never known, that in every family conversation and discussion his wife had invariably obtained the victory of the last word; although sometimes a half-triumphant look in her eyes had caused him to doubt.

So, upon this occasion, notwithstanding the decided tone in which her husband had closed the conversation, Mrs. Marvel bent her head over her worsted stocking, and whispered to herself, half tearfully and half triumphantly,—

"But if Josh does get shipwrecked, father, don't forget that I warned you beforehand."

CHAPTER VI.

THE ACTOR AND HIS DAUGHTER.

THAT night, as Joshua was lying half-awake and half-asleep, his mind being filled with pleasant sea-pictures, he was surprised to hear his bedroom-door creak. Without moving in his bed, he turned his eyes towards the door, and, in the indistinct light, he saw his mother enter the room. She opened the door very softly, as if fearful of disturbing him, and she paused for a moment or two in the open space, with her hand raised in a listening attitude. Joshua saw that she believed him to be asleep, and he closed his eyes as she approached the bed. Her movements were so quiet, that he did not know she was close to him, until she gently took his hand and placed it to her lips. Then he knew that she was kneeling by his bedside, and knew also, by a moisture on his hand, that she was crying. His heart yearned to her, but he did not move. He heard her whisper, "God protect you, my son!" Then his hand, wet with his mother's tears, was released, and when he re-opened his eyes, she was gone.

"Poor mother!" he thought. "She is unhappy because I am going to sea. I will ask the Old Sailor to come and tell her what a glorious thing the sea is. Perhaps that will make her more comfortable in her mind."

He acted upon his resolution the very next day, and his efforts were successful. In the evening, he wended his way homewards from the waterside, in a state of ineffable satisfaction because the Old Sailor had promised to come to Stepney, for the express purpose of proving to Mrs. Marvel how superior in every respect the sea was to the land, and what a wise thing Joshua had done in making up his mind to be a sailor.

The lad was in an idle happy humor as he walked down a narrow street, at no great distance from his home. It differed in no respect from the other common streets in the common neighborhood. All its characteristics were familiar to him. The sad-looking one-story brick houses; the slatternly girls nursing babies, whose name was legion; the troops of children of various ages and in various stages of dirtiness, one of their most distinguishing insignia being the yawning condition of their boots, there not being a sound boot-lace among the lot of them; and here and there the melancholy and desponding shops where sweet stuff and cheap provisions were sold. Joshua walked down this poor woe-begone street, making it bright with his bright fancies, when his attention was suddenly aroused by the occurrence of something unusual near the bottom of the street.

A large crowd of boys and girls and women was gathered around a person, who was gesticulating and declaiming with startling earnestness. Pushing his way through the throng, Joshua saw before him a tall, spare man, with light hair hanging down to his shoulders. So long and waving was his hair, that it might have belonged to a woman. His gaunt and furrowed face was as smooth as a woman's, and his mouth was large, as were also his teeth, which were peculiarly white and strong. But what most arrested attention were his eyes; they were of a light-gray color, large even for his large face, and they had a wandering look in them strangely at variance with the sense of power and firmness that dwelt in every other feature. He was acting the Ghost scenes in "Hamlet;" in his hand was a wooden sword, which he sheathed in his ragged coat, and drew and flourished when occasion needed. His fine voice, now deep as a man's, now tender as a woman's, expressed all the passions, and expressed them well. In the library which Dan and Joshua possessed there was an odd volume of Shakspeare's works, and when the street-actor said, in a melancholy dreamy tone, —

"It waves me still: — go on, I'll follow thee,"

Joshua remembered (as much from the intelligent action of the actor as from the words themselves) that it was a Ghost whom Hamlet was addressing. The words were so impressively spoken, that Joshua almost fancied he saw a Shade before the man's uplifted hand. Then, when Hamlet cried, —

"My fate cries out,
And makes each petty artery in this body
As hardy as the Nemean lion's nerve.
Still am I called. Unhand me, gentlemen!"

(struggling with his visionary opponents and breaking from them, and drawing his wooden sword)

"By heaven, I'll make a ghost of him that lets me!
I say, away! Go on, I'll follow thee;"

Joshua experienced a thrill of emotion that only the representation of true passion could have excited. As the man uttered the last words, Joshua heard a shuddering sigh close to him. Turning his head, he saw Susan, whose face was a perfect encyclopædia of wondering and terrified admiration.

"Who is he following, Joshua?" she asked in a whisper, clutching him by the sleeve.

"The Ghost! Hush!"

"The Ghost!" (with a violent shudder.) "Where?"

Joshua pressed her hand, and warned her to be silent, so as not to disturb the man. Susan held his hand tightly in hers, and obeyed.

The Ghost that the actor saw in his mind's eye was standing behind Susan. The man advanced a step in that direction, and stood with outstretched sword, gazing at the airy nothing. Susan trembled in every limb as the man glared over her shoulder, and she was frightened to move her head, lest she should see the awful vision whose presence was palpable to her senses. The man had commenced the platform-scene, where Hamlet says, "Speak; I'll go no further;" and the Ghost says, "Mark me!" when a tumult took place. At the words, "Mark me!" a vicious boy picked up a piece of mud, and threw it at the man's face, with the words, "Now you're marked;" at which several of the boys and girls laughed and clapped their hands. The actor made no answer, but, seizing the boy by the shoulder held him fast and proceeded with the scene. The boy tried to wriggle himself away, but at every fresh attempt the man's grasp tightened, until, thoroughly desperate, the boy broke into open rebellion.

Actor. Thus was I, sleeping, by a brother's hand
Of life, of crown, of queen, at once despatched.

Boy (struggling violently). Just you let me go, will you?

Actor. Cut off even in the blossoms of my sin, Unhousel'd, disappointed, unaneal'd.

Boy (beginning to cry). Come now, let me go will you? You're a hurting of me! Let me go you — (bad words).

Actor (calm and indifferent). No reckoning made,
 but sent to my account
With all my imperfections on my head.

A girl's voice. Pinch him, Billy!
A boy's voice. Kick him, Billy!
Billy did both, but the actor continued.

Actor. Oh, horrible! Oh, horrible! Most horrible

Billy. Throw a stone at him, some one!

Actor (sublimely unconscious). If thou hast nature in thee, bear it not.

A stone was thrown; and as if this were a signal for a general attack, a shower of stones was hurled at the actor. One of them hit him on the forehead; hit him so badly that he staggered, and, releasing his hold of Billy, raised his hand to his head, while an expression of pain passed into his face. Hooting and yelling, "Look at the mad actor!" "Hoo, hoo! look at the crazy fool!"—the crowd of boys and girls scampered away, and left the man standing in the road, with only Susan and Joshua for an audience. Joshua was hot with indignation, and Susan, spell-bound by awe and fear, stood motionless by Joshua's side, while large tears trickled from her eyes into her open mouth.

The blood was oozing from the wound in the man's forehead, and his long fair hair was crimson-stained. His eyes wandered around distressfully, and a sighing moan died upon his lips. The fire of enthusiasm had fled from his countenance, and in the place of the inspired actor, Joshua saw a man whose face was of a deathly hue, and from whose eyes the light seemed to have departed. With his hand pressed to his forehead, he staggered a dozen yards, and then leaned against the wall for support.

"He is badly hurt, I am afraid," said Joshua.

Susan walked swiftly up to the man.

"Shall we assist you home?" she said.

"Home!" he muttered. "No, no! Money! I want money!"

As he spoke he drooped, and would have fallen to the ground but for Joshua, who caught the man on his shoulder, and let him glide gently on to a door-step. Susan wiped the blood from his face with her apron. He looked at her vacantly, closed his eyes, and fainted.

"He is dying, Joshua!" cried Susan, her trembling fingers wandering about the man's face. "Oh, the wicked boys! Oh, the wicked boys!"

A woman here came out of a house with a cup of cold water, which she sprinkled upon his face. Presently the man sighed, and struggled to his feet, murmuring, "Yes, yes; I must go home."

"Where do you live?" asked Joshua. "We will assist you."

He did not answer, but walked slowly on like one in a dream. Assisting but not guiding his steps, Joshua and Susan walked on either side of him, and supported him. Although he scarcely seemed to be awake, he knew his way, and turning down a street even commoner than its fellows, he stopped at the entrance to a miserable court. Waving his hand as if dismissing them, he walked a few steps down the court, and entered a house, the door of which was open. Impelled partly by curiosity, but chiefly by compassion, Joshua and Susan followed the man into a dark passage, and up a rheumatic flight of stairs, into a room where want and wretchedness made grim holiday.

"Minnie!" he muttered hoarsely, and all his strength seemed to desert him as he spoke—"Minnie, child! where are you?"

He sank upon the ground with a wild shudder, and lay as if death had overtaken him. At the same moment there issued from the corner of the room where the deepest shadows gathered, a child-girl, so marvellously like him, with her fair waving hair, her large beautifully-shaped mouth, her white teeth, and her great restless gray eyes, that Joshua knew at once that they were father and daughter.

Minnie crept to the man, and sat beside him. She spoke to him, but he did not reply. And then she looked at Joshua and Susan, whose forms were dimly discernible in the gathering gloom.

"What is the matter with father?" she asked of them in a faint moaning voice.

"Some bad boys threw a stone at him, and hit him on the forehead," Joshua answered. "He will be better presently, I hope."

Minnie did not heed what he said, but felt eagerly in her father's pockets, and, not finding what she searched for, began to cry.

"No, no," she said, beating her hands together; "it is not that. He is weak and ill because he has had nothing to eat. I thought he would have brought home enough to buy some bread, but he hasn't a penny."

Joshua remembered the man's words, "Money! I want money!" and he immediately realized that the poor creatures were in want.

"Are you hungry, Minnie?" he asked.

"I have not had any breakfast," she answered wearily. "No more has father. Nor any dinner. We had some bread last night. We ate it all up. Father went out to-day, hoping to earn a little money, and he has come home without any. We shall die, I suppose. But I should like something to eat first."

"How do you know he has had nothing to eat?" asked Joshua; the words almost choked him.

Minnie looked up with a plaintive smile. "If he had had only a hard piece of bread given him," she said in a tender voice, "he would have put it into his pocket for me."

"Stop here, Susan," said Joshua, a great sob rising in his throat. "I will be back in ten minutes."

He ran out of the room and out of the house. Never in his life had he run so fast as he ran now. He rushed into Dan's room, and said, almost breathlessly,—

"Where is the money-box, Dan? How much is there in it?"

"Fourteen pence," said the faithful treasurer, producing the box. "What a heat you are in, Jo!"

"Never mind that. I want every farthing of the money, Dan. Don't ask me any questions. I will tell you all by and by."

Dan emptied the money-box upon the table, and Joshua seized the money, and tore out of the house as if for dear life. Soon he was in the actor's room again, with bread and tea. Susan had not been idle during his absence. She had bathed the man's wound, and had wiped the blood and mud from his face and hair. He had recovered from his swoon, and was looking at her gratefully.

Joshua placed the bread before him, and he broke a piece from the loaf and gave it to Minnie, who ate it greedily.

"'So fair and foul a day I have not seen,'" the man muttered; and both Joshua and Susan thought, "How strangely yet how beautifully he speaks!"

Susan made the tea down stairs, and she and Joshua sat quietly by, while the man and his daughter ate like starved wolves. It was a bitterly-painful sight to see.

"I think we had better go now, Susan," whispered Joshua.

They would have left the room without a word; but the man said,—

"What is your name, and what are you?"

"My name is Joshua Marvel, and I'm going to be a sailor."

"'There's a sweet little cherub that sits up aloft,'" said the actor, "'to keep watch for the life of poor Jack.'"

"That's what Praiseworthy Meddler says," said Joshua, laughing. "I shall come and see you again, if you will let me."

"Come and welcome."

"Good-night, sir."

"Good-night, and God bless you, Joshua Marvel!"

Minnie went to the door with Joshua and Susan, and looking at Joshua, with the tears in her strangely-beautiful eyes, said,

"Good-night, and God bless you, Joshua Marvel!"

She raised herself on tiptoe, and Joshua stooped and kissed her. After that, Susan gave her a hug, and she returned to her father, and lay down beside him.

When he arrived home, Joshua told Dan of the adventure, and how he had spent the fourteen pence. Dan nodded his head approvingly.

"You did right," he said,—"you always do. I should have done just the same."

Then they took the odd volume of Shakspeare from the shelf, and read the Ghost scenes in "Hamlet" before they said goodnight.

CHAPTER VII.

EXPLAINS WHY PRAISEWORTHY MEDDLER REMAINED A BACHELOR.

HERE is Praiseworthy Meddler, sitting in the best chair in a corner of the fireplace in the little kitchen in Stepney. In his low shoes and loose trousers, and blue shirt open at the throat, he looks every inch a sailor; and his great red pock-marked face is in keeping with his calling. On the other side of the fireplace, facing Praiseworthy Meddler, is Mr. George Marvel; next to Praiseworthy Meddler is Mrs. Marvel; on a stool at her father's feet sits Sarah; and Joshua sits at the table, watching every shade of expression that passes over his mother's face. The subject-matter of the conversation is the sea; and Praiseworthy Meddler has been "holding forth," as is evidenced by his drawing from the bosom of his shirt a blue-cotton pocket-handkerchief, upon which is imprinted a ship of twelve hundred tons burden, A 1 at Lloyd's for an indefinite number of years. The ship is in full sail, and all its canvas is set to a favorable breeze. Upon this blue vessel Praiseworthy Meddler dabs his red face in a manner curiously suggestive of his face being a deck, and the handkerchief a mop. When he has mopped his deck, which appears to be a perpetually-perspiring one, he spreads his handkerchief over his knee to dry, and says, as being an appropriate tag to what has gone before,—

"There is no place on earth like the sea."

The Old Sailor was not aware that any thing of a paradoxical nature was involved in the statement, or he might not have repeated it.

"There is no place on earth like the sea. Show me the man who says there is, and I'll despise him; if I don't, I'm a Dutchman;" adding, to strengthen his declaration, "or a double Dutchman."

The man not being forthcoming—probably he was not in the neighborhood, or, being there, did not wish to be openly despised—Praiseworthy Meddler looked around with the air of one who has the best of the argument, and then produced a piece of pigtail from a mysterious recess, and bit into it as if he were a savage boar biting into the heart of a foe.

"But the danger, Mr. Meddler," suggested Mrs. Marvel, in a trembling voice.

"There is more danger upon land, lady."

"There, mother," said Mr. Marvel; "didn't I tell you so, the other night?"

"You told her right," said Praiseworthy, with emphasis. "Danger on the sea, lady! What is it to danger on the land? A ship can ride over a wave, let it be ever so high; but a man can't step over a wagon. Are carts and drays and horses safe? Are gas-pipes safe? And if there is danger on the sea, lady — which I don't deny, mind you, altogether — what does it do? Why, it makes a man of a boy, and it makes a man more of a man."

"Hear, *hear*, HEAR!" exclaimed Mr. Marvel, rapping on the table.

"Look at me!" said the enthusiastic sailor. "Here am I — I don't know how many years old, and that's a fact — I've lived on the sea from when I was a boy; and I've been blown by rough winds, and I've been blinded by storms, and I've been wrecked on rocky coasts, and I've been as near death, ay, a score of times, as most men have been. Lord love you, my dear! All we've got to do is to do our duty; and when we're called aloft, we can say, 'Ay, ay, sir!' with a brave heart. What better life than a life on sea is there for boy or man? And doesn't Saturday night come round?

"For all the world's just like the ropes aboard a ship.
Each man's rigged out,
A vessel stout,
To take for life a trip.
The shrouds, the stays, the braces,
Are joys, and hopes, and fears;
The halliards, sheets, and traces,
Still as each passion veers,
And whim prevails,
Direct the sails,
As on the sea of life he steers.
Then let the storm
Heaven's face deform,
And danger press;
Of these in spite, there are some joys
Us jolly tars to bless;
For Saturday night still comes, my boys,
To drink to Poll and Bess.'"

Praiseworthy Meddler roared out the song at the top of his voice, as if it were the most natural and appropriate thing for him to do just there and then. The effect of his sudden inspiration was, that every member of the Marvel family, without being previously acquainted with the young ladies referred to, repeated in their honor the refrain of the last two lines, —

"For Saturday night still comes, my boys,
To drink to Poll and Bess,'"

with such extraordinary enthusiasm, that the carroty-haired cat rose to her feet in alarm, debating within herself the possibility of the Marvel family having suddenly caught a contagious madness from the Old Sailor. Convinced that the matter required looking into, puss walked softly to the door, with the intention of arousing the neighbors; but, silence ensuing at the conclusion of the refrain, she became reassured, and stole back to her warm space on the floor, and curled herself up again, and blinked at the fire.

After this exertion, Praiseworthy Meddler took the twelve-hundred-ton ship off his knee, and dubbed his face with it energetically.

"What does it amount to," he continued, "if the heart's brave? What does it amount to when it is all over, and when one gets to be as old as I am? I'm tough and firm;" and he gave his leg a great slap. "I'm as young as a younger man; and I know that there's no place on earth like the sea."

"And you can get promotion, can t you?" asked Joshua, eagerly. "A man needn't be a common sailor all his life?"

"No, Josh; he needn't stick at that, if he's willing and able, and does his duty. I know many a skipper who once on a time was only an able-bodied seaman."

"Do you hear that, mother?" cried Joshua. "Now are you satisfied?" and he jumped up and gave her a kiss.

"What is a skipper, Mr. Meddler?" asked Mrs. Marvel, with her arm round Joshua's waist. She had a dim notion that a skipper was connected with a skipping-rope, and that she might have been a skipper in her girlhood's days. If that were the case, she could not see what advantage it would be to Joshua to become one.

"A skipper's a captain, mother," whispered Joshua.

"Oh!" said Mrs. Marvel, but not quite clear in her mind on the point. "Then, if I might be so bold, Mr. Meddler" —

But here Mrs. Marvel stopped suddenly, and blushed like a girl.

"Ay, ay, lady, go on," said the Old Sailor, encouragingly.

"If I might make so bold," continued Mrs. Marvel, with an effort, "how is it that you never rose to be a skipper?"

"O mother!" cried Joshua.

"The question is a sensible one, Joshua," said Praiseworthy Meddler slowly, "and a right one too; though, if all able-bodied seamen rose to be skippers, there wouldn't be ships enough in the world for them. I should have been promoted, I have no doubt; but I was born with something unfortunate, which has stuck to me all my life, and which I have never been able to get rid of."

"Is it any thing painful?" asked Mrs. Marvel with womanly solicitude.

Praiseworthy Meddler looked at her with a droll expression on his face, and folded his twelve-hundred-ton ship into very small squares, and laid it in the palm of his left hand, and flattened it with the palm of his right, before he spoke again.

"It wasn't my fault, it was my misfortune. I couldn't help my father's name being Meddler, and I couldn't help being a Meddler myself, being his son, you see. My father didn't like his name any more than I did, but he didn't know how to change it; he was born a Meddler, and he died a Meddler. My being a Meddler is the only reason, I do believe, why I am not a skipper this present day of our Lord; and I don't think I am sorry that, when I die, I sha'n't leave any Meddlers behind me."

"You have never been married, Mr. Meddler?"

"No, lady; but I was very near it once, as you shall hear. It was all because of my name that I wasn't. My father didn't like his name, as I have told you. His Christian name was Andrew; he was a saddler. He got along well enough to set up shop for himself, and one morning he took the shutters down for the first time, and commenced business. Over his window was the sign, 'A. Meddler, saddler.' There was a rival saddler in the same town, whose name was Straight, and who didn't like my father setting up in opposition to him; and he put in his window a bill, with this on it: 'Have your saddles made and repaired by a Straightforward man, and not by A. Meddler.' That ruined my father: people laughed at him, instead of dealing with him; he soon had to shut up shop, and go to work again as a journeyman. He had two children; the first was a girl, the next was me. I heard that he was very pleased when my sister was born, because she was a girl. 'She can marry when she grows up,' he said, 'and then she will have her husband's name.' When I was born, my father wasn't pleased: he didn't want any more Meddlers, he said. But he couldn't help it; no more could I. He did what he thought was the very best thing for me — he gave me a fine Christian name to balance my surname: he had me christened Praiseworthy. Now that made it worse. If I was laughed at for being a Meddler, I was laughed at more for being a Praiseworthy Meddler. Once, when I was a young fellow, I did good service in a ship I was serving in. When we came into port, the skipper reported well of me, and the owners sent for me. I went to the office, thinking that I should be promoted for my good services. The firm owned at least a dozen merchant-ships; and I should have been promoted, if it hadn't been for my name. The owners spoke kindly to me; and after I had satisfied them that I was fit for promotion, the youngest partner asked my name. I told him Meddler. He smiled, and the other partners smiled. 'What other name?' he asked. 'Praiseworthy,' I answered; 'Praiseworthy Meddler.' He laughed at that, and said that I was the only Praiseworthy Meddler he had ever met. They seemed so tickled at it, that the serious part of the affair slipped clean out of their heads; they called me an honest fellow, and said that they would not forget me. They didn't forget me; they gave me five pounds over and above my pay. If it hadn't been for my name, they might have appointed me mate of one of their ships. I was so mad with thinking about it, that I began to hate myself because I was a Meddler. If the name had been something I could have got hold of, I would have strangled it. At last I made up my mind that I would get spliced, and that I would take my lass's name the day I was married. Being on leave, and stopping at my father's house, I told him what I had made up my mind to do. He was a melancholy man — it was his name that made him so, I do believe — and he told me, in his melancholy voice, that it was the best thing I could do, and that he wished he had thought of doing so before he married. 'Wipe it out, my boy,' he said, 'wipe out the unlucky name; sweep all the Meddlers out of the world. It would have been better you had been born with a hump than been born a Meddler.' He talked a little wild sometimes, but we were used to it. I began to look about me; and one day I caught sight of a lass who took my fancy. My leave was nearly expired, and I had to join my ship in a few days. I wanted to learn all about the girl, and I was too bashful to do it myself, which is not the usual way of sailors, my dear. So I pointed out the lass to a shipmate, and told him I had taken a fancy to her, and would he get me all the information he could about her. That very night, as I was bolting the street-door, just before going to bed, I heard my shipmate's voice outside in the street. 'Is that you, Meddler?' he asked. 'Yes, Jack,' I answered. 'I thought I'd come to tell you at once,' he cried; 'I've found out all about her. Her father's dead, and her mother's married again, and the lass isn't happy at home.' 'That makes it all the better for me,' I said. 'Has she got a sweetheart?' 'None that she cares a button for, or that a sailor couldn't cut out,' he answered. 'Hurrah!' I cried; 'I will go and see her to-morrow. Thank you, Jack; good-night.' 'Good-night,' he said, and I heard him walking away. Just then I remembered that I had forgotten the most important thing of all — her name. I unbolted the door, and called after him, 'What is her name, Jack?' 'Mary Gotobed!' he cried from a distance. 'Mary what?' I shouted. 'Gotobed!' he cried again. I bolted the door, and went."

Praiseworthy Meddler, pausing to take breath, cast another droll look upon his attentive auditors.

"Gotobed!" he then resumed. "Why, it was worse than Meddler! I couldn't marry a lass named Gotobed, and take her name; I didn't want to marry and keep my own name; I couldn't put them together and make one sensible name out of the two. Gotobed Meddler was as bad as Meddler Gotobed. And the worst of it all was, that I liked the lass. She was as pretty a lass as ever I set eyes on. She looked prettier than ever when I saw her the next day; and forgetting all about the names, I spoke to her and lost myself."

"Lost yourself!" exclaimed Mrs. Marvel.

"Yes, my dear," said the Old Sailor, with a bashfulness that did not set ill upon him. "I fell in love."

He said this in a confidential hoarse whisper to Mrs. Marvel, as if the youngsters ought not to hear it.

"Oh, that!" said Mrs. Marvel with a smile.

"But directly she heard what my name was," continued the Old Sailor, "she burst out laughing, and ran away. I had to go to my ship soon after that; and when I came back again, she was married to some one else. So I gave up the idea of marrying; and the name I was born to has stuck to me all my life. And that is the reason why I never married, and why I never became a skipper."

They made merry over the Old Sailor's story, and over other stories that he told of the sea, and of the chances it afforded a youngster like Joshua of getting on in the world. And towards the close of the evening Mrs. Marvel fairly gave in, and promised that she would not say another word against Joshua's determination to be a sailor. In token of which submission a large jug of grog was compounded, in honor of the Old Sailor; and when that was drunk, another was compounded in honor of Joshua. Of both of which Praiseworthy Meddler drank so freely, that he staggered home to his barge in a state of semi-inebriation, singing snatches of sea-songs without intermission, until he tumbled into his hammock and fell asleep.

CHAPTER VIII.

A HAPPY HOLIDAY.

IN after years, when Joshua was many thousands of miles away from Stepney, Dan loved to linger over the memory of one especially happy day which he, and Joshua, and Ellen, and the Old Sailor spent together. Upon that day the sun was rising now; and Dan, lying in bed, was waiting impatiently for the solemn and merry church-bells to strike the hour of seven. His Sunday clothes were smoothly laid out upon a chair, close to his bed. Had the day not been an eventful one, he would not have been allowed to wear his best suit in the middle of the week. When Joshua makes his appearance in Dan's bedroom, it will be seen that he will also be dressed in his best clothes. The secret of all this is, that the lads had received permission from their parents to spend the day with the Old Sailor at the waterside, and were to be taken in a cart to the Old Sailor's castle — the barge near the Tower Stairs. Twenty times at the least had Dan said to Joshua, "I should so like to see the Old Sailor, Jo!" And Joshua, in the most artful manner, had fished for the invitation, which would have been very readily given had the Old Sailor been aware of Joshua's desire. But Joshua, like a great many other diplomatists who think themselves wise in their generation, went to work in a subtle roundabout way, and so gave himself a vast deal of trouble, which would have been saved had he come straight to the point at once. At length, one day, when the Old Sailor had said, "And how is Dan, Josh?" and Joshua had answered that he thought Dan was beginning to grow strong, he ventured to add, with inward fear and trembling: " And he would so much like to see you, sir, and hear some of your sea-stories! When I tell them they don't sound the same as when you tell them. There's no salt in them." Artful Joshua! "Well, my lad," the Old Sailor had said with a chuckle (he was not insensible to flattery, the old dog!), " why not bring him here to spend the day?"

"When shall it be, sir?" asked Joshua secretly delighted.

"Next Wednesday, Josh," said the Old

Sailor. So next Wednesday it was. And Joshua ran to Dan's house wild with delight, and coaxed Dan's parents in to giving their permission.

It was on this very Wednesday morning that Dan was lying awake, waiting for seven o'clock to strike. He awoke at least two hours before the proper time to rise; and those hours appeared to him to be longer than hours ever were before. The ride itself would be an event in Dan's life; but it was not to be compared with what was to come afterwards — the spending of a whole day and night in a house on the water. During the past week Dan had been in a fever of pleasurable anticipation, and in a fever of fright also, lest it should rain upon this particular day. The previous night it *had* rained; and Dan, lying awake for a longer time than usual, had prayed for the rain to go away. Ellen — standing at the window in his bedroom, after she had got out his clean shirt and Sunday clothes, and brushed and smoothed them, and taken up a stitch in them here and there, as women (and girls after them) say — had seen the spots of rain falling, and, joining her prayer to his, had begged very earnestly to the rain to go away and come again another day.

And now the day was dawning; and Dan, opening his eyes, clapped his hands in delight to see the sun shining so brightly upon the broken jug which stood upon the window-sill, and in which was a handful of the sweet-smelling humble wall-flower. The pair of bullfinches which Joshua had bought for the Old Sailor were busily at work in their cage, which was hanging at the window, and were as conscious of the beauty of the morning as the most sensible human being could possibly be. Dan was so delighted that he whistled " Rule, Britannia! Britannia rules the waves!". And one of the bullfinches, after abstracting the last hemp-seed from the glass containing their morning meal, immediately piped out with fervid patriotism, " For Britons never, *never*, NE-*ver* shall be slaves!" From this episode the reader will learn that the education of the bullfinches was completed. "Rule, Britannia," was not their sole vocal accomplishment. They could whistle "And did you not hear of a jolly young waterman?" in a very superior manner. On that day the bullfinches were to be presented to their new master — to whom not a hint had been given of the pleasant surprise in store for him; which made it all the more delightful.

While the patriotic bullfinch was asserting in the most melodiously-persuasive notes that "Britons never, *never*, NE-*ver* shall be slaves," its mate was engaged drawing up water in the tiniest little bucket in the world — another of the accomplishments (coming, presumably, under the head of "extras") which patient Dan had taught the birds in order to win the heart of the Old Sailor. The industrious bullfinch had a remarkably rakish eye, which flashed saucily and impatiently as the music fell upon its ears. The slender rope which held the bucket being in its beak, it could not join in the harmony; but directly the bucket was hauled up and secured, it whetted its whistle, and piped out in opposition, —

"And did you not hear of a jolly young waterman,
Who at Blackfriars-bridge used for to ply?
He feathered his oars with such skill and dexterity,
Winning each heart and delighting each eye;"

repeating, as was its wont, the last line, "Winning each heart and delighting each eye," so as to produce a greater effect. I do not assert that the bullfinch actually uttered the words, but I *do* assert positively that it sang the music of them with the most beautiful trills that mortal ever heard.

But there was the solemn church-bell striking seven o'clock in tones less solemn than usual, and there was the joyous churchbell following suit. And as if the sound had conjured him up, there was Joshua, dressed in his best, and looking so fresh and handsome with his holiday-face on, that Dan might well be proud of him. He had his accordion under his arm, and in one hand was a bunch of flowers which Dan was to give to the Old Sailor, and in the other a glass containing some rape-seed soaked in canary-wine for the birds. They knew as well as possible — knowing little bullfinches! — that Joshua had something nice for them; and as he approached the cage they came as close to him as they could, and, to show their appreciation of his kindness, greeted him with a gush of the sweetest melody. What better beginning could there be for a happy holiday!

When Dan was dressed the lads went into the kitchen to have breakfast. And there was Ellen, as fresh as a daisy. The breakfast things were laid; and there was a clean cloth (not damask, mind!) on the deal table, and there, absolutely, were two new-laid eggs, one for Joshua and one for Dan, which Ellen had bought and paid for with her own money the day before, without saying a word about it. Ellen stooped and kissed Dan, and as she raised her head Joshua looked at her, and felt a huge longing to take her face between his two hands and kiss her, as he used to do in the time when they played sweethearts together. But he hadn't the courage. Yet he could not help looking at Ellen again and thinking, What a pretty girl Ellen is! and then, seeing Ellen's eyes fixed upon his, he turned away his head and blushed. And Ellen smiled at that, and, if she had been asked, really could not have told the reason why. Surely never was such a happy commencement to a holiday, and never was such a happy couple as Dan and Joshua! After all, are not simple pleasures the best? Are not those the sweetest pleasures that cost the least?

What put it into Joshua's head? Was it the sentiment of perfect happiness that actuated the wish? Or was it a passing shadow, lighter than the lightest cloud, that passed over Ellen's face, as the lads were talking of the coming delights of the day? It was there but a moment, but Joshua saw it, or thought he did, and thought also that there was regret in it. Or was it Ellen's pretty face, or the little piece of blue ribbon that she had put round her neck, the puss? For Ellen was fair, and knew what colors best suited her complexion. Whatever it was that actuated it, there was Joshua saying, just as they had sat down to breakfast and Ellen was pouring out the milk-and-water — you may imagine that there was not a great deal of tea drank in Stepney — there was Joshua saying, —

"Ellen, I wish you were coming with us."

Ellen's hand shook so that she spilt some of the milk-and-water, and a spasm rose in her throat, for she had wished the same thing fervently, but had never spoken of it. She checked the spasm, hoping that her emotion would not be noticed, and answered not a word. But she looked. Such a look!

Dan was biting into a slice of bread-and-butter, but directly he heard Joshua's wish, and saw the yearning look that sprang into Ellen's eyes, he ceased eating, and leaned his head upon his hand.

"I think I am very selfish," he said, and hot tears gushed into his eyes.

In an instant Ellen was by his side, and Ellen's face was close to his. Any one who saw that action, any one who could understand the quick sympathy that caused her to put her face so close to Dan's, to show that she knew what he was reproaching himself for, might have been able to comprehend the depth of unselfish tenderness that dwelt in the soul of that little maid. Ah! it was only in a kitchen, but how beautiful it was to see!

"Don't bother about me, my dear," she said almost in a whisper. "If you are happy, I am happy." And then she added, pretending to be comically indignant, "You stupid Dan! I've a good mind to rumple your hair! You selfish, indeed!"

"I am selfish!" exclaimed Dan, looking up and thinking — just as Joshua had thought — that he had never seen her look so pretty. "I am selfish, Joshua!" he cried, so energetically that Joshua was quite startled. "What would the Old Sailor say?"

"But, Dan" — said Ellen.

"Seriously, Jo" said Dan, putting his hand over Ellen's mouth, "what *would* the Old Sailor say?"

"The Old Sailor would be delighted."

"Now, look here," said Dan, with a determination almost comical in its intensity when one considered what inspired it; as if it were a question of tremendous national consequence, or something in which mighty interests were involved; "are you sure?"

"I am sure he would be delighted, Dan," replied Joshua without the slightest hesitation.

"It's of no use, Dan and Josh dear," said Ellen, shaking her head. "You musn't think of it. I can't go. Mother wouldn't be able to spare me. Why, don't you know"—

"Don't I know what, Ellen?" asked Dan.

"Don't you know that it's washing-day?" said Ellen with a sharp nod, as if that settled the question.

Dan's head was still resting upon his hand. He pondered for a few moments, and then raising his head, said, "Good little Ellen;" and kissed her. "Now let us have breakfast."

Breakfast being over, Dan said he wanted to see Susan.

"Tell her I want to speak to her most particularly," he said to Ellen. "And, Ellen! when Susan comes, you go out of the room, and Joshua as well. I want to speak to her quite privately."

Ellen and Joshua left Susan with Dan, and went into the passage; which gave Joshua opportunity to ask Ellen if she remembered when he used to be pushed into the coal-cellar. Yes, Ellen remembered it very well indeed; and they both laughed over the reminiscence.

"How black your face used to be!" exclaimed Ellen.

"And yours too, Ellen!" retorted Joshua saucily.

Whereat Ellen blushed, and did not reply.

What passed between Susan and Dan was never divulged. It was nothing very dreadful, you may be sure; for when Dan called to Joshua and Ellen to come in, they found him smiling. Susan was gone, but presently she entered again with a

radiant face and nodded to Dan, who nodded to Susan in return, and said gayly,—
"Thank you, Susey!"

When Susan went into the passage, she wiped her eyes, and did not once look round to see if any thing was behind her. That day, over the washing-tub, Susan was happier than she had been for a long time.

Then Dan rubbed his hands, and said, "I really think this is going to be the happiest day of my life."

The happiest day of my life! How often, and with what various meanings, are those words uttered! At dinner-parties when the invited guest rises to respond to the toast of his health, and commences by saying in tones which falter from emotion, "This is the happiest day of my life!" At wedding-feasts, if healths are being proposed, when the bridegroom, the bridegroom's father, and the bride's father, each in his turn declares, "This is the happiest day of my life!" At the presentation of testimonials, whether to humbug, worthy man, or fool, it is "The happiest day of my life!" with one and all of them. With copious use of pocket-handkerchief, and with face more suitable for a funeral than for a joyful occasion. But a fig for moralizing on such a day as this!

Dan's countenance was suffused with a flush of genuine delight, as he repeated,—
"Yes, Ellen, this is going to be the happiest day of my life."

She gave him a questioning, imploring look, which asked the reason why as plainly as any words could put the question.

"Come here, and I'll whisper," said Dan.

Ellen put her ear close to his mouth, but Dan, instead of whispering, blew into her ear, which caused her to start away with a pleasant shiver, and to cry out that he tickled her. Nothing daunted, however, she placed her ear a second time to his lips; and then he whispered something, which made Ellen jump for joy, and hug him round the neck, and tear out of the room as if she were mad. And almost before you could say "Jack Robinson!" there she was back again, her eyes all aglow with excitement, in her modest Sunday dress and pretty Sunday bonnet.

Susan's voice was heard calling out,—
"Here's the cart at the door!"

"She means our carriage, Jo," said Dan merrily, as Joshua carried him out.

And there they were, the three of them in the cart; Dan lying his full length on some straw between Joshua and Ellen, who sat upon a kind of bench in a state of perfect happiness. And there were the bullfinches in their cage, wondering what on earth it all meant, but very blithe and merry notwithstanding. And there was the cart moving along slowly, so that Dan should not be jolted. And there they were, presently, looking at each other, and laughing and nodding pleasantly without any apparent cause.

Not among all the stars that gem the heavens (which some wise men assert are really worlds in which forms that have life fulfil the task ordained by the Master of all the worlds) could there be found a more beautiful world than this was to our young holiday-folk on that bright summer morning. Whitechapel the Dingy was as a flower-garden in their eyes; and as they rode through the busy neighborhood a great many persons turned to look at the crazy cart—the springs in which were the only uneasy part of the whole affair—and at the three joyful faces that peered about, enjoying every thing, and thankful for every thing, from the flying clouds to the lazy gutters.

Soon they were at the waterside; and soon they were on the barge, with the Old Sailor welcoming them in downright sailor fashion. Directly Dan put out his little hand, and felt it imprisoned in the Old Sailor's immense palm, and directly he looked at the great open face, pock-marked as it was, and into the staring pleasant eyes, which returned his look honestly and pleasantly, he nodded to himself in satisfaction. His delight was unbounded when the Old Sailor lifted him tenderly, and placed him in a hammock specially prepared for him. He was deeply impressed by the Old Sailor's thoughtful kindness. The mere fact of his lying in a hammock was entrancing. And there Dan swung, and, gazing in wonder upon the busy life of the flowing river, fancied himself in dreamland.

Before he gave himself up to that trance, however, there was much to be done and much to be observed. When the Old Sailor lifted him into the hammock and arranged him comfortably—Dan was surprised that those great strong hands could be so light and tender—he said to the Old Sailor, "Thank you, sir;" and the Old Sailor replied, "Ay, ay, my lad," just as he had read of, and in just the kind of tone he imagined a sailor would use.

The next thing the Old Sailor did was to rest his hand upon Ellen's head. Thereupon Joshua said, "You don't mind, Mr. Praiseworthy, do you?" referring to the liberty they had taken in bringing Ellen without an invitation. "Mind!" the Old Sailor exclaimed. "A pretty little lass like this!" and he stooped and kissed her. And Ellen did not even blush, but seemed to like it. The Old Sailor seemed to like it too. There was something wonderfully charming in his manner of saying "Pretty little lass;" none but a downright thoroughbred old tar could have said it in such a way. And there was something wonderfully charming in the rough grace with which he accepted the bunch of flowers from Ellen. His first intention was to stick them in the bosom of his shirt; but second consideration led him to reflect that their circumference rendered such a resting-place inappropriate. So he placed them in a large tin mug, and sprinkled them with water, which glistened on their leaves as freshly as the dew-kisses which glisten in the early morning wherever Nature makes holiday. Then Dan took the cage containing the bullfinches, and asked the Old Sailor to accept the birds as a present from him and Joshua; and the Old Sailor thanked him in such cordial terms, that his heart was stirred with a fresh delight. Truth to tell, the Old Sailor was mightily gratified with the birds; but, at the same time, he was mightily puzzled as to what he was to do with them. Prettier little things he had never seen; but, small and beautiful as they were, they were a responsibility for which he was not prepared. He stood with his legs wide apart, regarding the birds with a perplexed expression on his face; and Dan divining what was in his mind, opened the door of the cage and out hopped the bullfinches, looking about them with an air of having been accustomed to the water all their lives. As if impelled by a sudden desire to fly away and join their mates in distant woodlands, they took wing and fluttered around the hammock in which Dan lay; now coming tantalizingly near, and now sailing away with an independent air, as much as to say, "We're off!" But when Dan held out his forefinger, they came and perched upon it contentedly. The Old Sailor gazed on the little comedy in admiration. His admiration was increased a hundred fold when Dan, taking his hand, transferred the birds on to his forefinger. He looked at the birds timorously; the birds looked at him confidently. He was afraid to move lest some mischief should happen to the delicate creatures.

"Put them in the cage, sir," said Dan. The Old Sailor did so. "Now," continued Dan, "I will send you food for them regularly; and it will not be too much trouble for you to fill this well with fresh water every morning, will it, sir?"

"No," said the Old Sailor. "But how will the birds get at the water, my lad? It is out of their reach."

"Ah! you think so, sir. But have you ever been in want of water?"

"Of fresh water, I have, my lad; not of salt. Was for three days on a raft, with not a drop of fresh water among thirty-seven of us. Two drank salt water, and went raving mad; one threw himself into the sea."

"And the others, sir?" inquired Dan, immensely interested.

"The others, my lad, waited and suffered, and prayed for rain. And it came, my lad, and we were saved, by the mercy of God. It was awful suffering; our very eyeballs were blazing with thirst. It would have been a relief to us if we could have cried."

"But the heavens cried for you, sir," said Dan tenderly.

"Ay, ay, my lad," said the Old Sailor; "that's well said. The heavens cried for us; and we lay on our backs with our mouths open to catch the blessed drops. The salt water that was death to us dashed up from below; and the fresh water that was life to us came down from above. In five minutes we were soaked with the rain; and we sucked at our clothes. We caught enough rain-water to last us until we were picked up by a merchantman, homeward bound from the Indies."

"That was good," said Dan, feeling as if he had known the Old Sailor all his life. "Now, supposing you were wrecked, sir, on a high rock. Here is the rock," pointing to the perch on which the bullfinches were standing.

"Here is the rock," repeated the Old Sailor, chiming in readily with Dan's fancy.

"And here you are, sir, with another sailor," identifying Praiseworthy Meddler and the other sailor with the two bullfinches.

"And here am I, with another sailor," said the Old Sailor attentively, nodding familiarly at his new shipmate in the cage, who, making much too light of the calamity which had befallen them, winked saucily in return.

"And you are very thirsty."

"And I am very thirsty," said the Old Sailor, smacking his parched lips.

"And here, out of your reach, is the water," indicating the well, "you want to drink."

"And here, out of my reach, is the water I want to drink," said the Old Sailor, growing more parched.

"Now, then," said Dan, "you can't get at the water with your beak — I mean your mouth — and you can't reach it with your claws — I mean your hands. Now what do you do?"

"Ah! what do I do?" repeated the Old Sailor, not seeing his way out of the difficulty.

"Why," exclaimed Dan enthusiastically, "you get a rope — or, if you haven't got one, you make one out of some strong grass, or out of strips of your clothes; and you get a bucket — or you make one out of a cocoanut," in his enthusiasm Dan took the cocoanut for granted; and the Old Sailor accepted its existence on the rock with most implicit faith — "and you attach the cocoanut to the rope, and you lower it into the water, and draw it up full. Here you are, doing it."

And, obedient to Dan's signal, the bullfinches lowered their tiny bucket into the well, and drew it up full, and dipped their beaks into the water, as if they were shipwrecked bullfinches, and were nearly dead with raging thirst.

A thoughtful expression stole into the Old Sailor's face.

"They are wise little creatures," he said. "I have seen a might of strange things and pretty things; but this is as pretty as any thing I have seen."

"You can learn them any thing almost, sir," said Dan, who was bent upon making the Old Sailor love the birds.

"To climb ropes like a sailor?"

"In a week they could. If I had a little ship, with two or three sails and a rope-ladder, I could teach them to climb the ladder and set the sails."

"I dare say, my lad, I dare say."

"Did you ever see a mermaid, sir?"

This was one of the questions Dan had made up his mind to ask the Old Sailor directly they grew familiar.

"Yes," answered the Old Sailor. "I wasn't very near her; and I was laughed at for saying I had seen her. But I saw her, for all that."

"Where was it that you saw her, sir?"

"In the South Pacific, where there are the ugliest images of men and women, and the most wonderful birds and flowers and trees, in the world. I have walked for miles through forests of wild flowers and strange trees, while thousands of parrots were flying about, with their feathers all blue and gold and scarlet and silver."

"Oh, how beautiful!" exclaimed Dan, twining his fingers together. "And they're there now, sir?"

"Surely. Your land-lubbers don't know any thing of the world."

"Those men and women, sir — are they very ugly?"

"As ugly as sin can make 'em — brown and copper-colored and nearly black; cannibals, they are."

"That's very dreadful!" said Dan with a shiver. "What else have you seen, sir?"

"What would you say to gardens in the sea?" asked the Old Sailor enthusiastically. "What would you say to fields in the sky?"

"No!" said Dan in wonder.

"Yes, my lad. Gardens in the sea, with the flowers growing and blooming. I only saw land in the sky once; but it was a sight that can't be forgot. We were thousands of miles away from land; but there in the sky was the country, with fields and forests and mountains. We saw it for near an hour; then it melted away. What would you say to flying fish — showers of 'em. I heard of a talking fish; but I never saw it. I shouldn't wonder, now, if these pretty little birds could talk."

"No, sir," said Dan; "they can't talk, but they can sing."

With that he whistled the first stave of "Rule, Britannia;" and the bullfinches piped the patriotic song so spiritedly, that the Old Sailor roared out in a hoarse voice, "Rule, Britannia! Britannia rules the waves!" and then stopped, and wiped the perspiration from his forehead, and exclaimed, "Lord, Lord!" with rapturous bewilderment. But when Dan whistled "And have you not heard of a jolly young waterman?" and the birds answered, "Oh, yes! we have heard of a jolly young waterman," and proceeded to narrate where that jolly young waterman plied, and how dexterously that jolly young waterman feathered his oars, the Old Sailor was fairly dumfoundered, and sat down in silence, and watched and listened, while Dan put the birds through the whole of their performances.

Ah, what a happy day was that — never, never to be forgotten! As he lay in his hammock, with a delicious sense of rest upon him, he saw pleasure-boats and barges floating down with the tide, with a happy indolence in keeping with every thing about him. What else? Bright visions in the clouds; not for himself, but for his friend, his brother Joshua; bright visions of beautiful lands and beautiful seas. What did the Old Sailor say? Gardens in the sea, with the flowers growing and blooming! He saw them in the clouds; and each flower was bright with beauty, and each petal was rimmed with light. Fields in the skies! There they were, stretching far, far away; and some one was walking through forests of wild flowers and strange trees. Who was it? Joshua! And there were the parrots that the Old Sailor had spoken of, with their feathers of blue and gold and scarlet and silver. But Dan happened to turn his eyes from the clouds to the water, and dreamland faded. Joshua was rowing on the river.

Bravo, Joshua! How strong he looked, with his shirt-sleeves tucked up to his shoulders; and how well he managed his oars! Not that Dan was much of a judge; but he knew what grace was, and surely he saw that before him when he saw Joshua rowing. Joshua looked at Dan, and smiled and nodded; and Dan clapped his hands. And Joshua, to show how clever he was, made a great sweep with the oars, and fell backwards in the boat, in a most ridiculous position, with his heels in the air. But he was up again like lightning, and recovered his oars, and made so light of it, that Dan, who had caught his breath for an instant, laughed merrily at the mishap, and thought it was good fun. His laugh was echoed by Ellen, who was sitting by his side, and who had also been a little alarmed at first. The industrious maid was making holiday in her own peculiar way. She was not accustomed to sit idly down with her hands in her lap. By some mysterious means she had obtained possession of two of the Old Sailor's shirts which required mending; and there she was stitching away at them, as if it were the most natural thing in the world for her to do when she came out for a holiday. Did she have a design upon the Old Sailor? It really looked suspiciously like it, if one might judge from the demure glances she cast upon him every now and then, and from the admiring manner in which he returned her artful glances. One thing was certain: she had fairly captivated him; and there is no telling what might have occurred, if he had been thirty years younger.

What more beautiful phase of human nature can be seen than that of an old man with a young heart? Place, side by side, two pictures of old manhood: one, with crafty face; with cautious eyes that never rove; with compressed lips that keep guard on every word; with puckered forehead and eyebrows, from every ugly crevice in which the spirit of "You can't take me in" peeps out, as if the essence of a fox were in hiding there; — the other, with open face, which says, "Read me; I am not afraid;" with eyes that, be they large or small, enjoy what they see; with full-fleshed wrinkles on forehead and eyebrows; with lips that smile when others smile.

No younger heart ever beat in the breast of an old man than that which beat in the breast of Praiseworthy Meddler. He had never mingled with children; yet here he was, at nearly seventy years of age, a hale and hearty old man, with a nature as simple as a child's. What was it that made him so? Was it because he had lived his youth and manhood away from cities, where the tricky webs of trade teach men to trick as their brethren do, or where the anxiety how to live, and with many, alas, how to get to-morrow's bread, stops the generous flow of a generous nature, and robs life's summer of its brightness? Or did he inherit it? If so, how deserving of pity are those children who are born of crafty parents!

There are human mysteries which science has not dared to probe, and there are inherited ills and calamities which philanthropists, up to the present time, have not tried to get to the root of.

Anyhow, here was Praiseworthy Meddler sitting upon the deck of his barge by the side of Ellen, showing her, in the intervals of stitching, how to splice a broken rope, and initiating her into the mysteries of short-splice, long-splice, and eye-splice. Dan, looking on, begged some rope, and proved himself a wonderfully-apt scholar, which caused the Old Sailor to remark, —

"You ought to be a sailor, my lad;" forgetting for the moment that Dan's legs were useless.

"I should have to work in a hammock, sir," said Dan cheerfully.

The Old Sailor blushed.

"I forgot," he said in a gentle voice.

"There's the sailor for you, if you like," said Dan, pointing to Joshua, who, a couple of hundred yards away, was pulling lazily towards the barge.

"Ay, ay, my lad; Joshua has the right stuff in him. He will be a fine strong man."

"He is better than strong, sir," said Dan; "he is noble and tender-hearted. If you knew, sir, how good he has been to me, you would admire and love him more. If you knew how gentle he has been to me — how tender, and how self-sacrificing — you would think even better of him than you do. We have been together all our lives; every day he has come to me as regularly as the sun, and has been to me what the sun is to the day. I look back now that he is going away, and I cannot remember that he has ever given me a cross word or a cross look. And I have been very troublesome sometimes, and very peevish; but he has borne with it all. Look, sir," and Dan drew the Old Sailor's attention to two pieces of rope, one thin and one thick, the strands of which he had been interweaving, "this thin rope is me; this thick rope is Joshua. Now we are spliced, and you can't pull us apart. Joshua and me are friends for ever and ever!"

The Old Sailor listened attentively, and nodded his head occasionally, to show that he was following Dan's words, and understood them. Ellen, having mended the Old Sailor's shirts, sat with her hands folded in her lap, indorsing every word that Dan uttered.

Just then Joshua reached the barge, and having secured the boat, climbed on to the deck. As he did so, eight bells struck.

"Eight bells," said the Old Sailor. "Dinner."

With that, he lifted Dan out of the hammock, and carried him to where dinner was laid on a table which extended fore and aft down the centre of what it would be the wildest extravagance of courtesy to call a saloon, and where every thing was prepared in expectation of a storm. Joshua and Ellen followed, and the four of them made a very merry party. Lobscouse and sea-pie were the only dishes, and they were brought in by a Lascar with rings in his ears, whom the Old Sailor called a "lubberly swab," because he was unmistakably drunk; and who in return, notwithstanding his drunken condition, cast upon the Old Sailor an evil look, which flashed from his eyes like a dagger-stroke. This Lascar was the man who had struck eight bells, and who cooked for the Old Sailor, and did odd work about the barge, in return for which he got his victuals and a bunk to sleep in. A lazy, indolent rogue, who would do any thing, never mind what, for rum and tobacco; a cringing, submissive, treacherous rogue, ripe for the execution of any villany on the promise of rum and tobacco; a rogue who would fawn, and lie, and stab, and humble himself and play Bombastes for rum and tobacco. They were all he seemed to live for; they were his Thirty-nine Articles, and he was ready to sell himself for them any day. Of what quality might be the work proposed to him to do, so as to earn the reward, was of the very smallest consequence to him. He gave Ellen such an ugly look of wicked admiration that she was glad when he was gone.

Dinner over, they returned to the deck, and the Old Sailor told them stories of the sea — stories so enthralling, that the afternoon glided by like a dream; and the setting sun was tinged with the glories of the distant lands whither it was wending. They had tea on deck — a delicious tea, of shrimps, water-cresses, and bread-and-butter. The task of preparing the tea was performed by Ellen and the Old Sailor; and during the performance of this task, it may be confidently stated that the conquest of the Old Sailor was completed, and that he was from that moment, and ever afterwards, her devoted slave. Then they went down, and sat two and two on each side of the table, Joshua and Dan being on one side, and Ellen and the Old Sailor on the other; and they had more sea-stories, and were altogether in a state of supreme happiness.

During the latter part of the evening the conversation turned upon Joshua's approaching voyage.

"Always bear in mind the sailor's watchword, my lad," said the Old Sailor. "'Along the line the signal ran: England expects that every man this day will do his duty.' That's meant not for this day alone, but for always. What a sailor's got to do is to obey. Many a voyage has had a bad ending because of a sailor's forgetting his watchword. Don't you forget it, Josh."

"I won't, sir."

"The 'Merry Andrew,' that you're going to make your first voyage in, is a fine ship; the skipper is a fine skipper — a man he is, and that's what a ship wants — a man, and not an image." The Old Sailor said this in a tone of exasperation, inspired, possibly, by some tantalizing remembrance of a ship commanded by an image instead of a man. "So stick to your watchword, my lad. It wouldn't be a bad thing now if we were to drink to it."

The cunning old rascal was only too glad of a chance to get at his grog.

"Bravo!" exclaimed Dan, clapping his hands.

No sooner said than done. Hot water, lemon, sugar, rum, compounded with the skill of an artist. A glass for Joshua, a glass for Dan, a glass for the Old Sailor, and a small glass for Ellen. Not one of them seemed afraid of it — not even Ellen.

"Now then," said the Old Sailor, smiling as the steam rose to his nostrils. "Now then; the sailor's watchword — Duty, and may Joshua never forget it!"

"Duty, Jo," said Dan, nodding over his glass to Joshua.

"Duty, Dan," said Joshua, nodding to Dan.

Ellen said nothing aloud, but whispered something into her glass. Then they drank and sipped their grog, and resumed the conversation.

"Have you been to New Holland, sir?" asked Dan. The "Merry Andrew" was bound for New Holland.

"I was there when I was a youngster," replied the Old Sailor, mixing a second glass of grog for himself. "It was a wild country then; I am told it is growing into a wonderful country now. We were six months going out. We had nearly four hundred convicts aboard, most of them in irons. A miserable lot of desperate wretches they were! They were not well treated, and they knew it. We had to keep close watch over them; if they could have set themselves free by any means — they talked of it many a time among themselves — they would have captured the ship, and flung us overboard, or something worse. We landed them at Port Phillip, where the British Government wanted to form a settlement."

"Why New Holland, sir?" asked Dan, always eager for information.

"Discovered by the Dutch in about

1600," replied the Old Sailor oratorically. "Victoria was discovered by Capt. Cook; let us drink to him." They took a sip — all but the Old Sailor, who scorned sips. "Discovered by Capt. Cook in 1770, after he had discovered New Zealand."

"Any savages, sir?"

"Swarms. We were out in a boat exploring, and when we were close in shore, two or three hundred savages came whooping down upon us. We weren't afraid of them; we pulled in to shore, and they stopped short about twenty yards from us, jabbering like a lot of black monkeys. They soon got courage enough to come closer to us, and we gave them some grog; but the ignorant lubbers spit it out of their mouths at first. Then they began to steal things from the boat; and when we gave them to understand that what was ours wasn't theirs, they grew saucy. A black fellow caught up the master's-mate, and ran away with him."

"What did they want with him, sir?"

"To eat him, of course. We fired over their heads, and they dropped the master's-mate, who ran back to us, glad enough to get free, for he didn't relish the idea of being made a meal of. But when the savages found that the guns didn't hurt them, they came whooping up to us again, flourishing their spears. Their faces were painted, and they had swans' feathers sticking out of their heads. Some of them had skin cloaks on, painted all over with figures of naked men, and some of them had bones stuck through their nostrils. On they came, yelling and leaping like so many devils, thinking what a fine roast the fattest of us would make. Then we fired and killed one of them. Directly they saw him fall, they scampered off like madmen."

When the conversation flagged, they had music and singing. Joshua played, and Dan sang a song, and the Old Sailor sang a good many. The best of the Old Sailor's songs was, that they were all about the sea, and that every one of them had a chorus in which the company could join. Of course he sang "Heave the Lead," and "Yeo, heave, ho! To the windlass let us go, with yo, heave ho!" and "Saturday Night at Sea;" and when "Saturday night did come, my boys, to drink to Poll and Bess," he flourished his glass, and drank to those young ladies with a will. The number of lovely ladies with whom the Old Sailor made them acquainted was something astonishing. Poor Jack had his Poll, whom he addressed in a not very dignified manner, when he said to her, —

"What argufies sniv'ling and piping your eye?
Why what a — (hem!) fool you must be!"

Out of respect for Ellen, the Old Sailor coughed over a good many words in the songs he sang; for it must be confessed that there was more swearing in them than was absolutely necessary. Poor Jack, however, who called his Poll a something fool, made up for it in the end by declaring that "his heart was his Poll's" (a very pretty though somewhat trite sentiment), and "his rhino's his friend's" (a very unwise and foolish sentiment, as the world goes). Then there was a Polly whom the lads called so pretty, and who entreated her sweetheart, before he sailed in the good ship the "Kitty" to be constant to her; and who, when he returned without any rhino, turned up her nose at him, as young women do now and then. Then there were Poll in 'My Poll and my partner Joe" (it was wonderful how faithless the Polls were), and Poll in "Every inch a Sailor," who, when poor Haulyard came home in tatters, swore (very unfeminine of her) that she had never seen his face. But honest Ned Haulyard was a philosophical sailor, for he something'd her for a faithless she, and singing went again to sea. The Nancies were a better class of female: —

"I love my duty, love my friend,
Love truth and merit to defend,
    To mourn their loss who hazard ran;
I love to take an honest part,
Love beauty with a spotless heart,
    By manners love to show the man;
To sail through life by honor's breeze —
'Twas all along of loving these
    First made me dote on lovely Nan."

And so on, and so on, with gentle Anna and buxom Nan; and poor Fanny, who drowned herself in the waves near to the place where hung the trembling pines; and poor Peggy, who loved a soldier lad (a marine, without doubt); and bonny Kate, who lived happily afterwards with Tom Clueline. Ellen joined in the choruses with her sweet voice; but, strange to say, she had not been asked to sing until the Old Sailor, struck perhaps by a sudden remorse at monopolizing the harmony, called upon her for a song. Ellen, nothing loth, asked what song; and Joshua said, —

"Sing the song you learned of mother, Ellen."

"'Bread-and-Cheese and Kisses?'" inquired Ellen.

"Yes, 'Bread-and-Cheese and Kisses.' Tisn't quite a girl's song, sir" (to the Old Sailor); "but it is a good song, and Ellen sings it nicely."

"Hooray, then, for 'Bread-and-Cheese and Kisses!'" cried the Old Sailor, casting a glance of intense admiration at Ellen, who, without more ado, sang as follows: —

BREAD-AND-CHEESE AND KISSES.

One day, when I came home fatigued,
  And I felt inclined to grumble,
Because my life was one of toil,
  Because my lot was humble,
I said to Kate, my darling wife,
  In whom my whole life's bliss is,
"What have you got for dinner, Kate?"
"Why, bread-and-cheese and kisses!"

Though worn and tired, my heart leaped up
  As those plain words she uttered.
Why should I envy those whose bread
  Than mine's more thickly buttered?
I said, "We'll have dessert at once."
  "What's that?" she asked. "Why, this is."
I kissed her. Ah, what sweeter meal
  Than bread-and-cheese and kisses!

I gazed at her with pure delight;
  She nodded and smiled gayly;
I said, "My love, on such a meal
  I'd dine with pleasure, daily.
When I but think of you, dear girl,
  I pity those fine misses
Who turn their noses up and pout
  At bread-and-cheese and kisses.

And when I look on your dear form,
  And on your face so homely;
And when I look in your dear eyes,
  And on your dress so comely;
And when I hold you in my arms,
  I laugh at Fortune's misses.
I'm blessed in you, content with you,
  And bread-and-cheese and kisses."

Thus ended the happy day.

CHAPTER IX.

MINNIE AND HER SHELL.

So the simple ways of Joshua's simple life were drawing to a close. He had chosen his career, and to-morrow he would be at the end of the quiet groove in which he had hitherto moved, and would step upon rougher roads, to commence the battle which dooms many a fair-promising life to a despairing death, and out of which no one comes without scars and wounds which art and time are powerless to heal. To-morrow he was to leave a father almost too indulgent; a mother whose heart was as true in its motherly affection for him as the needle is to the pole; a friend who gave him a love as tender and as pure as that which angels could feel.

During the past week he had been busily engaged in leave-taking, and he had been surprised to find what a number of friends he had. There was not one of the poor neighbors, in the poor locality in which he had passed his boyhood's days, who had not kind words and good wishes for him, and who did not give them heartily and without stint. Many a hearty hand-shake from men whose hands he had never touched before, and many a motherly kiss from women he had been in the habit of saying only "Good-morning" to, did Joshua receive. There is a stronger knitting of affection between poor people in poor neighborhoods than there is among the rich in their wider thoroughfares. Perhaps it is the narrow streets that draw them closer to each other; perhaps it is the common struggle to keep body and soul together in which they are all engaged; perhaps it is the unconscious recognition of a higher law of humanity than prevails elsewhere; perhaps it is the absence of the wider barriers of exclusiveness, among which the smaller and more beautiful flowers of feeling — being so humble and unassuming — are in danger of being lost or overlooked. Anyhow the ties of affection are stronger among the poor. Putting necessity and sickness aside, more mothers nurse their babes from love among the poor than among the rich.

The secret of this unanimity of goodwill towards Joshua lay in his uniformly quiet demeanor and affectionate disposition. The wonderful friendship that existed between Dan and Joshua was a household word in the poor homes round about; there was something so beautiful in it, that they felt a pride in the circumstance of its having been cemented in their midst; and many tender-hearted women said that night to their husbands, that they wondered what Dan would do now that Joshua was going away. "And Josh, too," the husband would reply; "do you think he won't miss Dan?" But the women thought mostly of Dan in that relationship. The romance of the thing had something to do with this general interest in his welfare. Here was a young man, one of their own order, born and bred among them, who, from no contempt of their humble ways of life, but from a distinct desire to do better than they (not to *be* better; that they would have resented), had resolved to go out into the world to carve a way for himself. It was brave and manly; it was daring and heroic. For the world was so wide! Cooped-up as *they* were, what did they know of it? What did they see of it? Those of them — the few — who worked at home in their once-a-week shirt-sleeves, could raise their eyes from their work, and see the dull prospect of over the way; or, resting wearily from their monotonous labor, could stroll to their street-doors, and look up and down the street in a meaningless, purposeless manner: like automatons in aprons, with dirty faces and very black finger-nails, coming out of a box and performing a task in which there was necessarily no sense of enjoyment.

Those of them — the many — who toiled in workshops other than their homes, saw with the rising and the setting of every sun a few narrow streets within the circumference of a mile, mayhap. Moving always in the same groove, trudging to their workshops every morning, trudging home every night — it was the same thing for them day after day. The humdrum course of time was only marked by the encroachment of gray hairs and white; or by the patching-up of the poor furniture, which grew more rheumatic, and groaned more dismally every succeeding season; or by the cracking and dismemberment of cups and saucers and plates; or by the slow death of the impossible figures on the tea-trays — figures which were bright and gay once upon a time, as their owners were upon a certain happy wedding-day. Here, as a type, are three small mugs, the letters upon which are either quite faded away, or are denoted by a very mockery of shrivelled lines, as if their lives were being drawn out to the last stage of miserable attenuation. Once they proclaimed themselves proudly, and in golden letters, "For George, a Birthday Present;" "For Mary Ann, with Mother's Love;" "Charley, for a Good Boy." George and Mary, Ann and Charley used to clap their little hands, and swing their little legs delightedly, when they and the mugs kept company at breakfast and tea-time; but now flesh and crockery have grown old, and are fading away in common. The hair on George's head is very thin, although he is not yet forty years of age; Mary Ann is an anxious-looking mother, with six dirty children, who, as she declares twenty times a day, are enough to worry the life out of her; and Charley has turned out any thing but "a Good Boy," being much too fond of public-houses. With such like uninteresting variations, the lives of George and Mary Ann and Charley were typical of the lives of all the poor people amongst whom the Marvels lived. From the cradle to the grave, every thing the same; the same streets, the same breakfasts, the same dinners, the same uneventful routine of existence, the only visible signs upon the record being the deepening of wrinkles and the whitening of hairs. But they were happy enough, notwithstanding; and if their pulses were stirred into quicker motion when they shook Joshua's hand and wished him good luck, there was no envy towards him in their minds, and no feeling of discontent marred the genuineness of their God-speed. When at candle-time they spoke of Joshua and of the world which he was going to see, some of the women said that it would have been better if "you, John," or "you, William,"

"had struck out for yourself when you were young;" and John and William assenting, sighed to think that it was too late for them to make a new start. Well, their time was past; the tide which they might have taken at the flood, but did not, would never come again to their life's shore. Joshua *had* taken it at the flood, and would be afloat to-morrow; good luck be with him! In the heartiness of their good wishes there was no expressed consciousness that there was as much heroism in their quiet lives as in the lives of great heroes and daring adventurers; which very unconsciousness and unexpressed abnegation made that heroism (begging Mr. Ruskin's pardon for calling it so) all the grander.

Joshua had bidden the Old Sailor good-by. The dear, simple old fellow had given Joshua some golden rules to go by; had enjoined him to be respectful and submissive; to learn all he could; to be cheerful always, and to do his work willingly, however hard it seemed; not to mix himself up in the men's quarrels or grumblings; had told him how that some officers were querulous, and some were tyrannical, but that he could always keep himself out of mischief by obeying orders; and had impressed upon him, more particularly than all, the value of the golden motto — Duty. "Keep that for your watchword, my lad," said the Old Sailor, "and you will do."

"I am glad it is nearly all over," said Joshua to Dan. "I have only two or three more to say good-by to, with the exception of mother and father, and Ellen and you, dear Dan."

"There's Susan, Jo," said Dan after a pause. "I wish you could see her before you go."

"I wish so, too. I am going now to say good-by to Minnie and her father."

"Is he better, Jo?"

"I haven't seen him for a week; but I don't think he is ever quite right here;" touching his forehead.

They were speaking of the street actor, whose name was Basil Kindred.

"And Minnie is very pretty, you say."

"Very pretty, but with such strange ways, Dan, as I have told you before."

"Yes," said Dan, looking earnestly at Joshua.

"Sometimes like a woman, which she is not; sometimes like a little child, which she is not. Yet for all she is so strange, one can't help loving her, and pitying her."

"Is she at all like Ellen, Jo?"

"Minnie is not like Ellen," said Joshua, considering. "Ellen's face is calm and peaceful; Minnie's is grander, larger,

Minnie is the kind of girl for a heroine, and Ellen is not, I think. She is too peaceful. Say that Ellen is like a lake, Minnie is like the sea.

A quiet smile passed over Dan's lips, yet a regretful one, too.

"You don't know Ellen, Jo," he said simply. "Give me the lake."

"And me the sea," said Joshua, not meaning it at all with reference to the girls, but literally, with reference to his choice of a profession.

From the first part of this conversation it will be gathered that Susan Taylor had left her home, and had chosen to keep her residence a secret from her family. She was not to blame for it; for she had been most unhappy in the family mansion of the Taylors. Although she earned her own living, and paid for her board and lodging, her father, a drunken, lazy mechanic, had lately been pestering her for small loans, to be spent, of course, at the public-house. These she could not afford to give him; and when he found that she would not assist him, he quarrelled with her. He twitted her about her ungainly person, jeered at her strange mannerisms, pricked her with domestic pins and needles, and made her life so miserable, that she was glad when the culminating quarrel gave her the opportunity to run away.

She had never had a friend. Nearly every girl has a girl-companion with whom she exchanges little confidences, and whom she consults as to the fashion of the new bonnet, and how it is to be trimmed, the pattern of the new dress, and how many flounces it is to have, the color of the new piece of ribbon, and how it should be worn, the personal appearance and intentions of the last new admirer, and how he is to be treated. Susan never had such a companion; worse than that, she never had a sweetheart. She had grown to woman's estate without ever having experienced the pleasures of courtship, either as a child or as a woman. No little boy had taken a liking to her when she was a little girl; and when she grew to be a young woman, no young man had cast a favorable eye upon her. Sooth to say, there was nothing singular in the circumstance; for she was as little attractive externally, as a young woman well could be.

If it were necessary to define and describe her with brevity, a happy definition and description might be given in two simple words — Joints and Knobs. Susan Taylor was all Joints and Knobs, from the crown of her head to the soles of her feet. There was not a straight line about her; every square inch of her frame was broken by a joint or intersected by a knob. Her face did not contain one perfect feature. Bones, with sharp rugged outlines, asserted themselves in her cheeks, in her chin, in her nose (most aggressively there), and in the arches of her eyes. Her shoulders were suggestive of nothing but salt-cellars; her fingers were covered with knuckles; her arms were all elbows; and her knees, as she walked, forced themselves into notice with offensive demonstrativeness. There was nothing round and soft about her. Every part of her was suggestive of Bone; she was so replete with mysterious and complicated angles that she might be said to resemble a mathematical torture. Her angular proportions, broken here by a joint, or intersected there by a knob, did not agree with one another. As not one of them would accept a subordinate position, they were necessarily on the very worst of terms: like a regiment in which every soldier insisted on being colonel, and struggled for the position. The result was Anatomical Confusion.

Cupid is popularly represented to be a mischievous young imp, who delights in tying persons together who are not in the least suited to each other, and as being so reckless and indiscriminate in the use of the metaphorical arrow, which he is everlastingly fixing to that metaphorical bow with such malicious nicety, that the right man seldom finds himself in the right place, and the right woman is similarly unfortunate. As a consequence of this eccentric and inhuman conduct, long men and short women and long women and short men, get absurdly matched, and the mental disparity is often found to be no less than the disparity in limb and bulk. But never, surely, did that tricksy youngster (who is so convenient to writers as a reference, and in various other ways, that they cannot be sufficiently grateful for his mythological existence) play a stranger prank than when he made Susan Taylor and Basil Kindred acquainted with each other. The evening on which Susan, for the first time, saw Basil Kindred act the Ghost scenes in "Hamlet," marked an era in her life not less important than that sad era which was commenced by her letting her brother Daniel fall from her arms out of the window on to the cruel stones. For if ever woman fell in love (which is so violently suggestive that it may well be doubted) with man, Susan Taylor, on that evening, fell in love with Basil Kindred.

But Susan was not the woman to exhibit her passion in words. In another fashion she did exhibit it: in the best fashion that devotion can show itself — in deeds. She was not a cunning woman, nor a wise one either. Being from the very infirmities of her nature a kind of social outcast, she was not likely to consider what the world would say of any action of hers. And here was an anomaly: she was neither foolish enough nor wise enough to consider what the world would say; yet had she considered that her conduct was open to censure, she would not have swerved a hair's breadth because of the world's opinion; and this very independence proceeded not from a hardened nature, but from a nature utterly simple. So she did what a very considerable majority of the busy bees in this busy world would consider either a very foolish thing or something worse. When she left her home she rented a room in the miserable house in which Basil Kindred and his daughter resided. She did this because she loved him; and yet looking for no return of her passion, she did it so that she might make herself useful to him and to Minnie. The living she earned as a dressmaker was a poor and a scanty one enough; but she managed, out of her small earnings, to contribute some little towards the comfort of the couple whose acquaintance she had so strangely made.

Joshua was always certain of a warm welcome from Basil and Minnie; an affectionate intimacy had sprung up between them, and he had spent many a pleasant hour in their company. But in the first flush of their intimacy he had been sorely puzzled by Basil Kindred's strange ways and oft-times stranger remarks; the wandering restlessness of his eyes, and the no less wandering nature of his speech, engendered grave doubts whether he was quite right in his mind. And as Joshua looked from Basil's fine mobile face to that of his daughter, so like her father's in all its grand and beautiful outlines, it distressed him to think that her intellect also might be tainted with her father's disease. It might not be; it might be merely the want of proper moral training that induced her to be so strangely incoherent, so reckless and defiant, and yet at the same time so singularly tender in her conduct. With Minnie every thing was right or wrong according to the way in which it affected herself. She recognized no general law as guiding such and such a principle or sentiment. There was this similarity and this difference between Minnie and Susan: they both ignored the world's opinion and the world's judgment of their actions. But where Susan would be meek, Minnie would be defiant; where Susan would offend through ignorance, Minnie would offend consciously, and be at the same time ready to justify herself and argue the point; which latter she would do, of course, only from her point of view. Supposing that it could be reduced to weights and measures, Minnie would have been content to place herself and her affections on one side of the scale, and all the world on the other, with the positive conviction that she would tip the scale. She was very affectionate and docile to Joshua; she looked up to him with a kind of adoration, and this tacit acknowledgment of his superiority was pleasing to his vanity. He was her hero, and she worshipped him, and showed that she did so; and he, too, dangerously regarding her as a child, received her worship, and was gratified by it. And so she drifted.

Now as he entered the room, Minnie sprang towards him with a joyous exclamation, and taking his hand, held it tightly clasped in hers as she led him to a seat. The room was not so bare of furniture as it was when he first saw it. He looked round for Basil Kindred.

"Father is not at home, Joshua," said Minnie. "He will be in soon, I dare say." She pushed him softly into a chair, and sat on the ground at his feet. "I am so glad you have come!"

"But I don't think I have time to stay."

"You mustn't go; you mustn't go," said Minnie, drawing his arm round her neck. "I shall be so lonely if you do."

"But you were alone before I came in, Minnie."

"Yes," returned Minnie; "but I did not feel lonely then. I shall now, if you go away."

"Then I will stop for a little while," said Joshua, humoring her.

"Always good!" said Minnie gratefully, resting her lips upon her hand, "always good!"

"Why did you not feel lonely before I came, Minnie?"

"I was thinking."

"Of what?"

"Of long, long ago, when father was different to what he is now."

"It could not have been so long, long ago, little Minnie,"—here came a little caressing action from the child,—"you are only — how old?"

"Fourteen."

"And fourteen years ago is not so long, long ago, little Minnie."

Minnie repeated her caressing action.

"To you it isn't perhaps, but it is to me. It seems almost," she said, placing Joshua's hand upon her eyes, and closing them, "as if I had nothing to do with it. Yet I must have had; for mother was mixed up with what I was thinking.

"But I shall think of something else now that you are here," she said presently. "I am going to listen."

With the hand that was free she took something from her pocket, and placing it to her ear, bent her head closer to the ground. She was so long in that attitude of watchful silence, that Joshua cried "Minnie!" to arouse her.

"Hush!" she said; "you must not interrupt me. I am listening. I can almost hear it speak."

"Hear what speak?" asked Joshua, wondering.

Minnie directed his fingers to her ear, and he felt something smooth and cold.

"It is a shell," she said softly, "and I am listening to the sea."

"Ah," said Joshua in a voice as soft as hers, "that is because I am going to be a sailor."

"For that reason. Yes. Call me little Minnie."

"Little Minnie!" said Joshua tenderly; for Minnie's voice and manner were very winsome, and he could not help thinking how quaintly pretty her fancy was.

"Little Minnie, little Minnie!" whispered Minnie in so soft a tone that Joshua could scarcely hear it, — "little Minnie, little Minnie! The sea is singing it. How kind the sea is! and how soft and gentle! I should like to go to sleep like this."

"Does the shell sing any thing else, little Minnie?"

"Listen! Ah, but you cannot hear! It is singing, 'Little Minnie, little Minnie, Joshua is going to be a sailor. Little Minnie, little Minnie, would you like to go with him?'"

"And you answer?"

"Yes, yes, yes! I should like to go with him, and hear the sea always singing like this. I should like to go with him because"— But here Minnie stopped.

"Because what?"

"Because nothing," said Minnie, taking the shell from her ear. "Now the sea is gone, and the singing is gone, and we are waiting at home for father."

"What for, Minnie? What am I waiting at home for father for?"

"To see him of course," answered Minnie.

"And to wish him and you good-by," said Joshua.

"Good-by!" echoed the child, with a sudden look of distress in her large gray eyes. "So soon!"

"Yes. My ship sails to-morrow."

"And this is the last day we shall see you," she said, her tears falling upon his hand.

"The last day for a little while, little Minnie," he said, striving to speak cheerfully.

"For how long?" asked the child, bending her head, so that her fair hair fell over her face.

"For a year, perhaps, Minnie," he answered.

"For a long, long year," she said sorrowfully. "You will not do as mother did, will you?"

"How was that?"

"She went away from us one afternoon, and was to come back at night. And it rained — oh, so dreadfully! — that night. We were lodging under some trees, father, mother, and I. Father was ill — very ill, but not with the same kind of illness that he has now sometimes. He had a fever. And mother went into the town to get something for us to eat — as you did that night when the bad boys threw a stone at father, and you brought him home. When father woke we went in search of her. But I never remember seeing mother again. And you are going away, and perhaps I shall never see you again."

"What does the shell say, Minnie?"

Minnie placed the shell to her ear.

"I cannot make out any thing," she said in a voice of pain. "It isn't singing now; it is moaning and sighing."

He took the shell and listened.

"It will speak to me, because I am a sailor."

"And it says?" asked Minnie anxiously.

"And it says — no, it sings —"Little Minnie, little Minnie, Joshua is going to sea, and Joshua will come back, please God, in a year, with beautiful shells and wonderful stories for you and all his friends. So, little Minnie, little Minnie, look happy; for there is nothing to be sorrowful at."

"Ah!" said Minnie in less sorrowful tones, "if I was a woman, and loved anybody very much, I would not let him go away by himself."

"Why, what would you do?"

"I would follow him." And she pulled Joshua's head down to hers, and whispered, "I should like to go to sea with you."

"Would you indeed, miss!"

"Yes; for I love you, oh, so much!" whispered the child innocently in the same low tones. "But you wouldn't let me go, would you?"

"I should think not. A nice sailor you would make; a weak little thing like you!"

The girl sprang from her crouching attitude, and stood upright. As she did so, expressing in her action what her meaning was, Joshua noticed for the first time that she was growing to be large-limbed and strong. She tossed her hair from her face, and said, —

"Father says I shall be a tall woman."

"Well?"

"Well," she repeated half-proudly and

half-bashfully, "I should not make such a bad sailor, after all." And then, with a motion thoroughly childlike, she knelt on the ground before him; and placing her elbows on his knees, rested her chin in her upturned palms, and looked steadily into his face. "If I was a woman," she said slowly and earnestly, "I would go with you, even if you would not let me."

"How would you manage that?"

"I would follow you secretly."

"You must not say so," said Joshua reprovingly; "it would be very, very wrong."

"To follow any one you loved?" questioned the child, shaking her head at the same time to denote that she had no doubt whether it would be right or wrong. "Wrong to wish to be with any one you loved? It would be wrong not to wish it. But"— and she looked round, as if fearful, although they were alone, lest her resolution should become known — "nobody should know; I would not tell a living soul."

Joshua was silent, puzzled at Minnie's earnestness. Minnie, with the shell at her ear, soon broke the silence, however.

"Has your friend — the boy you have told me about"—

"Dan?"

"Yes, Dan. Has Dan got a shell?"

"No. I don't suppose he ever thought of it."

"And yet he loves you very much, and a shell is the only thing that can bring the sea to him."

"Who gave you the shell, Minnie?"

"No one."

"How did you get it, then?"

"I took it from a stall."

"O Minnie!" exclaimed Joshua, grieved and shocked; "that was very wicked."

"I know it was," said Minnie simply; "but I did it for you. Two days afterwards, when father had money given to him, I asked him for some, and he gave it me. I went to the stall where the shells were, and asked the man how much each they were. 'A penny,' he said. I gave him two pence and ran away. That was good, wasn't it?"

Joshua shook his head.

"It was very wicked to steal the shell; and I don't think you made up for it by paying double what you got the money."

But Minnie set her teeth close, and said between them, "It was wicked at first, but it wasn't wicked afterwards, was it, shell?"

— She listened with a coaxing air to the shell's reply. — "The shell says it wasn't'. Besides, I did it for you; Dan wouldn't ave done it."

"No, that he wouldn't."

"Shows he doesn't love you as much as I do," muttered Minnie with jealous intonation. "If he did, he would have thought of a shell, and would have got it somehow. If he did, he would go with you, and would never, never leave you!"

"Now, Minnie, listen to me."

"I am listening, Joshua." She would have taken his hand; but he put it behind his back, and motioned her to be still. She knew by his voice that something unpleasant was coming, and she set her teeth close.

"You know that it is wrong to steal, and you stole the shell."

"I did it for you," she said doggedly.

"That does not make it right, Minnie. I want you to give me a promise."

"I will promise you any thing but one thing," she said.

"What is that."

"Never mind. You would never guess, so you will never ask me. What am I to promise?"

"That you will never steal any thing again."

"Do you think I ever stole any thing but the shell, then?" she asked, with an air that would have been stern in its pride if she had not been a child.

It was on the tip of Joshua's tongue to say, "I don't know what to think;" but her manner of putting the question gave the answer to it. "No," he said instead, "I don't think you ever did, Minnie."

Her head was stubbornly bent; and she had enough to do to keep back her tears. She would not have succeeded had his answer been different.

"No, I never stole any thing else. Stole is the proper word, I know; but it is a nasty one, and makes me ashamed."

"That is your punishment, Minnie," said Joshua, wondering at himself for his tenaciousness.

"That is my punishment, then," said Minnie not less doggedly than before; "but I did it for you"— nothing would drive her from that stand-point — "and I promise you, Joshua, that I will never steal any thing again —never, never!"

He gave her his hand, and she took it and caressed it.

"And now, Minnie, about Dan," he said. "You must not say or think any thing ill of him. He is the best-hearted and the dearest friend in the world; and I cannot tell you how much I love him, or how much he loves me."

"Why doesn't he go to sea with you, then?"

Joshua looked at her reproachfully.

"Your memory is not good, Minnie. He is lame, as I told you."

"I forgot. He can't go because he is lame. Would he go if his legs were sound?"

"I think he would."

"Don't think," Minnie said, with a sly look at him; "be sure."

"I am sure he would then."

"Caught!" cried Minnie, clapping her hands, the sly look, in which there was simplicity, changing to a cunning one, in which there was craft. "Caught, caught, caught!"

"I should like to know how," said Joshua.

"How ridiculous of you, Minnie, to cry 'Caught!' as if I was a fox!"

"No, I am the fox," she cried, shaking her hair over her face with enchanting grace. "I am in hiding — just peeping round the corner." She made an opening in her thick hair, and flashed a look at him; a look that was saucy, and cunning, and charming, and wilful, all at once. "Am I a good fox?"

"You are a goose. Tell me how I am caught."

"Listen, then," throwing her hair back, and becoming logical. "Dan loves you as well as any man or woman could love another, you said."

"Did I say as well? I thought I said better. I meant better."

"That's no matter. Dan loves you," — she held up her left hand, and checked off the items on her fingers — "that is one finger. And Dan would go to sea with you; and it would be right, because he loves you — that is two fingers. But Dan can't go because he is lame — that is three fingers. Now I love you, and I am not lame — that is four fingers. And it would not be wrong, in me to follow you — and that is my thumb, the largest reason of all. So you are caught, caught, caught, you see."

"I do not see," said Joshua in a very decided voice. "Dan is a boy, and you are a girl; and what is right for a boy to do is often wrong for a girl. I do not see that I am caught."

But Minnie had relinquished the argument. She was satisfied that she was right.

"And you would really be very angry with me if I did it?" she asked.

"I should be very angry with you now, Minnie, if it were not that you were a stupid little girl, just a trifle too fond of talking nonsense. Such nonsense, too! Why, there's Ellen, Dan's sister, *she* wouldn't talk so."

All the brightness went out of Minnie's face, and a dark cloud was there instead.

Joshua noticed it with surprise. He took her hand gently; but she snatched it away.

"Ellen would not behave like that," he said; "she is too mild and gentle." There came into his mind what he had said to Dan of the two girls — that Ellen was like a lake, and Minnie like the sea; and he thought how true it was. "It would do you good to know her."

"I don't want to know her," said Minnie sullenly, "and I don't want to be done good to."

"I didn't think you would be cross-tempered on my last day at home," said Joshua in a grave and gentle voice. He paused, as if expecting her to speak; but she remained silent. "Ah, well," he said, rising, "I shall go and see if I can find your father."

She jumped up and walked with him to the door.

"Say that you are not angry with me," she said in a voice of the softest pleading, raising her face to his.

He would have made a different reply, but he saw that her face was covered with tears.

"Angry with you!" he said kindly. "Who could be angry with you for long, little Minnie?"

She smiled gratefully and thoughtfully as he kissed her; and when he had gone, and she had heard his last footstep, she returned to her old place upon the floor, and crouching down, placed the shell to her ear, and listened to the singing of the sea.

CHAPTER X.

GOOD-BY.

Minnie's obliviousness of what was right had never before been presented so clearly to Joshua. He knew well enough that Minnie, although she was aware that it was wrong to steal, could not understand that she did wrong in stealing the shell. At the same time he could not help feeling tenderly towards her because of that wrong action. After all, how much she was to be pitied! Could it be wondered at that she was hard to teach, and that she was wayward and wilful, living such a lonely life as she lived, with no friend to counsel, no mother to guide her? How quaint was her fancy, and what a pretty thing it was to see her as he saw her in his imaginings — sitting alone in her room, with the shell at her ear, listening to the singing of the sea! With what a daintily-caressing motion she nestled to him when he called her "Little Minnie!" He repeated the words to himself, "Little Minnie, little Minnie!" as he walked along, and smiled. As for her telling him that she would like to go to sea with him, what was it but a childish whimsey? If he had not contradicted her, and made a matter of importance of it, she would have said it, and there an end. She would like to go to sea with him, and would follow him if she were a woman: Well! she was but a child, and the wish was as innocent as her declaration that she loved him.

When he had thought out all this, he thought of to-morrow, and looked round upon the familiar streets and the familiar houses with a pang of regret. To-morrow he would be far away from them, and every succeeding day would take him farther and farther away from them and all that he loved. From mother, father, the Old Sailor, his pet birds, and from Dan — ah! dear, dear Dan! Did ever boy or man have such a friend? Then there was Ellen, his dear little sweetheart in the days when they were children together. Was there ever such another unselfish little maid as that? So devoted, so tender, so loving! How quickly she had won the heart of the Old Sailor! He remembered that old salt saying, pointing his great finger at Ellen as he said it, "Joshua, my lad, that little lass there is the prettiest, the best, the truest and the kindest-hearted in these dominions." And he remembered himself looking at Ellen's mild face — peaceful as a lake — and saying, "So she is, sir," and meaning it heartily; and he remembered the Old Sailor saying, "That's right, my lad; all you've got to do is to mind your bearings." Although he had answered, "Yes, sir, I will," he wondered afterwards, and he found himself wondering now, what on earth the Old Sailor meant by saying. "Mind your bearings." But what matter? Ellen *was* the prettiest, the best, the truest, and the kindest-hearted lass in these or any other dominions. God bless her!

As he thought of these things, he felt himself growing so soft-hearted, that he stopped and stamped his feet upon the pavement, and thumped himself upon the chest, saying as he did so, between laughing and crying, "This won't do, Josh; this won't do."

He had given himself a score of thumps, and had said, "This won't do, Josh," half-a-score of times, when loud cries for help fell upon his ears. He had been walking in the direction of the river, through some of the streets where he would be most likely to find Basil Kindred; and he was in a locality where there was a number of low public-houses, patronized by the worst class of seamen. Turning in the direction of the cry, Joshua saw a woman run swiftly out of a narrow thoroughfare. Pursuing her was a man, a dark-looking fellow, with glittering eyes, and rings in his ears, and a knife in his hand, and with all his copper-colored fingers and black-serpent locks of hair flashing in the air with evil intent. Impelled by the unmistakable air of terror in the form of the flying girl, and the unmistakable air of mischief in the form of the pursuing man — partly, also, by the impulsion born of the hunting spirit implanted in man and beast, Joshua started off at a great pace, and flew after the flying couple.

It was that part of the day when the neighborhood was most quiet. All the men were at work in the dockyards, and the few women about (having a wholesome horror probably of a man with an open knife in his hand, and being perhaps accustomed to such diversions) seemed disinclined to take part in the chase. With the exception of one drunken creature, with a blotched and bloated face, who made a frantic motion to follow, but being tripped up by her draggling petticoats, stumbled, more like a heap of rags than a woman, into the gutter, where she lay growling indistinctly.

The flying woman and the pursuing man were fleet of foot, but Joshua was younger and more nimble than they. As he gained upon them, a dim consciousness stole upon him that he knew them; and, as he approached nearer, the doubt grew into conviction. The almost breathless woman, throwing affrighted looks behind her, as if a dozen men were pursuing her instead of one, was Susan; and the evil-looking man who was bent on running her down was the Lascar who served the Old Sailor, and who cooked for him, and would have poisoned him for rum and tobacco. Some other than those, the ruling cravings of his existence, influenced him now. All the passions of love and hate, and the desire to achieve his purpose by striking terror, were expressed in every motion of every limb: they were so eloquent and earnest in the savage pursuit that they seemed to proclaim their owner's intention, as he raced after the panting girl.

He was almost upon her, and she felt his ugly lips reeking their detestable flavor of rum and tobacco upon her neck, when Joshua, coming up to him, seized him by the throat. He had been so savagely vindictive in the pursuit, that Joshua's hand upon his throat was the first indication he received that he was being himself pursued; but, wasting no look upon his pursuer, he slipped from Joshua like an eel — his neck was redolent of grease — and with an inarticulate cry of rage and baffled lust, he sprang after Susan again, who had gained a few steps by Joshua's ineffectual interposition. But Susan, thoroughly bewildered and terrified, turned into a blind alley, and perceiving that there was no thoroughfare, and that she was trapped, fell upon the rough stones, prostrate from fear and exhaustion.

On one side of the blind alley were four or five houses, in which no signs of life were visible. They seemed stricken to death by disease. On the other side was a black dead wall, which shut out the sky. Before the Lascar could reach Susan — what the man's intention was, or what he would have done in his wild fury, he, being more beast than man, might probably not have been able to explain — Joshua had knocked the knife out of his hand, and had knocked him down with a blow, the force of which astonished Joshua himself, even in the midst of his excitement. Almost before Joshua could realize what had occurred, the cowardly Lascar was crouching by the side of the dead wall, as if his lair were there, and Joshua was on his knee assisting Susan to recover herself; keeping a wary look, however, upon the knife, which was lying in the road at an equal distance from him and the Lascar. The Lascar saw it too — saw it without looking at it, and without seeming to see it. A surprising change had taken place in him. A minute since a volcano of delirious lust was raging in his breast, and every nerve in his body was quivering with dangerous passion; now, as if by magic, he was coiled up like a snake, with no motion of life in him but the quiet glitter of his eyes, which watched every thing, but seemed to watch nothing.

"What is it all about, Susan?" asked Joshua in wonderment, after a pause. But, before Susan could reply, a crawling motion on the part of the Lascar towards the knife caused Joshua to spring into the road. The snake had no chance with the panther. The Lascar was knocked back to his position by the dead wall, and Joshua stood over him grasping the knife. This was the most eventful transaction that had ever occurred to Joshua; and, as he stood over his antagonist palming the knife, a strange sensation of pride in his own strength tingled through his veins. There was blood upon the Lascar's face; Joshua had struck him so fiercely as to loosen one of his teeth—so decidedly to loosen it, that the Lascar put his finger into his mouth and drew it out. He said nothing, however, but kept the tooth clasped in his hand.

"You black devil!" exclaimed Joshua, gazing upon the crouching figure with a kind of loathing amazement. "What do you mean by all this?"

The Lascar wiped the blood from his mouth with his sleeve, and shaking the hair from his eyes, threw upon Joshua a covert look of deadly malice — a look expressive of a bloody-minded craving to have Joshua helpless on the stones beneath him, that he might press the life out of his enemy. His eye spoke, but his tongue uttered no word. Raging inwardly as he was with bad passion, he had sufficient control over himself to suppress any spoken manifestation of it. But his attitude and demeanor were not less dangerous for all that.

"He follows me everywhere," said Susan, still gasping and panting for breath. "He dogs me by day and by night. He waylays me in the dark, and I can hardly get away from him."

"What for?" demanded Joshua, with his eye upon the Lascar, who was sitting cunningly quiet, nursing his wounded mouth.

"I don't know," replied Susan, with an appalled look over her shoulder, as if she were haunted by a fear that the spirit of the Lascar was there, notwithstanding that he was crouching before her in the ugly flesh. "I am afraid to think."

"Afraid! in broad daylight!"

"Day or night it is all the same," moaned Susan. "Whenever he sees me, he dogs me till I am ready to die. You don't know his power — you don't know his power!"

"What were you doing before I saw you?"

"I was looking for some one."

"For whom?"

"For Mr. Kindred," with a curious hesitation.

"For Mr. Kindred!" exclaimed Joshua, more amazed than ever; "why for him?"

"He is ill. I will tell you about it by and by," replied Susan nervously. "I thought I should find him in this neighborhood, and while I was looking for him, he" — pointing to the Lascar with a shudder — "he saw me and spoke to me, and would not leave me — wanted me to go with him and drink with him, and when I refused, he seized me, and then — then — I scratched him — and — I don't remember any thing more, except that I was afraid he wanted to kill me."

Joshua looked up at the Lascar's face, and observed the scratch for the first time. It was a long scratch downwards from the eye to the wounded mouth. The Lascar made no attempt to hide it, but sat still, with his hand on his mouth.

"Serve you right, you black dog!" exclaimed Joshua. "What do you mean by dogging her? What do you mean by following her with a knife? Why, you Lascar dog, for two pins" — he raised his hand indignantly, and advanced a step towards the Lascar, who made a shrinking movement backwards, although in truth he could not get nearer to the dead wall than he was already.

"Don't, Joshua, don't!" cried Susan, seizing his arm, and clinging to him imploringly. "Don't touch him, for God's sake, or "— with another scared look behind her —" he'll haunt you as he haunts me."

A taunting wicked smile crossed the Lascar's lips, but it was gone a moment afterwards. It might have been the shadow of an evil thought finding expression there.

"How does he haunt you more than you have already told me he does?" demanded Joshua in a great heat. "You don't think he can frighten me as he frightens you, Susan, do you? The black dog! Look at him! He's frightened of a white man's little finger!"

"Hush!" implored Susan. "He haunts me when he is not near me."

"How can he do that, you foolish girl?"

"He does it — he *can* do it — with his double!"

"His double?"

"He has a double — a spirit, a wicked spirit" — she turned her head slowly and trembled in every limb; "and he told me it should haunt me, and follow me wherever I go. And it does! I feel it behind me when I don't see him. It is there now! It is there now!" And wrought to the highest pitch of mental terror and excitement, Susan threw up her hands, and would have fallen to the ground but for Joshua's protecting arm.

The taunting smile came again upon the Lascar's lips, as he secretly watched Susan's terror. With a special maliciousness he flashed his fingers towards her, as if he were issuing a command to his double not to leave her. It was evidence of the power he possessed over her weak mind that, notwithstanding her almost fainting condition, a stronger shuddering came upon her when he made even that slight motion.

Feeling that, for Susan's sake, it was necessary to put an end to the scene, Joshua, with an indignant motion, commanded the Lascar to leave them. The Lascar rose submissively, like a whipped dog, and so stood with bent head before Joshua.

"Now then, what are you waiting for?" asked Joshua.

"My knife," answered the Lascar doggedly.

"Not likely," said Joshua; "I know you too well to let you have it."

"What do you know of me?" asked the Lascar in a low guttural voice.

"I have heard enough of you from Mr. Meddler"— the Lascar grated his teeth with tigerish ferocity —" you and the likes of you. I know how free you are with your knives, you Lascars, on land and on sea. Be off!"

"My knife!" again demanded the Lascar, with his eyes directed to Joshua's feet; but he saw Joshua's face and every motion of Joshua's body. "My knife! It is mine. I bought it and paid for it."

"Stole it more likely," said Joshua with a sneer.

"It is a lie. I bought it. Even if I did steal it, you have no right to it. Give me my knife, and let me go."

Joshua reflected. Clearly he had no just claim to the man's knife, and had no right to retain it. His mind was soon made up. Releasing his hold of Susan, he placed the blade beneath his foot, and broke it off close to the handle. Then he threw the handle and the blade over the Lascar's head. A dangerous fire gleamed in the man's downcast eyes, and a cold-blooded grating of teeth came from his mouth. He stood silent for a few moments, with his hands tightly pressed, striving to master the devil that was raging within him. But he could not restrain his passion.

"Curse you!" he hissed; "I owe you something; I will pay it you, by hell!"

He crouched to receive the blow which he expected Joshua would give him, in return for his curse. But no blow was given nor intended; yet he quivered as if he had been struck before he spoke again.

"See you!" he cried; "I never forget — never — never! My turn will come. You called me black devil"—

"So you are," said Joshua scornfully.

"And black dog — dog of a Lascar!"

"So you are."

"You shall pay for it! If it is years before I can pay you, you shall be paid for it! See you — remember!" With all his fingers menacingly, as if each was possessed with a distinct will, and was swearing vengeance against Joshua. "Your life shall pay for it!— more than your life shall pay for it!" He spat upon the ground and trod savagely upon the spittle. "I mark you — see!" With his forefinger he marked a cross in the air. "I put this cross against you — curse you!"

Susan, gazing on with sight terror-fixed, saw the infuriated man stamp upon the stones, as if he had Joshua's life-blood beneath his foot, and then saw the cross marked in the air. The fire of her fevered imagination gave red color to the shadowy lines; and when the Lascar lowered his forefinger, she saw the recorded cross standing unsupported in the air — a cross of bright red blood. Fascinated, she gazed until the bright color faded into two dusky lines, and so remained. Joshua laughed lightly at the vindictive action and the curse; yet he did not feel quite at his ease.

"Come, Susan," he said, "let us be going."

But Susan did not move. Every sense was absorbed in watching the dreadful cross and the Lascar's passion-distorted face. He, stooping to pick up the handle of the knife and the broken blade, turned again upon Joshua, and remained faithful to his theme.

"Don't forget," he said in his low, bad voice, the words coming slowly from a throat almost choked with passion. "By this "—placing his hand upon his wounded mouth—" and these "—holding up the pieces of the knife—"I will keep you in mind. If it is to-morrow, or next week, or next month, you shall be paid! The dog of a Lascar never forgets! See you —remember!"

"Storm away," said Joshua, drawing Susan aside to allow the Lascar to pass. "You will have to be very quick about it, for to-morrow I go to sea."

"You do, eh!" exclaimed the Lascar, with another harsh grating of his teeth, and stopping suddenly in his course. "See you now — take this with you for my good-by!" With a swift motion, he cut his finger with the broken blade, and shook the blood at Joshua. It fell in a sprinkle over his clothes, and a drop plashed into his face. The Lascar saw it, and laughed. "Take that with you for luck!" he cried. "By that mark I shall live to pay you, and you will live to be paid!"

So saying, he turned and fled. Joshua sprang after him, but the man was out of sight in a minute. Returning to Susan, Joshua found her sitting upon the pavement, nursing her knees and sobbing distressfully.

"O Josh!" she cried, "it is a bad omen."

"Not at all," said Joshua, cooling down a little, and wiping the spot of blood from his face. "What does the old proverb say? 'Curses always come home to roost.' Do you hear me?"

It was evident that she did not; her fright was still strong upon her. With a shrinking movement of her head, she looked slowly round, and clutching Joshua's hand, whispered, "For pity's sake, don't let him come near me! Hold me tight! Keep close to me! He is not gone!"

With a firm and gentle force, Joshua compelled her to stand upright.

"There is no one here but you and I," he said, in a firm voice. "You are letting your fancies make a baby of you. There is no one here but you and I. If you will not believe what I say — I can see, I suppose, and I am calm, while you are in a regular fever — if you will not believe what I say, I shall leave you."

"No, no!" she cried, clinging to him.

He compelled her to walk two or three times up and down the court. His decided action calmed her. She gave vent to a sigh of relief, and wiped her eyes.

"That's right," said Joshua as they walked out of the court. "Now I can tell you that I am glad I have met you. I join my ship to-morrow."

"I had no idea you were going away so soon."

"I am going now to see if Mr. Kindred is at home."

"I live in the same house as he does," she said, looking timidly at Joshua.

"That is strange. Are you and he intimate?"

"Yes. They are poor, you know, Joshua."

"So are you, Susey."

"But I can help them a little. He's often ill, and Minnie isn't strong enough to take care of him, and so I nurse him sometimes. Minnie and I are great friends."

When they arrived at Basil Kindred's poor lodging, Minnie met them at the door. With her finger to her lips, she motioned them to be quiet.

"Tread softly," she whispered; "father has come home, and is lying down."

They walked to the bed, and saw Basil Kindred lying on the bed in unquiet sleep. Susan placed her hand on his hot forehead, and said, —

"I have been afraid of this for a long time, Josh. He has got a fever. What would he do without me now?"

There was a touch of pride in her voice as she asked the question. The pride arose from the conviction that the man she loved really needed her help, and from the knowledge that she could make some little sacrifice for him.

"He is very, very ill, I think," whispered Minnie.

"We will make him well between us, Minnie," said Susan.

All the fears by which she was assailed but a few minutes since were gone. Joshua was glad to see that, at all events.

Minnie took Susan's hand gratefully, and kissed it.

"She has been so good to us, Joshua," she said.

Susan's eyes kindled, and she directed to Joshua a look which said, "Have I not done right in coming to live here? See how useful I can be, and how happy I am!"

"I shall tell them at home where you live, Susey," said Joshua.

"Very well. Give my love to Dan."

Joshua nodded, and bent over Basil Kindred. The action disturbed the sleeping man. He seized Joshua's wrist in his burning hand, and said, in a trembling voice, "She died in my arms, and the earth was her bed. The stars were ashamed to look upon her. Well they might be! Well they might be!"

"He is speaking of his wife," said Susan softly to Joshua. "He loved her very dearly, and would have died for her. When she died, his heart almost broke."

Sympathy and devotion made her voice like sweet music. Joshua looked at her with a feeling of wonder, and was amazed at the change that had come over her. An hour ago, she was crouching in drivelling terror, overpowered by absurd fancies; now she moved about cheerfully, strong in her purpose of love. But he had never in all his life seen her as he saw her now. He bade her good-by, and she wished him Godspeed, and kissed him. Minnie accompanied him to the door.

"Good-by, dear little Minnie," he said.

"Good-by," she said, with tears in her voice. "You forgive me, don't you, for what I said this afternoon?"

"Yes, my dear."

"Ah! I like to hear you speak like that; it sounds sweet and good. Say, 'I forgive you, little Minnie.'"

"But I haven't any thing to forgive, now I come to think of it."

"Yes, you have. You say that out of your good nature. You mustn't go away and leave me to think that you are angry with me."

"I am not angry with you, Minnie. After all, what you did, you did through love, and there could not be much wrong in it."

The brightest of bright expressions stole into her face, and she clasped her hands with joy.

"Say that again, Joshua, word for word, as you said it just now."

"What you did, you did through love," repeated Joshua to please her, "and there could not be much wrong in it."

"O Joshua!" she cried, pressing her hands to her face, "you have made me almost quite happy. I have heard father say the same thing, but in different words. Now I shall follow you to sea. Yes, I shall, with this" holding up her shell. "To-morrow night, and every night that you are at sea, I shall listen to my shell and think of you."

"Stupid little Minnie," he said affectionately.

"And you will come back in a year?"

"I hope so, please God."

"Then I shall be growing quite a woman," she said thoughtfully.

The next moment she raised her face quickly to his. The tears were streaming down it. As he bent to her, she caught him round the neck, and kissed him once, twice, thrice, with more than the passionate affection, but with all the innocence, of a child. Then she ran into the house; and Joshua, taking that as a farewell, walked slowly homewards, to go through the hardest trial of all.

That hardest trial through which he had to go awaited him at home. All the members of the Marvel family, and Dan and Ellen Taylor, were assembled together in the old familiar kitchen. They were all of them sad at heart, and made themselves sadder by vain little attempts to be cheerful. The tea was a very silent affair, and the two or three extra delicacies provided by Mrs. Marvel — as if it were a feast they were sitting down to — were failures. The most remarkable feature about the tea was the pretence they all made to eat and drink a great deal, and the miserableness of the result. They pretended to accomplish prodigies, and handed about the bread-and-butter and the cake very industriously, as if it were each person's duty to be mightily anxious about every other person's appetite, and to utterly ignore his own. But every thing in the way of eating and drinking was a mistake. The bread-and-butter was disregarded, and was taken away in disgrace; the cake was slighted, and retired in dudgeon. It was a relief when the tea-things were cleared. Mrs. Marvel was the bravest of the party; she who had so strongly protested against Joshua's going to sea, did all she could to administer little crumbs of comfort to every one of them, and especially to her husband, who had so heartily encouraged Joshua not to do as his father had done before him, but who was now the most outwardly miserable person in the kitchen. Thus, Mrs. Marvel sang snatches of songs, and bustled about as if she really enjoyed Joshua's going, and was glad to get rid of him. When she had accomplished a good deal of nothing, she rose and did nothing else; and when that was done, she sat down and remonstrated with her good man, and would even have rejoiced if she could have worried him into blowing her up.

"Don't take on so, George," she said; "you ought to be cheerful to-night of all nights. What is the use of fretting? Joshua's going to make a man of himself, and to do good for all of us — ain't you, my dear?"

"I intend it, mother, you may be sure."

"Of course you do; and here is father in the dumps when he ought to be up in the skies."

"Some day, I hope," said George Marvel, mustering up spirit to have his joke in the midst of his sadness; "not just now, though. I want to see what sort of a figure Josh will cut in the world first. Give me my pipe, Maggie."

Mrs. Marvel made a great fuss in getting the pipe, knocking down a chair, and clattering things about, and humming a verse of her favorite song, "Bread-and-Cheese and Kisses;" and really made matters a little less sad by her bustle. Then, instead of handing her husband the pipe without moving from her seat, as she might have done, she made a sweep round the table, and pinched Ellen's cheek, and patted Dan on the head, and wiped her eyes on the sly, and kissed Joshua, and so worked her way to George Marvel, and put the pipe between his lips.

"You are as active as a girl, Maggie," said George Marvel, putting his arm round her waist, and gently detaining her by his side.

She looked down into his eyes, and for the life of her could not help the tears gathering in her own. She made no further attempts to be cheerful; and what little conversation was indulged in occurred between long intervals of silence. They had an early supper; for Joshua was to rise at daybreak. When supper was over, George Marvel took out the Bible, and in an impressive voice read from it the one hundred and seventh Psalm. They all stood round the table with bent heads, Joshua standing between his mother and Dan, clasping a hand of each. Very solemn was George Marvel's voice when he came to the twenty-third verse:—

"They that go down to the sea in ships, that do business in great waters;

These see the works of the Lord, and His wonders in the deep.

For He commandeth and raiseth the stormy wind, which lifteth up the waves thereof.

They mount up to the heaven, they go down again to the depths; their soul is melted because of trouble.

They reel to and fro, and stagger like a drunken man, and are at their wits' end.

Then they cry unto the Lord in their trouble, and He bringeth them out of their distresses.

He maketh the storm a calm, so that the waves thereof are still.

Then are they glad because they be quiet; so He bringeth them unto their desired haven."

When the reading of the Psalm was over, and they had stood silent for a little while, they raised their heads, but could scarcely see each other for the tears in their eyes. Then they kissed, and said good-night; and Joshua, casting a wistful glance round the kitchen, every piece of furniture and crockery in which appeared to share in the general regret, assisted Dan up to his bedroom for the last time.

They had scarcely time to sit down before the handle was gently turned, and George Marvel entered. In the room were all Joshua's little household gods — his accordion, his favorite books, and his dear little feathered friends.

George Marvel threw his arm round Joshua's waist, and drew him close.

"What are you going to do with the birds, Josh?" he asked.

"Dan will take care of them, father."

"Don't fret at leaving them — or us. Be a man, Josh — be a man," he said, with the tears running down his face.

"Yes, dear father, I will," said Joshua with a great sob.

"And don't forget father and mother, my boy."

"No, father, never!"

"It's better than being a wood-turner, Josh. Don't you think so?" doubting at the last moment the wisdom of his having encouraged Joshua in the step he was about to take.

"A great deal better, father. You'll see!"

"That's right, Josh — that's right! I'm glad to hear you say so. Good-night, my boy. God bless you!" And pressing Joshua in his arms, and kissing him, George Marvel went away to bed.

He had not been gone two minutes before the handle of the door was turned again, and Mrs. Marvel's pale face appeared. She did not enter the room; and Joshua ran to her. She drew him on to the narrow landing, and shut the door, so that they were in darkness. She pressed him to her bosom, and kissed him many times, and cried over him quietly.

"O mother!" whispered Joshua, "shall I go? Shall I go?"

"Hush, dear child," Mrs. Marvel said. "It is the very best thing; and you must not doubt now. Bless you, my dear, dear child! You will come home a man; and we shall all be so proud of you — so proud — and happy!" She pressed him closer, and tried to speak cheerfully; but it was a poor attempt. "And write whenever you can, and tell us every thing."

"Yes; I will be sure."

"Be a good boy, Joshua."

"Yes, mother."

"And you will say your prayers every night?"

"I will, mother."

"Dear child, God will protect you. I shall think of you of a night saying your prayers, my dear, and it will comfort me so! And here I am, keeping my boy out of bed, like a selfish, selfish, selfish mother! Now, my dear, one more kiss, and say good-night."

He kissed her again, and she left his arms, and crept softly to her room. These heart-shocks were hard to bear, and he paused to recover himself before he re-entered the room. Dan did not look at him, nor ask him any questions. But Joshua sat down beside Dan, and said,—

"It was mother kept me, Dan."

"Yes, I know, Jo dear. There's somebody else at the door."

It was Sarah, who asked if she might come in. Of course she might. And might Ellen come in? Of course. So Ellen came in, and she and Sarah sat with their brothers for a few minutes. They talked quietly together, and Joshua drew close to Ellen, and grew calmer as he looked at her sweet peaceful face. She raised her eyes shyly to his, and told him she had a little present for him, and would he accept it? *There* was a question to ask him! Joshua answered almost gayly. She produced her present—a poor little purse, which she had herself worked for him— and Joshua kissed it, and kissed her afterwards, and she nestled to his side very tenderly and very prettily, and cast down her eyes, and was perfectly happy. The girls did not stay long. Good-night was said again and again, and Joshua asked Ellen to kiss him, and she did so without hesitation. When they were gone, Joshua sat down, and rested his head upon his hands. He was weary after the day's excitement, but although he was tired, he was wakeful, and did not feel inclined for sleep. So he and Dan had a long chat together, recalling the many tender memories that enriched their friendship.

"*I* have a present for you, too, Jo," said Dan, producing a Bible.

Joshua opened it, and read on the first page, "From Dan, to his dearest friend and brother, Joshua. With undying love and confidence."

"With undying love and confidence," mused Joshua. "Nothing could ever change our friendship, Dan, could it?"

"Nothing, Jo."

"Come, now," said Joshua, "suppose, for the sake of argument, that I was to turn out bad."

Dan smiled. "That couldn't happen, Jo."

Thereupon Joshua told Dan the adventure he had had that day with Susan and the Lascar. "And, do you know, Dan, that when I knocked him down, and saw his mouth bleeding, I was glad — savagely glad, I am sorry to say. Yet afterwards when I thought of it, and when I think of it now, it seems as if it was a bad feeling that possessed me."

"It doesn't seem so to me, Jo; it gives me greater confidence in you. If you had not acted so, what would have become of poor Susan?"

"That's true," said Joshua.

"I knew all along, Jo dear, that you were loving and tender and good, but I did not know until now that you were so bold and brave. And so strong too! I am proud of you. You can't tell what may happen. Think of this strange new world you are going to now, Jo, and of the strange things the Old Sailor has told us of it. You have no more idea of the wonders you will see than I have. But you will see them, and I shall see them through you. Listen now to me, Jo. I love you, my dearest friend and brother, and you have my undying love and confidence. I, a poor helpless cripple, had no future of my own; and you have given me one. I live in you. I shall follow you in my thoughts, in my dreams. Somehow, Jo, our minds have grown together, and I smile at your words that you might turn out bad. Could you believe it of me, if I was strong like you even?"

"No."

"You answer for me, Jo. You have always been noble and good to me, and you will always be the same. I would not think of thanking you, Jo, for what you have done for me — I would not think of thanking you for making my poor crippled legs a blessing to me instead of a burden. Not with words do I or can I repay you — but with undying love and confidence. Kiss me now, Jo, and say that you fully understand my friendship and truth."

"Fully, Dan;" kissing him. "And I have never forgotten what I promised you a long time ago, Dan. Wherever I am, and whatever I shall see, I will think, 'Dan is here with me, although I cannot see him.' Although we are parted, we shall be together."

"Yes, in spirit, Jo dear," said Dan, with a beautiful light of happiness upon his face. "And now, good-night."

"Good night, Dan."

"If I am asleep in the morning, Jo, do not wake me. I am content to part from you now with this good-night."

"Very well, Dan. Good-night."

"Good-night, MY FRIEND."

With that Dan turned to the wall, and Joshua, going to the bird-cages hanging in the room, said good-night to the birds. They were asleep on their perches, and he did not disturb them. "They will give me a chirrup in the morning," he thought, and, blowing out the candle, he said his prayers and went to bed. But he could not sleep; the events of the day presented themselves to his mind in the strangest forms. Minnie and her shell came and faded away, and her place was filled by Susan nursing Basil Kindred; then came the ugly figure of the Lascar crouching down, and afterwards making a cross against him, and cursing him; his father reading the Psalm, while they all stood round; he and his mother standing in the dark passage, and his mother sobbing over him; Ellen kissing him and nestling close to him, oh so prettily and innocently! All these pictures presented themselves to him consecutively at first; but presently they grew disturbed, and the Lascar, the evil genius of the group, was mischievously and triumphantly at work, now in one shape, now in another. Joshua and Ellen were sitting together when the Lascar came between them, and struck Ellen out of the picture. Then the two were locked in a deadly struggle on the ground, and the Lascar, overpowering him, knelt upon his chest and hissed, "I could take your life, but that won't satisfy me. More than your life shall pay for what you have done." Other phases of his fancies were, that Dan believed him to be false. "My doing!" hissed the Lascar. That Ellen believed him to be wicked. "My doing!" hissed the Lascar. That they all believed him to be bad. "My doing!" hissed the Lascar. That they were all grouped together, and were turning from him, and that the Lascar, holding him fast, whispered that that was his revenge. At length the combinations became so distressing, that Joshua, to shake off the fancies, rose in his bed and opened his eyes. The moonlight was streaming in through the window, and Joshua crept quietly to the water-jug and sprinkled some water over his face. Then, his mind being calmer, he knelt down by the side of the bed; and Dan, who had not slept, raised himself upon his elbow, and, seeing his friend in prayerful attitude, smiled softly to himself and was glad.

CHAPTER XI.

WHAT OCCURRED AFTER JOSHUA'S DEPARTURE.

THE nicest mathematical calculations of the probability of events are not uncommonly subjected to shocks which, to those dull and unreflective persons who cannot distinguish between rule and exceptions, seem to give the lie to science. Yesterday the world was at peace, and rulers and politicians were eloquent in phrases of friendship and good-will to the inhabitants of every nation on the face of the earth. To-day the world is at war, and rulers and politicians, hot with wrath at a cunningly-provoked insult, are eager to avenge traditional wrongs at any expense of blood and human suffering, and to resent what they choose to call national humiliation. Yesterday two nations clasped hands, and smiled upon one another. Suddenly, as thus they stood, a fire — kindled by the worst of secret passions and by the lust of self-aggrandizement — flashed into their palms, and they threw each other off, and drew the sword. A more serious shock was never given to the calculation of the probable course of events.

Yesterday peace was certain, and men were preparing to gather the harvests; today war is raging, and the cornfields are steeped in blood.

So have I seen in a far-off country — now almost in its infancy, but whose growth is swift, and whose manhood will be grand — a sluggish river rolling lazily to the sea. Walking inland along its banks, now broadened by fair plains, now narrowed by towering ranges, I have come suddenly upon the confluence of it and another river, whose waters, springing from cloud-tipped mountains of snow, rush laughingly down the grand old rocks. Here, in the narrow pass where the rivers meet, the gray sluggish stream of a sleeper opposes itself to the marvellously blue waters of a passionate life. One, dull and inert, rolls like a soulless sluggard sullenly to the sea; the other, with its snow-fringed lines reflected in its restless depths of blue, leaps and laughs as it flashes onwards, like a godlike hero, to the mightier waters of the Pacific. But a few hundred yards away from the confluence of the streams, no stranger, walking thitherward, could imagine the singular and grand contest that is eternally waging in that wonderful pass; and when he comes upon it suddenly, admiration impels him to stand in silent worship.

One of the commonest of common similes is the simile of life and a river. But as it is not because a thing is rare that it must needs be sweet, so it is not because a thing is common that it must needs be true. Every river fulfils its mission: does every life? More like a stream than a river is life. Trace the stream, from the inconsiderable bubbling of a mountain spring, down the hillsides, over rocks, through glades lighted by sunlight and moonlight, through tortuous defiles and rocky chasms, into a sparkling current, which swells and swells and grows into a lovely channel, or into a sullen rill, which drips and drips and loses itself in a puddle.

When Joshua's ship had sailed, gloom fell upon the house of the Marvels: the sunshine that used to warm it no longer shone on it. George Marvel showed his grief more plainly than did his good woman. He was more gentle towards her, and sometimes his gentleness of manner took the form of submission. Singularly enough she was seriously distressed at the change. She wished him to be positive and contradictory, as he used to be; to scold her and put her down, as he used to do; to be more masterful and less gentle. She strove in all sorts of ways to bring back his old humor; she tried his temper by opposing him in trivial matters; she contradicted him when he spoke; and she even ventured, on two or three occasions, to tell him that he would have to wait for his meals — which waiting for one's meals, as is well known, is one of the leading causes of domestic differences. But all her well-meant efforts were thrown away; and when she saw him sit down patiently on being told, with assumed snappishness, that tea wouldn't be ready for half an hour, she gave it up as a bad job, and, acting wisely, left time to cure him. It *did* cure him, as it cures greater griefs; but in the mean time he suffered greatly.

The fact of it was, George Marvel was troubled in his mind at the prominent part he had taken in influencing Joshua's choice of a profession. Having driven his son to sea, he felt as if he had a hand in every storm, and as if he were in some measure responsible for every gust of wind, inasmuch as it expressed danger to Joshua. Then the thought of Joshua's being shipwrecked haunted him. "Suppose Josh is shipwrecked, father," his wife had said, "what would you say then? You'd lie awake night after night, father — you know you would — and wish he had been a wood-turner."

"Maggie was right," he admitted to himself; "it would have been better for Josh, and happier for all us, if he had remained at home and been a wood-turner."

Being in pursuit of misery, he showed the doggedness of his nature by hunting for it assiduously. He read with remorseful eagerness every scrap of print relating to shipwreck that he could lay hands upon. He would go out of his way to borrow a paper which he had heard contained an account of disasters at sea, and when he obtained it, he would shut himself up, and read it and re-read it in secrecy, until he extracted as much misery from it as it could possibly yield him. The second Saturday night after Joshua's departure he saw a number of persons assembled round a sailor who was begging. The sailor had a patch over his eye and a wooden leg, and he was singing, in a voice of dismal enjoyment, a woful narration of his sufferings on a raft. George Marvel stopped until the song was finished, and then gave the man a penny. The following Saturday night he went in search of the sailor, and listened to his song, and gave him another penny. And so, for many successive Saturday nights, he went and enjoyed his penny-worth of misery, getting, it must be admitted, full value for his money.

On other evenings he smoked his pipe in the kitchen as usual. If the weather was boisterous, he would go restlessly to the street-door, and come back more low-spirited than ever.

"It's dreadfully windy to-night, Maggie," he would say.

"Do you think so, George?" Mrs. Marvel would ask, making light of the wind for his sake, although she too was thinking of Joshua.

"Not a star to be seen," he would add despondently.

Then would come a stronger gust, perhaps, and George Marvel would shiver and ask his wife if she thought it was stormy out at sea. She, becoming on the instant wonderfully weatherwise, would answer, No, she was sure it wasn't stormy at sea, for the sea was such a long way off, and it wasn't likely that a storm would be all over the world at once.

One night when a great storm was raging through London, and when the thunder was breaking loudly over the chimney-tops in Stepney, Mrs. Marvel lay awake, with all a mother's fears tugging at her heart-strings, praying silently for Joshua's safety, and clasping her hands more tightly in agony of love at every lightning-flash that darted past the window. She hoped that her husband was asleep, oblivious of the storm; but he was as wide awake as she was, and was following Joshua's ship through the fearful storm. At one time, the house shook in the wild blustering of the wind, and they heard a crash as of the blowing down of some chimneys.

"Maggie," whispered Mr. Marvel, wondering if his wife were awake.

"Yes, father," answered Mrs. Marvel, under her breath.

"It is an awful storm." Then, after a pause, "Have you been awake long, mother?"

"I have been listening to it for ever so long, dear," said Mrs. Marvel; adding, with a cunning attempt to comfort him, "And praying that it might spend out all its force over our heads, and not travel away to Joshua's ship. We ought to be thankful that Joshua is on the open sea.

Mr. Meddler says there's no danger for a ship in a storm when it isn't near land."

"And he knows better than us, mother."

"Yes, dear. All we can do is to pray for Joshua. God will bring him back to us, father."

"I hope so; I pray so. Good-night, Maggie. Go to sleep."

"Yes, George. Good-night."

But they lay awake for a long time after that, until the storm, sobbing like a child worn out with passion, sighed and moaned itself away.

As for Dan, for many days after Joshua was gone he felt as if a dear friend had died; not Joshua, but some unknown friend almost as dear. He had reason enough for feeling lonely and miserable. His dear friend's companionship had been inestimably precious to him; Joshua's very footfall had made his heart glad. The hours they had spent together were the summer of his life, and now that he and Joshua were parted he recognized that a great void had been made in his life, and that it behoved him to fill it up. That void was want of occupation. What was he to do now that Joshua was gone? When Joshua was at home, there had been every day something to do, something to talk about, something to argue upon. Then, time did not hang heavily upon his hands; now, when there was no Joshua to look forward to, he found himself falling into a state of listlessness which he knew was not good for him. He wanted something for his hands to do. What? He thought a great deal about it, and had not settled the difficulty when a domestic calamity occurred.

The drinking proclivities of Mr. Taylor have been incidentally referred to. These proclivities had unfortunately grown upon him to such an extent, that he was now an ardent and faithful slave of that demon to so many English homes among the poor — Gin. It has been spoken of often enough and truthfully enough, God knows! But it cannot, until it lie vanquished in the dust, be too often struck at. If there is a curse in this our mighty England which degrades it to a level so low that it is shame to think of, that curse is Gin! If vice, domestic misery, and prostitution have an English teacher, that teacher is Gin! And in this England, which we so glorify, so sing about and mouth about, no direct attempt has ever yet been made by statesmen who work as Jobbers to root this teacher out of our wretched courts and alleys, and replace it by something better. Perhaps one day, when a lull takes place in the jangle of Politics — amid the din of which so many strange sounds are heard; such as the wrangle of religious creeds, whose various exponents split worthless straws in Church-and-State bills for Heaven knows what purpose, unless it be for the triumph of their particular creeds; such as the wrangle of private members whose hearts and souls (literally) are wrapt up in private bills for the good of the people — perhaps one day amid the lull, a wise and beneficent statesman may turn his attention to the abominable curse, and earn for himself a statue, the design of which shall be — after the manner of St. George and the Dragon — Gin writhing on the ground in all its true deformity, pierced through by the spear of a wise legislation, which in this instance at least shall have legislated for the good of the many.

Mr. Taylor, one of the Gin Patriots, having enrolled himself as a soldier in the cause, was necessitated by the magnanimity of his nature to become a soldier leal and true. So he bowed himself down before Gin, and worshipped it morning, noon, and night. Even in his dreams he was faithful to the cause, mumbling out entreaties to his god. His devotion causing him to neglect all lesser worldly matters, he fell into a bad state of poverty, and his family fell with him. The worst form of Mr. Taylor's devotion did not appear until Joshua left home; hitherto he had been working up to his ambition's height. Having reached it, he rested on his oars, which, being composed of the frailest of timber, gave way and sent him rolling into the mud. As he declined to provide for his family, that duty devolved upon Mrs. Taylor, and she patiently and unmurmuringly performed her duty, and worked her fingers to the bone, until her strength gave way. She was one of those quiet souls who always do their best, and never complain; and having done her best, she closed her eyes upon the world, and passed without a murmur out of the hive of busy bees.

There was much sadness in the house when the event occurred, and there was much helpful sympathy among the neighbors. Not for Mr. Taylor — although they remembered the time when he was a respectable member of society, before he had fallen under the fatal influence of Gin — but for the children. During Mrs. Taylor's illness, which lasted but a very short time, Susan came to the house and helped Ellen in her household work and in nursing their mother. It was an anxious time for the poor little maid; but she did her work willingly, and with the patient spirit her mother had exhibited. Susan was a great help to her, and there was more sisterly love between them during that time than had ever before shown itself. At the funeral, Mr. Taylor presented himself in as decent a state of Gin as he could muster up for the occasion; drivelled a little, trembled a great deal, and proclaimed himself a most unfortunate man. Finding that he obtained no sympathy for his miserable position from his children or from the neighbors, he, when the funeral was over, pawned his waistcoat, and dissolving the proceeds, wept tears of Gin over the death of his wife. While he was employed in that process of drowning his grief, the three children were sitting together in Dan's room talking in hushed tones over their loss and over their prospects. After the funeral, Mrs. Marvel — who had helped to nurse Mrs. Taylor — quietly prepared tea in Dan's room, and with her usual sympathetic instinct of what was best, kept herself out of sight as much as possible. But at the last moment, when tea was ready and she was about to leave the children undisturbed, she placed her arm round Dan's neck, and whispered that Joshua's home was Dan's, and that he might come and occupy Joshua's room whenever he pleased. "And he another son to us, my dear," said good Mrs. Marvel, "so that we shall have two." Dan thanked her, and looked at Ellen thoughtfully, and then Mrs. Marvel left the children to their meal.

Said Dan, "Mrs. Marvel has asked me to live in her house, and sleep in Joshua's room."

"It would be a good thing," observed Susan.

Dan stole his hand into Ellen's, who had been looking down sadly; she felt the warm pressure, and her fingers tightened upon his. That little action was as good as words; they understood each other perfectly.

"No," he said, "it would not be a good thing. It was a good thing for Mrs. Marvel to offer, but then she is Jo's mother, and as kind and good as Jo is; but it would not be a good thing for me to accept. For there's Ellen here; she is half of me, Susey, and we mustn't be parted. But indeed there will be no reason for it. I have a wonderful scheme in my head, but it wants thinking over before I tell it."

Dan spoke bravely, as if he were a strong man, with all the world to choose from.

"O Dan!" exclaimed Susan, tears coming to her eyes at his brave confident manner, "if it hadn't been for me you wouldn't have been a cripple, and your poor legs might have been of some use to you."

"They will be of more use to me perhaps than if they were sound, Susey," said Dan cheerfully, "if I can make something out of the scheme I have got in my head — and I think I can. Let us talk sensibly. Now that poor dear mother's gone, we must all do something. I intend to commence doing something to-morrow."

"What, dear Dan?" asked Susan.

"You will see. What I should like is that we should all live together. Perhaps not just now, Susey, but by and by. What do you say to that, Susey?"

Susan thought of Basil and Minnie Kindred, and felt that it would be impossible for her to leave them. "It would be very good," she said, "but we can talk of that by and by, as you say."

"Very well. The first thing, then, we have to consider is bread-and-butter. Bread-and-butter," he repeated, in reply to their questioning looks. "We must have it, and we must earn it."

Susan nodded gravely, and said, "Ellen had better learn to be a dressmaker."

Ellen looked up with joyful gratitude.

"Oh, how good of you, Susey!" she exclaimed. "Then I could earn money. I wouldn't mind how hard I should have to work."

"It is a capital idea," said Dan, taking Susan's hand. "The best thing you can do, Susey, is to bring some of your work here every day for a couple of hours, and let Ellen help you — she will soon learn."

"That I will," said Ellen in a voice of quiet gladness.

These young people, you see, were not entirely unhappy.

"I wonder where Joshua is," remarked Ellen during the evening.

"Ah, where?" sighed Dan. "But wherever he is, he is doing his duty, and we will do ours. How happy we all were that night at Mr. Meddler's! What a beautiful day that was! Like a dream! Hark! There is the church-bell striking nine o'clock." They listened in silence. "That is like a wedding-bell. Now the other church is striking — how solemn it sounds! — like a funeral-bell."

The tears came to their eyes when Dan inadvertently made the last remark.

They did not speak for a long time after that, and then Dan said, —

"I feel now just as I felt the day after Jo went away."

They sat up talking until eleven o'clock. They spoke in low tones, and they sat in the dark.

"Don't you miss mother's step, Dan?" asked Susan.

"How strange it is to know that she is not in the house!" said Dan. "Hush!"

There was a step outside the door; it was the drunken step of their father, who stumbled through the passage and up the stairs, shedding tears of Gin as he staggered to bed, bemoaning the death of his wife. They listened with feelings of grief and fear until they heard his bedroom-door shut, and then turned to each other with deeper sighs. Shame for the living was more grievous to bear than sorrow for the dead.

CHAPTER XII.

DAN ENTERS INTO BUSINESS.

Their plans were commenced the very next day. Susan came round with her work, and gave Ellen her first lesson in dressmaking. Ellen was as skilful with the needle as Susan was, and made famous progress. A cheerful worker is sure to turn out a skilful one.

"I have been thinking in the night, Ellen," said Susan, "that we might go into partnership."

"Wait," said Dan the Just, looking up from the table, on which the birds were going through their performances; "there is time enough to talk of that. I don't intend that you shall sacrifice every thing for us."

"No sacrifice could be too great for me to make for you, Dan," replied Susan. "But I think that I should have all the advantage, if we were partners. Ellen has such a beautiful figure, that she would be sure to get customers. Stand up, dear — look at her, Dan!" And Susan turned Ellen about, and looked at her pretty sister's pretty figure without a tittle of envy. "If you are a judge of any thing but birds, Dan, you must confess that Ellen is a model."

Dan smiled and said, "If Ellen wasn't good, you would make her vain. Let the partnership question rest for a little while. Go on with your work, and don't talk. I've got something very particular to do."

Dan, with his birds before him, appeared to be perplexed with some more than usually difficult problem concerning them. There was a curious indecision also in his treatment of them. Now he issued a command, now he countermanded it; now he ordered a movement, and before it was executed threw the birds into confusion by giving the signal for something entirely different. Until at length the birds, especially the old stagers, stood looking irresolutely at each other, with the possible thought in their minds (if they have any) that their master had taken a drop too much to drink; and one young recruit — none but a young one and a tomtit, who is notoriously the sauciest of birds, would have dared to do it — advanced, alone and unsupported, to the edge of the table, and looking up in Dan's face, asked what he meant by it. Recalled to himself by this act of insubordination, Dan recovered his usual self-possession, and selected two bullfinches, somewhat similar to those which he had given to the Old Sailor. They were young untrained birds, and Dan at once commenced their education. But Ellen remarked with surprise that he was less tender in his manner towards them than towards the other birds. He spoke to them more sternly, and as if the business in which they were engaged was a serious business, with not a particle of nonsense in it.

"See, Ellen," he said after some days had passed — "see how clever they are! They draw up their own food and their own water; and directly I sound this whistle, they sing 'God save the King.'"

He blew through the tin whistle, and the birds sang the air through.

"Now you sound the whistle, Ellen."

Ellen blew through the whistle, and the birds repeated the air.

"So you see, Ellen, it doesn't matter who blows the whistle; the birds begin to sing directly they hear it. Here is another whistle — a wooden one, with a different note. Blow that softly."

Ellen blew, and the bullfinches immediately set to work hauling up water from the well.

"That is good, isn't it?" said Dan. "They will obey anybody."

"But tell me, Dan, why you don't speak to them as kindly as you do to the others?"

"Ah, you have noticed it, miss, have you? I thought you did. Well, then, in the first place, I wanted to teach them by a new system. I wanted to teach them so that anybody can make them do what I do, if he gives the proper signal; and I have succeeded, you see. If I had taught them by my voice, as I have taught the others, they wouldn't have been of use to any one but me. They are such cunning little things, and they have such delicate little ears! In the second place, Ellen, I did not want to grow fond of them."

"Why, Dan dear?"

"Because, if I had grown fond of them, it would almost break my heart to part with them. Who could help loving them, I wonder? They have been my world, you see, and they are such innocent little pets. I have grown to love them so, you can't tell. And we know each other's voices, and have made a language of our own, which no one else can understand."

He chirruped to them, and called to them in endearing tones; and all the birds, with the exception of the pair of bullfinches, fluttered to him, and perched about his shoulders and nestled in his breast. The two little bullfinches, standing alone in the centre of the table, looked more surprised than forlorn at the desertion.

Then Dan said: "This is part of my scheme. I commence business to-day as a bird-merchant. I have trained these two bullfinches to sell. You are earning money already, Ellen dear, and you are a girl. I am not quite a man in years, although I think I am here"—touching his forehead—"and I am not going to let you beat me at money-making."

He pulled out a paper, on which was written, in Roman letters, and neat round hand,

THIS PAIR OF BULLFINCHES
FOR SALE.

They draw up their own food and water; and they sing
" GOD SAVE THE KING,"
And other Tunes, to the Sound of a Whistle.

Inquire within of DAN TAYLOR.

"What I propose to do, Ellen, is to put the cage with the bullfinches in the parlor-window, with this announcement over the cage. Perhaps it will attract the attention of some one or other, and he will be curious about it, and will come in and make inquiries."

So the birds were exhibited in the parlor-window, and above their cage was hung the announcement that they were for sale. The neighbors saw the birds, and there was not a woman for a quarter of a mile around who did not make a pilgrimage to the parlor-window of the Taylors. "Dan is selling his birds," they said, "because of his brute of a father;" and they shook their heads sorrowfully, and admired Dan's writing, and said he was quite a scholar. Ellen, working in the parlor, would pause in the midst of her hemming, or stitching, or basting, as the shadow of a passer-by darkened the window, and pray that he would come in and buy the birds.

The exhibition was a great boon to the dirty little boys and girls in the neighborhood, who at first stood in open-mouthed admiration, and would have stood so for hours, neglectful of the gutters, if an occasional raid against their forces by anxious mothers had not scattered them now and then. Those of the children who could get near enough, would flatten their noses and mouths against the window-panes in the fervor of their enthusiasm. The bullfinches, looking down from their perch upon the queerly-distorted features, had the advantage of studying human nature from an entirely novel point of view, and were doubtless interested in the study. For the purpose of attracting the passers-by, Dan, at certain intervals during the day, caused the birds to draw up their water and food; and those exhibitions were the admiration of the entire neighborhood.

"I wish some one would come in and ask the price of them," sighed Ellen, wishing that she had a fairy-wand to turn the sight-gazers into customers.

Dan only smiled, and bade Ellen have patience.

In the mean time Mr. Taylor, becoming every day more devoted in his worship to his god, fell every day into a worse and worse condition. One evening, Ellen, being tired, went to bed soon after tea, and on that evening Mr. Taylor happened to come home earlier than usual. There was a reason for it: he had spent all his money, had quite exhausted his credit, and had been turned out of the public-houses. Being less drunk than usual, he was more ill-tempered than usual, and he stumbled into the parlor with the intention of venting his ill-humor upon Ellen. But Ellen was not there. Dan was the only occupant of the room, and he was reading. He raised his eyes, and seeing his father half-drunk, he lowered them to his book again. He was ashamed and grieved.

"Where is Ellen?" demanded Mr. Taylor.

"Gone to bed," replied Dan shortly.

"Why isn't she here to get my supper?" asked the gin-worshipper irritably. Dan made no reply; but, although he appeared to be continuing his reading, a quivering of his lips denoted that his attention was not wholly given to his book. "Do you hear me?" continued Mr. Taylor after a pause, thumping his fist upon the table. "Why isn't she here to get my supper? What business has she to go to bed without getting my supper?"

"She was up at five this morning to do the washing, and has been working all day."

Dan spoke very quietly, and did not look at his father.

"Her mother wouldn't have done it," whimpered Mr. Taylor. "Here am I without two pence in my pocket, and my very children rebel against me. Is there any thing in the house for supper?—tell me that."

"I don't know. I don't think there is."

"You don't know! You don't think there is!" sneered Mr. Taylor. "You've had yours, I suppose?"

"No, sir, I have not had any."

"What do you mean by 'sir'?" cried Mr. Taylor furiously. "How dare you call your father 'sir'? Is that what you learned from your friend Joshua?"

Dan clasped his hands nervously together; he was agitated and indignant, and he did not dare to give expression to his thoughts.

"Why don't you speak?" demanded Mr. Taylor with unreasoning anger. "What do you mean by sitting there mocking your father?"

"I am not mocking you," said Dan. "And as for speaking, I am too much ashamed to say what I think; so I had better remain silent."

"How dare you speak to me in that way? Haven't I kept you for years in idleness and luxury? Haven't I provided for you? And now when I am in bad luck, and haven't sixpence to get a quartern loaf"—he meant a quatern of gin, but the loaf was the more dignified way of putting it—"my children turn against me."

"It isn't my fault that you have had to keep me," Dan said quietly. "If I had been like other boys, I should have been glad to work and earn money; but I am crippled, and never felt that I was unfortunate until now. I don't think mother would have thrown my misfortune in my teeth as you have done."

Mr. Taylor was too much steeped in gin to feel the reproachful words. He continued to bemoan his hard fate and the ingratitude of his children. In the midst of his bemoaning he caught sight of an empty cage. An inspiration fell upon him. That bird-cage could probably be exchanged for a pint of gin. Present bliss was before him, and the prospect of it made him cunning.

He ordered Dan to bed, and Dan, who could crawl with the aid of his crutches, went, thankful to escape from so painful an interview. When Dan came down the next morning he discovered his loss. He was much grieved; not so much at the loss of the bird-cage, but at the thought that his other cages and the birds might be appropriated in like manner. He said nothing of what had occurred, but that night when he went to bed he had all his birds and cages removed to his bedroom, and he locked his door.

It was midnight when Mr. Taylor came home. Although he was drunk, he crept like a thief into the house. The proceeds of the cage had supplied him with drink for the day; and having conscientiously spent every penny, he was in the same impoverished condition as he had been the previous night. As he could not live without gin, he determined to appropriate another bird-cage. What right had Dan to them? They were his, the father's, who had kept his son in idleness, and who had clothed and sheltered him. Yet in the midst of his drunken muttering he was oppressed with a shamefaced consciousness of the villany of his logic, and it was with difficulty he obtained a light from the tinder-box. The poor little rush-light flickered when it was lighted, as if it also were oppressed with shame.

Unsteadily, and with much stumbling, Mr. Taylor groped his way to Dan's room. Looking around on the walls he discovered, to his dismay and astonishment, that the birds and the cages were gone. His first surprise over, he gave way to passion. The boy had no doubt taken the cages to his bedroom for fear his father should steal them. How dared Dan suspect him? He would teach Dan a lesson—a lesson that he would not forget. Working himself into a state of maudlin indignation, he stumbled up the stairs to Dan's bedroom, and tried the door. It was locked. Here was another proof of his son's ingratitude and want of confidence. What was he to do for gin the next day? He must have gin; he could not live without it. Ellen's bedroom was next to Dan's. The drunken father turned the handle of the door, and looked in. On the floor were Ellen's boots. He saw gin marked on them, and catching them up, he clutched them to his breast, and slunk guiltily to bed.

Ellen, rising the next morning, looked about in vain for her boots. She searched for them up stairs and down stairs, wondering what had become of them. The door of her father's room was open, and she entered it; but Mr. Taylor, knowing that Ellen was an early riser, had taken care to get out of the house before she was about. When Ellen saw the empty bed, some glimmering of the truth flashed upon her. At first the poor girl sat down upon the bed and began to cry ; the loss of her boots was a grievous loss indeed to her. She had no money to buy another pair with; they were such beautiful boots, too, and fitted her so nicely! What was she to do? How it would grieve Dan to know? That thought calmed her. Dan must not know—it would hurt him too much. She might be able to get an old pair from somebody during the day; perhaps Susan had an old pair to lend her. She dried her eyes and washed them well with cold water, and altogether managed so successfully, that breakfast was over, and she and Dan and the birds were alltogether in the parlor, without Dan ever suspecting what had occurred.

Those two children sitting there were fully aware that a grave crisis was approaching. Young as they were to bear the weight of serious trouble, they bore it cheerfully, and strove in their humble way to fight with the world and with the hard circumstances of their lives. Dan, cripple as he was, had much hope; and often when he was thinking over certain schemes which had been suggested by the stern necessity of his condition, a quaint smile would play upon his lips, and a humorous light would shine in his eyes. Ellen, looking up from her work, would sometimes see that smile, which, for all its quaintness, had a shade of thoughtfulness in it; and on her lips, too, a pleasant smile would wreathe in sympathy. They were very tender towards each other; and their love made them strong.

Ellen, busy with her needle, sat close to the table, so that Dan should not catch a glimpse of her shoeless feet. Dan was industriously at work training two birds, which were to replace those in the window when they were sold.

The education of this second pair of birds was almost completed, and Dan said as much to Ellen. He had taught them different tricks, and had fitted two ladders in the cage, up and down which they hopped, keeping time, step for step.

"But will they ever be sold?" exclaimed Ellen almost despairingly.

"It *is* a long time before we make a commencement," said Dan. "There's Susan."

When Susan entered, she examined the dress which Ellen was making, and suddenly exclaimed, —

"Why, Ellen, where are your boots?"

Dan looked up quickly, and then directed his eyes to Ellen's feet. Poor Ellen stammered a good deal, and striving to hide the truth from Dan, got into a sad bewilderment of words.

"Nay, but, Ellen," interposed Dan in a grave voice, "you don't mean to say that you have been sitting all the morning without your boots?"

"Yes, I have," said Ellen, compelled to confess.

"But why, my dear?"

"When I got up this morning, I looked for them, and could not find them. Perhaps I can find them now." And Ellen ran out of the room; but she soon returned, shaking her head, and saying, "No, they're gone. Never mind; it can't be helped."

"You really don't know what has become of them?"

"No, Dan."

"Did you see father last night?"

Ellen shook her head.

"Nor this morning?"

Ellen shook her head again.

"I can't quite see what is to be the end of all this," said Dan sadly. "It is almost too dreadful to think of. Father must have taken your boots, Ellen dear. The night before last he took a bird-cage; that was the reason I had all my birds in my bedroom last night. It is very, very dreadful. Poor dear mother! Poor dear Joshua! I do wish you were here now to advise us what to do!"

And the three children then drew closer together, and strove to comfort each other.

"Dry your eyes, Ellen," said Dan stoutly; "brighter days will come. Susan, have you a pair of old boots that you can lend to Ellen?"

Susan ran out of the house and returned with a pair of boots which she had bought at a second-hand clothes-shop, and which Ellen was very thankful for, although they were much too large for her.

Mr. Taylor came home at midnight in a state of drunken delirium. He had drunk deeply — so deeply, that when he slammed the street-door behind him, he found himself in the midst of a thousand mocking eyes, growing upon him and blasting him with their hideous looks; and as he groped his way in terror up the dark stairs, a thousand misshapen hands strove to bar his progress. They fastened on him and clung to him; and the faster his trembling hands beat them down and tore them away, the more thickly they multiplied. So, fighting and suffering and groaning in his agony, the drunkard staggered to his room, and Dan and Ellen shuddered as they lay and listened. Well for them that they could not see as well as hear; well for them that they could not see him pick the crawling things (existing only in his imagination) off his bed-clothes and throw them off with loathing; that they could not see him, bathed in perspiration, writhing in his bed and fighting with his punishment. He could not endure it. It was too horrible to bear.

The room was full of creeping shapes, visible in the midst of the darkness. He would go out into the streets, into the light, where they could not follow him. Where was the door? He felt about the walls for it. It was gone; he was closed in, imprisoned with his terrors. He beat about with his hands deliriously. The window! ah, they had not closed that! He dashed at the panes, and tearing open the casement with his bleeding fingers, fell from a height of twenty feet, and met a drunkard's death.

CHAPTER XIII.

DAN DECLARES THAT IT IS LIKE A ROMANCE.

THE old gentleman with the hour-glass who never sleeps does not look a day older, and yet four seasons have played their parts and have passed away. The white hairs in George Marvel's head are multiplying fast, and he grumbles at them as usual, but has given up the task of pulling them out. Great changes have taken place among Joshua's friends; and Dan, looking up from his work, remarks sometimes that it is almost like a romance. Judge if it is.

When Mr. Taylor was buried — when the shame of his death was forgotten and only sorrow for it remained — the children found themselves in one of those social difficulties from which many wiser persons than they are unable to extricate themselves. For the first three or four weeks after their father's death, Mrs. Marvel and Susan had between them managed to defray the small expenses of the house; but the tax was heavy — too heavy for them to continue to bear. One day, however, unexpected help came. George Marvel, in his quiet way, had conceived a great idea, and in his quiet way had carried it out. Here were these two children thrown upon the world. Not children exactly perhaps, for they were nearly seventeen years of age; but one was a cripple, and the other was a girl. They had been good children, and their character stood high in the neighborhood. Who ought to assist them? The neighbors. Some one must take it in hand, and why not he as well as any other person? No sooner had he made up his mind than he set to work. He went round to the neighbors personally, and told them what his errand was. Poor as they were, they gave their mites cheerfully, with scarcely an exception. When he had made the round of the neighbors, he went to the workshops, and the men there gave their penny each, and the boys their halfpence; and so swelled the total. His own employers and fellow-workmen were more liberal than any. He did not forget his tradesmen, his butcher and baker and grocer. They all gave; and the result was that, at the end of the three weeks during which he had been employed in his self-imposed task, he had a sum of not less than twelve pounds four shillings in his possession, to hand over to Dan and Ellen to assist them through their trouble. The night he made up his accounts, he told his wife what he had done, and she blessed him for it, and was silently and devoutly grateful that Providence had given her a husband with such a heart.

The following evening George Marvel visited the children, with his bag of money in his coat-tail pocket. Ellen was at work, and although she looked pale in her black dress, she looked very pretty. The goodness of the heart always shows itself in the face.

Now Dan had been thinking all day, and indeed for many previous days, that he ought to consult some mature person as to what he was to do. You must understand that Dan, notwithstanding that he was so much younger than Susan, considered himself the head of the family. He had his plans, but he wanted advice concerning them. Up to the present time, his business in trained birds had not flourished. It could not be said to have commenced, for he had not sold a bird. He had decided Mr. Marvel would be a proper person to ask advice of, and by good luck here Mr. Marvel was.

"Have you a few minutes to spare, sir?"

"Yes, surely, Dan," replied Mr. Marvel.

"I want to take your advice, sir," commenced Dan after a slight hesitation. "You know how we are situated, and how suddenly our misfortunes have come upon us. Well, sir, we must live; we must have bread-and-butter. Now the only scapegrace out of the lot of us is me — don't interrupt me, Ellen, nor you, sir, please. Susan is earning her bread-and-butter and something more. Ellen is earning enough to keep her; and I am the only idle one of all of us, and I am the only one who is eating bread-and-butter and is not earning it."

"But, Dan," interposed George Marvel.

"No, sir, please; let me go on. I have been eating the bread of idleness all my life, and I am eating it now. It isn't right that I should do so. I ought to earn my own living. But how? I am not like other boys, and cannot do what other boys can do. One thing is certain: I can't let Ellen work for me, and it would break my heart to part from her; and she would feel it quite as much as I should. — Yes, Ellen, keep your arm round my neck, but don't speak. — I tried to earn money, you know that. I trained some birds, and put them in the window, thinking that some one would buy them. But no one has. I havn't earned a penny-piece, and every bit of bread I put into my mouth has been paid for by Susan and Ellen."

Notwithstanding his eagerness, his tears choked him here, and he was compelled to pause before he resumed. In the mean time, obedient to his wish, neither Ellen nor Mr. Marvel spoke.

"Now, sir, this is my idea. I have got now twenty-two birds; they can do all sorts of tricks: they can whistle tunes; they can climb up ladders; some of them can march like soldiers and can let off guns; some of them can draw carts. Would it be considered begging, if I, a lame boy, who have no other way of getting bread-and-butter, made an exhibition of these birds, and got some one to wheel me about the streets, and stop now and then so that I might put the birds through their tricks? I shouldn't be ashamed to accept what kind persons might give me, or might drop into a little box which I would take care to have handy. I wouldn't do it in this neighborhood. I would go a long way off — three or four miles perhaps — into the rich parts of London, where people could better afford to give. But would it be considered begging? That is what I want to ask your advice upon, sir."

George Marvel's breath was completely taken away. The enthusiastic manner in which Dan had spoken, no less than his admiration of the proposed scheme, had caused him to forget his errand for the time. "Wait a minute," he said somewhat excitedly, "I must think; I must walk about a bit." But no sooner had he risen than the weight of the money in his coat-tail pocket brought him to his sober senses, and he sat down again.

"Dan," he said, taking the lad's hand affectionately in his, "you are a good boy, and I am glad that you are Joshua's friend. I will answer your question and give you my advice, as you ask it. In any other case than yours I think it would be begging; but I don't think it *would* be in yours."

"Thank you, sir," said Dan gratefully.

"Mind, I think even in your case it would not be exactly what I should approve of, if you had any other way of getting a living."

"You think as I do, sir; but I have tried, as you see, and I have not succeeded."

"Try a little longer, Dan."

"How about next week's rent, sir?"

"You can pay it," replied George Marvel, "and many more weeks' besides. I have a present for you in my pocket;" and he pulled out the bag of money and put it on the table. "In this bag is twelve pounds four shillings, which your friends — yours and your sisters' — have clubbed together for you, and that is what brought me here to-night."

"O sir!" cried Dan, covering his face with his hands.

"This money has been got together because all of us round about here love you. I sha'n't give it to you all at once. You shall have it so much every week; and I should advise you — as you ask for my advice — to continue training birds for sale and putting them in your window. Try a little while longer. A customer may come at any minute. And one customer is sure to bring another."

"How can I thank you and all the good people, sir?" said Dan, with a full heart.

"Never mind that now," said George Marvel.

If he had known that it would have been so difficult and painful a task, it is not unlikely he would have remitted it to his wife to accomplish. Pretending to be in a great hurry, he rose to go, and, pressing Dan's hand and kissing Ellen, went home to his wife and told her of Dan's wonderful idea.

Ellen and Dan were very happy the next morning, and set about their work cheerfully and hopefully. Dan wrote a new announcement concerning the birds, and the windows were cleaned, and presented a regular holiday appearance. In the midst of his work, Dan, looking up, saw a face at the window that he recognized. It was that of a young man who had been in the habit of looking in at the window nearly every day for the last week, and of whom Dan had observed more than once, that he looked like a customer.

"There he is again, Ellen," said Dan; "the same man. Why doesn't he come in and ask the price of them?"

He had no sooner spoken the words than the man's face disappeared from the window, and a knock came at the street-door.

"Run and open the door, Ellen. I shouldn't wonder if he has made up his mind at last." Dan's heart beat loud with excitement. "How much shall I ask for them?" he thought. "Oh, if he buys a couple of them, how happy I shall be!"

The parlor-door opened, and the man entered; decidedly good-looking, dark, with a fresh color in his face, and with black hair curling naturally. The first impression was favorable, and Dan nodded approvingly to himself. The man had curiously flat feet, which, when he walked, seemed to do all the work without any assistance from his legs; and although his eyes were keen and bright, they did not look long at one object, but shifted restlessly, as if seeking a hiding-place where they could retire from public gaze.

"I have been attracted by the birds in the window," he said, coming at once to to the point, much to Dan's satisfaction. "Can they really perform what the paper says? Can they really sing 'God save the King,' and draw up their own food and water?"

"They can do all that, sir; but you shall see for yourself. — Ellen! Where is Ellen?" Dan called; for he wanted her to assist him, and she had not followed the stranger into the room.

"Ah, Ellen," said the stranger, dwelling on the name. "Is that the young lady who opened the door for me?"

"Yes, sir. — Ellen!" Dan called again.

"Allow me," said the stranger; and he went to the door, and called in tones which slipped from his throat as if it was oiled, "Ellen! Ellen!" Then he turned to Dan, and questioned: "Your sister?"

"Yes, sir."

"Ah," said the man greasily, "she is extremely like you. Allow me. I will bring the cage to the table."

He brought the cage from the window, and placed it before Dan. At that moment Ellen entered the room. The man's eyes wandered all over her as she took her seat at the table. She did not return his gaze, but bent her head modestly to her work.

"Your sister's name is Ellen," he said, "and yours?"

"Daniel," said Dan; "Daniel Taylor."

"Daniel; a scriptural name. Mine is also a Scriptural name: Solomon, Solomon Fewster. Solomon was a wise man; I hope I take after him."

"I hope so, I am sure, sir," said Dan somewhat impatiently; for he was anxious to get to business. "Now, sir, if you will please to look and listen."

He blew through the tin whistle; and the bullfinches piped "God save the King."

"Very pretty, very pretty," said Solomon Fewster, nodding his head to the music. "And you taught them yourself?"

"Yes, sir. But it isn't as if they will only sing for me; they will sing for you, or for Ellen, or for any one who blows the whistle."

"And they will sing for Ellen if she breathes into the whistle?" said Solomon Fewster. "Will Ellen breathe into the whistle with her pretty red lips? Allow me."

He took the whistle from Dan and handed it to Ellen; and she reluctantly gave the signal to the birds, who willingly obeyed it. Mr. Fewster took the whistle from her and blew; and the birds for the third time piped the air. Then Dan directed his attention to the wooden whistle, and to the wonders performed by the birds at its dictation. Nothing would please Mr. Fewster but that Ellen should place the wooden whistle between her "pretty red lips," as he called them again, and "breathe into it." He said that "breathe" was more appropriate to Ellen's pretty lips than "blow." He, using the whistle after her, cast upon her such admiring looks, that he really made her uncomfortable. The performance being over,

Dan gazed at Mr. Fewster with undisguised anxiety. He had intended to be very cunning, and to appear as if he did not care whether he sold the birds or not; but the effort was unsuccessful.

"Well, well," said Mr. Fewster; "and they are really for sale? Poor little things! I asked the price of bullfinches yesterday at a bird-fancier's, and the man offered to sell them for four pence each. Not that these are not worth a little more. There is the trouble of training them: of course that is worth a trifle. Still bullfinches are bullfinches all the world over; and bullfinches, I believe, are very plentiful just now — quite a glut of them in the market." He paused, to allow this information to settle in Dan's mind, before he asked, "Now what do you want a pair for these?"

"What do you think they are worth, sir?" asked Dan, much depressed by Mr. Fewster's mode of bargaining.

"No, no, Daniel Taylor," said Mr. Fewster, in a bantering tone, "I am too old a bird for that; not to be caught. Remember my namesake. You couldn't have caught him, you know; even the Queen of Sheba couldn't catch *him*. I can't be buyer and seller too. Put your price upon the birds; and I will tell you if they suit me."

"You see, sir," said Dan frankly, "you puzzle me. The training of these birds has taken me a long time. You would be surprised if you knew how patient I have to be with them. And you puzzle me when you make so light a thing of my teaching, and when you tell me that bullfinches are a glut in the market. If the bullfinches you can get in the market will suit you, sir, why do you not buy them?"

"Well put, Daniel, well put," said Mr. Fewster good-humoredly. "Still, you *must* fix a price on them, you know. How much shall we say?"

"Fifteen shillings the pair," said Dan boldly.

Mr. Fewster gave a long whistle, and threw himself into an attitude of surprise. Dan shifted in his seat uneasily.

"A long price," said Mr. Fewster, when he had recovered himself; "a very long price."

"I couldn't take less, sir," said Dan.

"Not ten shillings? Couldn't you take ten shillings?" suggested Mr. Fewster, throwing his head on one side insinuatingly.

There was something almost imploring in the expression on Dan's face as he said, —

"No, sir, I don't think I could. You haven't any idea what a time they have taken me to train. I hoped to get more for them."

"I tell you what," said Mr. Fewster, with sudden animation. "Ellen shall decide with her pretty red lips. What do you say, Ellen? Shall I give fifteen shillings for them?"

"They are worth it, I am sure, sir," said Ellen timidly.

"That settles it," said Mr. Fewster gallantly. "Here is the money."

And laying the money on the table, Mr. Fewster took the cage, and shaking hands with Dan, and pressing Ellen's fingers tenderly, bade them good-morning.

Dan's delight may be imagined. It was intensified a few day's afterwards, when Mr. Fewster called again, and bought another pair of birds; Mr. Fewster at the same time informed Dan that it was likely he might become a constant customer; and so he proved to be.

In the course of a short time, Dan found himself in receipt of a regular income. Other customers came, but Dan could not supply them all, as Mr. Fewster bought the birds almost as soon as they were trained. Very soon Dan thought himself justified in making a proposal to Susan. The proposal was that they should all live together in the house where Dan carried on his business. The only obstacle to the carrying out of the arrangement was Susan's determination not to leave Basil and Minnie Kindred. But why should not Basil Kindred and his daughter come as well? asked Dan; there was plenty of room for them, and it would be such company. And after the lapse of a little time, the result that Dan wished for was accomplished, and Basil and Minnie and Susan were living with them. They were a very happy family. The parlor-window had been altered to allow more space for the bird-cages; and Dan, looking around sometimes upon the group of happy faces, would remark that it was almost like a romance.

And so indeed it was, notwithstanding that the scene was laid in the humblest of humble localities.

CHAPTER XIV.

THE STRANGE COURSES OF LOVE.

PERHAPS one of the most absurd questions that could be put to a person would be to ask him how old he was when he was born. Yet the little old-men's faces possessed by some babies might furnish an excuse for such a question. The shrewd look, the cunning twinkle, the pinched nose, the peaked chin, the very wrinkles — you see them all, though the child be but a few weeks old. All the signs of worldly cunning and worldly wisdom are there, ready made, unbought by worldly experience; and as you look at them and wonder how old the little child-man really is, the object of your curiosity returns your look with scarcely less speculation in his eye than you have in yours. You are conscious that you are no match, except in physical strength, for the little fellow lying in his mother's lap or sprawling in his cradle; and a curious compound of pity and humiliation afflicts you in consequence.

Some such a child as this was Solomon Fewster before he attained to the dignity of boyhood; his parents and their friends agreed in declaring that he was a cunning little fellow, a knowing little fellow; they would poke their fingers in the fat creases of his neck, and would sportively say, "Oh, you cunning little rogue!" "You knowing little rogue!" and he would crow and laugh, and endeavor to utter the words after them. He was so accustomed to the phrase, and grew to be so fond of it, that when he was old enough to understand its meaning, his chief desire seemed to be to prove himself worthy of it. It falls to the lot of but very few of us to compass our desires. Solomon Fewster was one of the fortunate exceptions. He was dubbed a cunning little rogue, before he knew what such praise meant; and (could it be that he was unwilling to trade under false pretences?) when he did know, he educated himself to deserve it, and succeeded. A small percentage of the old-men babies retain their old-men's looks as they grow to boyhood; specimens of these can be seen any day in our courts and alleys. This was not the case with Solomon Fewster; as he grew, the old-man look faded from his face, and the spirit of "a cunning little rogue" took root in his heart, and flourished there. His parents dying when he was a child, he was left to the charge of a bachelor uncle, an undertaker by trade, who adopted and educated him. When he was taken from school — where he was the cunningest boy of them all — he was initiated into the mysteries of the undertaking business, and when he was of age he was intrusted with a responsible position, and his uncle made a will leaving every thing to him. He proved himself an invaluable ally; was grieved to the heart at the losses sustained by his uncle's customers; wept when he assisted at measurements; was broken-hearted when the clay was taken from the house; and sobbed with an almost utter prostration of spirit when he receipted the account, and signed Payment in Full. He entered heart and soul into the business, and thoroughly enjoyed it. Whether it was because he looked upon himself as the future master of the establishment, or because it was congenial to his nature, he strove by every means in his power to extend the connection; and being as acute and sensible as a man of double his age, his efforts were successful and the business flourished. Death was most obliging to him, and waited and fawned upon him at every step he took. If his spirits became depressed because trade was slack, a fortunate epidemic restored him to his usual cheerfulness, and orders poured in ; and it is no disparagement of him, as an undertaker, to state that he buried his friends and acquaintances with melancholy satisfaction. When he was twenty-three years of age his uncle died. He paid the old gentleman every possible mark of respect: had the coffin lined with white satin; wept till his face was puffed; entered the expense of the funeral in the ledger to the debit of the deceased, and wiped off the amount at once as a bad debt. Then he set to work vigorously upon his own account. He had his name painted over the door, and issued circulars to every house for miles round. In those circulars he announced that he undertook and conducted funerals cheaper than any other undertaker in London ; said that one trial would prove the fact; and respectfully solicited the patronage of his friends and the public. His appeal was successful; his trade increased; and Solomon Fewster was generally spoken of as a man on the high-road to prosperity.

When Solomon Fewster first saw Ellen, she was seventeen years of age, and he was seized with a sudden admiration for her pretty face and graceful figure. He had never seen a girl so winsome; and when they met again, he followed her admiringly to her home, and saw the exhibition of the bullfinches in Dan's window. Here was an opportunity to stare at her; and he enjoyed the cheap pleasure again and again until Dan noticed his face at the window. Then a happy thought entered Mr. Fewster's mind. The birds certainly were wonderfully intelligent, and their clever tricks would most likely render them easy of disposal. He entered into communication with a West-end fashionable bird-fancier — the farther away from Dan the better, he thought — and the bird-fancier (who had a connection among fine ladies) informed him that if the birds could really do all that he stated, a profitable trade might be established between them. "What a fine opportunity," thought Solomon Fewster, "of introducing myself to the pretty girl in the light of a benefactor!" Then came the first interview and the first purchase. The pair of bullfinches he bought for fifteen shillings he sold for thirty; and the following week the fashionable bird-fancier asked for more. Thus it was that Solomon Fewster made his growing passion for Ellen a means of putting money in his purse; and thus it was that he came to be looked upon as a privileged visitor to the house.

The Old Sailor also found his way to the house. He was not as frequent a visitor as Mr. Fewster, but he was a more welcome one. The Old Sailor might have been a child, his heart was so green ; and he had such a fund of stories to tell, and he told them with such simplicity and enthusiasm, believing in them thoroughly, however wild they were, that his hearers would hang upon his words, and laugh with him, and sorrow with him according to the nature of his narrative. They spent the pleasantest of pleasant evenings together, and when Praiseworthy Meddler told his sea-stories, Minnie would sit very quiet on the floor — a favorite fashion of hers — listening eagerly to every word that dropped from his lips. Then Basil Kindred would read Shakspeare when he could be coaxed into the humor, and would keep them spell-bound by his eloquence. He had ceased wandering in the streets and begging for his living. Necessity was his master there. He was stricken down with rheumatic fever, which so prostrated him that he was unable to pursue his vagrant career. They had a very hard task in inducing him to remain with them.

"Live upon you, my dear lad!" he exclaimed loftily. "No; I will perish first!"

"There is enough for all, sir," replied Dan. "Do not go. I would take from you — indeed, indeed I would! — could we change places. And there is Minnie, sir," — with such a wistful tender glance towards Minnie, who was growing very beautiful, — "what would she do ? But not for her nor for you do I ask this, sir. It is for me; for Ellen and Susan and Joshua. How happy he will be to find you here when he returns! You and Minnie, that he talked of so often, and with such affection! Then think, sir. You would not like to be the means of breaking up our little happy circle; and it is happy, isn't it, Minnie ?"

"Ah, yes, Dan!" replied Minnie, with an anxious look at her father. "Only one is wanting to make it perfect."

"And that one is Joshua," said Dan, divining whom she meant, and grateful to her for the thought.

"And that one is Joshua," she repeated softly, placing her shell to his ear. "Do you hear it? Is it not sweet, the singing of the sea?"

But all argument and entreaty would have been thrown away upon Basil if it had not been for Minnie. It was she who, when they were alone, prevailed upon him to stay.

"Your mother suffered for me and died for me," he said to her, as he lay upon his bed of pain. "How like her you are growing, Minnie! Well, well, one is enough. I will stay, child, for your sake."

And she kissed him and thanked him, and whispered that he had made her happy.

The next day she told Dan in a whisper that father was not going away; and Dan clapped his hands, and quietly said, "Bravo!"

"And Joshua used to speak about us?" she remarked, with assumed carelessness.

"Often and often, Minnie," answered Dan.

"And really speak of us affectionately?"

"Ah! if you had only heard him! You know what a voice he has — like music."

A sudden flush in her face, a rapid beating at her heart, a rush of tears to her eyes. None of which did Dan notice, for her eyes were towards the ground. A little while afterwards she was singing about the house as blithe as a bird. Dan, stopping in the midst of his work, listened to the soft rustle of her dress in the passage, and to her soft singing as she went up the stairs; and a grateful look stole into his eyes.

"Not to hear that!" he said. "Ah, it would be worse than death! But she is going to stay, birdie," nodding gayly to one of his pets; "she is going to stay!"

Dan told Minnie of the pretty fancies he had in connection with his friend; of the manner in which his love had grown, until it was welded in his heart for ever and ever; of Joshua's care and self-devotion towards him, the poor useless cripple. He told her of his fancy about the dream-theory, and how he had believed in it, and of the experiments he had made. And Minnie listened with delight, and sympathized with Dan — ay, and shed tears with him — and showed in every word she uttered how thoroughly she understood his feelings.

"I have dreamed of him over and over again," said Dan; "but of course I don't know, and indeed I can't believe, that I have dreamed of him as he is. He is a man by this time, Minnie; and — let me see! — he is standing on his ship, with his bright eyes and handsome face" —

"Yes!" interrupted Minnie eagerly.

"Made brighter and handsomer by living on the open sea and away from narrow streets. I can see the spray dashing up into his eyes, and he shaking it off laughing the while."

"Yes, yes!" said Minnie enthusiastically. "You can see him too, Minnie. I feel that you can. Is he not handsome and brave? I can hear him say, as he looks round upon the grand sea and up at the beautiful clouds, — I can hear him say, 'Dan is here with me, although I cannot see him.' He has me in his heart, as I have him. It was a compact. We were to be always together, and we are. Dear Jo!"

He paused a while, and Minnie, her hands clasped in her lap, gazed before her, and saw the picture painted by Dan's words. Many such conversations they had, and the theme was always the same.

Shortly after the death of Mr. Taylor the Old Sailor came to see the children. He did not know of the loss they had sustained; and when he heard that both father and mother were dead, he was much grieved. The news so disconcerted him that he rose to go three or four times, and each time sat down again, as if he had something on his mind he wished to get rid of first. As a proof that he was mentally disturbed, he dabbed his face more frequently than usual with his blue-cotton pocket-handkerchief, folding it up carefully before he put it in the breast of his shirt, as if he were folding up his secret in it, and afterwards taking it out and unfolding it, as if he had made up his mind at last to disclose what that secret was. When he found courage to speak, Dan learned that the bullfinches which Joshua and he had presented to the Old Sailor were dead.

"Died yesterday morning, my lad," said the Old Sailor; "died just as we were beginning to understand each other. Sailor birds they were, and they could climb ropes as well as any bird in the service."

"I am sorry they are dead, sir," said Dan; "but I can give you another pair."

"No, Dan, no. I'll not have any more; they wouldn't be safe."

"Not safe?"

"There was a mutineer in the crew, my lad," said the Old Sailor, dropping his voice. "It comes awkward for me to tell you; but you ought to know — and duty before every thing. The pretty birds were poisoned."

"Who could have been so cruel as to poison the innocent creatures?" asked Dan sorrowfully.

"That damned copper-colored son of a thief who cooked for me!" replied the Old Sailor excitedly. "You saw him when you were on my ship. He had rings in his ears."

"I remember. He was a Lascar, you told us."

"The treacherous dog!" exclaimed the Old Sailor wrathfully, dabbing his face. "But I did what was right to him. I flogged him with a rope's end till he couldn't stand."

"He knew that Joshua gave you the birds, sir?"

"Ay, he knew it. To tell you the truth, my lad, I christened the birds Josh and Dan, and used to call them by their names. They were as sensible as human beings, and I gave them decent burial. I sewed them in canvas, and weighted it with shot, and slipped it off a plank. I'll not have any more of them, Dan. That lubberly thief would crawl on board one night and murder them too. No, no, my lad; no more birds for me."

"Well, then, I'll tell you what we'll do," said Dan. "I will give you another pair of birds, and I will keep them for you, and you will come here sometimes and see how they are getting along. That's a good idea, isn't it, sir?"

The Old Sailor admitted that it was, and thus it fell out that he became a visitor to the house. Dan bought a toy ship, with sails and masts and slender ropes all complete, and taught the birds to climb the ropes and masts, which they did deftly, although not in sailor fashion, hand-over-hand; and his thoughtful conceit filled the Old Sailor with infinite delight.

It was Susan's good fortune not to meet the Lascar for many months after the eventful occurrence in which Joshua had played so prominent a part. But one evening, when she and Ellen were returning home, she met him face to face.

"Stop!" cried the Lascar, noticing Susan's agitation with secret pleasure. "You don't forget me, do you?"

Ellen, raising her eyes, saw and recognized the Lascar, and was recognized by him at the same moment.

"Ah!" he said, "I remember you. You came one day with a lame boy and that young thief Joshua Marvel — curse him! — to see Mr. Meddler's boat."

Ellen tried to hurry Susan along, but the Lascar stood directly in their path.

"Not yet, my beauty. You are about the prettiest girl I've ever seen. What's your name?"

Ellen was not so overcome with fear as to entirely lose her self-possession. Had she been alone, she would have run away. But Susan was clinging to her, almost fainting with terror. On the opposite side of the road she saw a man walking towards them.

"Help!" she cried; but she could have bitten her lip with vexation when she found that it was Solomon Fewster who responded to her appeal. However, there Solomon Fewster was, ready to grapple with the enemy and to die in Ellen's defence. The occasion for a display of heroism was as good as he could have desired.

"Where is he?" he cried valiantly; "where's the villain who has dared to frighten my pretty Ellen?"

He said this with such a presumptuous air of being her defender by natural right, that Ellen was annoyed and displeased. But she could not be uncivil to him. She thanked him for coming to their help, and he asked to be allowed to see them home. But Ellen refused, and although he pleaded hard, she was firm.

She was especially angry because of his calling her his pretty Ellen. Glad as she would have been of a protector, she rightly thought that it would be giving Mr. Fewster encouragement if she allowed him to assume that office. So, with many distressingly-tender protestations, he took his departure, congratulating himself upon the adventure, and Susan and Ellen walked homewards.

Ellen was very anxious to know all about the Lascar, and why Susan was frightened at him. Susan told her all, and Ellen's face glowed with delight at Joshua's courage.

"Brave Joshua!" she exclaimed. "Isn't he a hero, Susan?"

Notwithstanding that she had not recovered from her fright at meeting the Lascar, Susan could not help smiling at Ellen's enthusiasm.

"He was to be away a year," said Ellen, "and it is now two years and four months."

"And how many weeks, and how many days, and how many hours?" interrupted Susan, half gayly. "You could tell, I dare say, Ellen, couldn't you, if you were put to it?" Ellen looked shyly at Susan. "What a change he will find in you, my dear!" Susan continued tenderly. "In the place of a plain little girl he will find a very pretty woman."

"O Susey! calling me a woman!"

"Well, you are, dear, or you will be when he comes back. I wonder"—

But Susan did not say what it was she wondered at, but stopped, most unaccountably, in the middle of the street and kissed Ellen in a motherly kind of way. The caress set Ellen a-blushing, and she fell into a state of happy musing. They were very near home when a voice at their side said,—

"You thought you had escaped me, eh?"

It was the voice of the Lascar, who had dogged them until he found an opportunity of speaking to them without attracting attention. Their hearts beat fast, but they did not turn their heads.

"Don't say a word," whispered Ellen, "don't speak, don't stop, don't look! We shall be home directly."

"So Joshua Marvel hasn't come back yet," he said with bitter emphasis. "He is a long time gone; but wait till he comes. I go every day to see the cross I put against him, and it grows brighter and brighter. I curse him every night. Perhaps he thinks that I forget. He shall see if I do." He gasped this at intervals, for the girls were now almost running in their terror. "Tell him," hissed the Lascar, "when he comes home that I poisoned that old thief's birds because Joshua gave them to him, and because the old thief used to call one of them by his name. Curse him! And you!" he exclaimed savagely, touching Susan's arm. "See you — remember! My shadow follows you from this day, you damned witch! for it was because of you that he came across me. Oh, you live there, do you? Dream of my shadow, you cat, to-night. It shall stand at your bedside. Blot it out if you can."

He had worked himself into a horrible rage; his passion made a madman of him; yet he did not attempt to stop them as they darted in at the door, but stood aside and looked at the house, and marked it and lingered about it for half an hour afterwards. In the mean time Ellen and Susan had run into their bedroom and locked the door. It was a long time before they recovered from their agitation. Susan was in an agony of terror; all her old fears came with stronger force upon her. She pressed her fingers upon her eyes and threw herself upon the ground, shuddering and moaning.

"Do you see his shadow, Ellen?" she moaned. "Do you see it?"

"There is nothing in the room but you and me, dear Susey," said Ellen, smoothing Susan's hair, and striving by every means to soothe her. "Why, I am braver than you, and I am ever so much younger. What have we to be afraid of? A drunken man! You stupid Susey! And as for shadows, who believes in them?"

"I do. I have seen them and felt them. I have heard them creeping after me in the dark, and I have been frightened to turn. I have felt their breath upon my face — and it is like death — like death!"

All Ellen's efforts to tranquillize her were unavailing. Susan did not leave her room again that evening, and during the night that followed she awoke a dozen times, and her fevered imagination conjured up the shadow of the Lascar standing at her bedside, pointing to a cross of blood which shone with cruel distinctness in the midst of the darkness.

CHAPTER XV.

SOLOMON FEWSTER GIVES THE LASCAR A FLOWER.

EARLY in the new year letters from Joshua reached home. With what joy they were read! In one of them he wrote: "I remember saying that I should be home in twelve months; but that time has passed, and another twelve months, and nearly another, and still there is no talk of returning. If I stay away much longer you won't know me when you see me. Upon my word, I think if I were to open the door now and walk in suddenly, you would be puzzled to know whether I was really myself or somebody else."

When they read this they all raised their heads and looked towards the door, wishing that Joshua would turn the handle and walk into the room.

The evening of the day on which the letters arrived was spent in grand state in Dan's house. Every member of the Marvel family was there, and the Old Sailor, and Solomon Fewster as well; so that the little parlor was quite full, and all the chairs had to be brought from the bedroom and the kitchen to provide seats for the company. The letters were read aloud, and commented upon and rejoiced over.

"It isn't as good as Joshua's being here," said Dan, looking round with a happy face; "but it is next door to it. I tell you what pleases me almost as much as any thing in the letters — it is that Jo's a favorite with the men. Hear what he says: "I play to them on my accordion two or three times a week, and according to them I am a splendid musician — which I am not, you know, for I only play simple tunes. Last week the captain sent for me and told me that some passengers who were on board wanted to dance, and wished me to play for them. Of course I fetched the accordion at once. You should have seen us! I played for them twice after that night; and yesterday when we arrived at Sydney — Oh, Dan! such a lovely place, with such a bay! — they gave me a sovereign, which I put into Ellen's purse. Tell Ellen that!"

A blush came into Ellen's face, and her heart beat more quickly, when she heard that Joshua was so careful of the purse she had worked for him.

Filled with such like matter, the letters could not fail to be a source of delight. Dan was commissioned to give Joshua's love to Ellen, and Ellen was asked to pay a visit to the Old Sailor, and to tell him that Joshua was doing his duty. Susan received messages for Basil and Minnie, and was to tell Minnie that Joshua would bring her some beautiful shells — "shells in which Minnie can hear the waves singing to each other in whispers," Joshua wrote, almost poetically.

Minnie, sitting in her corner, scarcely spoke a word; she was thinking of the sailor-lad who had been so kind to her, and she was looking with the eyes of her mind upon the picture which Dan had painted of Joshua, with his handsome face and free waving hair, standing on the deck, and laughingly shaking the spray from his eyes.

The Old Sailor nodded approval as the letters were read, and then traced Joshua's course on a map which he had brought with him, stopping many times to tell the eager on-lookers of the wonders and the glories of the beautiful South Pacific. The map was spread on the table, and it was not an unattractive picture to see them all clustered round the Old Sailor, peeping over his shoulders and under his arms, as with his great forefinger he followed the ship from port to port. Mrs. Marvel, who had taken to spectacles, found them of but little use to her on this occasion, for the obstinate tears came into her eyes and dropped into the ocean which the Old Sailor's forefinger was ploughing. Minnie leaned over Dan's shoulder, and the table was so small that she had to put her arm round Dan's neck and to put her face close to his, so that she might see. A strange feeling of happiness came upon Dan as her cheek nestled close to his; a feeling of happiness so exquisite that all his senses were merged in it. The common parlor, the eager faces peering at the map, the pleasant voice of the Old Sailor explaining the route, all faded from before him, and he was conscious of nothing but Minnie's presence. He felt the warm contact of a soft hand; it was Minnie's hand, which in her eager abstraction she had placed on his. He folded it in his, and she allowed it to rest there. It was like a dream. He feared to move, and held his breath lest he should awake. A sudden murmur of voices — voices that sounded for a moment as if they came from afar off — aroused him; he looked into Minnie's face, and saw it lighted up with a happiness that seemed to be a reflex of his own; and as she turned her eyes to his, so luminous a beauty dwelt in them that he could have fallen at her feet and worshipped her. But the dream was at an end — the blissful silence which had encompassed him, was invaded. Minnie had returned to her corner, and his friends were speaking together, and laughing, and appealing to him upon some point which he had not heard. Dan still felt the warm pressure of Minnie's hand and the soft contact of her cheek; and unobserved he rested his lips upon the palm which had clasped hers, and kissed it softly and wonderingly.

There was only one person in the party who did not feel happy. That one was Solomon Fewster. Directly he entered the room he had been greeted with the joyful tidings; and understanding that he was expected to share in the general excitement of pleasure, he professed a delight which he did not experience. That afternoon he had purchased a rare flower, which it was his intention to present to Ellen. He had brooded over the idea for several days, and had decided that it would be a good thing to do. As he entered the room with the flower in the button-hole of his coat, he was already primed with a few complimentary words which he had learned by heart to say to Ellen, when he presented his gift. Ellen had never before looked so pretty, he thought. Her eyes were brighter, and there was a more joyous animation than usual in her manner. She greeted him with a smile so much more gracious than he was accustomed to receive from her, that he congratulated himself upon the purchase of the flower. She gave him her hand with more than her usual warmth, and when he ventured gently to press it, she did not resent the liberty. The fact was, she did not notice it. She was full of joy, and, as is the case with all amiable natures, she dispensed gleams of her happiness to all with whom she came in contact. Unless we are too much engrossed in our own special cares, we sometimes meet with such like happy faces in the streets — faces which seem to say, "We are happy; be happy with us" — faces which, although quite strange to us, which we have never seen before and may never see again, will kindle with a smile of welcome upon the smallest encouragement.

But Solomon Fewster was terribly discomfited when he learned the reason of her cheerfulness and animation; it was because letters had been received from Joshua. He determined not to present his flower just then, for he read something in Ellen's blushes that sorely galled him. He could not help thinking that the fuss they were making about a common sailor-boy, and the laughing and the crying they indulged in over Joshua's stupid letters, were utterly ridiculous, and in a sort of way derogatory to himself, Dan's best patron.

As the night wore on, his anger and uneasiness increased; and yet he lingered until the last moment, torturing himself with all kinds of speculations as to what was the nature of the feeling that Ellen entertained for Joshua. Every expression of gladness that fell from her lips concerning Joshua and Joshua's career was painful to him, and it was with a bitter heart that he left the house, with the flower still in his coat. He was hot and feverish as he closed the street-door behind him, and he was not sorry to find that a heavy rain was falling. He took off his hat and bared his head to the rain. Within the house he had been compelled to repress expression of his feelings; it was a relief to him now to feel that no one was by, and that he could speak out at last. And the first words he uttered, as he smoothed his wet hair and put on his hat, were, "Damn Joshua Marvel! I would give money to drown him!" As he spoke the words aloud, he was conscious of a slouching figure at his side. Although it was raining, the night was not quite dark; there was enough light for him to notice that the man who had approached him was in rags — most probably a beggar. Muttering that he had nothing to give, Solomon Fewster walked on. But the man was not to be so easily shaken off, and Mr. Fewster being in an eminently quarrelsome mood turned upon him, and repeated in no civil tone that he had nothing to give.

"I have not asked you for any thing," said the man, surlily, "though if I had, you might speak to me more civilly, Mr. Fewster."

They were passing a lamp-post, and, attracted by the utterance of his name, Mr. Fewster stopped and said, —

"How do you know my name?"

"I know it; that is enough," was the answer.

"Ah!" said Mr. Fewster, regarding the Lascar with curiosity and recognizing him, "I have seen you before, my man."

"That is not saying much against me, master," said the Lascar, rather sneeringly. "I have seen *you* before; so we're equal."

"And whenever I have seen you, it has been in this street," continued Mr. Fewster.

"And pretty well whenever I have seen *you*, it has been in this street," retorted the Lascar; "you seem to be as fond of it as I am."

"And generally of a night."

"The same to you, master; and what then? The street is free to me as it is to you. Look you. I know more than you are aware of. If it comes to that, why do *you* go so often to that house?" The sudden look of discomposure that flashed into Mr. Fewster's face was not lost upon the Lascar, who had seen him walking by Ellen's side more than once, and who had stealthily followed them on every occasion. "Look you, master. What one man does for love, another man does for hate."

"Hate of whom? What do you mean?"

"The people in that house have received letters from Joshua Marvel to-day."

"Well, what of that?"

"What of that!" cried the Lascar, in a voice of suppressed passion, and yet with a cunning watchfulness of Mr. Fewster's face, as if he were watching for a cue to speak more plainly. "Well, nothing much, master; except that I should like to know when the cub is coming home."

Mr. Fewster could not help an expression of satisfaction passing into his eyes as he heard Joshua spoken of as a cub, and the Lascar saw it and took his cue from it.

"What do you want to know for? What is Joshua Marvel to you?"

"He is this to me," cried the Lascar, the dark blood rushing into his face and making it darker; "that if I had him here, I would stamp upon him with my feet, and spoil his beauty for him! He is this to me, that if I could twist his heart-strings I would do it, and laugh in his face the while! See me now, master; look at me well. I did not ask you for money, for I know you, and I know you don't give nothing for nothing. But I might have asked you, and with reason, for I want it. Look at my feet" (Mr. Fewster noticed, for the first time, that the Lascar's feet were bare); "look at my clothes — rags. That old thief, Praiseworthy Meddler, kicked me off his barge where I've lived and slept this many a year. And every blow he struck at me went down to Joshua Marvel's account, and makes it heavier against him. See you; the Lascar dog never forgets. I've sworn an oath, and I'll keep it. I've put a cross against him, and he shall see it when he is dying."

Solomon Fewster looked at the wretch before him, quivering with passion and shivering with cold, and deliberately cracked his fingers one after another. When the operation was concluded, he said, lightly, as taking no interest in what the Lascar had said, —

"That is your business, my friend; not mine. I will tell you as far as I know about this young gentleman who has served you so well. He is not coming home yet a while, I believe — not before the end of the year, perhaps. I dare say you'll manage to see him when he does come home."

"Yes, I'll manage to see him then," said the Lascar, with a sudden quietude of manner and with a furtive look at Mr. Fewster's face — a look which said, "You are trying to deceive me, master; let us see who is the more cunning — you or I." Then aloud, "Thank you for answering my question. You say it is not your business, this hate of mine for Joshua Marvel. Yet there may be something in common between us, for I've seen you walking with the girl who worships Joshua Marvel."

"How do you know that she worships him?" demanded Mr. Fewster, thrown off his guard, his heart beating loud and fast.

"Because I am not blind. I know that as well as I know that you have as much cause to hate him as I have. I am like a cat; I watch and watch. You are too young, my master, to mask your face; and I have seen that in it that you wouldn't like to speak."

"Mind what you are saying," said Mr. Fewster, with his knuckles at his teeth; "you are on dangerous ground."

"Why should I mind?" questioned the Lascar, with a curious mixture of fierceness and humility in his voice. My tongue's my own. I have nothing to lose: judge you if you have any thing to gain. Mind you, I stop at nothing. I am not squeamish. You are a gentleman; I am a vagabond. I can do what you daren't. I can help you to what you want, perhaps; and you can help me."

The cunning of the Lascar was too deep for Mr. Fewster. The Lascar saw as clearly as if he had been told that Solomon Fewster loved Ellen Taylor, and he seized instinctively upon Ellen's love for Joshua as the lever by which he was to gain power over Mr. Fewster. In the present conversation the men were not evenly matched; the Lascar had all the advantage on his side. Subtle as Mr. Fewster was, his love blinded his judgment, and his hate led him to consider that this man might be useful to him.

"I can help you, you tell me," he said. "How?"

"I am cold to the bone," said the shivering wretch. "Treat me to some rum."

They walked until they reached a public-house; then Mr. Fewster gave the Lascar money.

"Go in and drink, but don't get drunk."

"Ain't you coming in, master?"

"No," said Mr. Fewster, with a look of contempt at the Lascar's tatters. "You can buy a bottle of rum, and bring it out with you. And mind, when you come out, don't walk by my side; follow me."

Five minutes afterwards they were walking in single file towards Mr. Fewster's place of business, where he lived. When they arrived at the door, Mr. Fewster hesitated. He wanted to talk to the Lascar, to get out of him all he knew about Ellen and Joshua; yet, looking at the Lascar, he hesitated. The man divined what was in his mind, and said, —

"There is a policeman coming along on the other side of the way. Go to him and say, 'Look at this man; I have occasion to speak to him on a matter of business; but he is a disreputable dog, and I want you to watch the house. Knock in an hour, and if I don't answer, or if you hear any noise, force open the door.' Say that to him, or something like it, and give him a pint of beer, and you will be all right."

"Come along," said Mr. Fewster, stung by the Lascar's quiet sneer; "I am not frightened of you."

"You have no need to be, master. You can use me like a dog, if you give me to eat and drink."

"Like a dog!" echoed Mr. Fewster, with a laugh. "Well, suppose I regard you in that light; it may be useful."

Mr. Fewster struck a light in the shop, in which there were at least a score of coffins — respectable coffins, solemnly black as coffins should be, with respectable nails to match.

"Waiting for tenants," he remarked, pleasantly, to the Lascar. "The cheap ones — common deal — are in the workshop at the back." Mr. Fewster put the candle down upon a coffin, and looked complacently upon his wares. "Handsome, are they not? This one, now, with lacquered handles and silvered plate for name, age, and virtues, what should you say to that?"

"Shouldn't care much for it," said the Lascar, with evident repugnance. "It would be more suitable for such as you, master. A cheap one — of common deal — will be good enough for me, when my turn comes."

"Quite good enough, I should say."

"You are not going to stop here talking, are you?" inquired the Lascar, seeing that Mr. Fewster evinced no disposition to move.

"Why, don't you like it, you dog?" retorted Mr Fewster, with a spice of his native humor.

"No, I don't; it smells of worms."

With a pleasant laugh Mr. Fewster led the way into his sitting-room, and set light to the fire and lit a second candle.

"This is better," said the Lascar, huddling before the fire. "Ah, this is good, this warmth; it is life! Have you ever slept out in the cold, master?"

"No, you dog," answered Mr. Fewster. He had recovered his self-possession and much of his usual equanimity.

"I have; in the cold and wet, for two or three nights together."

"There was the Union," suggested Mr. Fewster.

"I have been there often enough. Sometimes I was too late; sometimes there were too many of us; sometimes I didn't care even for that shelter."

"Would you like to sleep in my shop? I think I could trust you there."

"I think you might. I shouldn't be likely to steal a coffin. I shouldn't care to sleep there, master, and that's flat. If I woke up in the dark, I should see dead men lying in the coffins. I wouldn't mind it so much if the coffins were plain deal ones; but black — ugh!"

Mr. Fewster laughed loud and long. Coffins were playthings to him — toys symbolical of the joys of life. He laughed merrily as he set food on the table, the Lascar watching him with greedy eyes the while.

"Fall to, you dog!" said Mr. Fewster; and like a dog, devoid though of a dog's generous nature, the Lascar fell to, and devoured the bread and cheese. Meanwhile Mr. Fewster helped himself to a large glass of rum. He was one of the soberest of undertakers, who, as a rule, are not the soberest of men. He drank but very rarely; but when he did, all the worst part of his nature disported itself, in revenge for being generally kept so much under control. Now as he drank his rum — and he drank it neat — he became savage, vengeful, desperate. He had never felt till now how deeply he loved Ellen Taylor. He had loved her in a light way from the first, and his love had grown quietly, and had been fed by her avoidance of his attentions. Her behavior towards him had deepened his love and intensified it. Yet all along, notwithstanding that he felt he was not as agreeable in her eyes as he would wish to be, he thought that to have he had only to ask. "They, poor working people," he thought, "earning just enough to keep them, living as it were from hand to mouth, *must* feel flattered and honored by my attention — by the attention of a man who has a prosperous business and an account at the bank." As for marriage, he had not thought of that till lately. But Ellen had so firmly and so steadily repulsed him in any advances he had plucked up courage to make, that he had resolved to lower himself and ask her to be his wife. Having determined to make the sacrifice, he considered that the road was clear to him. He reasoned with himself thus: "She thought perhaps that I did not mean honorably by her, and that is the cause of her treating me so coldly; but when she learns my real intentions she cannot but feel flattered, and must accept me."

He thought over these things as he sat before the fire entirely engrossed by love for Ellen and hate for Joshua. The Lascar had helped himself to the spirits, and as Mr. Fewster sat studying the fire, he sat studying his host. That it was a study that interested him and pleased him was evident from the satisfied expression in his face, and from the satisfied manner in which he rubbed his hands gently over one another.

"Well, you dog!" exclaimed Mr. Fewster insolently.

"Well, master?" replied the Lascar meekly.

"Have you had enough, you dog?"

"Plenty, thank you, master."

The Master took another drink of rum, and the Dog followed suit. The Master regarded the Dog with a contemptuous assumption of superiority. The Dog regarded the Master with becoming humbleness. But the Dog had the best of it, although he did cast down his eyes.

"Look up, you dog," said Mr. Fewster. The Dog looked up.

"What would you do to Joshua Marvel if you had him here, with no one by?"

The Lascar, who had been playing idly with the knife with which he had cut his supper, raised it, and with a fierce action struck at the air. Then, springing to his feet, he threw aside his chair, and kneeling on the ground, made motions with his fingers as if he were strangling an enemy.

"H-m!" exclaimed Mr. Fewster, looking at the upturned face, blazing with vindictiveness, that fronted his. "Dangerous."

"That's my business. I'll risk the danger of it. See you — shall I speak plainly?"

"Yes."

"This girl that you love worships the man that you and I hate" —

"Say that *you* hate, you dog," interrupted Mr. Fewster. "I'll have no partnership. I am master."

"I ask your pardon, master. The girl that you love worships the man that I hate. She is waiting for him to come home; so am I. I have sworn death to him. When he comes home, the girl that you love will have no eyes for any one but him. What chance will you have with her then?"

"Stop. You are too fast. Speak of yourself and of them without reference to me. Don't iterate with your damnable tongue about the girl that *I* love. The girl that I love, I'll have" —

"So you shall, master, if I can help you."

"When I want your help, I'll ask for it.

"Now go on with your story, and heed my caution."

With ready wit the Lascar fell into Mr. Fewster's humor.

"This girl that I speak of — as pretty a picture of flesh and blood as eyes ever saw — is loved by a gentleman who in a sort of way has lowered himself to think of her. But the gentleman has made up his mind to have her, and when a gentleman makes up his mind, who shall stop him? He goes one night to the house where this pretty girl lives — I shouldn't wonder if the very flower that the gentleman wore in his button-hole wasn't intended for her" —

"You are a clever dog, you!" said Mr. Fewster, half in anger, half in admiration.

"Thank you, master. With the flower in his button-hole the gentleman goes to the house where his pretty girl lives, and there he spends the evening, and hears read, I dare say, some letters, which she has received from his rival, who is a sailor — I only speak from fancy, master; set me right if you can."

"How can I set you right when I know nothing about it, you dog, except by saying that I shouldn't think it likely *she* received any letters?"

"Thank you, master. My fancy was wrong, I've no doubt. The gentleman, then, is obliged to listen to some letters which have been received from abroad, and is obliged to listen to affectionate words uttered by the girl he loves for his rival far away — mind, master, I don't know this, I only suspect it — and he sees, too, in her face, that when her sailor-boy comes home, she will open her arms to his rival, to his enemy, whom he hates, and would like to see put out of the way."

"How do you know that last?"

"I have seen it in his face; I have heard it in his voice. I happened to see the gentleman come out of his sweetheart's house one rainy night, not long ago; and I happened to hear the gentleman mutter that he would give money if that sailor-lover was drowned."

"If I were the gentleman, and you told me this to my face, I should say that you lied."

"Of course you would; but what should you know of it? Still, master, confess that the story is a likely one as far as it has gone."

"There is more of it to come, then?" asked Mr. Fewster, who had turned his back so that the Lascar should not see his face.

"There *is* more of it to come. But say, first, it is a likely story as far as I have told it," said the Lascar a little doggedly.

"It is likely enough. I have heard stories more strange."

"Where did I leave off? Oh! about my hearing this gentleman say, as he stood bareheaded in the rain, that he wished his rival were dead. Now that was a fortunate hearing for me. Not that I should take advantage of what I heard; not that I should go to the pretty girl's brother, and then tell him what I had heard the gentleman say about his sailor-friend; not that I should go to the pretty girl herself and say, 'Beware of the gentleman; he means mischief'; if he can ruin your lover he will.' That would be a mean thing to do; for it would upset the gentleman's chances with the girl that he loves. No; I should go to the gentleman and say, 'I hate this absent lover, and any thing that I could do to make him suffer, I would do cheerfully. You would do the same. But you are a gentleman, and I am a dog. You mustn't be seen in the matter. What you want done do through me. Never mind how mean it is, how dirty it is; do it through me. And all the return I want for it is enough to buy food and shelter, and perhaps a drop of grog and a bit of tobacco.' That wouldn't be much to ask in return for what I may be able to do for him."

"But no gentleman would compromise himself by entering into a bargain with a —a" —

"A dog, master — say a dog; it is good enough for me," interposed the Lascar with a careless laugh.

"With a dog like you, I don't see how the affair could be arranged with a proper understanding as to what was expected to be done."

"It could be arranged easily enough, master. I might ask the gentleman, supposing he had a flower in his button-hole, to give me that flower, and not say another word. That would be a proper understanding for both of us."

Mr. Fewster rose, and put aside the curtain of the window. The rain was coming down hard and fast, and the wind was tearing furiously through the streets."

"A fine storm for a ship to be in near rocks, master," said the Lascar, who had risen, and was standing by his side.

"It is time for you to be going," said Mr. Fewster, turning abruptly away from the window.

"In such a night as this!" exclaimed the Lascar. "And I with no place to put my head in?"

"You are homeless, then?" The Lascar nodded. "Well, I take you into my service. It would be hard if no one could be found to do a good turn for a poor devil like you."

"That it would, master," said the Lascar, standing in an attitude of expectation; "and thank you. Could you spare that flower out of your coat?"

Blinded by passion, inflamed by jealousy, Mr. Fewster detached the flower, and threw it to the Lascar, whose eyes gleamed with satisfaction as he put it in his pocket.

"You can sleep in the out-house," said Mr. Fewster; "and as every dog should have a kennel, I dare say you can find a coffin to lie in."

"No, thank you, master; I will lie on the ground." He poured what remained of the rum into his glass, and raised it to his lips. "Here's luck, and my faithful service to you. You may depend upon me, for my heart is in my work."

CHAPTER XVI.

CHRISTMAS-EVE AT HOME.

A HAPPIER party was never assembled within four walls than is now gathered together within the four walls of Mr. Marvel's kitchen. That it is Christmas-eve is proclaimed by the two little hoops which hang from the ceiling, circled by colored Christmas candles; and that the kindly influence of the time has fallen in full measure upon the wood-turner's house may be read in the faces of George Marvel and his family and guests. Sarah Marvel, whose place in this history is but a small one, has grown into a comely young woman; and, indeed, the four years which have elapsed since Joshua's departure have changed all his friends for the better. Those of them who were young when he left are no longer boys and girls, except in their hearts, which are as young as ever, and which are pulsing with love for the absent hero. Not to be absent for long now; for Joshua is coming home. They cannot tell the exact day of his arrival; it may be a week yet, or a month; but the sails of his ship are spread for dear home. So, as they sit round the fire, there is a happy light in their eyes, and they look at each other and smile, and laugh musical little laughs.

"It is more than four years ago," said George Marvel, "that one night as we were sitting round the fire, as it might be now, Josh said all of a sudden, 'I should like to go to sea.' Those were the very words he said 'I should like to go to sea.' And it came so sudden-like, that mother there began to cry. 'So you want to be a sailor, Josh?' I asked. 'Yes,' he answered; 'a sailor first, and then a captain.' Do you remember, mother? And now my boy is coming home a man; and here we are this happy Christmas-eve, talking of him, and thinking of him, and hoping to see him soon after the New Year. Said mother that night, 'Suppose Josh is shipwrecked, what would you say then?' What would I say then? What *did* I say then? I said that Josh wasn't going to get shipwrecked, and that there's more danger on the land than on the sea. And I was right, I was; and mother wasn't."

Mrs. Marvel smiled contentedly at the reproof, and nodded in confirmation of her husband's words.

"And when Mr. Praiseworthy Meddler came to see us for the first time," continued Mr. Marvel, "he said the very same thing that I said about the dangers of the sea. And talking of Mr. Meddler, here he is, I do believe; and that makes our party complete."

The last words had been suggested by a great stamping and puffing outside in the passage; and presently the door opened, and Praiseworthy Meddler, covered with snow, stood in the entrance.

"A merry Christmas to you all!" he said, peeling off his glazed coat. "No, no my lasses, don't come near me; you'll spoil your pretty ribbons."

But the girls would not be denied, and clustered round him, assisting him to take off his coat, and to shake the snow from his cap and hair. A pleasant figure he was to look at as he stood there, his honest face beaming with health and pleasure, encircling the waists of Ellen and Minnie, who nestled to him as confidingly and lovingly as if they were his daughters. A sprig of mistletoe hanging over the door caught his sight, and he stooped and gallantly kissed the girls, who pretended resistance, and sprang laughing from his arms. Then he shook hands all round, and taking the seat that was waiting for him near the warmest part of the fire, remarked that the snow was two inches thick on the pavement, and that it was coming down heavily still. It reminded him of a great snow-storm by which he was overtaken in a cruise in the north. That, of course, led to entreaties for a snow-story, and the Old Sailor, in his homely way, told them a story of icebergs and polar-bears, which kept them entranced for nearly an hour, and which was all the more delightful because it ended happily.

The story being concluded, they talked noisily and merrily as to what they should do next in honor of Christmas. In the midst of the conversation, Ellen, who was sitting next to Dan, felt her hand tightly clasped. Looking up, she saw upon his face a listening expression of such painful intensity that she asked him, in a whisper, what he was listening to. He put his finger to his lips and told her — with a strange abstractedness in his manner — that he was going out of the room, and that he wished her to come with him without attracting attention.

"We shall be back presently," said Ellen to Mrs. Marvel, as she assisted Dan with his crutches.

When they were in the passage, she felt that he was trembling, and she anxiously asked if he was unwell.

"Not bodily," he answered; "I want to look in the street."

They went to the street-door, and, opening it softly, looked out. The snow was falling fast, and the unpretentious houses, covered with their white mantle, looked surprisingly quaint and beautiful. A man, who passed on the opposite side of the way as they opened the door, was the only sign of life beside themselves in the street. The man slouched onwards, and dragged his feet along the pavement in a brutish kind of way, tearing a black gash in the pure white snow, out of sheer wantonness as it seemed. It looked like a desecration.

"Ellen," said Dan, when the man was out of sight, "I would not tell my fancies to any one but you. I am not happy. All last night I was dreaming of Joshua."

"That was good, dear," said Ellen.

"It was not good, Ellen. My dreams were bad ones. They were too confused and indistinct for me to remember them clearly. But the impression they left upon me was that Joshua was in danger; I cannot tell in what way or from whom. I did not hear a word of the story Mr. Meddler just told us. I was thinking of I don't know what — and all of a sudden, Ellen, I fancied that I heard Joshua's voice."

"That is because he is so near us."

"Near us? Yes. He is very near us; nearer than you imagine."

"How do you know, dear?"

"I feel that he is; and strange to say, Ellen, the feeling does not seem to bring me pleasure."

"O Dan!"

"It is so, Ellen; I cannot help it. That Joshua is near us, I am certain. See: is there anybody in the street?"

Ellen looked up and down. No; there was no person to be seen, and she said so.

"How beautiful the night is, Dan!"

"Yes, like fairyland, almost," said Dan. "It hurts me to see that black track on the other side, where the man was walking. Did you notice how he slouched along? Look at that shadow at the end of the street. Is it the same man, I wonder?"

The shadow lingered for a few moments, as if undecided which road to take, and then disappeared again.

"Dan, dear," whispered Ellen, "you said that you would not tell your fancies to any one but me."

"Well, Ellen?"

"May I whisper something, my dear?" she asked very tenderly.

"Yes."

"Would you not tell them to Minnie?"

She was supporting Dan, and his hand was round her neck; a nervous twitching of his fingers told her that her question was a momentous one.

"Dear Ellen," he answered in an agitated voice, "I do not think I would — at least just yet — because — because " —

"Because what, dear?"

"Because I am not sure, Ellen," he said, with a sob which he strove in vain to suppress. "Do not say any thing more, dear. My heart is very sad."

She obeyed him, and kissed him, and then, with a lingering look at the wondrous white outlines of eaves and roofs, and at the wondrous white carpet with which the earth was clad, they closed the street-door and re-entered the kitchen. There they were greeted with the news that Basil Kindred was going to describe and read a play to them. The play which Basil had selected was Shakspeare's "Tempest," with which none of them was acquainted but Minnie and Dan. Minnie clapped her hands in delight.

"We will all have characters," she said. "You," to her father, "shall be Prospero. You," to the Old Sailor, "shall be Stephano. You," to Ellen, "shall be Miranda; and I will be Ariel. What a pity it is that Mr. Fewster is not here! — he should be Caliban. If Joshua were here, he should be Ferdinand."

"Who is Ferdinand?" asked Ellen.

"Ferdinand is a prince, and is in love with Miran — no!" Minnie exclaimed suddenly and impetuously, the blood rising into her face, " he should not play Ferdinand; he should not play at all. Look at me. I am Ariel."

With a swift motion, she unloosed her hair and let it fall around her shoulders. Bewitchingly graceful and bewitchingly beautiful, she bent in obeisance to Prospero, and said with a happy inspiration, —

"Do you love me, master?"

And he, partly in accordance with her pretty conceit and partly from fatherly affection, placed his hand upon her head and answered, —

"Dearly, my delicate Ariel."

Then, motioning her to be silent, Basil Kindred, book in hand, commenced to tell the story, reading passages now and again in illustration of the beautiful fancy, and giving appropriate vocal distinctness to each character; so that his hearers could understand without difficulty who it was that was supposed to be speaking. He was in his happiest humor, and he lingered lovingly upon the theme. The fooling of Trinculo, the brutishness of Caliban, the tenderness of Miranda, the majesty of Prospero, the daintiness of Ariel, were all faithfully portrayed; and his audience followed the course of the story with eager delight. When he had given utterance to that grandest of poetical images,

> "We are such stuff
> As dreams are made of, and our little life
> Is rounded with a sleep."

he paused, and a deep silence fell upon the room, a silence that was broken by Dan exclaiming,—

"Hark! a knock at the door!"

Was it the magnetism of love that caused their hearts to flutter with joy — that caused Mrs. Marvel to rise tremblingly and say that she would go and open the door? But her limbs failed her, and Minnie, crying, "I will go!" ran out of the room. They below, listening in a state of strangely-anxious expectancy, heard Minnie ask "Who is there?" and heard her open the door. Almost at the same moment they heard a cry of joy, followed immediately by a sharp cry of pain. They ran up stairs and saw Minnie kneeling in the snow, supporting on her bosom the head of a man dressed in sailor-fashion, and pressing her lips to his neck, from which the blood was flowing. The pure snow was crimson-stained; and Mrs. Marvel, in an agony of fear falling on her knees by Minnie's side, looked into the face of the wounded man, and recognized the features of her sailor-boy just returned from sea.

CHAPTER XVII.

THE DOG AND HIS MASTER.

UPON that same Christmas-eve Solomon Fewster sat in his room a moody unhappy man. He was alone; but if angry thought could have found palpable shape, the room would have been thronged with ugly forms. He had refused the invitation which Mrs. Marvel had given him to join the Christmas party, simply because, when she invited him, she happened to say something in joyful tones of Joshua's expected return. The mere mention of Joshua's name was sufficient to inflame him; and he had at once refused her in a lofty manner, saying that he had another engagement for the evening. The Lascar had done his work well. There is no death for jealousy: it sleeps, but it never dies. And the Lascar had been careful that even the temporary bliss of forgetfulness should be denied to his master. Less force of cunning than he was endowed with would have served his purpose with such a man as Solomon Fewster.

The good influence of the time did not touch Solomon Fewster's heart. He was completely engrossed by two sentiments — love for Ellen, hate for Joshua. The very circumstance that upon this Christmas-eve he had wilfully deprived himself of the painful pleasure of being in Ellen's company he laid to Joshua's door. Every happy face he saw that day deepened the hate he bore to Joshua; for if it had not been for that absent enemy, he would have been as happy as the best of them. Once during the evening he went into the open space at the rear of his house, and saw his neighbors' windows lighted up, and heard sounds of merriment issue from the rooms. "Who is it that prevents me from being as happy as they are?" he muttered. "Who is the cause of my remaining here to-night, fretting my heart out, instead of sitting next to the girl that I love more than my life?" He unlocked the gate in the rear of his premises, and strolled along the narrow lane into which it opened. The houses in the lane were mere hovels, yet there was not one of them that was not brilliantly lighted, and the echoes of laughter and singing floating from their walls denoted that care had been sent to the right-about for that evening, at least. The sounds were so displeasing to him that he returned to his room and resting his face in his hands, raised up the picture of Ellen, fair and bright and beautiful. He was a calculating, unfeeling man; and if it had so happened that there had been no obstacle to the smooth course of his love, he might have remained so to the end of his days, and might never have suspected that there were points in his character which would not bear too close a scrutiny. But the means by which we are brought to a knowledge of ourselves are oftentimes very strange. The majority of us go down to our graves without suspecting that there are powerful forces hidden within us, which, had opportunity for display been allowed them, would have materially altered the tenor of our lives, whether for good or for evil. Solomon Fewster's love for Ellen was the most ennobling feeling he had ever experienced. His hatred for Joshua, and the thoughts and desires prompted by that hate were the most villanous. It is strange that the hate which disgraced him, not the love which ennobled him, should have made him conscious of his defects. It was that very hatred that brought to him the knowledge that he was not a good man ; and that caused him to reflect that, if his love were returned, it would be the means of making him better. His thoughts were taking this direction now, and he was still sitting with his face resting in his hands, when he was startled by the sound of the gate being violently dashed aside. He remembered that he had forgotten to fasten it. Before he had time to rise, the latch of the door was lifted, and the Lascar glided in like a white spectre. With a strange feverishness of manner, the Lascar turned the key in the door, and at the same moment stooped and listened, holding up a warning finger as a caution for Solomon Fewster to be silent. He remained in that position for two or three minutes ; then rose upright, and drew a long breath.

"What now ?" demanded Mr. Fewster angrily, and yet with a consciousness that the Lascar had sufficient cause for his abrupt entrance. "What thieves' trick have you been up to to-night, you dog! that you run in here as if the police were at your heels ?"

"They are not," said the Lascar, shaking the snow from his clothes, dog-like ; " and that's a good thing, master, for you and for me."

"For me, you dog ! You dare to say that !"

"I forgot to close the gate," said the Lascar, taking no notice of Mr. Fewster's exclamation. He went out, and having locked the gate, re-entered ; and, seeing a bottle on the table, said, "What's this ? Rum ? He did not wait to be invited, but helped himself freely, and spread his cold hands before the fire. "I am numbed to the bone. It's precious cold being out in the snow all day. I didn't hope to find you at home, master. I thought you would be enjoying yourself like a gentleman. I ran in here, finding the gate open, not knowing where to run. It is snowing fast—that's one comfort — and my footsteps will soon be filled up."

All the while he spoke he was busily occupied warming his fingers and blowing on his knuckles.

"Now, explain the meaning of all this," said Mr. Fewster.

"Give me something to eat first, master. I haven't tasted food since the morning."

Mr. Fewster pointed to the cupboard ; and the Lascar took bread and meat, and ate swiftly and ravenously.

"My service to you, master," he said, glass in hand, "and a merry Christmas." When he had emptied the glass, he threw a knife on the table. It was a clasp-knife, and the blade was open. There was a triumphant demonstrativeness in the action that instantly attracted Mr. Fewster's attention. He saw blood upon the blade — blood scarcely dried. Whose blood was it ? A mist floated before his eyes. It was there but a moment ; but in that moment a picture presented itself to him in the midst of a lurid cloud — a picture of a handsome sailor, smitten by an assassin's hand, falling to the ground. Then the figures were lost in a glare of bright blood and bright snow ; and they, in their turn, were lost in black shade. Although the vision lasted but a moment, it produced the curious effect upon him of having been enveloped in darkness for a long time ; and the sudden awakening to consciousness caused him to shade his eyes with his hand, as if the light in the room were too strong for him. Awake again, the Lascar's familiar action and bearing smote him with a sense of danger. The instinct of self-preservation whispered to him that his good name might be imperilled by further association with the man. It was clear that the Lascar had done a desperate deed — a deed which, although he shuddered to think of it, had perhaps removed his enemy from the scene. But if so, it was murder. The merest whisper, the faintest breath of suspicion, would be his ruin, not only with the world, but with Ellen. He would pay for services — yes ; but he would take no risk. It behoved him to be wary.

"They've had a merry party down yonder," said the Lascar, with a motion of his head in the direction of Mr. Marvel's house. "I made certain you were there, master. I've been hanging about the street all night in the cold. I've been on the watch ; shall I tell you for whom ?"

"No; I want to know nothing," replied Mr. Fewster, measuring his words carefully. "Understand me once and for all. Whatever you do you do on your own responsibility ; and I will in no way be associated with it or with you. If you presume to associate me with any acts of violence on your part, I wash my hands of you. Nay, more ; I will set those upon you who will not let you escape easily."

"I understand you, master," said the Lascar, without the least show of resentment. "But go on ; you have more to say. I'll wait till you've done."

"You dog, you ! You break into my house as if you had a right here ! You tell me, as if I were interested in knowing, that the police are at your heels, and that you are afraid of your very footsteps being tracked! You have the presumption to say that it is a good job for me that it is not so! You throw down this knife before me with blood upon it! What is it to me whose blood it is, or what crime you have committed? What if it were to be discovered that you had rendered yourself liable to the law, and then had been seen to come here? If I did my duty, I should go for a policeman, and hand you into his charge, and so be rid of you."

The Lascar listened without the slightest sign of discomposure. He even nodded approvingly as he said,—

"There's only you and me, master. You wouldn't speak so if anybody else was by. Don't fear; I know what you mean well enough. There's no chance of our misunderstanding each other, though you're a better actor than I am, and that's a fact. Rest you easy. No one saw me come here; and no one shall see me go out. As for the police, I know as well as you that it would suit your game as little to set them on me as it would suit my game for them to be set on. But you're right in threatening me with them. It belongs to your part; for you are master. And it belongs to my part to take what you say kindly; for I am a dog. I am satisfied so long as I get enough to keep me; and I'm not greedy, as you know."

Solomon Fewster was extremely disconcerted by the Lascar's coolness. It proved to him that he was in the Lascar's power, and that the Lascar knew it. He was disconcerted also by the conviction that forced itself upon him, that the Lascar measured his indignation at its proper worth. But he could not belie his nature. It was impossible for him to be straightforward; even in his villany he was compelled to be cunning. He would take care that he committed himself as little as possible by word of mouth. He was burning to hear what the Lascar had to tell, but he would not ask. He drew his breath hard, and it was with difficulty that he restrained his impatience during the long pause that followed; for the Lascar was as determined as he not to be the first to break the silence. At length, feeling that he was being mastered, he turned wrathfully upon the Lascar, and questioned, "Well?"

"Well!" was the quiet answer.

"If you have nothing more to say, you can go."

"I have something more to say, but I am waiting for permission to speak."

There was an assumption of insolent humility in the Lascar's tone; and Mr. Fewster bit his lip as he said, "Your tongue's your own; I can't stop you."

"Thank you, master;" with a cringing expression of satisfaction for the concession. "Since I was employed in my present service — I mean, since a certain night when a kind-hearted gentleman gave me a flower, the leaves of which I have kept carefully in paper, so that I shouldn't forget what I had to do — I have been more watchful than ever in the task I had set myself to perform. I have been better able to do that than I used to be, because the same kind-hearted gentleman has generously supplied me with money, so that I have had all my time at my own disposal. He also supplied me with information. The task I had to perform was to revenge myself upon Joshua Marvel for stepping between me and my affairs, and for doing me injury. A little while ago the gentleman told me that Joshua Marvel was expected home soon; and then I determined that not a night should pass and find me lagging. Not only my hate, but my faithful duty to my master, made me determined in this. I set myself to watch for the return of the sailor Joshua; and during my watch I discovered a curious thing. I discovered that the gentleman in whose service I am appeared very often in the street I was watching, and that he was in the habit of lingering there late at night. He never did any thing else but look up at the bedroom-window of a certain pretty girl, whose shadow I have often seen on the blind; and he never went away until the light in her room was extinguished. I was careful that he should not see me, for it was no business of mine; and I know when I ought to keep in the background. Besides, I admired him for it; for I knew that he loved this girl, and that Joshua Marvel stood in his way. Regularly every day I went to the docks to see if the Merry Andrew — Joshua Marvel's ship — had arrived; and as good luck would have it, the ship came in this very morning. When I learned that, I went back to my watch in the street the gentleman is so mightily fond of. I knew that Joshua Marvel wouldn't be able to get away from his ship directly it got into port; and I guessed that it was more likely than not that he wouldn't let his people at home know of his unexpected arrival. No; he would surprise them. It would be so pleasant on Christmas-eve to break in upon them suddenly, and be petted and kissed, especially by one" —

"The devil take you!" cried Solomon Fewster fiercely, grasping the table with such force that it trembled with the trembling of his hand. "Tell your story without preaching, can't you?"

"I'll try, master. I hung about the

street the whole day, eating nothing, and drinking very little. I might have been frozen, if my purpose hadn't kept me warm I didn't grumble because I had to wait. I wanted him to come at night, and he came when I wanted. It isn't much more than an hour ago"—here he dropped his voice to a whisper—"that I saw a sailor turn the corner of the street where pretty Ellen Taylor lives. He had an accordion under his arm, and a cage in his hand covered with a blue pocket-handkerchief; and he stopped two or three times to look at the houses, and nodded to them as if he was wishing them a merry Christmas. I followed him, like a cat, and opened my knife. He was singing—I couldn't catch the words—and to judge from that and from the way he walked, I should say he was as happy a man as any in London. He never once looked behind him; if he had, I would have struck him down. He stopped before the house where his father and mother lived, and stooped to the key-hole and listened. I was close upon him —waiting! If he hadn't been so much occupied, he might have smelt me at his back. But it wouldn't have saved him if he had seen me; he would only have been struck down the sooner. While he was listening at the keyhole, he laughed quietly, enjoying the surprise he was going to give his people. When he had his laugh out, he knocked at the door. Presently I heard a woman's voice inside the house ask, "Who's there?" "It's Josh," said my man. I heard a cry of pleasure; and as the door was being unfastened, I raised my knife, and stabbed him in the back.

"And killed him?" cried Solomon Fewster involuntarily.

"I don't know. He fell; and as I ran off, I caught a glimpse of a woman kneeling by him in the snow, and raising his head to her bosom."

Solomon Fewster groaned. Without another word he opened the door by which the Lascar had entered, and walked into the open air. The snow-fall had ceased, and the stars were shining. The moon, too, had risen, and clouds of light and deep shade were gliding swiftly across it, while everchanging shadows were playing on the snow. In the distance he heard the waits; they were a long way off, and the strains of music fell upon his ears chastened and mellowed. He was in danger; he had allied himself with this man, who made so light of the shedding of blood; and he had been made a confederate in perhaps a murder. Not that he had any compunction; not that he had any pity. Nothing would have rejoiced him more than to have heard that Joshua had been killed in a mutiny had been wrecked, or had lost his life on sea or on land by any means, so that he was not implicated in it. The feelings that disturbed him now were purely selfish; he had to save himself from suspicion, supposing any discovery were made. Perhaps it would be best, after all, to speak plainly to the Lascar. There were no witnesses, and it did not matter much what he said. If Joshua were dead, the Lascar must be got rid of at any sacrifice of money. Thus resolving, he returned to the room. The Lascar was sitting patiently before the fire, and did not even raise his eyes as Mr. Fewster entered. "He did not know what I went out for," thought Mr. Fewster. "I might have gone for a policeman, and if I had brought one in, he would have declared I was his accomplice."

"Has it left off snowing, master?" asked the Lascar.

"Yes."

"Then it wouldn't be quite safe for me to go away to-night—safe for you, I mean."

"You can stop here to-night."

"Thank you, master. Have I done well?"

"It doesn't matter whether I say you have done well or ill; so, to save argument, suppose I say you have done well. Now, attend. If what you have done to-night should turn out to be"—

"Say murder, master," said the Lascar, seeing that Mr. Fewster hesitated to speak plainly. "I don't mind."

"If it should turn out to be that, have you considered that you are in danger?"

"I haven't thought of it, master, and that's a fact. But if I am in danger, so are you."

"That may or may not be. The only danger I am in is from what you might say; and, supposing I had spoken to you only once in my life, you would be free to say any thing of me, or of any one else, for that matter. What you might say wouldn't be evidence, you know."

"True, master; but, at all events, I could ruin your chances with pretty Ellen Taylor."

"What satisfaction would that be to you?"

"Every satisfaction," said the Lascar with a kindling eye. "If any one hurts me, I hurt him."

"As you have hurt Joshua Marvel, because he hurt you."

"And because I am in your service," said the Lascar doggedly. "Don't forget that, please; I don't intend to forget it. If this is to be a fair argument, let it be fair. If it is to be acting, let it be acting.

What I have done to-night is half for me and half for you: equal shares."

"I told you once that I would have no partnerships," said Mr. Fewster in a steady voice, "and I will have none; but I don't mind coming to a distinct understanding. If what you have done to-night should turn out at its worst"—

"Or its best," interrupted the Lascar sneeringly.

"It will not be safe for you to remain in the country. To please you, I will say it will not be safe for you or for me."

"Ah!" exclaimed the Lascar thoughtfully. "I think I understand you. Well, in that case there are plenty of countries I shouldn't mind going to; or I might go aboard ship again. How much will you give me?"

"A hundred pounds."

"Agreed, master, — if it should turn out at its worst, as you say. But if it does not, I stay, mind you."

"That is your affair."

"As much yours as mine, master," said the Lascar with determination.

"What makes you harp upon that, you dog?" exclaimed Mr. Fewster, firing up.

"Necessity," replied the Lascar coolly. He liked the life of indolence he had been leading, and he did not intend to relinquish his hold of Solomon Fewster. "I have no money, and no means of living. You have acted fairly to me up to now, and you must continue to do so. You can afford it, that's certain. I know what it is you fear. You fear that it should be known that I am in your service. Well, no one shall know it from me; and I will never come here again. You know where I stay. What you have to give me, leave there for me; and when you want me, send for me. I am your dog, ready to do your bidding. I can't speak fairer. There's no occasion for any more palaver. I'm tired and sleepy; I can sleep here, before the fire." He stretched himself on the ground by the side of the fire. "Silence gives consent, they say. If you don't speak, I shall understand that the affair is settled. You wanted a distinct understanding, you know."

He closed his eyes, and listened for the answer. The answer came — in silence; for Solomon Fewster spoke not another word that night. The Lascar, made drowsy by the glare from the fire, courted sleep; and it came to him, as it comes to better men. And Solomon Fewster sat, looking down upon the form of the man who could blast his good name by a word, and thought — What? Once during the night the Lascar awoke with a shiver. The fire had gone out; but Solomon Fewster was still sitting at the table with a haggard look upon his face, as if he had suddenly grown old.

CHAPTER XVIII.

THE RIVALRY OF LOVE.

A SILENCE almost like the silence of the grave reigned in the house of the Marvels. If, by some chance, a blind man had found his way there, he might reasonably have wondered whether it was tenanted by ghosts or human beings. The persons in the house walked about it with such a ghostly motion that scarcely a footfall could be heard. The doors were opened and shut as tenderly as if wounds were being handled, and as if rough treatment would cause them to cry out with pain. The very voices were hushed and low, and what was said was said in whispers. The blow by which Joshua had been struck down was a severe one, and wounded many besides himself. Notwithstanding Minnie's efforts, Joshua had lost a great deal of blood, and was laid on a sick-bed for many weeks. For a long time the doctor feared for his life; but good nursing and a strong constitution were in his favor.

"But mind you, Mrs. Marvel," the doctor had said, half-a-dozen times, "nothing *would* have saved him — not even his constitution, and it's a good one; not even the nursing he has had, and no man ever had better — nothing *would* have saved him if Miss Kindred had not behaved like a heroine. You may thank that young lady for saving your son's life. If she hadn't stopped the flow of blood with her lips, all the doctors in London couldn't have kept him in the world for twenty-four hours."

When Minnie was told of this, she went to her room and locked herself in.

"I have saved him!" she said to herself, weeping tears of delicious joy. "I have saved his life! Oh, what happiness! I could die now, I am so happy!"

It might have been better for her if she had died then with those words upon her lips.

During the time that Joshua was in the greatest danger, Mrs. Marvel would allow no one but herself to sit up with him at night. She had a bed made up on the floor, and rested there, taking, indeed, but little sleep, until Joshua was out of danger. Minnie, especially, had pleaded hard to be allowed to sit up with her; but Mrs. Marvel was firm. Although she would not have confessed it even to herself, she was jealous of the girl's solicitude; and once expressed herself angrily because Minnie had offered to give Joshua his medicine. Afterwards, seeing Minnie in tears, Mrs. Marvel kissed her and begged her pardon in a gentle, motherly way, which made Minnie cry the more. Mrs. Marvel found Minnie more difficult to manage than Ellen. Ellen was wonderfully undemonstrative and wonderfully obedient. And besides, Ellen was never in the way when she was not wanted, and was always at hand the instant she was required. There was an instinctive sympathy between Mrs. Marvel and Ellen which did not exist between Mrs. Marvel and Minnie. The good mother loved both the girls, but she loved Ellen like a daughter. In the second week of Joshua's illness a circumstance occurred which, for a short time, occasioned Mrs. Marvel much anxious thought. Joshua being more feverish than usual — for three weeks he was delirious, and did not know where he was, or who were tending him — the girls hovered about the room (in their anxiety to be of some assistance) rather later than Mrs. Marvel generally allowed them.

"Go to bed, girls," said Mrs. Marvel. Ellen rose obediently, and kissing Mrs. Marvel, and asking to be called if Mrs. Marvel wanted assistance in the night, went softly out of the room. But Minnie lingered behind, and with a yearning, wistful look at Mrs. Marvel, begged, in the softest of whispers, to be allowed to sit up with her.

"No, child," said Mrs. Marvel, "I can't think of it. You would be of no use to me to-morrow if you were to sit up to-night."

"Oh, yes, I should!" said Minnie, still pleading; "you don't know what a strong girl I am. Do let me stop with you! Do let me think that I can do something to help you!"

"You can do a great deal if you obey me, Minnie; and you do assist me very much, my dear; but I will not let you sit up to-night. Hush!" For here Joshua said something aloud, and murmured feverishly in his sleep. When he was quiet, Mrs. Marvel said. "Don't distress me, dear Minnie; go to bed, like a good girl."

Minnie, with deep sighs, went to the bedside to look at Joshua and to bid him a silent good-night — Mrs. Marvel regarding her jealously the while — and then crept out of the room in tears. The girls being gone, Mrs. Marvel felt more contented. She sat down by her son's bedside, and, with that lightness of touch which nothing but a mother's pure love or that of a wife can impart, smoothed the bed-coverings, and brushed the hair from Joshua's eyes.

At about eleven o'clock the handle of the door was gently turned, and Mr. Marvel entered. He had no boots on, and she had not heard him come up from the kitchen. Clasping his wife's hand, he leaned over the bed to catch a glimpse of Joshua's face.

"He is better to-night, George," she said; "he is getting along nicely. The doctor said to-day that he will soon be sensible."

George Marvel nodded, and put his lips to his wife's cheek.

"You must be very tired, Maggie."

She replied by a bright smile.

"Shall I sit up for an hour while you lie down?"

"Yes, father," knowing it would please him. "Have you had supper?"

A nod.

"And your beer?"

Another nod.

"And your pipe?"

"Yes; Ellen got every thing ready nicely. She is like you were when you were a girl, Maggie."

"Better than me, father."

"That's not possible, wife." Ah! how her heart fluttered as he said the word! She trembled in his arms like a girl. "Now lie down; I'll wake you in an hour."

She had but to close her eyes — being satisfied that her darling son was in good hands — and she was asleep. George Marvel watched for an hour, and perhaps a little longer, and then touched his wife, who was instantly awake. Alone again, Mrs. Marvel resumed her loving vigil. Not a sound was to be heard except the occasional prattle of Joshua, now of Dan and the birds, now of "father" and "mother," now of Ellen, now of Minnie and her shell. Mrs. Marvel had already learned, through those unconscious confessions, that her son's heart was as tender and as good as it had been before he had started in life for himself. A few minutes after the church-clock had struck two, Mrs. Marvel fancied she heard a soft breathing outside the bedroom-door. She listened intently, thinking she must have been deceived; but no — the soft breathing, as of some one asleep, came distinctly to her ears. She went to the door and opened it, and, lying at the foot of the stairs in the narrow passage, she discovered Minnie, in her night-dress, fast asleep. The girl had evidently kept awake until Ellen and Sarah were asleep, and had then stolen down stairs, and had sat outside the door of the sick-room until she had been overpowered by fatigue. Mrs. Marvel stooped over the sleeping girl and whispered, —

"Minnie!"

The sound of her name, chiming in with

some dreaming fancy, brought a happy smile to the girl's lips, and she answered, —

"Yes, Joshua!"

A look of pain passed into Mrs. Marvel's face; she knelt by Minnie's side, and gently raising the girl's head, she whispered again, —

"Minnie! You'll catch your death of cold lying here."

Minnie, still sleeping, encircled Mrs. Marvel's neck with her arms, and murmured, as she nestled close to the anxious mother's breast, —

"Joshua! Love me! Love me, Joshua!"

Mrs. Marvel trembled as she looked upon the girl's fair face, made fairer by the happy smile playing about the lips, and she felt a sudden chill at her heart.

"Oh, my poor Minnie!" she said beneath her breath. "Oh, my poor, poor Minnie!"

Then by a strong effort, she raised the girl, and so awoke her.

Before Minnie had time to recover full consciousness, her name, uttered by Joshua in his fevered sleep, fell upon her ears. With a glad cry she sprang from Mrs. Marvel's arms into the sick-room; but Mrs. Marvel stepped swiftly before her, and taking her two hands prisoner, said, in a voice which, although very low, was stern and decided, "I am seriously angry with you, Minnie."

The sudden movements, the light in the room, and, above all, Mrs Marvel's stern voice, restored Minnie to her senses. She dropped her head, and a hot blush of shame stole over her neck and face, while the hands which Mrs. Marvel held turned cold as ice. All Mrs. Marvel's sternness was gone, and pity only remained.

"Forgive me," Minnie pleaded.

"I do, child," said Mrs. Marvel, more agitated than Minnie was. "I was obliged to speak sternly, or I should not have been able to wake you. Go to bed now, and be more obedient for the future."

Minnie walked humbly into the passage, whither Mrs. Marvel followed her.

"Ah, not like that!" sighed Minnie, as Mrs. Marvel turned to enter the room. "Not like that! Kiss me, and say again that you forgive me."

And Mrs. Marvel, distressed and pitiful, kissed Minnie, who clung to her for a few moments, sobbing quietly, and then crept to bed.

But who had struck the blow? Who was it that, waiting with malicious cunning until Joshua's foot was on the threshold of the home where so many loving hearts were eager to welcome him, had foully struck him down? Susan was the only one who had any suspicion; but she did not mention it, for she had not seen the Lascar for many months. When Minnie was questioned, she declared that she saw no one in the street. A neighbor asked why one of the men in the house did not look for footsteps in the snow and follow up the track. They could not tell why they had not done so; it would have been the right thing to do, undoubtedly, but it had not occurred to them. When Joshua was sufficiently recovered, he could not assist them. He was examined and cross-examined closely. Did he suspect any of the sailors? No; he was good friends with every person on board; was even a favorite with the captain and officers. Ah! perhaps it sprang from that, they said; one of his mates might have been jealous of him. No; he was certain not one of them was. His own opinion was that he had been stabbed by a thief who wanted to rob him. But there! what was the use of bothering about it? Here he was, getting well and strong again, when it might have been so much worse. Thank God, in a few weeks he would be as well as ever! The day that Joshua was out of danger, the doctor told him that his life had been saved by Minnie.

"In what way, sir?" asked Joshua.

"Don't you remember that, when you were struck"—commenced the doctor.

But Joshua interrupted him by saying that he remembered nothing from that moment.

"I was walking along, too much occupied with the happiness of coming home to think of any thing else. I remember looking at the houses in the street, and stopping before our house. I heard voices inside, or I thought I did. Indeed, it might have been fancy. I stooped to listen, and then knocked. Some one asked — ah, now I remember! It was Minnie's voice asking who was there. Just as I answered, a dizziness came over me; I did not even know that I was struck."

"As you answered," said the doctor, taking up the narrative where Joshua dropped it, "Minnie opened the door. She saw you falling, and saw blood flowing from your neck. She threw herself by your side, and put her lips to the wound, and pressed so as to cause the blood to flow less freely. I honestly believe that if she had not done that, your life would not have been saved."

Joshua did not pursue the conversation, and the doctor did not recur to the subject again. The following afternoon Joshua said to his mother, —

"Mother, I want to speak to Minnie."

Mrs. Marvel, a little uneasily, went for Minnie, who came and sat by Joshua's bed.

"Are you better, Joshua?" asked the girl.

"Yes, dear Minnie," answered Joshua. They spoke in whispers. Joshua put out his big hand, and Minnie clasped it.

"Your hand is quite cold, Minnie." Minnie, indeed, was very agitated. "I owe you my life, dear Minnie, and I want to thank you for it. It almost seems to me, after what I have been told, as if my life belonged to you. Thank you, dear little Minnie — you used to like me to call you that! — thank you a thousand thousand times. I shall never be able to repay you!"

"I don't want payment, Joshua," said Minnie, when the wild beating of her heart was subdued. "It brought its own payment with it. It is, and ever will be, my sweetest remembrance. O Joshua! as the greatest unhappiness that ever could occur to me would be" — (to lose you, she was about to say, but she checked the words in time) — " to know that you would not recover, so the greatest happiness that I have ever experienced is to think that I have done you some little service."

"Little service! The greatest service, the most devoted action that woman could do to man! Perhaps — who knows? — one day I may be able to repay you in my own way." As if those words were not sufficient for her, who would have given her life for his. "Stoop down Minnie!" She inclined her head to the pillow. "Little Minnie, little Minnie!" he whispered tenderly, and he placed his lips to her cheek. "Thank you for your devotion."

It was fortunate for Minnie that it was dusk, and that her back was towards Mrs. Marvel, or the good mother would have had further cause for anxiety and uneasiness in Minnie's trembling form and flushed face. As it was, there was a long silence in the room; and Mrs. Marvel, approaching softly to the bed to see if Joshua was asleep, broke the happy reverie into which Minnie had fallen.

Solomon Fewster came to the house every day to inquire after Joshua, and went away every day with content in his face and despair in his heart. If ever a man played a double part, he played it during that time. "If he would but die!" he thought many and many a time. "If mortification would set in, or erysipelas, or something that would kill him!" And "I am truly happy to hear it," he said, many and many a time, to Mrs. Marvel, as in answer to his inquiries she told him that Joshua was improving rapidly. "I have brought a little jelly for him," which Mrs. Marvel received thankfully. At other times he would bring a chicken or some other delicacy to tempt Joshua's appetite, and would walk from the house with earnest wishes that what he left would choke the invalid. "I shall never forget Mr. Fewster's kindness," said Mrs. Marvel. "I feel quite angry with myself; for I did not give him credit for so much good feeling. But it is just in such times as these that a man shows the real goodness of his heart." And Mr. Fewster met with his reward immediately; for they were all grateful to him for his attention to Joshua. Mr. Marvel always had a hearty word for him, Minnie always a bright look, Ellen always a kind welcome now. But it was both sweet and bitter to him. "Ellen looks kindly upon me," he thought, and thought truly, "because I profess myself kind to Joshua. Will it ever be otherwise? Yes; if money can make it so, it shall be. And money can do much."

Yes, money can do much; but it cannot buy love, although it is often paid for it.

The most delicious three months of Joshua's life dated from the day on which the doctor declared him to be out of danger. He lived in an atmosphere of love. Loving hearts, loving hands, loving looks, loving thoughts, surrounded him. Is it better to have those than to be great and rich and powerful? Too modest for ambition are such blessings. Yet are they the sweetest, the holiest attributes of life. Of life, which is nothing without pleasures which cost money. Of life, which is not worth the living without fine linen and rich food. Of life, which is useless without the restless striving, the absorbing ambition, which make up the sum of human progress. Of Life, the Paradox!

Something which has fallen out of its proper place may be mentioned here. When Joshua was carried into the house on that memorable Christmas night, two things that had fallen from his hands were picked up from the snow and carried in after him. One of these was his accordion, the other was a white cockatoo in a cage, which Joshua had brought home from the South Seas. Whether it was that the cockatoo was overwhelmed at finding itself in a strange land, or that it deemed it necessary to be silent in the distressing circumstances of the case, it certainly behaved itself in a most exemplary manner, and gave no indication that it possessed a tongue. The cockatoo was taken to Dan's house, which was but a very few doors from Joshua's, and two or three days afterwards Dan was startled by hearing his name called in a strange loud voice. He looked up at Ellen, and asked if she had spoken. She had just time to say "No" when *her* name was called in the same strange loud voice.

"Why, it's the cockatoo!" exclaimed Dan.

Sure enough, it was the cockatoo, which, now that its tongue was loosened, made as much use of it as a woman could have done. Its stock of language was not large, consisting only of a shrill "Dan!" a shrill "Dan and Jo!" a shrill "Ellen!" a shrill "Minnie!" and a softer articulation of "Bread-and-cheese and kisses! and kisses! and kisses!" winding up with a volley of kisses, which it continued until it was completely out of breath. No stronger proof of Joshua's attachment could have been received by Dan and Ellen. Dan was much affected by it.

"You see how he was thinking of us all the time he was away," he said to Ellen, with tears in his eyes. "What shall I do if he dies!"

But Joshua did not die, and it was not very long afterwards that Dan was sitting in his friend's bedroom, surrounded by his birds as usual. It was like the old time come over again. Here they were, man and man, talking often as if they were boys. So much had to be told! The loss of Dan's parents, Dan entering into business, and how they all came to be living together. "Wonderful, wonderful!" said Joshua, again and again. "Like a story in a book."

"Just what I said," said Dan; "like a romance."

Who should come to the house one day but the captain of Joshua's ship, the "Merry Andrew"? The part he plays in this story is a small one, but eventful enough in all conscience. He was a shrewd man of business and a good officer. It was to his interest to have good men about him; for he was the principal owner of the ship, and he was remarkably sensible in any matter affecting his interests. He had heard of what had occurred to Joshua, and he was very sorry for it, because he had been so satisfied with Joshua's conduct on board his ship, that he had determined to make the young sailor his third mate on the next voyage. Therein he showed his eccentricity; most other captains would have chosen a man who had already filled that position satisfactorily. But Captain Liddle liked to judge for himself, and Joshua had found favor in his eyes. The young sailor was steady and attentive, and had made some progress in the study of navigation. There was one especial reason why Captain Liddle wanted steady men with him on his next voyage. He was about to get married, and he was going to take his young wife with him. There was great excitement in the house when Captain Liddle announced himself. Joshua, who was in bed, wanted to rise, but Captain Liddle would not allow him.

"Lie easy, lie easy, Marvel," he said: "you'll get better all the sooner."

"I hoped to come with you, sir, on your next voyage," said Joshua.

"Well, I had some thought of that myself," said Captain Liddle.

"Do you go out soon, sir?"

"Not for three months, Marvel; perhaps not for four. The ship's undergoing a thorough overhauling. She'll have a precious freight in her next trip."

"What loading, sir?"

Captain Liddle's eyes twinkled. "Female. Lie easy, lie easy, Marvel;" for Joshua had given another start. "Mrs. Captain Liddle. I shall be married soon, and my wife goes out with me."

Joshua murmured respectful congratulations.

"Thank you, thank you, Marvel. Now, I'll tell you what I have come especially for. First, though, how long before you are well?"

"I am well now, sir."

"Strong, I mean; able to get about and do your work like a man."

"Not for two months, I am afraid, sir."

"That will do. Now, then. You get strong in two months, and you shall go out with me in my next trip as third mate of the 'Merry Andrew.' Lie easy, lie easy, Marvel. What do you say to it, eh?"

"Say to it, sir! O—"

"Lie easy, lie easy, my lad. When you get strong come to the ship, and write a few lines soon telling me how strong you are getting. Mrs. Marvel, your son is a good sailor, and will make a good officer. And this is Dan, that you told me of once? A good head; but not so strong in the legs as Marvel, eh?"

"No, sir," said Dan with a bright smile, for he was overjoyed at Joshua's good fortune; "but it wouldn't do for all of us to be strong, sir; consider the doctors."

"Why, here is a ship, ropes and sails and all! And birds!"

Obedient to Dan's signal, the sailor-birds flew up the ropes, and stood on the slender cross-trees, as proud as if they had passed their lives in the service.

"Good—good!" said Captain Liddle. "For sale, eh?"

"No; they are not mine sir; they belong to an old sailor."

"Very proper. Ah, young lady," to Minnie, who had been in the room, but in the background, during the captain's visit; "and what do you think of the sea?"

"If I had been a man, sir," said Minnie modestly and quietly, "I should like to have been a sailor."

"Very proper — very proper. Good-day, Marvel. Get strong as quickly as you can. You'll have to superintend cargo."

Mr. Marvel, coming home at night, was told the good news before he had time to take the comforter from his neck. He ran up stairs at once to his son's room. "A sailor first, and then a captain," he exclaimed, recalling Joshua's words when he first announced his wish. "Do you remember, Josh?"

"Yes, father, yes," said Joshua eagerly. "It's better than being a wood-turner, Josh," said George Marvel triumphantly.

"I should think so, indeed. You'll see!"

"There, Maggie!" observed Mr. Marvel to his wife later on in the evening. "What did I tell you? And you was against it all the while, and wanted him to be a wood-turner. He'll be a captain before he's thirty."

"He is spared, I hope, for great things," said Mrs. Marvel meekly; "and to be a blessing to us all."

That same night, Dan and Joshua and Ellen spent some very happy hours together. Minnie was with Susan attending her father, so that the three were undisturbed. Mrs. Marvel opened the door once; but seeing the group, and observing how engrossed they were, she shut it softly, and went down again into the kitchen. Once, also, George Marvel was going out of the kitchen, when his wife called to him,—

"Where are you going, father?"

"To Joshua's room."

"Don't go, George. Come and sit down; I want to speak to you."

Mr. Marvel resumed his seat, and Mrs. Marvel refilled his pipe and handed it to him, with a light, "There! smoke your pipe, and don't be so restless."

He took a few whiffs, and asked who was with Joshua.

"Ellen and Dan; and they are very happy and comfortable. I peeped in once, and I wouldn't disturb them."

"Oh!" said Mr. Marvel reflectively dwelling lengthily upon that smallest of words.

"I have reasons, George," said Mrs. Marvel quietly. "I never saw Ellen look so happy and pretty as she looks to-night."

Mr. Marvel nodded two or three times with an expression of satisfaction. "Do you think, mother," he commenced; and then he paused, and repeated, "Do you think, mother, that"— and then he paused

again, as if he had said enough to make his meaning clear.

"Yes, I do, George," said Mrs. Marvel. "I had my doubts, but now I really think it will be so."

"That will be a real good thing;" rubbing his hands. "Here's hoping so!" and he drank a full glass of beer to his mysterious toast.

What was going on up stairs that the wood-turner and his wife were loath to interrupt? Merely a recalling of old reminiscences and a closer drawing together of three hearts, which might have been one, for the undivided affection for each other with which they were filled.

"Thinking of then, when every thing before us was so uncertain, and of now, when every thing before us is so bright and clear," said Joshua, "makes me almost believe that our ways are shaped for us, and that, if we strive to do our duty, our reward is certain."

"It is too deep a question for us, Jo," said Dan; "so many considerations spring out of it. As to whether every good man is happy. . As to whether every man who strives to do right is spared pain and misery. At all events, it is certain that the very best thing to do is to do what is right, and to be straightforward and honest. It is not too often done, I am afraid. I haven't seen any thing of the world, but it strikes me that that is not the way of it."

"If ever I am captain of a ship — and I may be, Dan — it looks promising " —

"That it does, Jo."

"You shall come with me a voyage. I will have every thing snug for you; hammock on deck the same as that day we spent with the Old Sailor — ah, what a day was that!"

"I can recall every moment of it; from the night before, when Ellen stood at the window watching the rain, and my waking up in the morning waiting for you to come — oh, so anxiously! And the flowers, and the birds — the poor birds! — and the breakfast, and the ride! I tell you what, Jo, stories could be made out of these things. But the day wouldn't have been the day it was if Ellen had not been with us."

Ellen smiled, and her eyes sparkled.

"Every thing connected with it is so vivid to my mind just now," said Joshua, "that it only wants one thing to make it complete; and that is for Ellen to sing 'Bread-and-Cheese and Kisses,' as she sang it in the Old Sailor's cabin."

Ellen, in a low voice, sang the song; and they were silent for a long while, musing happily. Then Joshua made a remark that his pillow was not nicely arranged, and

Ellen smoothed it for him. Her arm necessarily was round his neck for a moment — only for a moment by her own will; for when she would have withdrawn it, Joshua held it there, and she, with impulse as pure as pure heart and mind could make it, allowed it to remain. What wonder that a silence of longer duration followed?

Ah! if a magic spell had fallen upon them then, a spell that would have transfixed them and made their happiness eternal!

Not one of them knew how long that blissful trance lasted. It was broken by the slightest sound — it might have been the opening of a door, or even the light tread of our old friend the tortoise-shell cat — but whatever the sound was, the trance was at an end, and they were all awake again. Ellen withdrew her arm, and, with downcast eyes, hurriedly left the room. Joshua turned to Dan, and holding out his hand, said, " Dan, take my hand, and say, Brother Jo."

"I do. Brother Jo!"

"That's good; isn't it, Dan?"

"Yes, Jo."

"Brothers more than in heart, Dan, as we have always been. But Brothers really and truly, if Ellen says yes."

"Ellen loves you, Jo. You have but to ask." He paused for a little while before he spoke again. "There is something in my mind that it is right you should know. It is the only thing I have ever kept from you; but now, since you have told me about yourself and Ellen"—

"Did you ever doubt it, Dan?"

"I wasn't certain, Jo. You have removed a great weight from my heart. It seems strange that now, when I see the almost certain prospect of your future being as bright as we used to hope it would be — it seems strange that I cannot say I am happy. Yet one thing would make me so perfectly."

"There is no cloud between you and me, Dan?"

"None — nor ever will be, brother of my heart. But a great hope, shadowed by a great fear, has entered into my soul — a hope which fulfilled, would make earth heaven for me. Is it too precious a thing to pray for? It seems so to me. I tremble as I think of it. But if it is not to be, I hope I shall soon die."

"Dan!" cried Joshua in alarm, for Dan's last words were like a cry of agony.

"Haven't you seen it, Jo? Haven't you suspected it? I love her so that, if I knew she were lost to me, I scarcely think I could live. I love her so that, if she were lost to me, some stronger motive, some stronger feeling than any I can now think of, would have to animate me to make my future less black than the blackest night."

"You mean Minnie, Dan?"

"Yes; she is my light. Ah, Jo! How I love her! I have never spoken of it till now; I have never dared to breathe it. And now that I speak of it for the first time, it frightens me."

"Nay, Dan, take courage. You are frightened by shadows."

"If I could think so!" mused Dan in a less agitated voice. "What can I, a cripple, offer her? Love? Yes, I can offer her that, pure and undefiled. Nothing more — nothing more! Keep my secret, Jo."

"Yes, Dan," said Joshua sadly.

"If all should come right in the end, Jo! You and Ellen, and me and Minnie!"

He trembled, and burying his face in his hands, thought of the happy night when the Old Sailor traced Joshua's course on the map, and when Minnie's arm was round his neck and her cheek had touched his. How many times had he thought of those few blissful moments, and what balm and comfort had the memory brought him!

CHAPTER XIX.

SUNSHINE AND CLOUD.

"GEORGE," said Mrs. Marvel to her husband one night, when they were alone in their room, "what has come over Mr. Kindred? He is quite changed."

"I've noticed it too, mother," said Mr. Marvel, "but I haven't thought of it much, because, to tell you the truth, I don't believe he is quite right here"— touching his forehead.

Mrs. Marvel had not mentioned to any one — not even to her husband — how Minnie had distressed her during Joshua's illness. The girl had not asked her to keep silence upon the subject; indeed, no word had passed between them about it; but Mrs. Marvel judged that it would be best for Minnie's sake, and for Joshua's also, to let the matter rest. Since the night when Mrs. Marvel had discovered Minnie lying asleep at Joshua's door, the girl had given her no further cause for displeasure. Mrs. Marvel's fears were dispelled; for Minnie showed nothing more than a friendly interest in Joshua's recovery. But if the good mother had been less openly observant of Minnie's every look and action, her fears would have grown stronger. For after the interview between Joshua and Minnie, when Joshua had thanked her and kissed her, Mrs. Marvel set herself the task of closely observing Minnie's conduct towards Joshua. And Minnie discovered it, and so behaved herself that Mrs. Marvel was thrown completely off her guard. Minnie displayed a carelessness and an indifference concerning Joshua's health, at which Mrs. Marvel at any other time would have been hurt; but now she was silently grateful, in the belief that her fears were groundless.

Joshua was better. With the exception of a scar upon his neck, where the Lascar had stabbed him, he was as well and strong as ever he had been. He had grown into a fine handsome man; and the affectionate disposition which had characterized him as a boy seemed to have become stronger with his strength. The affection that existed between him and Dan was unchanged and unchangeable. He took as much delight in the birds as ever he had done; and, notwithstanding that he and Dan were men now, with deepened passions and stronger aspirations, their hearts were as tender to each other as in the younger days of their friendship, when they mingled their tears together over the death of Golden Cloud.

Every thing was bright before them. Dan had not spoken to Minnie of his love for her; but he was made happy by a gradual change in her behavior towards him. She grew more and more affectionate, spoke softly to him, looked kindly at him, and did not repulse the little tender advances he dared to make to her now and then.

"When you are gone to sea, Jo," he said to Joshua in the course of a conversation in which, in the fulness of his joy at Minnie's kindness, he had unbosomed himself to his friend, "I shall speak to her, and tell her I love her." He spoke very slowly, and his eyes were toward the ground; it was so sacred a subject with him, that his voice trembled when he spoke of it. "Once on a time, before I knew her, Jo, you, and you alone, filled my heart; but I had no idea then of a man's passions and a man's fears. I think I should have disbelieved any person then who told me that you would have a rival in my heart. But you have, Jo; although you are not less loved for all that."

"I understand you, Dan, and am content. I am proud of your love. If I were to lose it, the sweetness would go out of life."

"So it would be with me, Jo; but you can never lose it — never, never. I think you and I know what love is. In the midst of all our trouble when you first went away — trouble that came upon us so suddenly that I began to be frightened of it — I found consolation in thinking of our love for each other. Misfortunes came. Never mind, I thought; Joshua loves me. Moth-

er died, father died; we were left penniless; and I thought of you, and was comforted. You had grown so in my heart — like the roots of a tree, Jo — that if it had ceased to love you, my heart would have ceased to beat. It is the same now; but Minnie is in my heart side by side with you. I shall tell her, you know, by and by. By and by," he repeated softly. "The thought of it is like heaven to me; for I have begun to hope."

It was on that same afternoon that Ellen was sitting in her bedroom looking at her face in the looking-glass. She was fair; and she knew it, and was proud of it. But it was not vanity that caused her to sit, with her chin upon her hands, looking into the glass. Of a very modest type of womanhood was Ellen; not a heroine of the Joan-of-Arc order, who, with all her false glitter about her, would have been a woman after very few men's hearts. Ellen was of the quiet order of women, of whom there are thousands growing up in happy English homes, thank Heaven! and who are blessed and contented and happy, notwithstanding their sisters' unwomanly cries about woman's rights. May English women like Ellen, modest and constant and loving, increase and multiply with every succeeding year! Ellen was thinking of herself a little, as she looked into the glass, and of Joshua a great deal. He had not spoken to her yet; but he would soon, she knew. And as she sat and saw her pretty face looking at her, whose step but Joshua's should she hear coming up the stairs? He went into the adjoining room — Dan's room; and she heard him moving about, and — yes; singing! Singing what? Why, "Bread-and-Cheese and Kisses." The heroine's name in the song is Kate; but Joshua sang, —

"I said to Nell, my darling wife,
In whom my whole life's bliss is,
'What have you got for dinner, Nell?'
'Why, bread-and-cheese and kisses!'"

He said to Nell, his darling wife! The happy tears ran down Ellen's face; but they were soon dried; and Ellen kept very quiet, fearing that Joshua might hear her move. But Joshua went down stairs singing; and then Ellen smiled at herself in the glass, and peeped at herself through her fingers; and it wasn't an ugly picture to look at, if any one had been there to see.

It was all settled without a word passing between them. I don't believe there ever was such another courtship. They were sitting in Mrs. Marvel's kitchen: only four of them — father, mother, Ellen, and Joshua. It really looked like a conspiracy that no other person came into the kitchen that night; but there they were, conspiracy or no conspiracy. There was Mrs. Marvel, knitting a pair of stockings for Joshua; not getting along very fast with them, it must be confessed: for her spectacles required a great deal of rubbing. And there was Mr. Marvel, smoking his pipe, throwing many a furtive look in the direction of Joshua and Ellen, who were sitting next to each other, happy and silent. There is no record of how long they sat thus without speaking; but suddenly, although not abruptly, Joshua put his arm round Ellen's waist, and drew her closer to him. It was only a look that passed between them; and then Joshua kissed Ellen's lips, and she laid her head upon his breast.

"Mother! father! look here!"

Mrs. Marvel rose, all of a tremble, and laid her hand upon Ellen's head, and kissed the young lovers. But Mr. Marvel behaved quite differently. He cast one quick satisfied look at the two youngsters; and then turned from them, and continued smoking as if nothing unusual had occurred.

"Well, father?" exclaimed Joshua, rather surprised at his father's silence.

"Well, Josh!" replied Mr. Marvel.

"Do you see this?" asked Joshua, with his arm round Ellen's waist.

Ellen, blushing rosy red, looked shyly at Mr. Marvel; but he looked stolidly at her in return.

"Yes; I see it, Josh," said Mr. Marvel, without any show of emotion.

"And what do you say to it?"

"What do I say to it, Josh?" replied Mr. Marvel with dignity. "Well, I believe I'm your father; and, as such, I think you should ask me if I was agreeable. I thought it proper to ask *my* father, Josh. It isn't because I'm a wood-turner"—

"No, no, father," interrupted Joshua; "I made a mistake. Ellen and I thought"—

"Ellen and you thought," repeated Mr. Marvel.

"That if you were agreeable"—continued Joshua.

"That if I was agreeable," repeated Mr. Marvel.

"And if you would please to give your consent"—said Joshua, purposely prolonging his preamble.

"And if I would be pleased to give my consent," repeated Mr. Marvel with a slight chuckle of satisfaction.

"That as we love each other very much, we would like to get married."

"That's dutiful," said Mr. Marvel, laying down his pipe, oracularly. "I'm only agreeable, Josh, because I am old, and because I am married. As I said to mother the other night, when we was talking the matter over — ah! you may stare; but we knew all about it long ago. Didn't we, mother? Well, as I was saying to mother the other night, if I was a young man, and mother wasn't in the way, I'd marry her myself and you might go a-whistling. Shiver my timbers, my lass!" he cried, breaking through the trammels of wood-turning, and becoming suddenly nautical, "come and give me a kiss."

Which Ellen did; and so the little comedy ended happily. Joshua, having a right now to sit with his arm round Ellen's waist, availed himself of it, you may be sure. If Ellen went out of the room, he had also a right to go and inquire where she was going; and this, curiously enough, happened four or five times during the night. If anything could have added to the happiness of Mr. Marvel — except being anything but a wood-turner, which, at his age, was out of the question — it was this proceeding of Joshua's. Every time Joshua followed Ellen out of the room, Mr. Marvel looked at his wife with pleasure beaming from his eyes.

"It puts me in mind of the time when I came a-courting you, mother," he said. "How the world spins round! It might have been last night when you and me were saying good-by at the street-door."

Mrs. Marvel had not spoken to her husband without cause of the change that had taken place in Basil Kindred. A very remarkable change had indeed taken place in him. A mistrustful expression had settled itself upon his face, accompanied by a keen hungry watchfulness of all that occurred around him. He gave short answers, and was snappish and morose. Yet not a look, not a word, not a gesture escape his notice. He did not avoid his friends; he rather courted their society. He repelled their advances, but he sat among them, watching. Every sense was employed in that all-absorbing task. What was it that he was trying to discover?

The change was so sudden. A few days ago he was, as he had ever been hitherto, frank and cheerful, — even gay sometimes. Now, all that was gone. In place of frankness, mistrust; in place of cheerfulness, gloom. Susan was the only one, with the exception of his daughter, to whom he did not speak with a certain bitterness. His manner to all the others was as though some sensitive chord in his nature had been sorely wounded — as though all men were his foes — as though his faith in what was good and noble in human nature had been violently disturbed.

See him now. He and Minnie have been sitting together for hours. He has been strangely stern and strangely tender to her in turns, but she is used to his wayward moods. He has detained her by his side all the morning, upon one and another idle pretext; and she, as if wishful to please him, has humored him, and been wonderfully submissive and obedient. But once she had fallen into a reverie — not a happy one — and he had broken it by asking her in a harsh voice what she was dreaming about. She replied only by a startled look, and resumed her work, which had been lying idly in her lap. Repentant of his harshness, he turned his head from her to hide the sudden spasm which passed into his face.

"Are you ill?" she asked.

"No, dear child."

"In pain?"

"No, dear child."

Presently she put aside her work, and rose to leave the room.

"Where are you going?" he asked in a strangely anxious voice.

"To see Mrs. Marvel," was her answer.

"Sit you down," he cried sternly.

She hesitated and lingered by the door, beating the ground with her foot irresolutely. Seeing that, he grasped her wrist firmly, and hurt her without intending to do so. The muscles of her face quivered, but not from the pain.

"O Minnie, my child!" he cried; then, releasing her, "have I hurt you?"

"No," she answered in a hard voice. "Why do you not wish me to go to Mrs. Marvel's house? You have forbidden me before."

"You trouble them too much."

"That is not your reason, father," she said in the same hard voice. "You are hiding something from me."

"Are you not hiding something from me, Minnie?" he asked, looking anxiously into her face.

"What should I hide from you?" she asked, in reply, coldly and evasively. "I am not well, father. I can't stop in this room. I will not go where you do not wish me."

He did not detain her, and she glided swiftly out of the room. He was about to follow her, when a dizziness came upon him, and he sank into a chair. It was only by a strong effort of will that he kept himself from fainting.

"My strength is deserting me," he muttered, his breath coming thick and fast; "scarcely a day passes but this weakness comes upon me." He held up his hand; it trembled like a leaf. "Have I failed in my duty to her? Is it my fault that she does not confide in me? Or is this a wicked lie?" He took a letter from his pocket and read it, not once, but many times. "No," he groaned; "it is true. I feel that it is true." He rose to his feet and felt like one just risen from a sick bed. He was as weak as a child; so weak, indeed, that the consciousness of his weakness brought tears into his eyes; and he said in a voice of anguish, "Now, when my child's happiness — her honor, perhaps — depends upon my watchful care, I am helpless. If I had some one that I could trust! some one to help me!" He heard a step upon the stairs. It was like an answer to his wish. "It is Susan," he muttered; "the one being that I know in the world who would serve me faithfully. Susan, Susan!"

She heard him, although his voice was faint and low, and entered the room. Alarmed by the traces of illness in his face, she hastened to his side.

"You are ill," she said, assisting him to a seat. "Can I do any thing for you?"

"Yes," he answered. "You can do much. You can be my friend."

"Your friend!" she exclaimed. Had she not always been his friend? But there was a deeper meaning in his voice than she had ever heard before, and his appeal sent thrills of pleasure to her heart.

"I am ill," he continued; "but it is more from weakness than any thing else. I am not in pain. A dizziness seizes me, as it seized me just now, and I feel as if my senses were leaving me. I can scarcely stand; and I have no one to trust to."

"Not Minnie?" she said softly and wonderingly.

"Hush! Minnie, of all others, must not be told of this. Can I trust you?"

"I would work till I dropped to serve you."

A flush came into his face.

"To serve me and Minnie?" he said.

"Yes; to serve you and Minnie."

"Give me your sacred promise that what passes between us now will never be divulged, will never be spoken of, by you, unless my tongue is sealed, and the time comes when it may be necessary to speak."

"Does it concern you?" she asked with a natural hesitation; for there was a feverishness in his manner that alarmed her.

"It concerns me and Minnie."

"I promise."

"Faithfully and sacredly?"

"Faithfully and sacredly."

He took her hand and pressed it, and then gave her the letter, and asked her to read it. It contained but a few words, but they were sufficient to cause a look of horror to start into her eyes.

"Can it be true?" she asked, more of herself than of him; and her trembling lips turned white and parched in an instant.

"Susan," said Basil Kindred, "I have lived long enough in the world to know its falseness. In years gone by, men have smiled in my face and shaken me by the hand, and I have learned afterwards, that while their manner spoke me fair, there was treachery in their hearts. My life has been a hard one, what with false friends and bitter poverty; but I bore it all patiently, and lived — lived, when a hundred times voices have whispered in my ear, 'Die, and be at peace!' I had an object to live for — Minnie, my darling child! So I lived and suffered, rather than die and leave her unprotected. It was a bitter, bitter life. You can guess how hard a thing it was for me to find food for her, and how often she had to go without it, before the day when you and that boy — I cannot utter his name — came to our rescue. From that time until this dark cloud" — he placed his hand on the letter — "fell upon me, I have been happy. And now, when I need all my strength to fulfil my duty as a father — when it seems to me a crime that I should allow her to go from my side — this weakness strikes me down."

"Does she know?"

"She knows, and must know, nothing. But she must be watched. If there be no truth in this letter — and there may not be" —

"I pray not! Oh, I pray not!" cried Susan. "For others' sakes as well as yours."

"I understand you; if there be no truth in it, no one need know of it but you and I."

"What shall I do?"

"Watch her and him, without seeming to do so," said Basil Kindred. "If she goes out, follow her if you can without letting her see you, and let me know all you see and hear. Mind, I say *all*; keep nothing from me. You have promised sacredly."

"I will do what you bid me."

He raised her hand to his lips, and in the midst of her great sorrow his action brought a happy feeling to her heart. When she was gone, Basil Kindred unlocked a desk and took out a clasped book, in which he wrote a few lines. "It is necessary," he sighed, "for my memory is lost to me sometimes, and I cannot recall events; and it may save me from doing an injustice." Then he replaced the book and locked the desk.

That night, in her room, Susan sat upon her bed and bowed her head to her knees, sobbing, "O my poor Dan! O my poor, poor Ellen! if, after all these years, you should find him false!"

CHAPTER XX.

THE ONLY DUTY THAT MINNIE CAN UNDERSTAND.

The "Merry Andrew" was nearly ready for sea again, and Joshua, having been duly installed as third mate, was busily employed superintending cargo. The Old Sailor was immensely delighted, and took an active interest in Joshua's doings. When he was told of the engagement between Joshua and Ellen, he smacked Joshua on the back and shook his hand again and again, and kissed Ellen a dozen times, the old rogue! as if he were the lucky man, and Joshua had nothing to do with it. He took a private opportunity of entering into a confidential conversation with the young lovers, and told them he had made over his barge and all his little property to Ellen and Joshua jointly, "for better or worse," he added, with a vague idea that those words were necessary in the circumstances of the case. And he took many other opportunities of instructing Joshua in the duties of mate and master, and also in navigation and astronomy. He was more exacting than any Marine Board would have been, and his instructions and examinations were of a very severe and precise character. But he had a willing and apt pupil in Joshua; and he delighted Ellen by whispering to her confidentially that Joshua would make as fine a mariner as could be found in the service. The examinations generally took place when only the Old Sailor, Joshua, and Ellen were together; and then Joshua propounded, to the satisfaction of his teacher, such problems as, how he would send a top-gallant yard down in a gale of wind; what he would do if he wanted to shiver his main-topsail yard when the leeches were taut and the main yard could not be touched: how to turn in a dead-eye; what he would do if he wanted to tack on a lee shore, and the ship wouldn't come round, and there was not room to wear; and so on, and so on. The Old Sailor was not satisfied with simple answers, but insisted upon the why and the wherefore; so that what with working and studying and sweethearting, Joshua's time was well taken up. Ellen herself became quite learned in certain matters concerning Joshua's profession, and made him laugh heartily by the wise air she assumed when she repeated the twelve signs of the Zodiac, which she had learned by heart perfectly, from Aries to Pisces. Joshua, repeating after her, would purposely leave out Gemini or Aquarius, or another sign, and would instantly be taken to account. In this simple way many happy hours were passed. The Old Sailor had a great liking for Captain Liddle, because he was a thorough sailor, and Captain Liddle admired the Old Sailor for the simplicity of his character.

"You are in luck's way," said the Old Sailor to Joshua: "you are sailing under a good master — not a land saint and sea devil — but a good officer and a kind man; and you have the dearest and the truest-hearted lass in the world to stand by you through life. Do your duty, Josh, to her and to your ship."

"I will do my duty to both, sir, you may depend."

The Old Sailor took out his pocket-handkerchief, and thoughtfully dabbed his face. "I don't doubt that you will, my lad," he said, "and to Dan as well." Now the Old Sailor uttered these last words with a significance that seemed intended to convey a deep meaning. His action was appropriately mysterious. He looked round cautiously, after the best manner of stage robbers, and hooked Joshua nearer to him by a motion of his forefinger. "Hark ye, my lad," he whispered, guiding the words to Joshua's ear by placing his open palm on one side of his mouth; "Hark ye. Do you suspect any thing?"

Joshua opened his eyes very wide at this; he had not the slightest consciousness of the Old Sailor's meaning.

"You don't?" continued the Old Sailor in the same mysterious manner. "So much the better. I didn't suppose you did. Now, supposing — mind, I only say supposing, my lad — supposing you were asked to do a very out-of-the-way thing for Dan's sake, but a thing notwithstanding that you would be very glad to do " — this with a chuckle expressive of intense enjoyment — "would you do it?"

"Would I do it, sir!" exclaimed Joshua warmly. "I don't think you or any one could ask me to do a thing for Dan's sake, that I shouldn't be glad to do."

"Just my opinion," said the Old Sailor, still in the same charnel-house whisper; "and if Dan's happiness depended upon your doing this out-of-the-way thing"—

"Why, then, sir, more eagerly and willingly than ever."

"That's plain sailing; it might come to pass, or it mightn't," said the Old Sailor, returning his handkerchief to its abiding-place in the bosom of his shirt, to denote that the conversation was at an end.

But this did not satisfy Joshua. "What might come to pass, sir?" he asked.

The Old Sailor winked craftily at Joshua, and said, "All I've got to say is, that it might come to pass or it mightn't."

And try as he would, that was all the satisfaction Joshua could obtain from the Old Sailor.

In the mean time Basil Kindred's condition had become so serious, that he was unable to leave his room, and he was unreasonably obstinate in his refusal to see a doctor. He knew well enough what was the matter with him, he said, and doctors could not relieve him. But one day, urged by Dan, Minnie brought a doctor to his bedside without consulting him.

"Your daughter brought me," said the doctor, seeing that Basil was displeased, and wisely judging that mention of his daughter would calm him.

Basil called Minnie to him and kissed her. "Go out of the room, child," he said; "what passes between me and the doctor must be private."

Minnie obeyed, and went down stairs to sit with Dan, and the doctor remained with his patient for half an hour. As the doctor came down, Minnie opened the door of Dan's room, and the doctor entered.

"Well, sir?" asked Dan.

"Your father is suffering from rheumatism and low fever," said the doctor, addressing Minnie. "I have left a prescription in his room; run and get it."

Minnie went up stairs, and the doctor said to Dan, "You are very anxious about Mr. Kindred."

"Yes, sir, very anxious, both for his sake and for Minnie's."

"Minnie — ah! yes, his daughter. Well, I may tell you in confidence what I must not tell her. He is suffering from something more than rheumatic fever. He has a disease which may prove fatal at any moment. A strong mental shock would very likely prove fatal to him. His mind is far from tranquil at the present time, and it is absolutely necessary that he should have quiet and repose. Good-morning."

Grieved as Dan was to hear this, it relieved him, for it enabled him to account for the sudden change in Basil Kindred's manner which had so perplexed him. It also served to account for a change he had observed in Minnie. It was not that she was less friendly towards him; on the contrary, she had on many occasions been more tender to him than usual. But the frank cordiality of her manner was gone; she was more reserved, and an engrossed expression, evidently born of painful thought, had settled upon her face. Dan had watched it with the sensitive eye of love, wondering what had brought it into her face. Now he knew the cause: her father's illness brought gloomy forebodings to her heart and made her anxious. "Does she ever think that I love her?" thought Dan, "and that I am only waiting for the proper time to tell her that my life is devoted to her?" He would have spoken that very day, but a sentiment of true delicacy restrained him. The feeling that closed his lips upon the subject for the present could not have existed in any but a chivalrous nature.

When Joshua came home in the evening, Dan told him what the doctor had said. Joshua was silent for a little while before he spoke. "It is very singular," he then said, "that what you have told me should make me easier in my mind. Both Minnie's and Mr. Kindred's manner lately have given me great pain, filling me with uneasiness, which I have vainly struggled against. It is made clear to me now."

"Why, that was also my feeling, Jo," exclaimed Dan almost gayly. "Another proof of the sympathy between us."

"I shall go and see Mr. Kindred. I am ashamed of myself to have allowed such small feelings to exist. I ought to have made more allowance for his sufferings." His hand was resting upon Dan's shoulder. He inclined himself so that he could see the face of his friend. "And Minnie?" he asked in that attitude. "How is it with you and her?"

"I am more hopeful than ever, Jo; but it would not be right for me to speak to her in her trouble."

"That is like you, Dan," said Joshua approvingly. "Ever tender — ever considerate — ever just. No; you must not speak until Mr. Kindred is better. You must wait."

Dan nodded assent, and Joshua went up stairs to Basil Kindred's room. He paused at the door and listened. No sound came from within, and he received no answer to his knock. He opened the door softly. The room was in darkness.

"Who is there?" was asked in the abstracted voice of one just aroused from sleep.

"It is I — Joshua. Shall I get a light?"

"No;" with a sudden fierceness. "What brings you here?"

The want of friendliness in Basil Kindred's voice was very painful to Joshua, and it was only by a great effort that he was enabled to maintain his composure. "What is the meaning of this, sir?" he asked, very gently.

"Of what?"

"Of your changed manner towards me, sir. And not to me only, but to all of us. Have we done any thing wrong — have I done any thing wrong? If I have, it has been done unconsciously, and it is but just that you should not leave me in ignorance of my fault. I came up to you now, sir, to ask that we should be to each other as we once were — as we were before I went to sea — as we were on the first day of our meeting, when you said, 'God bless you, Joshua Marvel.' I have never forgotten that, sir. I do not speak to you for myself alone; I speak for all of us, who hold you, I am sure, in the tenderest respect and regard." Joshua spoke feelingly, and his words had the effect of softening Mr. Kindred's manner.

"You are right," he said softly and very slowly; "it is not just. Sit here by my side." Joshua sat where he was bidden, and waited for Mr. Kindred to resume. "Distemper of the mind accompanies distemper of the body," continued the sick man, "and you must lay some part of my unfriendliness to that cause. I am sick in body, and therefore peevish, and therefore, perhaps, unjust. Sick men have sick fancies. They magnify straws, even as, lying here in the dark, I can, by the power of my will, magnify the shadows that rest within this room and make them 'palpable to feeling as to sight.' Joshua Marvel, I owe you much; you saved me and mine from starvation. I am glad that you are here now, and that you met my fretfulness with patience; for there is that within my mind, not newly born, but newly risen, that I would gladly not forget again. All the happiness of the last few years I owe to you, for it was for your sake we were welcomed here."

"The pleasure your society has given to all those dearest to my heart, sir, is recompense a thousand-fold."

"Those dearest to your heart!" repeated Basil Kindred musingly. "Who are they?"

"You ought to know, sir," replied Joshua, surprised at the question.

"It is but a whim — a sick man's whim — but tell me: of all those dearest to your heart, whom would you place first? Do not hesitate to answer me. We are in the dark, and I cannot see your face."

"In the dark or in the light, before all the world, if it were necessary, I could name but one, whom you know well."

"Still, to satisfy me, name her."

"Ellen, sir. You know that she is to be my wife."

"I have heard so. Take my hand. I wish you the happiness that faithful love deserves. No worldly happiness can be greater. It makes a heaven of earth, in whatever sphere of life it comes. And if, as it was with me, the partner of your faithful love is called away before you, the remembrance of her goodness and purity will dwell forever in your heart, like a divine star." His voice had grown so solemn, that Joshua could only press his hand in reply. Presently Basil Kindred spoke again. "Your past life should be a guarantee for the future. You have been faithful in your friendship; you should be faithful in your love."

"You do not doubt it, sir?"

"I cannot doubt it; your conduct gives doubt the lie. The shadows seem to be clearing away. I have much to say yet, if you will sit with me a little while."

"I am glad to do so, and happy to hear you speaking to me again in your old kind manner."

"It is so hard to reconcile," mused Basil speaking as much to himself as to Joshua. "From whom can the accusation have come? And the motive — what can be the motive? Joshua, answer me — have you an enemy?"

"No, sir, not one that I know of."

"Reflect a little. Can you bring to mind any circumstance that occurred during the years that you have been away to induce you to suppose that some one is conspiring to do you injury?"

"I am more than surprised at your question, sir; I am grieved that you should ask it, and apparently with reason. To my knowledge I have not a bad friend in the world."

"Your surprise is natural," said Basil; "but though you may think my remarks strange, do not think they are prompted by unkindness. I have good reasons for what I say. I hold this conversation sacred, Joshua. As it may be the last we shall ever have, let what is said between us be said in perfect confidence."

"Agreed as to that, sir; but you must not say that this is the last conversation we shall ever have."

"When do you go to sea again?" asked Basil Kindred, taking no heed of Joshua's remonstrance.

"In less than a fortnight. We set sail first for Sydney, New South Wales, then for China, then for home. A short trip. We shall not be away long this time."

"Before you return, I shall have gone on a longer voyage than you are about to take. Nay, do not interrupt me. I have received warning — bodily, not spiritual, and therefore not open to doubt. It is impossible that I can live much longer. And with this conviction strong within me, I am tortured by an anxiety that racks me with a mightier pain than that which even as I speak pierces me to the marrow."

Joshua was profoundly shocked at the disclosure; he had not thought it was so bad as that. Instinctively he knew what the anxiety was by which Basil was tortured, and Basil answered his thought.

"You guess what my anxiety springs from. What will become of Minnie when I am gone?"

If he had seen! If in that darkened room a vision had appeared to answer him, could he have believed that it would come to pass? But silence was his only answer for a time; for Joshua was revolving in his mind whether it would be wise and merciful — whether he had any right to speak to Basil Kindred about Dan's love for Minnie. The conversation between them was sacred and confidential, and the sick man's tone when he spoke of the bodily warnings he had received was so impressive, that it carried conviction with it. It would be like speaking to a dying man, and it would be serving his friend.

"That is my great anxiety," continued Basil; "were my mind relieved upon that point, I should fear nothing, for death is my smallest terror. I suffer deserved misery when I say that even I, her father, do not know her nature thoroughly, and that I fear to think to what extent her impulse might carry her. But I know that she needs guidance, and that she cannot control herself. I have taught her ill, or rather have not taught her at all. I have been remiss in my fatherly duty — not intentionally, God knows! But I see it now — I see it now." Even in the dark he turned his face from Joshua, the more completely to hide his tribulation. "There is but one duty she can understand — the duty of love. She knows no higher. She comprehends that, because it is instinctive. She has her mother's devoted nature, and would sacrifice herself for the only duty she can comprehend, as her mother sacrificed herself for me. But she could not be made to understand that under certain circumstances love may be sinful."

Joshua, following his train of thought, heard Basil's words, but scarcely understood their sense. Still he said, —

"She loves you, sir."

"Yes, she loves me as a father, and by that love I have unconsciously controlled her. But that power has gone from me. Our minds are strangers; they used not to be so. Once she hid nothing from me; now as I watch her I see in her eyes the attempt to hide her thoughts, and I cannot express to you my agony in knowing that her heart and mind are not open to me, as they have hitherto been. If I knew — if I only knew, I should be satisfied; for then I might protect her. Sometimes I think that another kind of love has come to her, and has shadowed the love she bore for me. But for whom? Do you know?"

He asked the question in a singular tone of fierceness and entreaty; but Joshua was thinking of Dan, and did not reply. Have I the right to speak? he thought;

and an affirmative answer did not come clearly to his mind.

"You are silent," continued Basil in a quieter tone. "Are you concealing any thing from me?"

"What should I conceal from you, sir?" asked Joshua in reply, after a pause.

Basil Kindred sighed, as the words so hesitatingly spoken came from Joshua's lips.

"Young men are often thoughtless in their actions," he said mildly, as if wishful to rob the remark of direct significance; "they do not know the depth and earnestness of some womanly natures. Listen, I will tell you my story; it may be a lesson and a warning to you."

CHAPTER XXI.

LOVE'S SACRIFICE.

WHEN I was a young man, I was an enthusiast. My mother had died when I was a child. My father was a clergyman, and wished to educate me for the church. But my heart was not in my studies, and I did not satisfy his expectations. I was too fond of poetry and plays, my tutors told him; sterner studies were distasteful to me, and they met with nothing but disappointment from so unwilling a pupil. I was also difficult to control; would indeed submit to no control. On several occasions when a company of players came to the place in which I was being educated, I had stolen away to the theatre, remaining there until nearly midnight. My tutors spoke the truth. From the first night that I stepped inside the walls of a theatre and saw a tragedy, my fate was fixed. I was fascinated, entranced. I had never conceived any thing so grand, so noble, so heroic. Mine was a pure passion; glitter possibly had its effect upon my mind, but no base ingredient was mixed with my determination to become an actor. What nobler calling could there be than that which clothed the noblest of all the arts with living fire, which made dead heroes speak and move and live again? My father received the report with displeasure. He looked upon a theatre as the abode of all the vices. He spoke to me and expostulated with me, and I argued with him until I angered him. Then he took me from school, and kept me at home, so that he might wean me from my wicked notions. I had not been home a month before a company of players paid our town a visit. I was aglow with excitement. My father warned me not to go; I told him frankly that I would. He locked me in my bedroom; and I made a rope of the sheets, and let myself out of the window. I came home late, and my father opened the door for me. He was so strict a disciplinarian, that my disobedience was a crime in his eyes. He told me so sternly, and told me also that unless I complied with the rules of his house, and with his commands as a father, I must find a home elsewhere. He had other children, and he declared that I should not contaminate them by my example. When I ventured to expostulate with him, he stopped me peremptorily. There was no sign of tenderness in his manner. He was harsh and hard. He forgot that I inherited some share of his own determination, and that I was as likely to be immovable in my ideas as he was in his. I felt that I could have answered him by arguments as forcible as his, and, with the not uncommon egotism of youth, I believed that I could have convinced him. But he would not listen to me, and I was compelled to sit silent and inwardly rebellious while he laid down the hard rules by which my life was to be guided. The glittering splendor of the play I had witnessed that night was vivid to my mind while his cold words fell upon my ears. The tragedian upon whose musical impassioned utterances I had hung entranced, was one of the greatest that ever trod the stage; the play I had seen was one of the grandest of England's grandest poet. What! was it a crime to come within the influence of such a teacher? I could not believe it; I would not believe it. My father said my inclinations were sinful, impious, misbegotten, and preached to me sternly, uncompromisingly, until my heart —beating with indignation at his injustice —was as hard to him as his was to me. Then he left the room with a cold goodnight, and I went to bed. But before I went to sleep, I took from my box the volume of Shakspeare containing the play that I had seen, and as I read the noble verse, the men and women who took part therein came and inspired me with the nobility of their speech.

On the ensuing Sabbath my father preached against play-houses and players. It is not necessary for me here to dilate upon his arguments; they were the common arguments generally used against actors and their abominations. Players were creatures of the devil, working in his service for the damnation of souls. There was no heaven for them; by their lives they earned damnation, and they received their wages in another life. It was a strong sermon—"a beautiful sermon," as I heard many men and women say to each other as they walked from the place of worship; but it filled me with indignation. It was a challenge thrown out to me, and I accepted it. I do not attempt to justify what I did; but it seemed to me as if I should be false to myself if I did not do it. On the following evening I went to the theatre early, and secured a seat in the most conspicuous position, and sitting there the whole night through, I applauded with more than my usual enthusiasm, and even — perhaps I should be ashamed to say it — with purposed demonstrativeness. It was like giving the lie to my father's teaching; but I did not think of it then in that light. I was bound in honor to a certain course of action, and I pursued it. When the play was over, I walked about the town for an hour, filled with fervent passionate admiration for what I had witnessed. It was past midnight when I knocked at my father's door. No answer came. I knocked again. Still no answer. I was standing in perplexity as to what I should do, when a piece of paper fluttered on to the pavement from a window above. I picked it up, and saw that it was addressed to me. It was in my father's handwriting, and it told me in a few simple words that, as I had chosen to commit a sinful outrage upon his cloth, and upon his sermon of the previous day, he disowned me as a son and cast me off. A postscript was added, to the effect that, upon my calling at or sending to a certain place every week, I could receive a small sum of money sufficient to keep me from want, but that if I adopted the stage as a calling, the money would be withheld. In the event of my adopting the stage, my father asked me as a favor to change my name. I never received a farthing of the money; I would have died rather than have taken it. I started that night from my native town, and I have never seen one of my family since.

I need not dwell upon the details of the next few years. The recollection is too painful to me. When I walked away from my father's house, I solemnly resolved never to set foot in it again; I renounced all claims of kindred, and said to myself proudly and confidently, "I am alone in the world, without friends, without family. I am free to adopt what course in life I think best. I will show my father, by my career, that I am right, and he is wrong." I changed my name to the name by which you know me. Speaking to you as I am speaking now, with the solemn darkness around us, with something like a sense of death upon me, I cannot hide from you any thing that comes to my recollection. The simple reason for my changing my name was, that it laid my father under an obligation to me. The motive was unworthy; but it is hard to reconcile the lofty aspirations and the despicable sentiment that in the same moment may animate a single mind. Well, I marched into the world friendless and unknown, filled with an arrogant courage, almost with defiance. I had a watch and a little money; I sold my watch to increase my wealth, and before I had spent my last shilling, I gained admission to a company of players, and commenced life as an actor. I had seen these actors on the stage, and had been inspired by them; but my amazement was great when their private lives were open to me. The men and women who had inspired me were poor struggling creatures, living almost begging lives, and suffering almost incredible hardships. The salaries they were supposed to receive were barely sufficient to pay for food and lodging; but the money that was taken at the doors of the theatre was often of such trifling amount, that at the end of the week the players were compelled to be content with half, ay, with a fourth the sum due to them. They all shared alike; there was none among them who took the lion's share while the others starved. The leading tragedian received a guinea a week, and was thankful when he got it. I have seen him play Macbeth, knowing that he had not tasted food since breakfast; and have seen him come off the stage at the end of the play and faint, not from enthusiasm and excitement, but from sheer hunger. From this you can form some idea of my sufferings; but I never wavered. I was indomitable in my resolve. Disenchanted as I was to some extent, I saw fame and glory before me, and I followed the beckoning shadows that lured me on. And then I saw so much to admire in the lives of my poor companions — so much self-sacrifice, so much devotion, so much virtue — that I was proud to suffer with them. "Children of the devil," I had heard my father call them. A strong resentment against him possessed me when I became a witness of their privations patiently borne, of their self-sacrifices cheerfully made. All this while — though I endured hunger and every species of worldly misery; though I had to walk, many and many a time, forty, fifty, and sixty miles, through wet and mud, in boots and shoes that scarcely held together; though I often slept in the open air, by the side of hay-stacks and under hedges — all this while I was advancing in my profession, and enthusiastically believed that the day would come when I should be famous and prosperous. So I grew to be a man, more firmly hoping, more firmly believing. I was what is called leading man;

I was at the head of my profession, and was only waiting for the tide — being prepared for it — that was to lead me to fame and fortune. But young as I was, the life I had led had already destroyed my constitution. Rheumatism had planted itself firmly in my bones, and want of nourishing food had so weakened me, that I felt like an old man. It was only the fire of enthusiasm that sustained me. I believed myself to be what I represented at night; I lost all consciousness of my poor self while I was acting; and would often come from the theatre with the dream strong upon me, and in my sleep weave fancies sufficiently bright and beautiful to recompense me for the material hardships of my working life.

I was at the height of my powers, when it was both my happiness and my misery to come to a town where we had arranged to stop for a fortnight, and where I gained such honors in the shape of applause as had never before fallen to my lot. It was a prosperous town, and our two weeks' stay was so remunerative, that we thought it advisable to lengthen our visit. We staid for six weeks — for six happy weeks. The place rang with my praises. I was a wonder, a genius; such acting had never been seen. Throughout the whole of my career I had preserved my self-respect; what I suffered, I suffered in silence. I complained to no one, and I never forgot my determination to prove, what perhaps my father might one day be forced to own, that an actor may be as good a man as a clergyman. Being therefore, in my habits of life, somewhat above my companions, and having been so successful in the town, I was courted by some of the towns-people, and received invitations to their houses. I was what is termed, I believe, a social success; and I was proud of it. Here was I, an actor, moving in as good society as was my father, a clergyman. Who was right now, he or I. During the second week of our stay, I was invited to an evening party; and as my part in the performance for that night would be finished by nine o'clock, I was enabled to accept the invitation. Fatal night — happy night! That night was the real commencement of my life; it shaped my career in this world, and it makes me look forward with joy unspeakable to the world beyond, where I shall rejoin the mother of my darling child. Her family were well born, and occupied a high position in the town. They were looked upon as leaders of fashion; and I learned that night that they were among the principal patrons of the theatre, and that her father had passed the highest encomiums upon me. They were not present at the party, and their daughter was accompanied by her aunt, an eccentric wealthy lady, with whom she resided during the greater part of the year. I had the good fortune to find favor in the eyes of this lady, who had a passion for celebrities, and she invited me to her house. The invitation arose in this way; she had been to the theatre on the previous evening, and a gentleman in her company had taken exception to one of my readings. She mentioned it to me, telling me that she had insisted that I was right, and at the same time confessed to me, that she had not the slightest idea upon the subject, and had been prompted to side with me only for the reason that the gentleman was the most insufferably-conceited person on the face of the earth.

"He is not satisfied unless he is master in every thing," said the old lady with wonderful warmth; "he is dictatorial, self-willed, ungenerous, and supercilious — so much so, that he will scarcely condescend to argue a point upon which he has expressed an opinion. Nothing would please me more than to be able to bring evidence against him respecting your reading."

It so happened that my reading was the correct one, and that the emendation made by the gentleman was unsupported by authority. I told her so, and she was delighted.

"But it will be of no use my telling him what you say," she said; "and it would not be proper to bring you together for the purpose of quarrelling about it."

Then I suggested a way. I would consult two or three old editions of Shakspeare we had in the company, and have fair copies of the passage made from them, with my notes or annotations that might be attached to it. There was no occasion, I said, to let the gentleman know that I supplied the evidence; it would be sufficient for him to see the quotations and the authorities, and he would be able to test their correctness for himself. She thanked me warmly, and I frankly owned to her that I was almost as much interested in the matter as she was herself.

"Ah! you are a student," she said, tapping me with her fan, "and are not actuated by such small motives as I am."

I told her that it had been my nature, ever since I remembered myself, to be in earnest in what I did. Success could not be attained without earnestness, I said; and such a spirit was not thrown away even when exhibited in the smallest matters. The old lady was pleased with my conversation, and asked me to bring the written quotations to her house the following day. She then introduced me to her niece.

Bear with me for a little while. When I commenced, I intended to be more brief, but I have been carried away by a tide of memories. These things that I have spoken of have dwelt in my mind, but mention of them has not passed my tongue; not even my daughter has ever heard from me the story of my life. All the memories that are dearest to me are stirred into life by my speech; and in the midst of the darkness in this room, where nothing human exists but ourselves, I see my wife as I saw her that night for the first time — as I shall see her soon in a better land.

Good and evil, consciously wrought, are not of this world alone; mind you that, Joshua Marvel. They bear their fruit hereafter. In what way or in what shape we do not know — but they bear their fruit. I never loved but one woman in my life, and never was false to her, even in thought. I never harbored an unworthy sentiment towards her. I loved her truly, purely, solely, as she loved me. If I had done her wrong, and, loving her, had played false with another by a single act, by a single word of encouragement, even if it were weakly given in a moment of weakness, I could not look into this darkness as I do now without fear and shuddering.

(What was it that passed into the room? The deep darkness that prevailed, no less than the intense interest with which Joshua followed the course of Basil's story, prevented him from seeing. Yet it was no less certain that the door was gently opened, and that a person with noiseless footfall entered the room, and, wrapped in shade, stood silent in listening attitude.)

She loved me, and sacrificed herself for me. Loving me, she conceived it to be her duty to follow me; she forsook friends and family, and imperilled her good name for me; and in this solemn moment, when all the dearest memories of my life give life to my words, life to my thoughts, I bless her for it! Her devotion, unworldly as it was, was sanctified by love. There is no earthly sacrifice that love will not sanctify!

(A sound, half sigh, half sob, floated on the air, but so light that Joshua doubted if he had heard it. It reached Basil's ears. Rising in bed, he clutched Joshua by the shoulder, and whispered in trembling tones, "Can spirits speak, and make themselves heard? Did you hear any thing?"

"Something like a sigh, I thought," said Joshua; "and yet it is not possible."

Rising, he walked to the door; but whoever it was that had entered so noiselessly had so departed.

"There is no one here; it must have been fancy."

Basil sank down in the bed, exhausted by emotion, and it was long before he resumed his story. During the silence, Joshua thought of Ellen, and was happy. Such love as Basil Kindred had spoken of, Ellen had given to him. "But she will not have to sacrifice herself for me," he thought; "hers and mine will be a happier lot, I hope." Yet Basil's life was grand and noble. "Like a great storm at sea," thought Joshua, "and two small boats, lashed together, contending against it vainly." His thoughts were interrupted by Basil's voice.)

I need not describe her. Minnie is like her; but she was more beautiful even than Minnie. I went to the aunt's house, and was a frequent visitor there. Alice and I loved each other from the first. How I won her pure heart, I do not know. I will not say I was unworthy of her; for I was animated by a true ambition, and I was earnest and conscientious in all I did. I did not deceive her; I told her exactly what I was, what I had suffered, and what I hoped to gain. She paid no heed to worldly matters; she loved me, and that was enough. She sympathized with me in my ambition, and said it was a noble one. Her words were like wine to me; they strengthened and encouraged me. During the last week of our contemplated stay in the town I was stricken down by rheumatic fever, and was confined to my bed for nearly two months. The other members of the dramatic company waited for me for a few days, hoping I would get well; but I grew worse, and they were too poor to remain idle; so they left without me, and I was alone in the place.

I was delirious for a long time, and knew no one about me. How well I remember the day when consciousness returned! I opened my eyes, wondering where I was, and what had occurred yesterday to cause me to feel so deliciously weak; but I could not understand it, and I lay contented and happy, as if newly born into a world of peace and blissful repose. But as I lay — it might have been for a few moments or a few hours — a soft murmur of voices fell on my ear. I did not turn immediately in the direction of the sound; I was content to lie and listen to the murmur, and had no desire to analyze it — it so harmonized with my condition — there was such a sense of luxurious ease in it: it was like the soft lapping of the sea upon a shore of velvet sand. But with returning consciousness, my mind was gradually aroused into activity; and in the whispering of voices, a familiar note, sweeter and more musical than the rest, came to me. Lazily I turned my head, and saw my darling Alice. Our eyes met, and it was like a flash of light. I understood in that instant that she had been my ministering angel during my sickness. A look of pity and love was in her eyes as I turned to her, and she glided to my side and took my hand in hers.

"Alice darling!" I whispered. My voice was tremulous as a blade of grass in the summer air.

"Dear Basil!" she said in reply.

No heavenly happiness can be greater than that which entered my grateful heart at that moment. All sense of sight and touch and hearing — all heart and soul and mind — were merged in the exquisite belief that inwrapped me then — in the faith that constituted itself a part of me, inseparable, indissoluble, that is mine through all time — that she and I were one for ever and ever!

She sat with me until my landlady warned her that it was time to go. When she was gone, I learned that not a day had passed since my sickness that she had not come to see me.

"Alone?" I asked.

"Yes, alone," my landlady said, adding that she had not spoken to any one of the young lady's visits, as they might have been misconstrued.

The significant tone in which she said this caused me to reflect that Alice's visits, if discovered, would expose her to the world's censure, and I begged my landlady to preserve silence upon the subject.

I will not linger upon this part of my story. Alice's visits were discovered; and one day, when I was nearly well, and when I was sitting by the window waiting for her beloved presence, I received a visit from her aunt.

I saw the unpleasant news in her face directly she entered the room. She commenced by saying she was glad to see I was nearly well, and that she trusted I would not take advantage of a young girl's indiscretion.

"It was by the merest accident I discovered that my niece has been in the habit of coming to see you every day," said the old lady; "and she has been very rash and indiscreet; you must see that, I'm sure."

I did not see it, and I told her so.

"Nonsense!" exclaimed the old lady; "you are a man, and you know the ways of the world and its judgment. As a man of honor, you must not encourage my niece in her folly."

"Is it a folly to love?" I asked.

But the old lady would not listen to argument, and she demanded my promise that I would not see my darling again.

Firmly I refused to give it, unless Alice asked me to do so. We were pledged to each other, I said, and it was out of my power to break the engagement, unless Alice wished it broken.

The old lady was terrified by my firmness; and when she asked me what I meant to do, and I told her that I meant to marry her niece, she exclaimed aghast,—

"Marry her! and you an actor!"

"Yes; and I am an actor," I answered proudly.

She kept with me for more than an hour, begging and entreating; but she could not move me. I was contending for what was dearer to me than life, and an old woman's worldly arguments could not make me false to myself and to my love. She tempted me too — offered me money to leave the town. After that, I was silent; I would speak to her no more upon the subject. When she had exhausted herself, and rose to go, I opened the door for her; and before she went out, I thanked her for her hospitality to me, and expressed my regret that I should have been the means of causing her pain. She made no reply; but I fancied I saw a pitying expression on her face as she passed out.

I was overwhelmed by despair, and might have been guilty of I don't know what extravagance, had not my darling love seen my misery, and provided against it. Within an hour of the departure of Alice's aunt, a note was given to me by my landlady. It was from my darling herself. She knew her aunt's errand; she knew that I was true to her; and she told me not to lose heart, for she was mine, and mine only, and would be true to me till death. Truly, those words were like oil upon the troubled waters; my mind was instantly composed, and a deep peace and joy fell upon me. The last words of her little note were to the effect that she would find means to write to me again soon; and she begged me not to go away until she saw me.

So I waited, and grew strong; and time passed, until there came an evening when we met — met never to part again. It was a solemn meeting; there was no hesitation on one side, or entreaty on the other. We walked up and down in the rear of a woodside inn; and my landlady, whom I had asked to accompany me, stood a little distance from us. My darling told me that her family were about to take her to the Continent, and that she saw no way of resisting. "There is one," I said. And as I said this, I stood by the side of an old elm, and she stood with drooping head before me. "There is one. We are pledged to each other till death. If I parted from you now in the belief that we should not meet again, I would pray to God to end my life here where I stand."

"Tell me what I shall do," she answered, "and I will do it."

"Follow me," I said. "Share my life, hard though it may be. Be mine, as I am yours. Let us walk together till death, and after it."

She placed her hand in mine, and answered me in the words of Ruth, and I folded her to my breast, and kissed her.

So, accompanied by my landlady, we turned our backs to the town where we first met, and the next day we were married.

Ah, how happy we were, and how our lives seemed spread before us like a bright holiday, which was to be spent in a land where the air was always sweet — where the flowers were always blooming! No thought of winter; but it came, with its frost and snow, and racked me with a renewal of the old pains. I could have borne them cheerfully, if they had not sometimes prevented me from working. We fell into poverty; and through all its bitterness she never complained, and never gave me one word of reproach. Nay, often and often, when she saw that my sufferings were increased by the thought that I had asked her to share my poor life, she comforted me and cheered me with tender speech, that fell like balm upon my soul. I struggled on in my profession, gaining applause always, but never seeming to mount a step nearer to the goal where fame and fortune stood beckoning me. My wife had written to her family without my knowledge; but not one of them replied except her good aunt, who sent her a small sum of money. When Minnie was born she wrote again, but the old lady was dead. Still, somehow we managed: our wants were small, and our happiness was perfect. We had to travel about a great deal; and when we had not sufficient money to pay our coach-fares, we walked, and made the way light for each other by cheering words. Many scores of miles have I — the great tragedian, as they called me in the bills — carried our little Minnie in my arms, lulling her to sleep, or pointing out to her the beauties of nature, as they peeped at us out of hedgerows, or as they sprang up in the gardens of great mansions, where they were not hidden by grim walls, as if their owners were jealous lest the poor toilers on the road should enjoy their lovely forms and colors. Now and then we got a lift on a wagon, and the music of the bells on the horses' necks often lulled Minnie to sleep. We seldom staid in one place longer than a fortnight; but once we stopped in a town for nearly four months, playing three nights a week. That was a happy time. I used to come home from the theatre when my work was done, and Alice and I would sit in our humble lodgings until late in the night, talking of such matters as were nearest to our hearts; painting the future in bright colors, and weaving fancies about our Minnie, who would sometimes be lying awake on her mother's lap, and whose little fingers would clasp one of mine as the ivy clasps the oak. We made many friends — false friends most of them, attracted by my wife's beauty — friends whose speech was fair, but whose thoughts were treacherous. But rocks on which many a woman's good name and happiness have been wrecked melted like snow before my wife's purity. And still we struggled on, hoping against hope, until there came a time which cast a shadow on me never to be removed except by death. It was in the autumn of the year. My wife had been ill, and I had to nurse her and carry her about, and study and work, while my heart was almost breaking; for the doctors had told me she required wine and nourishing food, and I was earning barely sufficient to pay for the commonest necessaries. One night when I left the theatre, the rain was pouring down like a second deluge. I had been playing the principal parts in tragedy and comedy, and I came into the street hot and flushed with my exertions. It was the last night I ever played. The rain soaked me to the skin; but I took no heed of that; I was too anxious to reach home. I crept into our one room, and found my wife asleep. I sat by her side and looked at her pale face, and recalled the past. I saw her as she had been five years before, a bright and beautiful girl; and as she was now, pale and wan as a ghost. I heard her whisper, "Until death, Basil — until death!" I threw myself on my knees by the bedside, and hid my face on the bed in utter prostration; and while I knelt, my body turned cold as ice, then hot as fire, and a feeling like the feeling of death came upon me. "Is it death?" I asked myself; and I almost rejoiced at the thought that we might pass away together. When I raised my head, the room seemed to be thronged with visible fancies. The light and brilliancy of the theatre; the dark night with its down-pour of rain; Alice as she was when I first met her; my father's study, and he and I looking defiantly at each other; all these pictures, and many others, were before me, and for a moment seemed to be in harmony with each other. Unutterable confusion among them followed; and then a darkness fell upon me.

Weeks passed before the darkness cleared away. When I recovered my senses, I found my patient angel nursing me, although she was scarcely stronger than I was. But what will not a woman's love accomplish? We were not in the same town in which I had fallen sick. She had removed me to a village some twenty miles distant from my native place. I did not discover this until I was able to rise and move about. I was but a shadow of myself; all my strength had left me, and I was like a child. I was to discover something worse than that. I was to discover that my memory was gone, and that, although I could repeat snatches of parts I had played, I could not, study as hard as I would — and I tried diligently during my convalescence — get the complete parts into my head. My wife helped me — looked at the book while I stumbled on — prompted me, encouraged me, bade me rest for a day and try again. All in vain. If I was rehearsing the scenes in "Hamlet," speeches and lines uttered by Macbeth and Lear, interpolated themselves, and I grew hopelessly confused.

So, then — my occupation was gone; my ambition was at an end. The knowledge would have been bitter enough to bear had I been by myself; but there were my wife and daughter, my darling Minnie, my patient suffering Alice, to provide for, and I in debt, without a penny in the world, and without any means of driving white-faced hunger from my dear ones. The despairing conviction almost brought on a relapse, and it was only by the strongest effort of will that I kept my senses. But I could not get strong; rheumatism had fastened itself too firmly in my bones, and would not be driven away; and I was afflicted with distressful shudderings and with feverish attacks, during which I knew no one about me. Winter was coming on fast. Every atom of clothing that could be spared had been sold by my wife; what she must have suffered, dear angel! can never be told. Was it my selfishness or blindness that prevented me from seeing death written in her face? I did not see it — I did not suspect it — until the time when her cold body lay before me. She suffered — yes; she could not disguise that from me; but the pleasant smile and the cheerful look of content and hope with which she always answered my wistful gaze, blinded me to her condition and to the extent of her sufferings. I did not ask her why she had brought me to the village — I guessed that it was because I had known it in my happier days, and because it might induce me to think of my father, and of the advisability of asking help from him. She did not say a word upon the subject. She knew the story of my boyish life, and was content that I should do as I thought best. But she was a mother as well as a wife, and she deemed it to be her duty to bring me where, if I so pleased, I might possibly obtain assistance. I thought over it, and, bitter as it was, I saw that my duty lay clear before me. I would sacrifice my pride and humble myself to my father. And yet I hesitated — hesitated until one morning my wife came into the room looking so strange that I passed my hand before my eyes, wondering if I were awake.

"Alice!" I cried.

She came to my side with a cheerful look. Her beautiful hair, that had hung down to her waist was gone. I took her upon my knee, and folded her in my arms, and sobbed like a little child. She soothed and comforted me.

"It will grow again," she said, knowing but too well that before that time came she would be beneath the daisies. "The landlady wanted money, and every thing was sold but that. See, I can pay her."

"All?" I asked.

"No, not all," she said cheerfully; "but perhaps some good fortune will come to us."

That morning I wrote to my father. I told him that I was married to a gentlewoman, noble, good, and pure, that we had a child, and that I was ill and in want. But no answer came. I wrote again, begging him to reply and to assist us. Still no answer. And meanwhile my wife was fading before my eyes, and our landlady clamored for what was due to her. Oh, if I could have sold my blood for money, I would have done it, when I heard her coarse tongue revile my wife! I tottered into the passage.

"Woman!" I cried, "you shall be paid. I will go and get money."

"Where?" asked my wife in a faint voice.

"At my father's," I answered. "Come, we will go and lay our sorrows at his feet."

I took Minnie in my arms, and we started in the direction of my native town. It was not until we had walked four or five miles that we discovered how weak we were. We were penniless and hungry, and Minnie was crying for food. I went into a public-house, and begged for some. I was turned out without ceremony; but a common woman, who was drinking with a tinker, ran after me — God bless her for it! — and put a biscuit into Minnie's hand. We struggled on. A mile nearer. My wife grew white in the face, and her lips were black. And as I looked at her, there came by her side the image of what she was, ruddy, bright-eyed, rosy-lipped. I saw it, I tell you. The impalpable shape of the beautiful girl, radiant with health, walked with light step by the side of the careworn haggard-faced woman. I must have been crazed. She saw in my face the disturbed condition of my mind.

"Courage!" she whispered, taking my arm.

I laughed, and looked around. Fortunately, no one was near us, or I should have robbed him — weak as I was, despair would have given me strength. I have asked myself since, if it would have been a crime, and have not found the answer. Ten miles were compassed when a storm came on — a dreadful pitiless storm, in which the slanting wall of rain before us seemed to shut out hope. We toiled through it, fainting from weariness and hunger; we toiled through it, until I fell prone to the earth. My wife knelt by me in the wet grass, and implored me to make another effort for her sake, for our child's. I tried to rise, but could not. All that I could do was to drag myself to a clump of trees, where I lay exhausted. Every word that passed between us from that time is too deeply engraven on my mind ever to be forgotten.

"Wife," I said, "the struggle is over. Kiss me and forgive me."

In the midst of her agony, a sweet smile irradiated her face. I could not see it, but I knew it was there by her voice.

"Forgive you, husband!" she exclaimed, as she kissed me. "We have nothing to forgive each other. Pity and love are all that I feel now. Love for you and our darling Minnie," — and she placed our little darling's hand on my aching eyes — "and pity for your great sufferings."

Not a word of herself! Her pure unselfish nature was triumphant over all. As surely as we have hands to feel and eyes to see, such love as hers is heavenborn, and dies not with the flesh!

"Rest here," she said, placing our child in my arms. "I will go and seek help. Keep up your heart while I am gone."

I had no power to stop her, and she left me and was lost in the gloom. Hours must have passed, though it was night when I awoke. I had fallen into sleep, and in my dreams all the circumstances of my life played their miserable parts; from the dawn of my ambition down to the words of my wife, "I will go and seek help. Keep up your heart while I am gone." When those words were uttered, I followed my wife, in my dream, as she stumbled on through the darkness. Suddenly I lost her; then a whisper of pain stole upon me, and I heard her murmur, "Come to me, Basil; I am dying." A strength born of fear enabled me to rise shuddering to my feet. "Alice!" I cried. No voice answered me, but I still seemed to hear the echo of the words, "Come to me, Basil; I am dying." With Minnie in my arms, I followed the sound. Some wonderful chance directed my steps aright. How far I walked, I do not know. The rain was still falling, but there was a glimmering light in the sky to guide me. The trees, past which I crept painfully and wearily, were bare of leaves; their naked branches were emblematical of the desolation of my heart. I crept onward until I came to a spot where I saw a form lying on the ground. No need to tell me whose form it was that I saw before me. No sound came from the lips, no sign of life was observable in the limbs. The ghostly echo of the cry, "Come to me, Basil; I am dying!" died away upon the wind as I fell by the side of my darling, who had sacrificed her life for me. I raised her head on my lap, and looked into her white face. The eyelids quivered, opened; a look of joy leaped into her eyes.

"Oh, my darling, my darling!" I wailed; "wait for me."

I inclined my head to her lips, for they were moving.

"I will wait for you, Basil. There!" And she looked up to heaven, while the cruel rain poured down upon her face.

I placed Minnie's lips to hers, and the child clasped her little arms round her mother's neck.

"Live, Basil," she said slowly and painfully, "live for her. No, no!" fearing that I was going from her, "do not leave me yet!"

Her fingers tightened on mine, and she closed her eyes. I leaned over her to protect her from the rain. In that supreme moment of sacrifice a smile rested on her lips.

"Till death, and after it, Basil, my love!" she whispered.

And her soul passed away into the wintry night.

"You are crying," said Basil Kindred, after a long pause. "My story has touched your heart. I have told it to you for the purpose of opening your eyes to Minnie's nature. She is like her mother, without her mother's teaching. She is a wild flower; the impulse of her mind is under the control of the impulse of her heart. She is oblivious of all else, defiant of all else. Those of her friends who have the consciousness of a higher wisdom than she possesses — those of them who can recognize that the promptings of such a heart as hers may possibly lead her into dangerous paths — must guide her gently, tenderly. If any betray her, he will have to answer for it at the Judgment-seat. Joshua, you said to me, when you entered this room, that you had not forgotten the blessing I gave you on the first day of our meeting. I repeat that blessing. In all your actions that deserve blessings and prosperity, I say, God bless and prosper you, Joshua Marvel! Now leave me."

Joshua's face was wet with tears, and his heart was throbbing with sympathy for Basil as he walked down stairs. In the passage he heard a footfall that he knew to be Minnie's. It was too dark to see her face.

"Is that you, Minnie?"

"Yes, Joshua," she answered, in a low voice. "You have been sitting with father."

"Yes."

"I have been wishing to speak to you, and I was afraid I might not get the opportunity, for father is very strange to me. When does your ship sail, Joshua?"

"In a very few days, Minnie."

"I should so much like to see it, if there was no harm in my coming."

"What harm can there be, Minnie?" exclaimed Joshua. "Come to-morrow to the docks at twelve o'clock when the men are at their dinner. Bring Ellen or Susan with you, and ask for the "Merry Andrew," and I will show you over it."

"Thank you, Joshua. Good-night."

"Good-night, Minnie."

As their hands met, Susan, carrying a light, came from the kitchen. Joshua did not wish Susan to see the tears on his face, and he turned hastily away as she approached. But she did not appear to notice either him or Minnie, as she passed to the upper part of the house; and the next moment Minnie glided away, and Joshua entered the room where Dan and Ellen were sitting.

The following day Joshua, looking over the bulwarks of the " Merry Andrew," saw Minnie standing in bewilderment amidst the busy life and the confusion of bales and cases on the wharf. He was surprised to find that she was alone. He hastened to her side, and asked her why Ellen or Susan had not come with her, and received for reply that she had thought they were both too busy, and had not liked to ask them.

"But you don't mind my coming by myself, Joshua, do you?" she said, looking into his face.

"No," he said, returning her gaze. Her eyes were sparkling with youth and health, and her cheeks had a bright color in them from the brisk walk she had taken in the crisp air. "But I would have preferred your not coming alone."

"I will go back rather than offend you."

"Offend me!" he exclaimed. "You are a stupid to talk of offending me. And as for going back, that would be sheer nonsense now you have taken the trouble to come."

It was impossible to look at her without pleasure; she was as beautiful as the spring. A good many of the sailors turned to take another peep at her, and thought what a lucky fellow the third mate of the "Merry Andrew" was to have such a lass as that to come and see him. But he was in luck's way right round, they said to each other as they walked along. Joshua, not wishing to submit Minnie to their prying looks—although, being human, he was proud of them a little bit, it must be confessed—took her hand to lead her up the gangway. It was not easy for Minnie to get aboard, and Joshua had almost to carry her.

"How strong you are," she said, "to be able to carry a big girl like me! And this is your ship."

"It is lumbered up at present, Minnie," he said; "but when we are at sea, and the decks are cleared, and the sails are set, and we are flying along before a fair wind, it is a little better than this, I can tell you. I can smell the sweet spray now, as it comes dashing up." His nostrils dilated at the mere thought of the ocean, and involuntarily he passed his hand before his eyes, clearing away imaginary spray.

"How beautiful it must be!" exclaimed Minnie.

Joshua abated a little of his enthusiasm. "It's all very well in fine weather, when the wind and sea are kind; but you would be frightened at storms."

"Not if you were on the ship, Joshua," she said dreamingly, but in so soft and low a voice that he did not catch the words; yet he looked at her keenly; but she did not notice his gaze, for she was wrapped in thought, and her eyes were turned from him. So still did she stand, that Joshua touched her sleeve to attract her attention. She started, as if he had aroused her from sleep, and then they went over the ship together. She was very anxious to see everything, and they had a busy half-hour. The last part of the ship they went into was the saloon.

"Captain Liddle has been very particular about the saloon," Joshua said, " for his wife is coming with us this voyage. Here are their cabins—one for the captain and his wife, and this little one adjoining for her maid."

Minnie peeped into the cabins, and wondered how ladies could live in such a dark place. Joshua had to explain that the cabins were dark because the ship was in dock, and that when they got out at sea there was light enough for any thing. Then they ascended to the deck again, and Minnie thanked Joshua and prepared to go. Just at that moment Joshua saw—or fancied he saw—Susan standing on the wharf.

She was standing quite still, and her eyes were fixed on the poop of the "Merry Andrew."

"Why, there's Susan!" he exclaimed; and, leaving Minnie on deck, he hurried down the gangway. But the woman was gone, and he could find no trace of her. He returned to Minnie in a state of perplexity.

"I thought I saw Susan on the wharf," he said.

"You must have been mistaken, Joshua," said Minnie; "she was hard at work at home when I left. If it had been Susan, she would not have gone away when you went towards her."

"I suppose I *must* have been mistaken. Good-morning, Minnie; take care of yourself going home."

He led her down the gangway, and Minnie made her way, like a gleam of sunshine among the throng of rough working-men, who stood aside to let her pass, and sent admiring looks after her. During his work that afternoon Joshua thought much of her, and of her father's anxiety concerning her. "Mr. Kindred is right," he thought. "Minnie requires gentle tender guidance; such guidance as Dan can give her, and will have the right to do soon, I hope. She can have no better teacher, wiser counsellor, than Dan!"

So he mused and worked, and saw no signs of the dark clouds that were gathering about him.

CHAPTER XXII.

NEVER TO RETURN.

COULD a map be made of the mental life of a man whose career has been marked by the commonest of commonplace incidents, and from that map a tale were woven, it would transcend in interest the most eventful story that can be found in the wonder-world of fiction. Space, matter, and all the abstract relations of the Great System, affect the meanest order of mind, and produce the strangest of contrasts between the outer and inner life of men. Not more strange perhaps, but certainly more beautiful, are the contrasts presented in men of a high order of intelligence. As in the case of Dan. Quiet as were the grooves in which his material life moved, compassed as it was by a few narrow streets, his ideal life was a romance. It glowed with poetic beauty, and was filled with graceful images, like a peaceful lake in whose waters are reflected the glories of grand sunsets and the delicate lines and colors of light clouds and overhanging trees. Had it been Dan's fate to mix with the world, his sensitive nature would have rendered him the most unhappy of beings. The selfishness with which the world abounds, and with which he would have been brought in contact, would have made his life a misery. Wishful to see good in every thing, he would have seen its reverse in so many things, that his enduring faith in the purity and goodness of those upon whom he fixed his affections might have been weakened. His friends were few, but all his heart was theirs, and no doubt of their truth found place in his mind. Not to suspect belonged to the nobility of his nature.

Otherwise, he might have found cause for suspicion in what was occurring around him. Three days before Joshua's final departure from home, Basil Kindred locked himself in his room, and denied himself and Minnie to every person but Susan. She, and she only, attended to his wants, and faithfully obeyed his wishes. To all inquiries the one answer received, through Susan's lips, was, that he was too ill to be seen, and that he required the constant attendance of his daughter, who could not leave his room. Even Mrs. Marvel could not shake his resolution, and was surprised to find that Susan encouraged him, and would not assist her in her kind endeavors.

"It is not good for Minnie," remonstrated Mrs. Marvel, "to be cooped-up in that room all day. She can nurse her father — it is only right she should — but her health will suffer if she does not have fresh air."

"Mr. Kindred knows what is best for himself and Minnie," returned Susan in a voice that trembled, despite her efforts to be firm. "He has asked me to nurse him, and to keep everybody out of his room until he is better; and I mean to do it. If I can't do it here, I shall take him away where he won't be disturbed."

"Let me go up and see him," persisted Mrs. Marvel. "I may be able to do him some good."

"You can't do him a bit of good," replied Susan uncompromisingly," and he won't let anybody but me go into his room."

"Sick people don't always know what is best for them, my dear. We are all of us very much distressed and anxious about Minnie and her father. They are more than friends to us, and perhaps you do not guess what Minnie is to" — But Mrs. Marvel was stopped in her speech by a fierce exclamation from Susan. The good mother was not sorry for the interruption; she had been about to refer to Dan's love for Minnie, which her delicate and keen instinct had discovered, and the thought came to her that perhaps it would not be wise to speak of it. She was not the less surprised at Susan's agitation, and at the frightened look which immediately afterwards flashed into Susan's eyes—a look which asked, "What have I said? Have I betrayed my trust?" But the next moment Susan resumed her determined manner, and no entreaties of Mrs. Marvel could move her. When Mrs. Marvel told her husband of the interview, he said he was sure that Basil Kindred was not right in his head, and that the best thing to do would be to let the sick man have his own way. As for Susan, Mr. Marvel said, was always strange — they were a pair, she and Basil Kindred.

So no further attempt was made by any of them to see Basil Kindred and Minnie until the day when Joshua was going to sea. On that day Joshua went to Basil's room, and knocked. Susan came out of the room into the passage, and stood with her back to the door.

"I have come to say good-by," said Joshua; "and I should like much to speak to Minnie and Mr. Kindred before I leave. Go in Susey, and ask him to see me."

Susan returned the usual answer, but Joshua's entreaties caused her to waver. She re-entered the room, and Joshua heard Basil's voice speaking to her. Then Susan came out again, and said, —

"Mr. Kindred is too ill to see you — he told me to say so."

"And Minnie?"

"Minnie!" echoed Susan; and then in a low troubled voice, "Minnie is asleep."

Joshua was inexpressibly pained.

"I must be content, I suppose," he said, sighing; "but I am deeply grieved. Something seems to have come between us lately, and I shall go away leaving a mystery behind. I wonder sometimes if I am the cause of this estrangement. If I am, I hope all will be set right when I am out of the way."

"I hope so," said Susan, with a singularly earnest look.

"You hope so! Then I am the cause, and you believe it. Take care, Susan, that you are not assisting in bringing unhappiness among us."

"It is for you to take care," said Susan, with bitter emphasis, "that you do not do so."

"What do you mean?" asked Joshua, in amazement. "Tell me. I have a right to ask, Susan, for you will one day be my sister."

Joshua had taken her hand as he spoke, but she snatched it from him angrily.

"I can tell you nothing that you do not know," she said hurriedly. "If I am to be your sister, I have only one thing to say to you."

"Well?" he inquired, in an offended tone, for he was angered by Susan's manner.

"Be true to Ellen," she said, with quivering lips and in a softer voice.

"Is that your fear?" he exclaimed almost gayly. "Be true to Ellen! Why, Susey, I love her with all my heart and soul. But there! words go for nothing. Time will show. Bid Minnie and Mr. Kindred good-by for me, and say I was sorry I could not see them before I went away."

He put out his hand, and mechanically she took it in hers; but she unloosed it immediately with a shudder, and left him abruptly. He was compelled to be content with that good-by, unsatisfactory as it was, and he walked to his home, where Dan had been staying for the last few days, eating there, and sleeping, in Joshua's room. Sitting in their bedroom alone on those last few nights, when all but themselves in the house were sleeping the friends renewed their vows of faithful love, and spoke of many things in the future which both of them desired. In one of these conversations Joshua put into Dan's hands a written paper, which made Dan and Joshua's father masters of his small savings and of wages that would be due to him from the London owners of the "Merry Andrew."

"In case any thing happens to me," said Joshua, in explanation.

"Not for any other reason, Jo," said Dan, "for I shall never want the money."

"Father may want a little. It is all his and yours. As to your never wanting money, I wish I could feel sure of it."

"You may, Jo; I am earning quite enough with my birds. Mr. Fewster gave me an order yesterday for four canaries thoroughly trained to do all the best and newest tricks."

Joshua uttered a dissatisfied "Hm!" at the mention of Mr. Fewster's name. Dan understood it, for Joshua had contracted what Dan said was an unreasonable dislike for Solomon Fewster. Now, in reply to a remonstrance from Dan, Joshua said, —

"But you don't like him, Dan."

"I don't know that," said Dan, considering. "When you put it to me so plainly, I am rather inclined to say I do like him; for I cannot give a reason for not doing so. I can give a reason for liking him; he buys my birds" —

"And sells them at a profit, I'll be bound."

"Perhaps; he has a right to do so, if he pleases. I did think at first that he bought them for himself, but of course I was mistaken. However, whatever he does with them, he buys them and pays for them: that's enough for me. You could give as good a reason for liking him. He was kind to you when you were ill."

"Oh, yes! brought me jellies and things"—

"And you ate them and relished them," said Dan, laughing.

"I didn't know that he had brought them, or I wouldn't have touched them. I remember in one of our coasting-trips we had a passenger on board who wrote for newspapers, and who was said to be a very clever man. Certainly he talked like one. He used to talk to me, as much perhaps because I was a good listener, as for any other reason. Well, a favorite subject with him was what he called magnetic sympathy. He would just have suited you, Dan! He said that the natural magnetism which makes persons like or dislike one another, without apparent reason, is never wrongly directed."

"A kind of instinct," remarked Dan reflectively.

"He said, too, that as there are certain things in chemicals that won't mix, being opposed in their natures, so there are persons who have natural antipathies"—

"And won't mix — like you and Mr. Fewster," interpolated Dan.

"Just so. Besides that, I have a good many little reasons for not liking Mr. Fewster."

"Firstly," prompted Dan.

"He never looks me in the face."

"Secondly."

"He has a horribly smooth voice."

"Thirdly."

"He has flat feet — ugly flat feet. I shall always hate men with flat feet. Then everything about him shifts and shuffles. But don't let us talk about him any more. I can't keep my temper when he is in my thoughts."

The conversation drifted into other subjects, and Solomon Fewster was dismissed.

It was Dan's whim to have all his birds on a table for Joshua's inspection on the morning of his friend's departure.

"Although we are men now, Jo," he said, "I should wish us to keep our boyish fancies fresh and green always in our hearts. There is plenty of room for them, notwithstanding that life is a more serious thing to us than it was."

There they were, the modest linnets, the saucy tomtits, the defiant blackbirds, the handsome canaries. Among the latter were four which Dan pronounced to be "real beauties;" they were of a beautiful orange color, and the feathers in their tails and wings were of a deep black. These were the canaries which Dan had spoken of as having been "ordered" for Solomon Fewster. As they were admiring them, Solomon Fewster's step was heard in the passage, and the man himself entered to wish Joshua good-by. He was profuse in his good wishes, to which Joshua listened in silence, uttering no word but "good-by" as Fewster quitted the room. It so happened that, during the pauses in his expressions of good will to Joshua, Solomon Fewster looked at the canaries which Dan had purchased for him, and handled them with words of approval. When he was gone, Joshua, who had thrown his handkerchief carelessly upon the table, said, —

"That man hates me, Dan, more than I hate him."

"My dear Jo," said Dan, "how can you be so fanciful?"

"Forewarned is fore-armed, Dan. I beg of you not to trust him; I beg of you not to believe he is any thing but a cruel false man. He wishes me ill — else why do I instinctively shrink from the touch of his hand? He wishes me ill — else why is this?" Joshua removed his handkerchief, and Dan saw one of his beautiful canaries dead upon the table. "As he talked to me with his smooth tongue," continued Joshua, "wishing me well in his hateful voice, he crushed the life out of this poor bird. Is that no sign of a false bad heart? Had his thoughts been as gentle as his words, would this have happened?" Dan was silent; he could not defend Solomon Fewster by another word. "Let us say good-by here, dear Dan. Mother and father are waiting for me, and many of the neighbors also, to give me God-speed in a better fashion and with kinder hearts than that cruel man. Good-by, dearest friend. God send you all that your heart desires!"

"Thank you, dear friend. You know the one thing I desire to render me perfectly happy — Minnie's love. Say, ' God speed you in that venture!' Jo."

"God speed you! Dan, it comes upon me now to ask you one question. You do not doubt me, do you?"

"Doubt you, Jo! No, nor never can."

"The answer is from your heart. I should not have asked but that some things have distressed me lately, and I should indeed be unhappy if I thought you had the shadow of a doubt of me. It may be that our voyage will not be prosperous; it may be that I may never live to return. If I do not — nay, Dan, I am impelled to speak thus — if I do not, believe me to have been always the same to you. Believe that I never wavered in my love or my truth, and that to the last I held you in my heart, as I hold you now, gentlest, dearest, best of friends."

Dan drew Joshua's face to his and kissed it.

"We are one, Jo," he said softly; "nothing can divide our hearts. God bless and protect you, and bring you safely back."

The leave-taking between Joshua and his parents was of a very different nature from the last, when he was leaving home for the first time in his life. Then Mr. and Mrs. Marvel were beset with doubts as to whether the step Joshua was about to take was for the best. Now, these doubts were dissolved. He had gone on his venture a bright happy boy, and had returned a bright happy man. He had started on the lowest round of the ladder, and had already mounted many steps. Third mate already! What might he not attain to? They were proud of him, and with just cause. All the neighbors were proud of him, too; he was a prince among them. The family were quite a distinguished family in the neighborhood, as having for their representative a young man who had been all over the world — a man who had not only seen the sea, but who had been on it. A little crowd of neighbors had gathered about the house to give Joshua a parting handshake. The information of their having gathered for that purpose was imparted to Joshua by his father with an air of pride.

"I've lived in this neighborhood for nearly fifty years, Josh," said George Marvel, "and I've never but once seen so many of the neighbors on the lookout at one time."

"When was that, father?" asked Joshua, humoring his father's vanity.

"That was when a carriage with two white horses came through the street, and stopped in it for full five minutes. It was the first carriage that ever was seen here, and the last, for that matter. You remember, mother!"

"Yes, George."

"I wish you could have stopped with us until the last minute, Josh," continued George Marvel; "but Mr. Meddler was so mightily anxious that you should spend to-night and to-morrow with him at Gravesend, that he couldn't well be refused, being so good a friend. Do you think your ship will sail to-morrow?"

"To-morrow or next day, daddy." And Joshua put his arm round his mother's neck, and she looked up at her big son with affectionate pride.

"In three or four months you'll be among the savages again," observed George Marvel contemplatively and admiringly.

"I shall see plenty of them, I dare say, father. They come down to Sydney from what the people call the interior."

"And they are black all over, eh, Josh?" asked George Marvel, who was never tired of a repetition of Joshua's adventures.

"A kind of brown-black rather," answered Joshua, "with eyes like pieces of lighted coal."

"And not a bit of clothing?"

"An old blanket, some of them; nothing at all, a good many. A sailor gave one a pair of trousers, and the fellow tied them round his neck by the legs."

"D'ye see what strange things there are in the world, mother, that we never knew of?" observed George Marvel to his wife. "That comes of being a wood-turner all one's life. — Josh, if you have children, don't make wood-turners of 'em."

"I won't, father," said Joshua, laughing; "but I'm not certain either that I'd make sailors of them."

"There, father!" Mrs. Marvel could not help saying triumphantly, "what do you say to that? Joshua is coming round to my old way of thinking."

"Now, one would think," said George Marvel, appealing to an invisible audience, "that Joshua's done a bad thing by being a sailor."

"Well, no," said Joshua; "I've nothing to grumble at; I've been very lucky, and I'm thankful for it. But it is a hard life for a common sailor. He's bullied here and buffeted there, and is obliged to be up at all times of the night and day sometimes, and he gets soaked and soaked until he hasn't a dry thing to put on. Then, when he's dead-beat and turns in, he hasn't been asleep an hour perhaps when all the watches are called on deck, and there he is again, half dead with sleep, wondering whether he is dreaming or not, till he is woke up with a vengeance by the water trickling down his back, and the wind blowing as if it would blow his eyes clean out of his head."

Mrs. Marvel shivered with apprehension at Joshua's description; and he with ready tact continued, —

"But that's not often; and even when an inexperienced man would suppose there was great danger, there really is none at all. For the most part, it is fair and beautiful; and when you are bowling along under a steady breeze, with all sails set, surrounded by a bright cloud and bright water, there isn't a more glorious life in the world. If you were to see the ship, mother dear, on a calm day, with the sails like birds' white wings, with a deck as clean as this kitchen, and the sailors sitting about mending sails and splicing ropes, while the grand albatrosses are flying over us, and shoals of beautiful fish are leaping like deer in the sea — if you were to see it then, you would almost wish you had been a man, so that you might be a sailor. And through all 'there's a sweet little cherub that sits up aloft, to keep watch for the life of poor Jack.'"

"Indeed, my dear," exclaimed Mrs. Marvel, satisfied with the sentiment of the quotation, though its meaning was not quite clear to her; "I'm glad to hear that."

"Dear old mother!" said Joshua, in secret delight at her simplicity, kissing her.

"But the best of it all is," said George Marvel, "it makes a man of you; your muscle's like a bit of iron. Feel mine, Josh — like a bit of soft putty. That comes of being a wood-turner."

"Ellen and Mr. Meddler went down to Gravesend two hours ago," said Mrs. Marvel to Joshua, who was tying his accordion in his pocket-handkerchief.

Joshua nodded. Brave as he had intended to be, spasms were rising in his throat.

"You have all your things, dear?"

"Yes, every thing."

He turned to take a last look at the homely kitchen, noting in that momentary glance the position of every piece of furniture and of the crockery on the dresser. The yellow-haired cat was too old now to do any thing but lie on the hearth before the fire; and Joshua stooped and patted its head. When he rose and put his hand on the back of a chair, it seemed to him as if that common piece of wood and every other inanimate thing in the room were familiar friends. The very shape of the room was dear to him. The dear old kitchen! how many happy hours had he passed in it! He could have knelt and kissed the floor, his heart was so tender. As it was, he touched the table and the mantle-shelf, over which the bright saucepan-lids were hanging, lovingly with his fingers, and with dim eyes walked slowly away. His arm was round his mother's waist as they went up stairs to the street-door, and he put his face to her neck and kissed it — a favorite trick of his when he was a child. It brought to her suddenly the fancy that her son was a baby-boy still; and she caressed his curly head as a young mother might have done. Mr. Marvel of course was too manly to give way to such weakness; but nevertheless he clasped Joshua's hand with a clinging fondness, and the tune he was humming in proof of his manliness came rather huskily from his throat. It was a triumphant moment for him when he opened the street-door, and stood on the step with his wife and Joshua; for there in the street were many of his neighbors, who pushed forward to shake Joshua's hand, and to wish him God-speed; while some of the women slyly gave him "a lucky touch."

"One word, dear mother," said Joshua, drawing mother and father into the passage, whereat all the neighbors fell away, and turned their backs to the door, there being nothing there really worth noticing. "Take care of my darling Ellen for me. And Dan too; he may need it."

"They are our children, Joshua, next to you," said Mrs. Marvel.

"You think to yourself, when you are away, Josh," said Mr. Marvel, with his finger in a button-hole in Joshua's jacket. "'There is Ellen, my wife that is to be; and there is Dan, my dearest friend; and there is father and mother with them every day, loving them almost as much as they love me, and almost as proud of them.' You think that, Josh, and you'll think right."

"I am sure of it. Once more, good-by; God bless you all!"

And so, with tender embraces, hearty neighborly farewells, and waving of hands, Joshua, with his accordion under his arm, bade farewell to his dear old humble home.

———

CHAPTER XXIII.

THE OLD SAILOR SETS MATTERS STRAIGHT.

HAVING made over the whole of his worldly property to Joshua and Ellen "for better or worse," it was reasonable that Praiseworthy Meddler should have considerable weight in the family council of the Marvels. The arrangement whereby Joshua left his home a day before his ship was to sail was entirely of the Old Sailor's making; he and he alone was responsible for it. Naturally enough, when he had at first proposed it, he had met with opposition — especially from Mrs. Marvel, who wished Joshua to remain with them until the last moment. But, after a private conversation with the Old Sailor, she had yielded to his wish, and had even used arguments to induce Joshua's readier compliance. That being obtained, the Old Sailor informed them that he had a lady-friend at Gravesend, name Mrs. Eliza Friswell, who was a married woman herself with a family, and who kept a respectable boarding-house, with whom he had arranged that Ellen should stay until the anchor of the "Merry Andrew" was weighed; substantiating his statement by a letter from Mrs. Eliza Friswell to Mrs. Marvel, in which Mrs. Eliza — as the Old Sailor called her — undertook to look after Ellen as "one of her own." On the morning of Joshua's departure from Stepney, the Old Sailor, dressed in his best, and decorated with a bunch of flowers in honor of Ellen, had called for his pretty lass and had taken her away, leaving a message that if Joshua did not arrive at Gravesend exactly at the appointed time, Ellen had consented to run away with him — to wit, Praiseworthy Meddler — and get married. Very proud was the Old Sailor of his charge, and very tender and confidential was the nature of his communications to her as they made their way to Gravesend. What it was that made her blush and laugh and cry in turns — what it was that made her serious one moment and glad the next — was known only to themselves. Certainly no one was taken into their confidence until they arrived at Mrs. Eliza's, when, with a fatherly kiss, he delivered Ellen into the charge of that estimable matron. Mrs. Eliza's husband was a boatman, rough and strong as a boatman should be: with a great red face and great red hands, and with a voice that rumbled from his great deep chest with such thunderous power as to render such a thing as a whisper physically impossible. He was the owner of a fleet of four boats, which had been bought and paid for in shrimps and watercresses, or, at all events, with the profits made by Mrs. Eliza out of those delicacies, which she purveyed to the easily-satisfied amorous British public, with stale bread-and-butter and an imitation of tea, at nine pence per head.

Praiseworthy Meddler was fraternizing with Mrs. Eliza's husband when Joshua made his appearance. Mrs. Eliza's husband immediately sheered off, and the Old Sailor took Joshua in tow. In response to the Old Sailor's remark that he was late, Joshua, who felt very despondent, said that parting from those at home took a longer time than he had expected.

"Ay, my lad," said the Old Sailor gravely, "'tis a hard word, good-by, when said to those we love. A long time with Dan, I dare say now?"

"Yes, sir; but it didn't seem long. Time flies faster at some times than others."

"Ay; flies fastest when we most want it to hold out. Mother and father all right?"

"As right as may be, sir. Crying more now, I know by my own feelings, than when I was with them. Kept up for my sake, sir, to give me courage." And Joshua turned aside.

"No need to be ashamed of your tears, my lad. Gentle thoughts and a gentle heart go together. Some people say 'tis unmanly to cry, but I wouldn't give much for the man who never cried, or who wasn't sometimes so near it as to feel a gulping in the throat. 'Tis as much crying, that is, as if the tears were rolling down his face. I've felt like it myself, I'm glad to say."

"You are very kind to me, sir."

"You deserve it, Josh. you deserve it, though I've a doubt that you're a bit blind to some things."

"To what things, sir?"

"Gently my lad, gently. Plenty of time to talk."

The gravity of the Old Sailor was contagious, and Joshua felt that the good old fellow was about to say something which he deemed of importance.

"Where is Ellen, sir?"

"In the house with Mrs. Eliza. She is happy and comfortable, my lad; and when you and me have had our bit of talk, we will go in to her. She knows that we're together, and that we've got something to speak about. As you turned the street, she put her pretty head out of window there — you didn't know the house or you'd have seen her do it, like a true sailor as you are — and when she saw us together, she put her pretty head in again, satisfied. And you left everybody at home all right, eh? Grieving naturally to be sure, but otherways all right?"

"Yes, sir."

"Let us walk as we talk," said the Old Sailor, hooking his arm in Joshua's, and walking in the direction of the river. "Or we shall talk better in a boat, perhaps; Mrs. Eliza's husband shall paddle us about the while."

"But I should like to see Ellen just for one minute first."

"To begin your kissing, eh, my lad?" said the Old Sailor, with a roguish laugh. "No, no; you'll have plenty of time for that. I'm in command now, and I'll have no mutineering, or I'll put you in irons. You'll not like them as well as Ellen's pretty arms." Notwithstanding the light nature of the Old Sailor's words, Joshua detected a serious mood beneath them, and with a good grace he walked to the landing-place and stepped into the boat which Mrs. Eliza's husband held ready.

"So you were a long time with Dan, my lad," remarked the Old Sailor, when they were launched. "What did you talk about mostly?"

"The old things, sir, — ourselves mostly?"

"You have no secrets from Dan, my lad?"

"No, sir, none."
"And he has none from you?"
"None, sir."
"And yet I'll be bound," said the Old Sailor, looking steadily at Joshua, and compelling Joshua to return his gaze, "that there was something which you might have spoken of had you not been restrained by a feeling, say, of kindness to Dan. What, now?"

"There *was* something, sir," replied Joshua, wondering what this conversation, so singularly commenced, would lead to.

"Ah!" ejaculated the Old Sailor, rubbing his knees in a satisfied manner; "let us hear what that something was."

"You speak so earnestly, sir," said Joshua, inwardly questioning himself, "that I must be careful not to conceal any thing from you — not that I have any reason nor that I wish to do so, but something might escape me. I must first say, though that you must not expect me to break any confidence — that supposing Dan had a secret, and had imparted it to me, I should not be justified in telling that secret to any one else."

"Fair and honest, my lad; what I expected from you."

"Well, then, I have been sorry to find that Mr. Kindred —"

"Minnie's father — yes," interrupted the Old Sailor, with a sharp look at Joshua. "Has been changed to all of us lately, and especially to me; and I have been sorry to think that it is because of something which I have done that he is so changed."

"You know of nothing, Josh?"

"Nothing — absolutely nothing; and that's what grieves me. If I did know, I should be able to justify myself. Why, sir, this morning he refused to see me when I went to wish him good-by, and refused to let me see Minnie. I did not speak of this thing to Dan because of my love for him."

"And because," said the Old Sailor, "supposing that Dan had a secret and had imparted it to you, you thought that Dan would be easier in his mind — in consequence of his secret — if he did not know of Mr. Kindred's strange refusal to see you."

"Just so, sir."

"Could I guess this secret of Dan's?" questioned the Old Sailor. "Could an old tar like me, who wouldn't be supposed to know much of boys and girls and their whims and whams, venture to guess that this secret of our dear friend Dan's was all about a woman?"

Joshua did not reply.

"And such a woman!" continued the Old Sailor. "With eyes as bright as the stars, and with hair like a mermaid's. As cunning as a mermaid too; not wickedly cunning — no, no; but 'tis in her to be so; and she needs weaning from it, like a babe."

Very gentle was the Old Sailor's voice; and greatly did Joshua wonder, not at its gentleness, for that was natural to the old man, but at the wisdom of the words that came from his lips. All his roughness was gone; all his pleasantry was gone; all his simplicity was laid aside for the time; and the Old Sailor spoke as if all his life he had been studying woman's nature until he was master of its complexities. But such deep wisdom often comes from very simplicity.

"Lord love you, my lad!" he said, "how blind you have been! Here has been a woman's heart laid bare to you, and you have not suspected it."

Joshua trembled with apprehension.

"For Heaven's sake, sir," he implored, "speak more plainly!"

"I intend to do so, Joshua; for this is the solemnest time of your life. I have considered the matter deeply, and I can see but one right thing to do; but I am running ahead too fast. Steady there, steady. As I said a time ago, here has been a woman's heart laid bare to you, and you have not suspected it. What woman, now? But 'tis not right to ask, mayhap."

"Ask me any thing, sir; I will answer truly."

"What woman do you love?"

"Ellen."

"Ellen? And Ellen only?"

"And Ellen only. None other; nor ever shall, if it is given to man to know his heart."

"Good! Answered like yourself; answered like the lad I used to see looking out on the river that runs to the sea; like the lad my old heart warmed to because there was honesty in his face; like the lad who has grown to be a man, and who sits afore me now with truth in his eyes."

"Thank you for that, sir."

"What woman does this lad, now grown to be a man, love? Ellen — the pretty Ellen, the truest-hearted, gentlest-hearted, kindest-hearted, dearest lass on all the high seas. What woman does Joshua's friend Dan love? That's a question I ask myself. 'Tis easily answered. Minnie — Minnie with the mermaid's hair, and with eyes bright as the stars. Does Minnie love Dan? Yes; but not as Dan wants her to love him. Why? Because there is some one in the way."

"Who, sir?" Joshua was constrained to ask, but dreading the answer.

"She loves Dan's friend Joshua better than she loves Dan. Let that friend, who sits afore me now, search his heart and his mind, and let him say what he thinks. He knows her nature; has been her friend since she was a girl; and, cunning as a woman may be, no woman can be cunning enough to hide her love always from the man she loves, though she may hide it from all the rest of the world. It happens sometimes in a man's life that he may be unconscious of a thing for years perhaps, it being present to him all the time, until, sometimes in one way, sometimes in another, a sudden light is thrown upon it, and he sees in a flash what he has been blind to all his life before."

"You are right, sir," said Joshua sadly. "It has happened to me now. I have been blind."

As he sat, sadly looking at the evening shadows reflected in the river, every circumstance connected with his intimacy with Minnie came to his mind with an interpretation different from that it had borne before. Her pretty fancy of the shell, which he had thought of often as a childish conceit, bore a different meaning now. Tender looks and simple acts, which had pleased him at the time, gathered strength, and became more than tokens of mere friendship. Child as she was when he first went to sea, he recognized now that she had more than the strength of a child; that even then, indeed, she was almost a woman. When he came back, a man, she had saved his life; and when he thanked her for it—surely he could do no less!—she told him that she did not want thanks, for the having saved his life would ever be her sweetest remembrance. "Little Minnie, little Minnie," he had said, kissing her, "thank you for your devotion." He remembered that she trembled, and that something like a sob escaped her when he had kissed her. Had he done wrong? Was he to blame? All he had done had been innocently done, as from a brother to a sister. And her feelings were known to others when they had been hidden from him. Minnie's secret was known to her father and to Susan. That was the reason why Basil Kindred had questioned him so strangely, and had told him the story of his life. Words uttered by Basil, which had borne no direct signification when they were spoken, came to him now with startling vividness. "Young men are often thoughtless in their actions," Basil had said; "they do not know the depth and earnestness of some womanly natures." The revelation that had come to him served also to account for Susan's singular conduct that very morning.

"So," he thought; "they believe I have been playing with Minnie's feelings; and both of them have condemned me. And I at the same time engaged to Ellen! It is too dreadful to think of. What can I do? Oh, what can I do?"

The unspoken words rended him to the soul; he was enveloped in a despairing darkness. But a greater terror than all fell upon him when he thought of Dan. In such a momentous crisis as that through which Joshua's mind was passing, nothing of the past is unremembered. Words which otherwise are borne in mind only by their sense come back as if they were just being uttered. When Dan had imparted to Joshua the secret of his love for Minnie, he had said, "A great hope, shadowed by a great fear, has entered my soul; a hope which, fulfilled, would make earth heaven for me. Is it too precious a thing to pray for? It seems so to me. I tremble as I think of it. But if it is not to be, I hope I shall soon die." And Joshua heard again that cry from Dan's soul, almost word for word. The sacred nature of the love existing between Dan and Joshua needs to be understood to realize the terrible fear that smote Joshua at the present time. If Dan should ever come to believe him false, he would not wish to live: for the salt would have gone out of his life forever.

For full a quarter of an hour Joshua was wrapped in painful thought; and the Old Sailor had not disturbed him. But now, as he raised his tearful eyes to the Old Sailor's face, the Old Sailor laid his hand gently upon Joshua's knee, and said,—

"Well, Joshua, and how do you make it out?"

"As bad as it well can be, sir. This is the hardest stroke I have ever had. I do not think that even you can understand how hard it is for me."

"Because of Dan?"

"Because of Dan, sir. I have no need to hide Dan's secret from you now—you know it; but if Dan should be disappointed in his love for Minnie, I don't know what effect it would have upon him. All this is very terrible. I don't need to assure you, sir, that I have been entirely blameless, and that I have never treated Minnie in any way but that of an honored sister."

"You do not, my lad," said the Old Sailor, with an evident brightening up in his manner; "I am satisfied of that. But what do we do when a storm comes? Do we run and bury our heads in our hammocks, or do we stand up like men to meet it and battle with it?—as we are going to meet this storm, which has come upon us unaware, and from no fault of our'n. Like men, Josh; we're going to meet it like men. I am looking it straight in the face. No wonder it made you stagger when it come upon you sudden. It set my old head a-thinking when I found it out — though it only come upon me by degrees, and after a deal of watching. Just you think a bit now, Josh, and tell me if you don't see any way of getting the ship off the rocks."

"I can see no way, sir," said Joshua, after a little anxious pondering; "all is dark around me."

The Old Sailor laughed a quiet little laugh.

"Lord, Lord! how blind these youngsters are! Here's a sailor that's lost his reckoning, and running the danger of seeing his ship break up before his eyes; and all the while there's a smooth-water bay close alongside him, and a friendly craft waiting to give him a hand."

"Where is that bay, sir?"

"Steady, my lad, steady. Let's see what we've got to do. Firstly, our duty to everybody, right round. Next, to make two persons, who ought to know better, ashamed of themselves for misjudging of us. Next, to make every thing so snug that our friend Dan sha'n't suffer from any fault of our'n. Next, to teach a gentle lesson to a mermaid of a girl who's got a notion in her head that's no business to be there, but who otherways is as good as gold. It's a riddle, my lad, and I've got the key to it in my pocket."

"May I see it, sir?"

"You may, and shall, Josh," said the Old Sailor, with a sly chuckle. "It was to give you the key, that I brought you out here to talk."

And the Old Sailor took from his breast his blue-cotton pocket-handkerchief, upon which was imprinted the twelve-hundred-ton ship, with all its sails set to a favorable breeze. There was a knot in the handkerchief, which the Old Sailor undid with his teeth, keeping his eyes fixed upon Joshua's face all the while. The knot being untied, the Old Sailor took from the handkerchief a very small parcel in silver paper, and handed it to Joshua in perfect silence.

Joshua opened the silver paper, and found in it a wedding-ring.

He looked at the tiny symbol with a beating heart, and a glimmering of the Old Sailor's meaning dawned upon his mind.

"That's the key, my lad," said the Old Sailor, with a triumphant expression on his honest, weatherbeaten face; "that's the key to it all. You put that ring upon pretty Ellen's finger to-morrow morning early, and what happens? Why, you spend your honeymoon here in Gravesend with your little wife; and when the 'Merry Andrew' sets sail, — which won't be to-morrow, Josh; I've found that out, —

Ellen goes back to Stepney with that pretty bit of gold on her finger. Says she, 'I'm married — married to Joshua.' 'Married!' says they, all but one of 'em; 'married!' And surprised they are, all but one of 'em. 'Who made you do it?' says they, all but one of 'em. 'Mr. Meddler,' says she; 'Mr. Meddler made me do it. He's a hard-hearted old shark, and he *made* me do it. But I'm not sorry for it,' says she; 'I'm glad of it. And I'd do it over again to-morrow; for I've got a true-hearted man for a husband, and all I've got to do is to pray that he may come back safe to me and to all of us.' With that they all fall a-kissing one another, which is but right under the circumstances. What happens then? Says Susan, 'I was mistaken; Joshua is as he always was.' Says Mr. Kindred, 'Minnie is safe. God bless Joshua for doing what he has done.' Says Minnie to herself, 'It's no use my loving a married man. I've been a foolish girl, and what I've got to do is to love Joshua like a brother, as he has always loved me — like brother and sister; that's all we can ever be to one another.' Then she turns to Dan, and loves that tenderhearted friend, — who ought to have been a man six foot high, with his limbs as sound as our'n, — and loves him as he ought to be loved. And I shouldn't wonder, my lad, that when you come home from this trip, Dan will say to you, 'Here is my wife, Jo, my own dear Minnie; and we're as happy as the day is long.' The consequence of all of which is, that every thing turns out as it ought to turn out, and as we all want it to turn out."

The Old Sailor drew a long breath after this peroration, and dabbed his face in a manner expressive of a high state of exultation and excitement. Joshua was no less moved. He toyed with the wedding-ring as gently and affectionately as if it were already on Ellen's finger. Truly, to him it was more than a piece of plain gold; it was a symbol of love. If it had been a precious life, he could not have handled it more tenderly. Tears came into his eyes as he looked at it, and his heart beat more strongly with love for Ellen as he pressed the ring to his lips. At which action the Old Sailor gave his knee a great slap; and falling back, in the excitement of his triumph, upon Mrs. Eliza's husband, nearly upset a boat for the first and only time in his life.

"And that is the reason, sir," said Joshua, "that you wished me to spend my last day at Gravesend with Ellen?"

"That is the reason, my lad, and no other."

"But how did you find all this out?"

"The fact of it is, my lad," replied the most unsuspicious and guileless old tar that ever crossed salt water, "I put this and that together. I put this and that together," he repeated with an air of amazing cunning. "It came first in a simple way. When you were ill, I went one day to see Minnie's father; and when I went into his room, I found that he was out. Minnie was there, though: but she didn't see me. She was sitting on the ground by her father's bed, with a shell at her ear, and was singing some words softly to herself; and I heard her repeat your name, Joshua, over and over again. It might have been a babe singing, her voice was so low and sweet. But I didn't like to hear it, for all that; and from that time, my lad, I began to watch, and to put this and that together. Lord love you! if you hadn't been so wrapped up with Ellen, you would have found it out yourself soon enough. You see, if Minnie had been a little girl, that shell and her singing wouldn't have mattered; but being a woman, it did."

"And Ellen, sir. Have you told her what you have told me?"

"Just as much as wouldn't wound her sensitive heart, the dear lass. Not a word about Minnie. I've put it more as if it was your doing and my wish, being an unreasonable old shark, you know, and because I had a right to have my own unreasonable way. I told her I'd set my heart on it, and so had you."

"And her answer?"

"That pretty little lass says, 'If Joshua, that I love dearer than all the world'— them's her very words, 'dearer than all the world'— 'wishes me to marry him down here at Gravesend, it will be my pride and my joy to do as he wishes, now and always.' Something else she says too. But before I tell you what that something else was, let me know what you think about it, Josh."

"What can I think, sir, after what you have told me, but that I believe it is the best and only way to set all matters straight? It is a task both of love and duty — love to Ellen, duty to Dan and Minnie. Yet I have one regret. I have often pictured in my mind what a proud day our wedding-day would be to mother," — his voice faltered here, — "and how her dear face would have brightened when our hands were joined!"

"That's the very something else that Ellen says to me, Josh," said the Old Sailor, beaming with satisfaction. "Says she, 'I should like to have Josh's mother at the wedding.' Says I, 'My dear, Josh's mother *will* be at the wedding.'"

"No!" exclaimed Joshua with a sudden start of surprise.

"Yes," cried the Old Sailor dabbing his face gleefully. "Says I, 'My dear Josh's mother *will* be at the wedding. She will come down to Gravesend to-morrow morning early, and will go back quietly in the afternoon.' And when Ellen tells 'em at home all about it, mother will be the only one among 'em who won't be surprised."

"Enough said, sir," said Joshua, his heart filled with wondering happiness. "I don't know what I have done to deserve such friends as I've got. Let us get back to Ellen."

With that, Mrs. Eliza's husband, who had behaved more like a machine than a man during the long interview, pulled briskly to shore.

It was dusk when they walked along the street where Mrs. Eliza lived; but Joshua saw Ellen standing at the door waiting for them. He hastened to her eagerly, and with his arm around her waist, drew her away from the little light that was left. She was trembling; but his strong arm supported her.

"So you are to be my little wife to-morrow?" he said in a voice of exceeding tenderness.

She clung closer to him, and hiding her face, although it was dark, answered him in the softest of soft whispers, "Yes, if you are satisfied that it shall be so."

"It will be for the best, darling," he whispered, embracing her.

How proud he was of her! and what a memorable night they passed with the Old Sailor! The best room in the house had been brightened up for them to have tea in; and after tea, Joshua and Ellen strolled by the waterside for an hour, which seemed about five minutes long, talking as lovers have talked since the Creation. Meanwhile, the Old Sailor stood at the door, smoking his pipe with infinite satisfaction at the thought of having set all matters straight. While he thus stood, a man approached with the evident intention of making an inquiry of him; but catching sight of the Old Sailor's face, the man uttered a hasty exclamation and abruptly crossed the road, making a pretence of being intoxicated. It was but a pretence, but it deceived the Old Sailor, who set it down in his mind that the man was a sailor on the spree. "Going to join the 'Merry Andrew' to-morrow, perhaps," he thought; "and fuddling himself, as most of 'em do the first and last nights ashore. A rare old swiller is Jack! Never knows when he has had enough. Must always take another drop."

The man's thoughts were of a different kind. When he had turned the corner of the street, he walked more leisurely, and drew such a breath as one draws when he has escaped a danger. His first muttered words were "He didn't see me;" his next, "What the devil brings him here?" That his mind was disturbed by the sight of the Old Sailor was evident from his manner; and it was evident also, by the wary looks he cast about him, that he was bent already on no idle mission and needed nothing fresh to occupy him. "A good job it was dark," he muttered, directing his steps to the waterside; "if he had seen me, he would have been sure to tell Marvel, and it might have given rise to suspicion. Where is that dog of a Lascar, and what the devil does he mean by keeping me waiting?" The words were scarcely uttered when his face grew deadly white, and an ugly twitching came about the corners of his lips, at what he saw before him. It was merely a man and woman—evidently lovers—who were walking slowly along, in earnest conversation. He was about to follow them, when his arm was touched by a new-comer, in a sailor's dress.

"Here I am, master," said the new-comer.

"See there, you dog!" exclaimed Solomon Fewster, pointing to the lovers. "See there! What brings her here?"

The Lascar looked after them, shading his eyes with his hand, and shrugged his shoulders. "Joshua Marvel and Ellen Taylor!" he said, with a careless laugh. "Doing a little sweethearting on the sly. If you had the chance, you'd do the same yourself. See, they're turning back this way; let us get out of sight."

They stood aside, and as the lovers passed, heedful of nothing, conscious of nothing, but their own great happiness, their faces met, and a kiss passed between them. In his torment of jealousy, Solomon Fewster grasped the Lascar's shoulder so tightly as to make the man wince. The dog shook himself free from his master, and said, "Well, he'll be away soon, and you'll have the pretty Ellen all to yourself. Come, now; I don't want to stop here all night. Let us say what we've got to say, and be done with it."

Solomon Fewster walked away a few steps to recover his composure, and when he had mastered his agitation, returned to the Lascar.

"I shipped this morning, through an agent," said the Lascar; "here are my papers."

"It is too dark for me to see them; I must take your word that you have done what you say."

"You have taken my word before, master, and you have found me faithful. You keep your part of the bargain; I shall keep mine. It is my interest to do so."

"Yes, your interest," said Solomon Fewster, with somewhat of a bitter emphasis. "You have cost me enough, you dog."

Notwithstanding that their positions of master and dog might have been appropriately reversed, the old fiction was kept up between them, with insolent arrogance on one side, and with mock humility on the other. Neither of them deceived the other.

"I might have cost you more, master," replied the Lascar; "but go on."

"Let us see, then, if we are agreed upon the position of matters, and if we understand one another. When a certain thing happened last Christmas, which nearly cost a whelp his life, you thought it necessary for your safety"—

"We thought it necessary for our safety," corrected the Lascar.

"To take yourself off somewhere, so as not to be seen, and therefore not suspected. Out of sight out of mind. In accordance with that understanding you went to a certain watering-place, and lived at my expense until you got into a drunken quarrel with your drunken mates, in which one of them received a cut across the face. The same night—being within a week of the present time—you thought it advisable to leave that district, and you accordingly did so, coming down here to Gravesend, and apprising me that you were in danger of arrest and in want of money."

"You talk like a book," said the admiring Lascar, with a laugh.

"I came down to see you, and to advise you"—

"Taking such an interest in me, master!" interrupted the Lascar, with another and a louder laugh.

"And I told you that as in England a man who is too free with his knife is likely to be deprived of his liberty for a longer time than he would probably consider pleasant, the best thing you could do—the police being on the lookout for you—would be to join a ship bound for a distant port, and so get clear of danger. Is that fairly stated?"

"Pretty fairly for you, master. It is for me to say, that so long as I am out of danger your safety is secured. But that's a matter, of course, that you don't think much of."

"It happening, as it does not often happen with such dogs as you," continued Solomon Fewster, taking no other notice of the Lascar's taunt than was indicated by a contemptuous emphasis on the word "dogs," "that you were for once open to reason, you agreed with me that it would be best for you to get out of the country. As luck would have it, Joshua Marvel's ship, the 'Merry Andrew,' was shortly to start for New South Wales, and as part of the crew was to be engaged at Gravesend, where you were skulking about, you set your mind very strangely upon going in the same ship with the whelp, and according to your own statement, have accomplished your desire to-day."

"I didn't find it a very difficult thing, master. Sailors are none so plentiful. Go on."

"When I found that you were determined to go in Joshua Marvel's ship, I bearing in mind that you have been as faithful as it is in the nature of such a dog as you to be, told you that the night before the ship sails, I would come down and give you a few necessaries which you said you required."

"Such as twenty-five pounds in gold," said the Lascar.

"Such as twenty-five pounds in gold," repeated Solomon Fewster, taking some packets from his pocket.

"Such as a six-bladed knife."
"Such as a six-bladed knife."
"Such as another knife with one blade."
"Such as another knife with one blade."
"Such as a silver watch and a silver chain."
"Such as a silver watch and a silver chain."

"Bah!" exclaimed the Lascar, in a voice of intense scorn, as he received the articles, one after another. "Look at the sky, master."

It was intensely dark; the clouds were black, there was no moon, and not a star was discernible. Solomon Fewster looked up, and said, "Well?"

"What can you see, master?"
"Nothing."
"Look at me" — he had walked away a few paces. "Can you see me?"
"I can see your form."
"Not my face, nor my eyes?"
"No, you dog!" answered Solomon Fewster hotly, for the Lascar's voice was contemptuously insolent.

"Bah! you are worse than I am. Too free with my knife, am I? I wonder whether you would be too free with your knife — in the dark? In the light I know you wouldn't be. You wouldn't have the pluck to use it. Look you, master: the first part of what you said was pretty well as things happened; but the last part — Well, you and me know all about that. And yet, although we're in the dark, and can't see each other's face, nor each other's eyes, you haven't pluck enough to tell the truth; you haven't pluck enough to say even to me,

here in the dark, with no one by, that when I found that the 'Merry Andrew' was going to sea, I said to you, 'What a fine thing it would be for me to go in the same ship as Joshua Marvel, and to take advantage of any thing that might happen to do him a good turn!' and that then you mentioned — quite accidentally, of course — that if any thing should happen to him through me, you would give me fifty pounds if the 'Merry Andrew' came home without Joshua Marvel. You haven't pluck enough to say that then I said, 'Done!' and done it was; but that I — knowing you, master — made a point of having something in earnest of the bargain — such as twenty-five pounds in gold; such as a six-bladed knife; such as another knife with one blade; such as a silver watch and chain. Bah! If it wasn't that I was such a cursed fool when my blood is up, that I don't know what I do, and that, because of that, it is safer for me to leave the country than to remain in it, I would stop and feed upon you — I would, by God! — and worry the heart out of such a coward."

"You've been drinking," said Solomon Fewster, with difficulty suppressing his anger.

"What if I have? I know what I am saying well enough. I have had too much of your airs of superiority, and of your lies and your acting. Why, do you think that I would ever have done your dirty work, if it hadn't served my purpose? Do you think that if I hadn't sworn an oath, and marked it with my blood, to be revenged upon that damned upstart, Joshua Marvel, for what he did to me, I would go in his ship? Look you! I will do my share of the work, never fear, master; but I would have done it for next to nothing, if you were a man instead of a sneak!"

"You dog!" cried Solomon Fewster, in an uncontrollable burst of passion. "You have my money, my knives, and my watch upon you at this moment. I have half a mind to give you into custody for robbing me."

An exclamation of anger escaped the Lascar, and Solomon Fewster cursed himself inwardly for his injudiciousness the moment the words had passed his lips. A long silence followed, a silence lengthened by Solomon Fewster's fears; for he knew that he was in the Lascar's power, and could not consider himself safe while his dog was in the country.

"I didn't mean that," he said, with an awkward effort at conciliation; "but you were wrong to provoke me."

The Lascar did not reply, and Solomon Fewster's alarm increased every moment.

"Why don't you speak?" he asked.

THE OLD SAILOR SETS MATTERS STRAIGHT.

"I've been thinking, master," then said the Lascar with a quiet laugh — "I've been thinking that a man isn't safe with such a sneak as you, and I've made up my mind."

"To what?"

"To this; and if you don't do it, I'll go straight to Joshua Marvel and his pretty Ellen, and open their eyes to what you are."

"And ruin yourself," said Solomon Fewster, trembling in every limb like the coward he was.

"And ruin myself," said the Lascar composedly, "and you along with me."

"You do not know what you are saying."

"You shall see," said the Lascar, moving slowly away.

"Stop! What is it you want me to do?"

"If the 'Merry Andrew' returns without Joshua Marvel, and I, having done my work, come to you for my wages, it isn't unlikely that you'll hatch some charge against me which I sha'n't be able to face, for you are rich and I am poor. I will prevent this. You shall come with me now to my lodging-house, and you shall scratch upon the inside of my watch, "From Solomon Fewster to his Lascar friend," and you shall give me a paper saying as how you made me a present of the knives and the money because I have earned them. This is what I have made up my mind to, and what I intend to have done, as sure as there is a sky above us. What's more, I'm not going to have any palaver about it. If you don't follow me to my lodgings, where I am going this very minute, I'll peach upon you, by God!"

Without another word, he walked towards the town; and Solomon Fewster, in a tumult of fear and vain passion, followed him to his lodging, and unwillingly gave him his bond. That being done, the Lascar repeated that he might be depended upon for fulfilling his task; and Solomon Fewster took his leave with the consciousness that the basest of dogs considered himself superior to the master who used him.

Early the following morning Mrs. Marvel came down to Gravesend, and all preparations having been made by the Old Sailor, Joshua and Ellen were married. It was the quietest and happiest of weddings. There were but two guests — Mrs. Eliza, in a blaze of red ribbons, and Mrs. Eliza's husband, whose futile efforts to speak in whispers were the only evidences to Joshua and Ellen that the events of the morning were real. Every thing but that irrepressible voice was so hushed and subdued, that it seemed to belong more to a dream than any thing else. But it was a happy dream, marred by no cloud, made bright by perfect love. There was no happier person in the party than Mrs. Marvel.

"Now you are truly my daughter," she whispered to Ellen, "and really belong to me."

"I can't believe that I am awake, mother," said Joshua to Mrs. Marvel, as they two stood a little apart from the others; "yesterday I had no thought of this. I wonder if Dan is thinking of me! When will you tell him?"

"None of them will know, dear, until Ellen comes back, and that won't be until your ship is gone. Mr. Meddler says it will not sail for two days, so your honeymoon will be longer than you expected."

"And father! how surprised he will be!"

"He will approve, my dear, when I tell him all."

When she told him all! That means, thought Joshua, when she tells him about Minnie. But he said nothing aloud in answer. Minnie was in both his and his mother's thoughts, but neither of them mentioned her name.

"Look at her, Josh," said Mrs. Marvel, turning with affectionate pride to where Ellen stood, hanging tearfully upon the Old Sailor's arm; "no man ever had a greater treasure."

Joshua, gazing at the modest figure of his dear little woman, thought of the comparison he had once drawn between Ellen and Minnie. "Minnie is like the sea; Ellen like a peaceful lake." Every thing about her — her dress, her trustful face, the calm light in her eyes — was suggestive of peaceful love, a haven of refuge from the storms of life. She turned to him, and he hurried to her side, and took her arm on his.

"Darling," he whispered, "it seems too wonderful to be real. I am afraid that I shall wake up presently, and find that it is all a dream."

Thank God, that while this world of ours is pulsing with mean ambitions and unworthy strivings, with heartless pleasures and vicious desires, flowers of circumstance such as this bloom sometimes in the lives of the poorest among us.

Dinner was taken in Mrs. Eliza's private parlor which abounded in family relics of great price, among which were especially conspicuous two brown-stone mandarins, who wagged their heads upon the mantleshelf; two large pieces of white coral under glass shades; some stuffed parrots similarly protected from the ravages of time; and an impossible castle made with small shells. It was April weather with all the company, and smiles and tears alternately chased one another. Mrs. Eliza's husband proposed the toast of "The new-married couple," but, attempting to make a speech, could only get out the words, "And may they ever," which he repeated four or five times, without being able to explain himself. However, the toast was drunk not the less cordially, Mrs. Eliza's husband and the Old Sailor giving three times three in hearty sailor fashion. Then, it being nearly time for Mrs. Marvel to go back to Stepney, the Old Sailor rose, glass in hand, and said, —

"Mrs. Marvel, lady, if you was my own mother, my dear, which you couldn't be, seeing that I am old enough to be your father, but if you was my own mother, I couldn't honor you more. Some women are sent into the world expressly to be mothers; you're one of 'em, and a noble one you are, and a credit to Britannia. Here's may Josh and his lass ever be a pride to your heart, lady, as they have ever been, and may Josh be a skipper before he's thirty! And if a rusty old sailor like me, lady, can ever serve you, my dear, I shall be proud to be commanded by such a commander."

With that he drained his glass, and turning it upside down, took Mrs. Marvel's hand and kissed it, like the gallant knight he was. Amid tears and embraces and blessings, Mrs. Marvel took her departure, escorted by the Old Sailor; and the lovers were left to their quiet honeymoon. The "Merry Andrew" did not sail until two days afterwards, as the Old Sailor had said. All too swiftly flew by the hours in that brief time: and Joshua and Ellen found it harder to part than they had ever done before.

"I am pledged to you forever, darling," said Joshua, as they stood together during the last few minutes.

"And I to you, dear."

"I want a curl, Ellen; not to remind me of you, but to have something of you always near me."

She cut off one of her brown curls, and he kissed her and it, and placed it in the Bible Dan had given him.

"How shall I count the days, darling! But I shall see you through all my work. It is time for me to go. My undying faithful love for you. My undying faithful love for Dan. And now, put your arms about my neck, and say 'God bless you, and bring you safely back!'"

"God bless you, and bring you safely back, my dear, my heart's treasure!"

Her strength failed her here, and she was sinking to the ground.

"Take her, sir," said Joshua to the Old Sailor, who was standing a little apart. "May Heaven reward you for all your kindness!" He stooped and kissed her once more, and whispering, "I leave my heart behind me," hurried with uneven steps to the boat in waiting for him.

CHAPTER XXIV.

FALSE FRIEND OR TRUE?

"I WISH Ellen was at home," said Dan to himself, as he sat alone in the parlor which served as his training-room; "the house is quite lonely without her." Joshua had been gone from Stepney for four days, and, knowing how Dan would miss Ellen, Mrs. Marvel had insisted that he should stop at her house during that time. "There will be no one to attend to you, my dear," Mrs. Marvel had said to him; "Mr. Kindred is ill, and Minnie and Susan are fully employed waiting upon him." Dan acknowledged the superior claims of Mr. Kindred on Minnie's and Susan's attention, and consented to stop at Mrs. Marvel's house until Ellen returned. Now that Joshua was gone, however, he could not help thinking it strange that Minnie had not found time to run in and see him, if only for two or three minutes. He expressed this to Mrs. Marvel, who replied that Mr. Kindred was suffering much, she believed, and did not like Minnie to be away from him, loving her so dearly. "But it will be all right, my dear, when Ellen comes back," she said, "she will be able to assist the girls in their nursing." The uneasiness which Dan would have otherwise experienced at not seeing Minnie was allayed by the knowledge that she was doing her duty. Still he was glad when the morning came upon which Ellen was to return; for patient as he was, he was hungering to see Minnie. And now at last he was at home in his own little parlor, waiting almost impatiently for Ellen. He heard a sound in the passage, and he raised his hand in a listening attitude.

"Ellen? No; Susan." The door opened, and Susan entered. Accustomed as he was to Susan's strange manner and to the alterations in it — morose one day and remorsefully affectionate the next — he had never seen her as as he saw her now. Her face was pinched as with some great agony, her hands wandered restlessly about her dress and over one another, her eyes dilated as he remembered them in the old days when she was tormented by the fear that terrible shapes were stealing upon her unaware. Yet, notwithstanding these distressing symptoms of a mind disturbed to its very uttermost, there was something still more painful in her appearance. This was the effort to appear calm and self-possessed, evidenced in the attempts she made to keep her hands still and her eyes from wandering around. But she could not bring color to her white face, nor composure to her quivering lips. No nerves are more difficult to master than those which directly affect the mouth, and many a hard-grained strong-minded man has betrayed himself by a twitching of his lips, which he has found it impossible to control. Dan had not seen Susan for more than a week, and he was appalled at the change in her. His first thought was of Minnie.

"What has happened, Susan?" he cried. "Minnie is not ill?"

He betrayed himself in the tone of anguish in which he made the inquiry. Susan twisted her fingers so tightly together that the blood left them, but she felt no pain.

"Why should Minnie be ill?" she asked. "You have not seen her, then?"

"Thank God!" Dan thought to himself; "it is not anxiety for Minnie that has changed her so."

"And her father, Susan?" he said aloud, more softly.

"Her father!" exclaimed Susan, approaching Dan so that he could take her hand; it was like ice. "Basil! He is stricken almost to death. I don't know what to do; and I am pledged, miserable woman that I am — I am pledged not to speak; not to divulge what I know!"

"Poor Susey!" said Dan soothingly, and in a tone of earnest sympathy, thinking that Susan's last words referred to what the doctor had told him of Basil's heart-disease. "Poor Mr. Kindred! I am grieved to the soul to hear it."

She strove to free her hand from his grasp; but he retained it.

"Tell me about Minnie, Susey," he implored. "Ah, if you knew how I am yearning to see her — how I am yearning to console her!"

At this appeal, so strong a trembling took possession of her, that her words, to any but the acutest sense, would not have been distinguishable.

"You, Dan!" she said, tightening her grasp upon his hand. "You yearning to see her! You yearning to console her! Why?"

"Susey, you will help me when I tell you. You will let me see her when I tell you. I love her!"

"My God!"

A deathlike silence followed, and Dan was almost frightened to break it, but he was constrained by his fears to speak.

"There is a hidden meaning in your words, Susan," he said in hushed tones, "that I cannot fathom. Give me some clew, if you have any love for me."

"I can give you none," she answered hurriedly, "until I am released from my pledge. Do not ask me any thing else — I don't think I am conscious of what I am saying. I will go up to Basil — to Mr. Kindred — and beg of him to see you. What is that?"

It was merely a knock at the street-door; but in Susan's nervous condition the sound was sufficient to cause her to start in alarm from Dan's side.

"Only a knock at the door, Susey. You have overtasked yourself, my dear, with nursing."

Susan hastened to the street-door, and Dan heard a voice ask if Mr. Basil Kindred lived there. "Yes," answered Susan. "Here is a letter for him; is it right?" "Quite right." And taking the letter from the messenger, Susan went upstairs to Basil Kindred's room. She had left the street-door open, and before another minute had passed, sunshine entered the house — sunshine, in the person of Ellen, who, radiant with joy, ran into the house and into the parlor, and clasping Dan round the neck, called him by the dearest of names, and kissed him again and again. What a bright flower she was! What a lovely flower she was! What nameless beauty had passed into her face, that caused Dan to thrill with pride that she was his sister, and caused him to wonder at the same time what change it was that had come over her and added to her loveliness? The sombre aspect of the room was gone; the chill, the fear, the dread of Susan's meaning was gone; the terror that had no reason in it, as far as he could see, was gone. For sunshine had entered the house.

"O my dear, dear Dan!" she cried, shedding tears in the fulness of her joy. "O my darling, darling brother! I am so happy to be with you again!"

She kissed his face a dozen times again, and hid hers on his neck, and kissed that too, until from Dan's heart, infected by her happiness, every particle of fear planted there by Susan's manner had fled. Truly, she was sunshine — the best, the dearest, the warmest.

"My dear, dear Ellen!" said Dan, returning her affectionate embrace, "how happy I am that you are back! I have been thinking how lonely the house is without you. But" — holding her face between his hands and looking at it, bright and blushing and beautiful — "you have grown positively lovely. What have you been doing with yourself these last four days?"

What had she been doing with herself? She laughed softly at the question, then ran and shut the door, and came back and sat on the floor at his feet, tucking up her dress to save it from the dust. She was in such a flutter even then — taking Dan's hand and fondling it — that he waited to speak until she was more composed. Presently she grew quieter, and resting her head on his knees, said, —

"Now, Dan, I am quiet. Ask me questions."

"To commence, then, when did you come back?"

"This very minute."

"Who brought you back?"

"Mr. Meddler."

"The dear old friend! Why didn't he come in to see me?"

"For reasons. He said that we had best be left alone, so that we might chat. He is coming to see you to-night."

"When did Joshua's ship go away?"

"The day before yesterday."

"Why, you little puss, you've been playing truant!"

"Mr. Meddler persuaded me; and yesterday Mr. Meddler and Mrs. Eliza and me went for a ride in the country."

"What a grand young lady you've got to be! And Jo! What about Jo?"

She nestled to him more caressingly; and he, passing his hand over her face, drew it away, with tears upon it.

"Crying, Nell?"

"For happiness, Dan — for very happiness, my dear! What about Jo, you ask. I will speak his exact words — almost his last, dear — " 'My undying faithful love for Dan.' "

"Dear Jo! my dear, dearest brother!"

"That was not all he said, Dan; we were speaking of you all the day — you were never out of our thoughts, never out of his, I am sure. He is the dearest friend, the truest friend, the most faithful, the most constant, that happy man or woman ever had!"

"He is all that you say, dear Ellen, and I thank Heaven for giving him to us."

"Any more questions, Dan?"

"No; I can't think of any."

"Then I must tell you something without being asked," said Ellen: "I am the happiest woman in the world."

She arose, and standing at the back of his chair, clasped him round the neck, folding her hands one in the other, so that he should not see her wedding-ring. Then she inclined her lips to his ear, and was about to whisper the precious secret which made her the happiest woman in the world, when an agonized scream rang through the house. With affrighted looks they turned to each other for an explanation.

"It is Susan," said Dan, all his fears returning. "I have not had time to tell you, Ellen, but her manner just now frightened me. For Heaven's sake assist me up stairs!"

With his crutch under one arm, and his other round Ellen's neck, he went to Basil Kindred's room, and, pushing open the door, entered. Basil Kindred was sitting motionless in his chair, before a table on which were writing-materials; his head was thrown back as if he were asleep; one hand was on his heart, and the other, from which a letter had fallen, was hanging listlessly down. And kneeling by his side was Susan, with a look of horror on her white face. But Minnie! where was Minnie? No one had gone out of the house; if she had come down stairs, Dan must have heard her. He sank into a chair and gazed about him vacantly. It was not that the power of thought had left him, but that he was afraid to think. Susan, rocking herself to and fro, her face turned away, had taken no notice of their entrance.

"Ask her where Minnie is," said Dan to Ellen. He had tried to utter the words two or three times, but his throat was parched; and now his voice sounded so strange to him, that he wondered if he or some one else had spoken.

"Susan!" said Ellen, placing her hand on Susan's shoulder. "Susan, where is Minnie?"

But Susan did not heed her; and Ellen raising her eyes from Susan's face to that of Basil Kindred, retreated appalled to Dan's side. It looked like the face of one to whom death had come suddenly; perfectly peaceful, but terrible to see. Still she found strength to whisper to Dan, "Be strong, my dear, be strong. Shall I run and fetch mother?"

"Mother!" echoed Dan, with the same doubt upon him as to whether he or some one else were speaking. "Mother! Oh! Mrs. Marvel you mean — Jo's mother."

"Yes, dear, Jo's mother and ours. Shall I run and fetch her?"

"No, not yet. What is that paper by his side? Pick it up; give it to me."

Averting her eyes from Basil's face, Ellen picked up the letter and gave it to Dan. "It is Minnie's writing," she whispered.

"Hark!" said Dan.

It was the cockatoo that Joshua had brought home that startled him. It was screeching down stairs, "Dan, Ellen, Minnie! Bread-and-cheese and kisses! and kisses, and kisses!" ending with the usual running fire of kisses, until it lost its breath. When the bird was quiet, Dan looked at the letter in his hand.

"Minnie's writing," he said, trying to read it; but the words swam in his fading sight. "Read it, Ellen; I cannot make it out."

Ellen took the letter from his trembling hand, and read:—

"FATHER,—I have not gone from you because I do not love you, but because it was my fate to do what I have done. I could not resist it. I have nothing to say in justification of my conduct, except the words I heard you use to Joshua when you were telling him of my mother. I came into the room while you were speaking; it was dark, and neither you nor Joshua saw me. What you said of my mother then sank into my mind, and I can never forget it. Do you remember? 'She loved me and sacrificed herself for me. Loving me, she conceived it to be her duty to follow me; she forsook friends and family for me, and I bless her for it. Her devotion, unworldly as it was, was sanctified by love. There is no earthly sacrifice that love will not sanctify.' As my mother did, so I have done. It will be useless searching for me; for when you read this, I shall be hundreds of miles away on the sea. If you guess my secret, keep it for the sake of my good name; and for the sake of my good name do not let any other eyes but yours see this letter. If it were possible for me to have a wish fulfilled, I would pray that I might die before this reaches you. On my knees I ask you to forgive your unhappy
"MINNIE."

No one but Ellen noticed the entrance of Solomon Fewster while the letter was being read; and she, with a warning finger to her lips, restrained him by that gesture from coming forward. So he stood silent and attentive within the doorway. As the words came slowly and painfully from Ellen's lips, each of them cut into Dan's heart like a knife. Ellen had seen his sufferings, and would have ceased reading, but that he motioned her to proceed.

"So, then," said Dan, after a long and painful pause, "Minnie is gone. What have I to live for now? I would have been content if she had only been near me; if I could have heard her voice or the rustle of her dress to assure me of her beloved presence. Without that, my life is dark indeed. But where has she gone?"

He asked the question of himself; but Susan, starting to her feet, answered him.

"Where has she gone? Where else but to sea in the 'Merry Andrew,' with your false friend Joshua Marvel? And the knowledge of it has killed her father!"

"It is false!" cried Dan in a clear ringing voice. "It is false, you bad sister!"

"It is true, Daniel Taylor," said Solomon Fewster in his smooth oily voice. "I have here a letter from a sailor on board the 'Merry Andrew,' informing me that Minnie and Joshua are on the same ship."

At this corroborative testimony, Susan fell upon her knees, and raised her arms.

"Curse that false friend!" she cried.

But Ellen fell at her side, exclaiming, "O Susan, Susan, restrain your tongue! For all our sakes—for my sake! He is my husband!"

Whereat Solomon Fewster, upon whose face there had hitherto been an ill-concealed expression of triumph, crushed the letter he held in his hand, and muttered a bitter curse.

And Dan, folding Ellen in his arms, said,—

"Hush, my sister, hush! Blessings on your wedding-ring! Blessings on your husband and my true friend! We shall live to see him give the lie to slanderous tongues. I have something to live for now—to defend the honor of my brother!"

CHAPTER XXV.

THE DEAD WITNESS.

WHEN Ellen felt the comforting protection of Dan's arms, and heard the words to which he gave utterance in the nobility of his soul, the despair by which she had been overwhelmed vanished like snow before the sun, and left her an unhappy, but not a hopeless woman.

"This, then, was your secret," said Dan to her, as she lay in his arms; "your marriage with Jo. It is the proof of his faithfulness, my dear. For me, I needed none. No heart but mine can judge my friend; no tongue shall malign him unanswered while I am by."

"Good, noble brother," she sobbed, "to comfort me thus in the midst of your own great grief! I do not doubt him; I love him—love him—love him! My faithful darling!

The reproachful looks she cast at Solomon Fewster, no less than the passionate tenderness of her words, stung him to the soul. In truth he had received a severe blow. When the Lascar's letter was delivered to him, and he read the amazing news that Minnie was on board the "Merry Andrew," he exulted in the triumph that awaited him. "Ellen is mine," he thought. "That fool of a whelp has played straight into my hand!" As such mean souls as Fewster's delight in detecting the meanness of others, he was rejoiced at the thought that Joshua had been playing false with Minnie, although, before reading the Lascar's scrawl, he had no suspicion of it. He walked to Dan's house exultant, and deemed himself fortunate in being in time to witness the tragic scene in Basil Kindred's chamber. But when he heard Ellen's declaration that Joshua was her husband, a groan of despair escaped him, and he became almost desperate in the sudden and unexpected dashing down of all his hopes. This feeling lasted but a very little while. His scheming mind was busy at work calculating the chances for and against him, and rays of light soon illumined the darkness. "If the Lascar keeps his word, and Joshua does not return," he thought, "all may yet be well." Even when Ellen flung at him the words, "I love him—love him —love him!" he said to himself, "Believing that he will come back to vindicate himself. We shall see."

Notwithstanding this conflict of thought, his professional instinct led him to the side of the inanimate form of Basil Kindred. He placed his ear and hand to the dead man's heart; and then, with heartless solemnity he lifted the gaunt form in his arms, and laid it on the bed. Susan's eyes asked him, "Dead?"

"Dead," he answered aloud. "It looks like a sudden stroke."

Dan covered his face; and Ellen shudderingly turned her eyes from Solomon Fewster.

"It is not my fault," he said, as if Ellen's looks conveyed an accusation. "Neither this, nor the letter I have received. It would not have been the act of a friend to keep such a thing to himself. What would you have thought of me, if you had discovered that I had received such a letter, and had concealed it?"

"No one accuses you, sir," said Dan sadly. "Indeed how could you be to blame? These things have come of themselves, and from no fault of ours. But," and his eyes kindled, and he laid his hand soothingly on Ellen's head, "we will have no word spoken against Jo. He is dearer to us absent than present; he is dearer to us now, when Susan's voice accuses him, and when you come to add your testimony to hers, than he has ever been before."

"I have not come to add my testimony to hers," said Solomon Fewster, with a well-assumed warmth of manner. "It is no testimony of mine; it is no accusation of mine. This letter surprised and grieved me almost as much as it has you."

"May I see the letter, sir?"

"Certainly." He had almost said "with pleasure," but checked himself in time.

Dan took the letter, which was written an an uneven and dirty piece of paper, and read aloud:—

"MASTER,—Joshua Marvel has run away with a young woman that lives in Daniel Taylor's house—him as trains the birds. They are both of 'em on board the 'Merry Andrew.' I send this by the pilot, and told him that you would pay him for putting it into your hands. My faithful service to you. When I come back, I hope to get what you promised me.

"Aboard the 'Merry Andrew.'"

"There is no name to it," said Dan. "Who sent it?"

"A sailor on the ship," replied Solomon Fewster; "a man who has done odd jobs for me, and whom I have assisted."

"But how does he know me?"

"Through the birds, and through my telling him of you, I suppose. He has been in the street often, and knows who live in the house. He is a faithful honest fellow, and I dare say thought it his duty to tell me about Miss Kindred, so that I might acquaint her friends."

"'When I come back, I hope to get what you promised me,'" said Dan, reading from the letter.

"I promised him money if he brought home some foreign birds," answered Solomon Fewster readily, "such as parrots and cockatoos, and other likely birds, for you to train for me."

Meanwhile Susan had covered the dead man's face, and sat moaning on the floor. To her Dan addressed himself, calling her by name; but it was not until he had repeated it two or three times that her attention was aroused. She took her hands from before her eyes, and looked at him vacantly. There was no sign of intelligence in her face as she spoke; it seemed as if the light of reason had fled, and as if the words she uttered belonged to a lesson she had learned and was forced to repeat.

"I promised him faithfully and sacredly —yes; they are the very words; he made me say them after him, 'Faithfully and sacredly,'—that I would never tell unless his tongue was sealed, and the time came when it was necessary to speak. Is the time come?"

"It is, Susan," said Dan, a new fear at his heart; "it is come."

"Is the time come?" she repeated, turning to the motionless form on the bed, and waiting for the answer in the awful silence that followed. "I was the only one he trusted. Not a soul but me was to come into the room; and they didn't—no I kept my promise faithfully and sacredly. He said to me, 'If I die, and Joshua Marvel has betrayed my daughter, give this book to Dan, and tell him it contains the words of a dying man.'" She rose to her feet, and taking a book which was lying on the desk, gave it to Dan. "Now you can tell him, when he asks you, that I obeyed him to the last, faithfully and sacredly."

A listening expression flashed into her face, and she inclined her body to the door. With feverish haste she ran down stairs and into the street; but returned presently, muttering, "She is not come; there's no sign of her;" and resumed her station by the side of the bed.

It is night, and Dan is sitting alone in his bedroom. An unopened book is before him: it is the book that Susan gave him by Basil Kindred's desire. He has not read a line in it. Between him and Ellen it has been tacitly agreed that whatever is written in it shall be read by them, and by them alone, at night. Another book is also before him: it is a Bible, and it is open.

Dan is waiting for Ellen. The grief that reigns in the house, and in that of Mrs. Marvel, cannot be written here. It is too deep, too overwhelming for expression. Mrs. Marvel is in the house now. All that she knows is that Basil Kindred is dead, and that Minnie is gone: she has no knowledge of the terrible suspicion that hangs like a deadly cloud over the good name of her beloved son. But the news of the death and the flight: they could not be concealed, although no one is aware how they became known: has gone forth into the neighborhood; and little knots of the neighbors have hung about the house all the evening and night, discussing the strange events. Even now, notwithstanding that it is near midnight, a dozen street-doors are open, each with its assemblage of gossippers, chiefly feminine, prattling, not at all sorrowfully, about the wonderful news. There is much head-shaking and raising of hands; but whatever may be the meaning of this play of heads and hands, it certainly does not express grief. The neighborhood is rather bare of historical events; and those that have just occurred are godsends. Given to the neighbors round about the merit of all the kindliness of heart they deserve, they really enjoy their gossip, and show their enjoyment of it. A stranger walking through the street might have reasonably supposed that the dwellers therein had been making general holiday.

Dan's face is very pale as he sits, with no sign of impatience upon him, expectant of Ellen's coming. The door opens, and Mrs. Marvel enters. She draws down the blind — the moonlight has been streaming in upon his face, giving it a more painful pallor than that which rests on it when the moon is shut out — and sits down by his side in silence for a while. She draws his head upon her breast, and kisses him; his arm steals round her neck, and he sheds tears, and kisses her in return; but few words pass between them.

"Susan?" he asks.

"She is in bed, my dear," she answers.

"Has she said any thing?" he asks anxiously.

"She has not spoken, my dear."

He gives a soft sigh of relief. She knows that he is waiting for Ellen, and she will not linger. She kisses him again in her motherly way, and bids him good-night; and soon after Ellen enters the room.

A great change has taken place in Ellen. All the girlishness has gone out of her face, and in its stead is an expression of quiet trustfulness in which there is much sadness, but no doubt. It is as though she is prepared to defend and believe in her husband's honor, though all the world condemn him. She closes the door gently, and draws a chair next to Dan. Then those two faithful souls, to each of whom the bitterest of trials has come, look into each other's eyes, and are comforted by what they see. They exchange no words of sympathy; none are needed from one to the other. They make no effort to conceal their sorrow; it must be borne, and they must suffer. But for Joshua's sake, and for Minnie's, they must be brave and hopeful.

Does Ellen acknowledge this, and in her heart of hearts is she disposed to be generous to the unhappy girl who has brought this great misery upon them? Yes — she feels nothing but pity for Minnie. The influences which actuate mental feeling are so delicate and various, that it is difficult even to the most profound of pathognomists to dissect the commonest of motives, and rightly account for it. We all pride ourselves in a greater or less degree, upon our knowledge of character, and believe that we know full well what prompted So-and-so to do such-and-such a thing. But in truth, in nothing do we show more ignorance than in arrogating to ourselves the power of divining character and motive. Strive as we may to be just and calm and reasonable — strive as we may to banish for the time the small feelings of uncharitableness which we are conscious of harboring, and which necessarily warp our judgment — we must from very necessity argue in a certain measure from our own point of view. Otherwise we should be infallible, and juries would never return a wrong verdict, and judges would never commit an error of judgment. Otherwise rogues would have their due; and some of them would not, as they do now, live in fine houses, and eat and drink of the best. It is impossible to put yourself in another man's place.

Most women in Ellen's situation would have thought of Minnie with inexorable animosity. Not so Ellen. The knowledge that Dan loves Minnie would alone have been sufficient to disarm harsh or bitter feeling. But that influence is not necessary. She has the firmest faith in Joshua's honesty and virtue, and firmly believes that when he returns home, please God, all will be explained. In the mean time, her duty is clear. Joshua's good name is at stake. In face of all adverse circumstance and sentiment, she must uphold it, and defend it if necessary.

Thus it is that as she and Dan sit looking sadly at each other, Dan is comforted by what he sees, and she is no less so. Their mutual faith in the purity of the absent dear ones is inexpressibly consoling to them. Unconsciously each gives to the other strength to bear the bitterness of the shock. But when their eyes turn to the book which they are to read to-night, they hesitate and tremble, What may not those dumb pages reveal! The place, the time, and all its surrounding circumstances are solemn and mournful. The presence of Death; the silence that strikes greater terror than brazen tongue of accusation; the gloom of the mean apartment, in the corners of which lurk fears made awful by the black shadow which inwraps them— these things and their influence impress with a deeper sadness those two young hearts. What wonder that they hesitate and tremble as they look upon the book in which the words of their dead friend are recorded? Joshua is on the sea, and each moment adds to the distance that separates him from his friends; Minnie is gone also; Basil, alas, is dead; and all that remains to light the mystery is the dumb witness that lies before them. But hesitation soon yields to indomitable faith.

"Ellen," says Dan, laying his hand upon the book, "perhaps the worst of this day's trials is here. Are you prepared for it?"

"Yes, Dan," answers Ellen with a steady light in her eyes.

"Susan's words were very dreadful," continues Dan; "but she does not know Jo as we know him. Come, we will read what is here written. And if it accuses your dear husband and my dear friend, our hearts will defend him. His memory will be dearer to us because he is unjustly accused; and we will wait hopefully and patiently for his return, please God, and never, never waver."

And drawing Ellen closer to him, Dan opened the book, and in a subdued voice read what follows.

———◆———

CHAPTER XXVI.

BASIL KINDRED'S DIARY.

I MAKE this record for various reasons, the strongest of which is the conviction that I have not long to live. Although my mind is in a state of sad confusion, what I write shall be no phantasy of the brain. I pledge myself to this. And I pledge myself also to throw down my pen when the suspicion comes upon me that, because of my fears and my agony, I am writing what is not strictly the fact. If I do not thus pledge myself, and death comes upon me unaware, this mute witness might be the cause of bringing undeserved unhappiness to persons whose conduct towards me has been wonderfully good and noble.

Let me read what I have written. Yes, it is clear, and it gives me the assurance that, to-day at least, I shall be able to express myself clearly. I pause over every word. I am careful of the construction of every sentence. For I must be just. I could not rest in my grave if my fear spoke instead of my reason.

What is it that immediately prompts me to commence this record? A letter— signed by no name, delivered by I know not whom. The writing is strange to me; I have never before seen its like. It lies before me now, upon my desk.

It is night. I am alone, and Minnie is at Mrs. Marvel's house. Let me carry back my thoughts to the time when I first made the acquaintance of the good people with whom I have lived for years— for many happy years—during which Minnie has grown from a child to a woman.

I had left her at home, poor child! hungry and unhappy. She had asked me in the morning for food, and I had none to give her, nor any money to buy it for her. The previous night we had eaten our last piece of bread. I went out of our little room, telling her I was going to get food for her. I toiled in the streets all the day, and was not fortunate enough to receive a penny. My sufferings were great, almost too great for human endurance, but I was compelled to bear them for the sake of Minnie. Nothing but the consciousness that, if I went home without food, my child might die from want, supported me. Late in the afternoon I was in the streets declaiming, when some boys among the crowd which surrounded me threw stones at me. One of the stones wounded me in the forehead, and I think I must have fainted. Two persons came to my assistance — a woman and a boy. The woman was Susan Taylor, the boy was Joshua Marvel. They assisted me home, and the next thing I remember was Susan bathing my wound and making tea for me. The boy Joshua had brought in some food for us. My gratitude was great, for his charity had saved my child. I blessed him that night before he left us.

From that time he was a constant visitor to our wretched lodging, and from that time I never knew want. I grew to love him. He was to be a sailor, and it was a pleasure to me to listen to the enthusiastic outpourings of his mind. He had a friend, Dan, whom I had not then seen; and the loving manner in which he spoke of that friend, seemed to me to be an assurance of the goodness of his own heart. He was the principal subject of conversation between me and my daughter, and she, dear child! grew to love him too. Before he went to sea, the woman Susan Taylor — the sister of Joshua's friend Dan — came to live in the house in which I lodged, and was very kind to us. Joshua went to sea, and I felt a void in my heart as if I had lost a son. Minnie grieved as much as I did — perhaps more — for she had never had a companion, and Joshua's visits were looked upon as a kind of holiday. We consoled ourselves for our loss by speaking of him often and by looking forward to his return home. Minnie derived much pleasure from a childish conceit in which she indulged. She had a shell, and she used to place it to her ear and listen to the soft singing, to remind her of the sea and of Joshua, she said. I thought it was a pretty fancy; but had I feared then what I fear now, I would have crushed the shell to powder beneath my heel.

Some time after Joshua left, circumstances occurred which caused me to remove to the house of Joshua's friend Dan. I was loath to do so when it was first proposed by Susan; but the argument used by Susan, who was devoted to us, that Minnie would have a companion of a suitable age in her sister Ellen, prevailed upon me. That was the sole cause of my removal to the house in which I am now living. I had reason to be grateful for the change. Minnie, who used to have many unhappy moods, was happy and cheerful in the society of her new friends. And I was no less so. I found that Joshua's parents were good simple people whom to know was to love. A girl could have had no better companion than Ellen, who is one of the pearls of womanhood. But before them all, I learned to love Dan. I had never met with so pure a mind, with so constant a nature. A cripple almost from his birth, it seemed as if the good God had endued him with the purest thought and the sweetest disposition to compensate for the misfortune he had met with. He might truly say, with our great poet, "Sweet are the uses of adversity."

Some happy years passed, during the whole of which Joshua was at sea. At rare intervals letters from him were received, and the perusal of these letters gave us all — for we were like one family — the greatest pleasure. At length he returned. It is not long since — but a few short weeks — that he arrived home. He was expected, but not so soon. His coming was eagerly looked for — he was the hero of the two houses. The night of his return was memorable. It was Christmas-eve, and we were all assembled in Mrs. Marvel's kitchen, celebrating the blessed time with joyful, grateful hearts. Minnie persuaded me to read a play. I chose the "Tempest," that loveliest creation of the poet's mind. She is not present, but I can see her as she unloosed her hair and stood before me, bright and bewitching as Ariel could have been. "Do you love me, master?" she asked. I answered in the words of Prospero, "Dearly, my delicate Ariel." . . . I resume my pen, which I had laid aside, thinking that I was being betrayed by my feelings, and that I was indulging in an exaggeration of sentiment. But no. I have read over what I have written, and I am satisfied.

I was in the midst of the lovely story when a knock came at the street-door. Minnie went out of the room to open the door. A silence followed. Presently a scream struck fear to all our hearts. We ran up stairs, and found that Joshua, having returned sooner than he was expected, had been stabbed by a coward's hand when his foot was on the threshold of his home. The house of joy was turned into a house of mourning. I have no need to set down here the events of the next few weeks, that bring me to the present day. Sufficient to say that Joshua lingered for some time between life and death, and to the joy of all of us was declared out of danger three weeks ago. I have been confined to my chamber with my old complaint nearly the whole of that time. Susan has attended to me chiefly; for seeing Minnie's anxiety to assist Mrs. Marvel in her trouble, I have allowed her to be much away from me. Although Minnie has not spoken of it, I have learned that she, according to the doctor's statement, saved Joshua's life by pressing her lips to the wound in his neck and stopping in some measure the effusion of blood, which might have been fatal to him. It gave me pleasure to hear this; for no service, purposed or accidental, could pay for the kindness we have received from the good people with whom we have lived so happily.

So! I have temperately set down all that has occurred up to the present, or rather up to four days ago, when I received the letter which lies before me now. I will not attempt to describe the effect it had upon me. It seemed to change the current of my blood. If there be truth in it, is there, can there be, truth in man? Before pinning it in the book, I copy it word for word: —

"A well-wisher warns Mr. Basil Kindred that Joshua Marvel is playing false with his daughter. The writer has no purpose to serve in writing this, and does not wish to be known. The information he gives is given in kindness. Minnie Kindred loves Joshua Marvel, who takes every secret opportunity that presents itself to prosecute his bad designs upon a simple girl. It is right that Mr. Basil Kindred should be made acquainted with the real character of the hypocrite, who is fair to a man's face and false behind his back."

With some girls and with some people, the best way to do with such a letter would be to show it to those concerned. But I dare not do this. It would bring unhappiness and mistrust among these confiding good people.

And I fear for Minnie. I fear that the writer, whoever he may be, is right when he says that my darling child loves Joshua. And I, knowing her nature, feel that if unhappily she has contracted a love for Joshua, the discovery of it in this manner would bring misery upon her for life. No; she must not see the letter — must not have a suspicion of it.

All Joshua's previous life contradicts the accusation. It was the simplicity and kindliness of his nature that attracted me to him. If he is fair to a man's face and false behind his back, he is false to his friend Dan; and I, knowing Dan's heart, know that there could be no blacker treachery than that; for I have at times suspected that Dan loves my Minnie. Yes; I may tell that secret to this mute friend, although I have never otherwise whispered it. On one particular night when we were all assembled together, reading a letter from Joshua, and when Mr. Praiseworthy Meddler was tracing the course of Joshua's ship upon the map, I detected in Dan's manner something more than a feeling of friendship for Minnie. Since then, other small evidences have forced themselves upon me, and I have not been unprepared for the disclosure of Dan's love. Would it be a good thing for Minnie? Yes; if she returned his love. Although he is a cripple, she could have no better mate: he is all that is noble and good, and he would make her happy, if she could learn to love him.

If she could learn to love him! These words have caused me to think if Minnie could ever *learn* to love — have caused me to ask myself if love is not intuitive to her, as it was to her mother. My anxiety is deepened by the thought. I am afraid to think further.

Every thing depends upon Joshua. If she loves him, and he encourages her, he is false to his friend, false to honor. My duty is plain. I must watch first, and discover if or there be any foundation for the accusation, if it emanates from spite and vindictiveness.

I close the book and lock it in my desk, for fear other eyes than mine should see what I have written.

Notwithstanding the bodily pain I have suffered, I have so far controlled it as to visit Mrs. Marvel's house during the last three days, and to sit with the young people as if nothing ailed me. I am beset with doubt. I know not what to think. I have watched every look, every movement; and I am afraid that my anxiety has caused me to be uncivil and abrupt. I do not think that any one but Mrs. Marvel has noticed my anxiety or any change in me; but I have observed her sometimes look at me questioningly, as if wondering at my changed manner.

That Minnie has an affection for Joshua is certain: she strives to prevent it being observed, and I think no one suspects her. if there is any secret understanding between her and Joshua, I have not discovered it. He treats her kindly and affectionately, but he is chiefly attentive to Ellen. But still the letter says that he avails himself of " every secret opportunity" to see her. If that be true, it is not likely that he would betray himself in the presence of his friends. I must act upon the results of my observation. I must endeavor to keep Minnie from visiting Mrs. Marvel's house so frequently; it may prevent her feelings from ripening into love. In a few weeks Joshua will be away, and then all danger will be over for a time. I am, indeed, loath to believe any wrong of him; he seems to have preserved the simplicity of character and the goodness of heart for which I used to admire him.

I am glad I commenced this record; for my thoughts are often very confused, and my memory is impaired.

Although my uneasiness increases with respect to Minnie, I have heard good news: Joshua is engaged to be married to Ellen. Do I need any other proof of Joshua's honesty? It would be monstrous if I did; and yet I cannot regard him with the old feelings of affection, for Minnie is unhappy, and he is the cause. One day I accuse myself of injustice towards him; another day I almost hate him, and curse the circumstance that made me and Minnie acquainted with him. Would to God that he were gone! Every hour that he stops is an additional agony to me.

Minnie has been sullen and rebellious because I have sometimes prevented her from going to Mrs. Marvel's house. She has not always obeyed me. I must speak more firmly to her; "I must be cruel only to be kind."

A day of agony. I have not been able to leave my room. Minnie was with me all the morning: but before she came to me, I had received another communication, in the same handwriting as the last. It contained but a few words, — "The friend who warned Mr. Basil Kindred before, warns him again. Joshua Marvel is a smooth-tongued villain. In his character of a hero he is playing false with two simple girls at one time."

Who can this friend be? I have no friends out of these two houses. But whoever he is, he is right, I fear, as to Minnie, and may be right as to Joshua — the mere writing of the name gives me pain. The receipt of the few words I have just copied opened my wounds, and they bled afresh. I detained Minnie with me all the morning; and when she wanted to quit the room, I invented pretexts to induce her to remain. She was not at her ease; I saw that plainly. Once or twice I am afraid that I spoke harshly to her; but she was painfully submissive — almost humble. At length she rose, with the intention of leaving the room. I asked her where she was going. She answered, to see Mrs. Marvel. I grasped her hand, and bade her resume her seat. She asked me why I did not wish her to go to Mrs. Marvel's house; and when I said it was because I thought she troubled the Marvels too much, all the hardness and obstinacy in her nature came into play, and she answered in a voice that might have come from lips of stone, that that was not my reason, and that I was hiding something from her. For the first time I betrayed myself. I asked her if she was not hiding a secret from me; and she returned me an evasive reply. She left the room, and I was about to follow her, when I was seized with a terrible dizziness. My strength deserted me, and I was afraid I was about to die. The attack passed away, and left me as weak as a child.

I pause in my recital of the day's events to make two declarations. The first is, that I am certain, from my sensations this day, that a sudden shock would be fatal to me; I am afraid that my heart is diseased. The second is, that if I die suddenly, and Joshua has betrayed my child, he is my murderer in the sight of God and man — as much my murderer as if he were to come into the room this moment and plunge a dagger in my heart!

How awful are these words! As I look at them, they seem to rise in judgment against me. "Thou shalt not bear false witness against thy neighbor." Am I bearing false witness against Joshua? Am I to be the cause of bringing unhappiness to friends but for whom Minnie and I might have perished from hunger? Still do I cling to the hope that lives in uncertainty. Still do I strive to believe that my fears have grown without reason, and that they are like the monstrous shadows that mock us on the walls and ceiling of a room whose only light is a flickering fire. Above every other consideration, I must be just. If no eye but mine reads these lines, I shall have done no harm in writing them. If it should happily result that Minnie's love is not deeply rooted — if it should happily result that Joshua has not been tampering with her affections, and that he goes away spotless, as I would fain believe him to be — let me determine to destroy this record. It *must* be done. Determining to do this — *willing* it with the whole strength of my mind — I shall be able to do it even before I am stricken down, if it be fated that I am to die suddenly. Should it be otherwise — should he prove to be false — this record shall remain as an evidence of his treacherous heart.

When Minnie left me, and I discovered that I was too feeble to follow her, I thought, Oh, if I had some one I could trust — some one to help me! And as I thought, Susan entered the room. In her I confided; to her I told my fears; and after pledging her sacredly to secrecy, I showed her the letter I have received. She has promised to watch Joshua, and she will be faithful. Now I shall know whether I have cause for fear; now I shall know whether Joshua Marvel is false or true.

I do not think I shall ever be able to leave my room. It is more than a week since I wrote in this book. True, I have had nothing to say until now. Minnie has been tender and affectionate to me; she has been absent at various times during the day; but when she is with me, she is all that a child should be. I have left her free to come and go, knowing that Susan was watching that she should come to no harm. I sometimes think that she is fighting with her soul; for a new-born sadness has settled upon her face. Yesterday I saw her sitting by the window, with her hands clasped in her lap, and a deep-seated sorrow in her eyes. I have seen her mother sit so in the old days long, long ago — in the old days that seem to belong to another life. I had been asleep; and when I awoke, I saw Minnie wrestling with her sorrow. I called to her twice before she heard me; and when she came to my side, she had the air of one who has been suddenly aroused from a dream. Darling child, I pray to God to give you strength to bear affliction, if it comes to you! If any sacrifice that I could make would lessen your pain, how gladly would I make it!

Last night Susan slept with her, and in her sleep heard her murmur Joshua's name. It proves that he is in her thoughts; but it proves nothing more. I hear a step upon the stairs. Good-night, dumb witness of my grief!

How shall I commence? All my pulses are throbbing with rage and apprehension. Proof has come. Joshua Marvel is a damned false-hearted villain!

I write with pain and difficulty. My heart is beating so violently, that I am obliged to stop to calm myself, for fear of consequences. Calm myself! Can I do it? I must. I will lay down my pen, and wait until I have subdued the tumult of passion which rages within me.

So! I am calmer. It is well that I stopped, or what the doctor warned me of might have occurred. And I want to live — Oh, how I want to live!

Susan is sitting in the room with me; for I am afraid of being alone, to-night of all nights. I am glad that I have kept this record; I am glad that, if I die suddenly, the guilt of an infamous recreant will be brought to light by means of this evidence.

About noon to-day — I am writing this at night — Minnie brought a doctor to my bedside. I had steadily refused to see one before; for I knew what I was suffering from, and I knew that the doctor's art was powerless to cure me. But I was not displeased that Minnie brought him; it was her anxiety and love — for she does love me — that caused her to disobey my wishes. I sent Minnie out of the room, so that I might speak to the doctor in private. He told me nothing new; as well as suffering from rheumatism and low fever, I have heart-disease. He told me what I already knew — that I might die suddenly, without any other forewarnings than those I have already received. He went away after uttering the usual platitudes. Late in the afternoon I fell asleep; and when it was dark, I heard a step in the room; asking who was there, Joshua's voice answered me. I spoke to him bitterly out of the bitterness of my heart, and he answered me quietly and feelingly. He said he had noticed with sorrow that I was changed; that he was not conscious of having done any wrong. He begged that I would be to him as I was before he first went to sea, and when I had blessed him. I could not see his face; but his voice was tremulous with emotion; and when he appealed to my sense of justice, I softened to him, for I had no evidence against him but the suspicion which had been created by the warning letters I had received. I had it first in my mind to tell him all; but my pride and my consideration for Minnie's feelings restrained me. Instead of doing that, I resolved to probe him; and, that my agitation might not betray me, I refused to have a light. We spoke in the dark. I elicited from him that he was engaged to Ellen, whom he declared he loved before all the world. Upon that, his hand in mine, I wished him the happiness that faithful love deserves. When, after that, Minnie became the subject of conversation, there was a hesitancy in his manner that aroused my slumbering suspicions. Then I spoke so plainly to him — though telling him nothing about the letters — that he could not have misunderstood me. I told him that my heart was diseased, and that I could not live much longer. I told him that I was tortured by anxiety for Minnie's future; that she needed guidance and control; that she knew only one duty — the duty of love; and that she could scarcely understand that, under certain circumstances, love may be sinful. I told him that she was changed, that she was hiding something from me, and that I was afraid some such love as I had spoken of had come to her. And when I asked him if he knew or suspected to whom that love was given, he was silent, and did not answer me. Was not that silence sufficiently damning? I asked him if he were concealing anything from me, and he equivocated. What should he conceal from me? he asked. At that answer I almost gave up hope; but my child's happiness was at stake, and I persevered. I resolved to tell him the story of my life, that he might learn how Minnie's mother sacrificed herself for love; that he might learn what Minnie's nature, being like her mother's, really was; and to what extent she would go where her heart was engaged. It was an appeal to him for mercy. How has he treated that appeal? I told him the story of my life; I laid bare my heart to him. I lived over again the agony of my wife's death. I told him that Minnie was like her mother, without her mother's teaching; that the impulse of her mind was under the control of the impulse of her heart; that those who knew it must guide her gently, tenderly; and that if any man betrayed her, he would have to answer for it at the Judgment-seat. Could tongue speak more plainly than mine did? Could any man who was not totally devoid of honor and humanity have listened to my trembling words unheedingly? I appreciate at its proper worth the code of morality by which many heartless men are guided; but I never believed it possible that man could be so base as Joshua has proved himself to be. Here is a proof of his villany. Within a few minutes after my story was ended — within a few minutes after he left my room, crying in sympathy with me — he was fondling Minnie in the passage below. Susan can prove it. They were in the dark, and Susan came up from the kitchen with a lighted candle, and discovered them. Their hands were in each other's clasp; and when Joshua Marvel saw the light and Susan, he turned away his head, so that she should not see his face. They parted on the moment; and Susan, not appearing to notice them, passed them by, and, faithful woman as she is, came straight to me, and told me what she had seen.

"Fair to a man's face, and false behind his back" — ay, that he is! But not for him, for whom my indignation can find no fitting name, do I care. For Minnie are all my thoughts. How can I act towards her? How can I warn her? Tell her that he is false! that he is lying to her! that to listen to him is shame! She would smile at my words; and if she dared not scorn, would pity the tongue that uttered the calumny. I must think; I must think. In the mean time, she must not be allowed to go about without being closely watched. Susan will do that for me. It will not be for long. He will be away soon, thank God; and when he is gone, I can resolve what to do. Perhaps he may never come back. With all my heart I pray — No, I dare not pen the words. The thought of Ellen and Dan, and his gentle mother, stops me. I give them here my heartfelt thanks, for all their noble kindness to me and Minnie. But for him — the treacherous son, the false friend, the perjured lover — I vow never willingly to look upon his face again.

My passion has exhausted me. I turn to the first page of this record, and I see there the pledge that I would throw down my pen when the suspicion came upon me that because of my fear and my agony I am writing what is not strictly the fact. I read over what I have written this night; and I solemnly declare that every word is true, as I hope to meet my wife in heaven! But a few words more. When I return this book to my desk, I shall tell Susan to place it in Dan's hands, if I die before Minnie is safe. A step upon the stairs! It is my darling child's! —

Another day of misery has passed, and I have received farther damning proof that Joshua Marvel is tampering with Minnie's affections. In my present state of mind, it will be best for me to write down Susan's statement, word for word. I cannot trust myself. I call her to me, and bid her relate, without passion, and without prejudice, what she saw to-day. What follows is from her own lips.

SUSAN'S STATEMENT.

"I noticed this morning that Minnie was more restless than usual. Whenever I looked at her, she looked at me back again; as much as to say, what do you mean by staring at me in that way? I couldn't help thinking that she knew I was watching her and I felt uncomfortable. But I watched her for all that, as I promised you I would. When she went out of the room, I made believe that I wanted to go out too. Now I think of it, she must have gone out of the room on purpose to try me; because the second time I followed her, she turned upon me in the passage, and looked at me in such a manner that I was frightened. Between eleven and twelve o'clock I was in the kitchen, helping to cook the dinner; and when I came up stairs, Minnie was gone from the house. I ran round to Mrs. Marvel's, and she wasn't there. Scarcely knowing what to do, I slipped on my bonnet and shawl, and went into the streets to look for her. All at once it came into my mind, that if I should find her anywhere it would be at the docks, where Joshua's ship was, and where Joshua was working. I ran there as hard as ever I could, and just at the entrance of the docks I caught sight of Minnie. I was regularly out of breath, and my only fear now was that she might see me. So I kept out of the way as much as I could, and followed her quietly. When she got near the ships she stopped short; and presently Joshua, who was looking over the side of his ship, as if he was expecting some one, came down to where she was standing, and began talking to her.

He seemed a little bit uneasy — perhaps, because there were so many people about, and because, I thought, he didn't want Minnie to be noticed, for all the workmen and sailors were staring at her. They went up a plank on to Joshua's ship; and Joshua had his arm round her waist. They stood by the side of the ship, looking towards the river, talking together. I never took my eyes off them, and I am certain — though, of course, I couldn't hear them — that they were talking of something very particular. All at once I lost sight of them; they had gone to a part of the ship where I couldn't see them. I think they must have been out of my sight for nearly a quarter of an hour; and when they returned, Joshua looked to the place where I was standing by the side of some large cases, and came off the ship towards me. I was frightened that he would catch me, and I ran away. When I was safe, I turned, and saw Joshua and Minnie together coming from the ship. Minnie walked out of the docks by herself, and I followed her home, and waited in the street a little before I went into the house after her. But I no sooner got inside the door, than Minnie met me in the passage; she hadn't taken her bonnet off. I didn't seem to notice her; but she came into the kitchen after me. 'Where have you been, Susan?' she asked me, so sudden-like that I was almost taken off my guard. 'Out for a walk,' I said. 'Have you been to the docks?' she asked me. 'No,' I said; but I felt my face turning red as I told the story. I thought she was done with her questions; but she soon commenced again. 'Are you going out again?' she asked. I said, No, I wasn't. '*I* am,' she said; 'I am going out for a walk.' And she ran upstairs and out of the house. I didn't know what to do; and I came to you, and you told me not to watch her any more to-day."

It is evident that Minnie is suspicious of Susan, and I know that Susan is no match for her. Ill as I am, I can see but one thing to do — I must wait and hope. That the innate goodness and purity of Minnie's heart will keep her from harm, is my earnest prayer. I will be, if possible, more tender and loving to her than I have hitherto been. I dare not speak plainly to her; I believe, if I did, that she would go away from us, and we should never see her again. If I were well, it would be different. I should take her from here until Joshua Marvel had sailed.

What can I say of him? It is clear that Minnie went to the docks by appointment, and that he expected her. I have appealed to him vainly. After what passed between us — after the knowledge he has gained that I am aware of his treachery — he has shown himself, in this clandestine meeting with Minnie, to be totally devoid of honor. I leave him to his conscience and to the judgment of his friends. May occasion never come for them to learn how they are deceived in him!

Two days more have passed. In a week Joshua Marvel's ship sails. I believe from that moment I shall begin to grow better. Then I shall make new plans for the future. The future! Alas, my future on earth will soon come to an end! See how I contradict myself. One moment saying that I shall begin to get better when Joshua is gone; the next, that my end must soon come. But 'tis in the nature of such a state of feeling as mine to be hopeful one minute, and despondent the next. The best thing for Minnie would be, that she should be impressed and touched by Dan's love for her — of the existence of which I am sure, having thought much of Dan's manner towards her — and that she should consent to marry him. It is not certain that she loves Joshua; after all, nearly the whole — nay, the whole — of the evidence is circumstantial. It is but natural that she should have an affection for him; the nature of the intimacy, his kindness to her and me, the very circumstances attendant upon his return home, make that a necessity. Indeed, indeed, it would be most unnatural if an affection did not exist between them. The mere writing of these words is comforting to me. I know that they are at variance with much that I have previously written; but at one time I am writing out of my despair, at another time out of my hope. I write now out of my hope. Joshua Marvel will soon be gone, and I am assured that no farther meeting has taken place between him and Minnie. Minnie's behavior to me has been most kind. She is growing more and more like her mother every day. There appears to have arisen in her some consciousness that my claims to her love are more binding upon her than those of any other person. I have passed some very happy hours with her.

She said a strange thing to me this morning. "Father, do you think I should make a good actress?" The question startled me, for it brought back to me some memories of my past life. Minnie, when a little child, was often in her mother's arms in the theatre where I happened to be playing; her mother would be waiting for me perhaps, and would not leave our little darling alone in the room. Minnie has no definite remembrance of those times and circumstances, I think; but shadowy impressions of the scenes she then almost unconsciously witnessed are stamped upon her mind. Upon this theme I questioned her somewhat curiously this morning, and found that these experiences had had their effect upon her, and that she has vague remembrances of beautiful creatures beautifully dressed, walking in gardens in the midst of light. Ah, if she were aware of the reality! If she knew what poor struggling men and women these beautiful creatures were, and what a mockery were the beautiful dresses and the lovely gardens in which they lived their artificial lives! But I did not disenchant her. Life is bitter enough; if a gleam of brightness can be thrown upon it by the indulgence of a harmless fancy, it is good. In the midst of our conversation, Minnie suddenly left the room, and in about half an hour returned completely metamorphosed. She went out of the room a fair lovely girl; she returned a dark tawny woman, looking at least half a dozen years older; but still beautiful, very beautiful. I gazed at her in wonder. By what means had she effected such a marvellous change in herself? She explained, first asking me if I knew her again. Knew her again? Could she by any disguise hide herself from my knowledge? But suppose I had only seen her once in my life, she asked, then did I think I should have known her again? I did not exactly know how to answer that, and although she pressed me to give her an answer, I could not. I was delighted to see her in the new light in which she presented herself to me; it was almost an assurance that some portion of my fears was groundless. She explained to me that in the box containing her clothes were some remnants of the wherewithals I once used in my profession, such as colors and a few wigs. I had forgotten them, not having had occasion for them for so long a time. And she confessed that she had often amused herself with these things. Indeed, in the middle of her explanation she stooped and hid herself from my sight, and rose in the wig I used to wear when I played "Hamlet." She had tucked up her beautiful hair with the skill of an actress, so that it was completely hidden by the wig; and as she stood before me, I saw in her some shadowy resemblance of myself as I was in days gone by. I could not but be delighted with her light humor; it almost entirely dispelled my fears. Then she took off the wig, and washed the color out of her face, and sat by my bedside quietly. I am used to her variable moods, and therefore, although I was sorry to see that her sportiveness had fled, and that a more serious mood took its place, I was not surprised. Never in all her life has she shown me such tenderness as she exhibited towards me this day. "I shall always love you, father," she said to me, more than once. Dear child! Darling treasure of my heart! All good angels guard you.

The cup of happiness is dashed from my lips. Something so strange, so unexpected, has happened, that, simple as it is, I scarcely know how to set it down, or what to augur from it.

Minnie has gone!

Where — for how long — for what purpose — I do not know. She has gone from her home, from me.

Early this morning, while I was waiting to see her dear face, I was thinking of something strange that occurred in the night, wondering whether it formed part of my dreaming fancies or had actually occurred. It was this:—

The house was very quiet. It was the most solemn part of the night, when troubled life is most like peaceful death. The healthfulness of dreamless sleep is denied me, as it is denied to all men whose minds are harassed. For many weeks I have not enjoyed an hour's repose, and so confused are the images that pass through my mind when I am alone, that I am often in doubt whether the scenes in which I am taking part are real or fanciful. I was in this condition last night at the time of which I am writing. While I was thinking or dreaming of Minnie and her mother, I heard a soft footfall in the room. The impression that some one was in the room was strong upon me, and when I felt a kiss upon my face, and my pillow being smoothed by a gentle hand, I was almost convinced that it was Minnie. The presence remained with me for I know not what length of time; I do not know when I lost it, or when it departed, but when I called "Minnie!" no voice answered me. When daylight came, I determined to ask Minnie if it was she who had entered my room in the night. I waited impatiently for her appearance, but she did not come. Susan came, and I asked her if Minnie was down yet; Susan had not seen her. I bade her go and tell Minnie to come to me; she returned and said that Minnie was not in bed, nor in any part of the house. As Susan told me this, she came to my bedside, and, stooping, picked up a paper which must have fallen from beneath my pillow. There was writing on it — Minnie's writing. It was addressed to me, and it told me that Minnie had left me, not from any want of love, but because she was miserable and unhappy. She said said she knew that she had been watched; that a feeling she could not control had compelled her to leave for a time; that she would write again or see me in a few days; and she begged me to believe that no one but herself was to blame for what she had done. She asked me, too, not to be anxious as to how she would live, for she had provided for that.

The first thing I did was to desire Susan to lock the door, and on no account to allow a person to enter the room. For the thought flashed upon me, that if it were known that Minnie had left her home clandestinely, her good name would suffer. She had done a foolish thing,— ay, it was a cruel thing to leave me thus; but it was done in all innocence, I am sure, and in ignorance of the world's judgment upon such an act. I, her father, must protect her good name; no breath of slander must be allowed to touch her. Therefore I judged it imperative that the secret of her departure should be known only to Susan and me. I gave Susan the letter to read, and when her tears were dried, my plan was formed. It is well for me that I have such an attached and faithful friend as Susan. Without her, I should be helpless indeed. I explained my wishes to her, and she promised to obey them implicitly — and she will. The Marvels and Dan and Ellen are to be told that Minnie cannot leave me; that my illness has increased, and I require her constant attendance. And on no pretence whatever is any one of them to be allowed to come into the room. The door is to be always locked, and when Susan goes out of the room, she is to lock the door and take the key with her. I am afraid that Susan judges Joshua even more harshly than I do; for she suggested that she should watch his movements, in the expectation that some clew might be gained. Her evidence of to-day is all in his favor. She ascertained that he went this morning direct from home to his ship; that he worked there for six hours, and that he came home direct to Ellen. No, I cannot associate him with Minnie's disappearance. I have been thinking as coherently as I could as to what is most likely the cause of her leaving home, and the most hopeful conclusion I can arrive at is this: That Minnie has an attachment for Joshua, which, in the face of his engagement with Ellen, she feels it is her duty to subdue; that it is painful to her to be a witness of Ellen's happiness; and that, fearful lest she should betray her attachment, she has left the neighborhood until Joshua has gone upon his voyage.

I am re-assured. This conclusion is reasonable as well as hopeful. I must bear with the misery of her absence — ah, how I miss her beloved face! — in the hope that my darling will return to me when he is gone, and that she will regain her peace of mind, and be to me as she has hitherto been; chastened perhaps, but not entirely unhappy.

Are you thinking of me, Minnie? Can you realize the depth of my love for you, my dearest? If such a thing exists in the flesh as spiritual communion with those we love, you will know, darling treasure of my heart! that my thoughts, my blessings, my prayers are with you now.

In two days Joshua's ship will sail, and then my darling will come home. The secret of her departure has been well kept. No one knows or suspects. There is a rare faithfulness in Susan's nature. If she possessed all the graces of womanhood, she could not be nobler than she is.

I need all my strength to enable me to bear with Minnie's absence; so constantly do my thoughts dwell upon her, that at certain times I lose consciousness of what has taken place, and detect myself listening for her footstep. At other times I am engrossed by the idea that many years have passed since I last saw Minnie. When this impression is upon me, Minnie appears to me not as a woman, but as a child.

Joshua Marvel has gone. Thank God! Now I may expect Minnie to return. Any moment may bring her to my loving arms again. I am haunted by the ghosts of footsteps on the stairs. I know afterwards that my fancy has conjured them up; but if they were real, I could not hear them more plainly. They are Minnie's footsteps always. I hear them first in the passage leading from the street — I stop and listen. Softly yet swiftly they come nearer and nearer to me, till they are outside my door. Then I say to myself, "She is lingering for a while, thinking of the happiness I shall feel when she opens the door and runs to my side." But the long silence that follows tells me that the steps I heard were created by my fancy, and that I have still to wait for the accomplishment of my dearest hope.

Before Joshua left, he came to the door, and asked to see me and Minnie to bid us good-by. His desire to see Minnie was assuring, for it convinced me that the reasons I assigned for her leaving are correct. But I would not see him — I could not; for if he came into the room, he would discover Minnie's absence.

I am thankful to think that my forced seclusion will soon be at an end. How the minutes lag! Come, Minnie! Come, my darling child!

How shall I be able to endure this agony? It is night; yesterday morning Joshua Marvel left to go on his voyage, and there is no sign of Minnie. What can I think? Has any calamity befallen her? Is she lying sick, helpless anywhere, and must I remain here, gnawing my heart away with the knowledge that I am powerless to help her? O God, who only witnesseth my sufferings, send my darling home to me to-night! If in my life I have erred, and deserve punishment — if the injunction I laid upon the woman who loved me, and whom I loved with all my strength, was a crime, and if I am to suffer for the misery of her wedded life, being the cause of it — deal with me as thou wilt; but let me look once more upon the face of my darling!

The third day. My life is being tortured away. I believe that I shall die before seeing Minnie. The prescience of death is upon me. Every few minutes Susan runs into the street to see if Minnie is coming; but there is no sign of her. The slightest sound in the house causes my heart to beat so violently that I am afraid. I try to think, but I cannot; I can only fear. These few words have taken me long to write. I cannot read what I have previously written. I have tried to do so, but the words swim before my eyes. I can write no more to-day.

With a despairing mind I trace these words slowly and painfully. They are powerless to express my feelings.

Death is near. I know it. Not by physical pain am I warned, but I know it. I saw my wife last night. She stood by my side for full an hour. It is a sign that my hour is come.

Susan is below, looking for Minnie, perhaps — looking for Minnie, who will never, never come. . . .

I take up my pen again. What lies before me? A letter. Susan brought it up a while ago, and gave it to me. But when I saw the writing on the cover, I had not courage to open it, so I placed it in the desk. It is addressed to me in Minnie's writing. And on the cover are these words: "The 'Merry Andrew;' John Steele, pilot." The letter, then, comes from the "Merry Andrew," and is in Minnie's writing. What follows? That Minnie is on board the "Merry Andrew" with Joshua Marvel! I must read it — I *must*, if it strike me dead!

That was all that was written. Dan read every word of the manuscript aloud, but was compelled by emotion to pause many times. During the silence that followed, one thought rose uppermost in their minds. Ellen thought, "How will Dan bear this?" And Dan had the same thought with respect to Ellen. Is such noble unselfishness rare? Let us hope not. For the first and only time in the course of this narrative, the writer pauses to speak of a personal experience of devotion and unselfishness. It was before him during his boyhood in the person of his mother; and it is to her, and to the patient, unmurmuring gentleness with which she bore the trials of her life, that her children owe whatever little of good there may be in their nature. It is from his experience of his mother's life of goodness and self-sacrifice that he knows that the noble unselfishness of Dan and Ellen is not, thank God, a creation of his fancy. And as he writes these words in the midst of a great city, with all the whirl of its busy life around him, he is glad to think that in it — in great mansions and mean houses, in sight of gardens where Nature makes holiday, and of dirty streets and courts where bright leaf never grows — flowers of human life which the world shall never see are blossoming tenderly and holily, and living gentle lives for others' good.

For a long time no word was spoken by Ellen and Dan. Then Dan turned and looked in Ellen's face. She met his gaze pityingly, almost appealingly. He answered her with a sad smile, in which there was much sweetness.

"You were the first to guess my love for Minnie," he said; "and only to Jo did I ever confess it. But do not fret for me, my dear; she can never be to me what I was daring enough to hope she would be one day. My love for her is not less strong, but my hope is buried now."

She could say nothing but "Oh, my poor Dan! Oh, my poor Dan!"

"Nay, why?" he answered in his gentle voice; "what could I have offered her? What right had I, a cripple, to entertain the hope? I dared to hope that she, bright, strong, and full of healthful life, would tie herself to a weak, sickly thing like me. I dared to hope that she would love me. I fed my heart upon delusions; I can see it now. But I can love her still — can believe in her still — shall have faith in her purity as long as my heart shall beat, and after that — ay, who knows?" He paused for a little while before he resumed: "What you and I have in our thoughts, my dear, we must speak of; in that lies our only consolation. And we must not shrink from it; for our duty, no less than our love, demands it."

And yet she did shrink, fearing what was coming.

"What wonder that she should love Joshua?" continued Dan, unflinchingly determined to look the truth in the face, and not to spare himself, although as he spoke his quivering lips and tremulous voice betrayed his agitation. "We who know how good and brave he is are able to understand that she could not help loving him. But he — no, he played no false part by her." He placed his hand upon the Bible, and the action gave a deeper solemnity to the declaration. "Some suspicion he may have entertained that her feelings towards him were warmer than they ought to have been; and I well know the grief such suspicion brought to him. But he could not mention it — he dared not speak of it for Minnie's sake — for mine. I can trace a meaning now in the last words he said to me. 'You do not doubt me, Dan?' he asked. I answered, 'No, nor never could.' And then he said he should not have asked, but that certain things had distressed him lately. Poor Jo! Yes, he must have guessed Minnie's secret, and, knowing my love for her, trembled lest I should turn against him. Turn against him! my best, my dearest friend! When I do, it will be time for me to die. Believe that I never wavered in my love or my truth, and that to the last I held you in my heart as I hold you now, gentlest, dearest, best of friends!"

Unconsciously he had uttered the very words which Joshua addressed to him, and he spoke them as if Joshua were standing before him.

"As for what we have read to-night, we, and we alone, can rightly understand it. He who wrote it in his agony knows now that Joshua's heart is as pure as Minnie's honor."

"Those strange letters poor Minnie's father received," whispered Ellen; "who wrote them?"

"Who stabbed Jo when he came home?" asked Dan in reply. "Whoever did that wrote the letters. Jo has an enemy." Then, with a sudden remembrance of Joshua's warning against Solomon Fewster, he cried in a louder tone than he had hitherto used, "Mr. Fewster!" With eager impatience he turned over the pages of Basil Kindred's diary, and lighted upon the original letters. They were pinned on blank pages at the end of the diary, and were written on soiled sheets of blue letter-paper. "No," said Dan, examining them; "the writing is strange to me. We must wait until Jo comes back; all will be explained then."

The candle had burnt low in the socket by this time, and Dan had just said, "I think we had better try to sleep for a little while, Ellen," when they heard sounds of some one walking softly about the house.

"There is no one here but Susan," said Ellen, in a tone of quiet surprise.

"No one but" — said Dan, and then paused, awestruck by the thought of that only other one in the house, who lay stark and dead in the room above.

They listened to Susan's footsteps, and a new fear entered their hearts. There was a soft stealthiness in the footfall, as if Susan were hunting for some one who was hiding from her.

"Shall I go and see?" asked Ellen.

"Hush!" whispered Dan.

Susan's footsteps, soft and stealthy as those of a cat, were in the passage. Presently the door was opened cautiously, and Susan entered, and softly closed the door behind her. She did not notice either Dan or Ellen, but looked about the room inquiringly, then went to the window and pulled up the blind. The moon was high in the heavens, and the light streamed down upon her face, making it ghastly.

"Susan!" cried Dan.

But she did not heed him; she peered anxiously through the window into the street, shading her eyes with her hand.

"Is she asleep?" whispered Ellen.

"I don't know," said Dan in a troubled voice; "it is dreadful to see her with that expression on her face."

It was an expression of suppressed watchfulness; that her firmly-compressed lips and wandering eyes were at variance might have been due to the peculiar circumstances of her life; but in the cunning and revengeful determination in her face there was no sign of indecision. It was as though she had staked her life on the accomplishment of a task.

As she turned from the window and approached Dan, he seized her hand.

"Susan," he said, gently, "speak to me, my dear. What is the meaning of this?"

She laid her hand upon his head, and said, "Poor Dan! And you loved her, and she is lost to you."

"Not lost, Susey," he said, detaining her hand and humoring her, for he was afraid that her reason was gone; "not lost. She will come back."

"She will never come back — never, never! When she hears that he is dead — he is lying dead up stairs, Dan — she will never come back; she will drown herself first; for she loved him, and me too; and would have loved you, Dan, but for that false-hearted friend."

"You must not say that, Susey," said Dan, pointing to Ellen, who had turned aside weeping. "Look at Ellen. He is her husband, and he is not false-hearted. For her sake you must have kinder, juster thoughts towards Jo."

But Susan did not catch the sense of his words. All that she understood was, that he was speaking in defence of Joshua.

"All in his favor," she muttered. "If any one is to blame, it is Minnie — that's what all of you will say. But I know better; I know better. Didn't I watch them? Didn't I see him making love to her on the ship? Didn't I see the poor dear that's lying dead up stairs tortured slowly to death? And don't I know who killed him?"

"Who, Susan, who?" asked Dan, holding his breath.

"Joshua Marvel," said Susan, between her set teeth, with no change upon her face. "And as God's my judge, I will bring him to justice! You are his friends — I know that: you'll try to hide him from me; but I'll do what I've made up my mind to, if I drop down dead the minute after."

She twisted her hand from Dan's grasp, and crept slowly into the passage, and thence into the street. And there she stood for many minutes, with the same expression of implacable animosity on her face, waiting for the return of Basil Kindred's murderer.

CHAPTER XXVII.

WHAT THE NEIGHBORS THINK OF IT.

THE events that have been described, proved to be something more than a nine-days' wonder. The neighborhood was remarkably bare of exciting incidents, and nothing so stirring as the sudden death of Basil Kindred and the flight of Minnie had happened within the memory of the oldest inhabitant. Besides that, there was one element in the occurrences which, above all others, added zest and flavor to them — this was the element of mystery. Here was a family, which might be looked upon as the most respected family in the neighborhood; for there was no question about the position held by the Marvels. Every one of the neighbors liked them, and every one of the neighbors had a good word for them. They had lived in the neighborhood — they and their fathers and grandfathers before them — for many scores of years, and no shadow of reproach had ever rested upon a single member of the family. They had always been steady, industrious, and sober, and had been held up as examples, time out of mind, by wives to their husbands, and parents to their children. They were homely, hospitable, and sociable, and, although they might very well have done it, had never held their heads above their fellows. If any male acquaintance wanted a word of advice, he went to Mr. Marvel for it; and the advice received was generally found to be sound, and was always admitted to be good. If any one was sick, Mrs. Marvel always came forward to help and assist, in her small way, and was always ready to sit up of a night if it were necessary, and to do some portion of the household work if it were needed. And what she did was done so unostentatiously and quietly that it never left a sting behind it, and never — strange as it may sound — elicited any thing but gratitude. Joshua was a model of a son, and the neighbors had been proud of him. Take them for all in all, the Marvels were a credit to the locality. And yet, as you shall presently see, notwithstanding their irreproachable character, notwithstanding the credit in which they were held, notwithstanding that they were famous for all the virtues under the sun, a very remarkable change was to take place in the estimation in which they were held.

Then as to the Taylors. There had been many transitions of feeling regarding them when the parents were alive. They had not been a credit to the neighborhood. The meek uncomplaining life which Mrs. Taylor had led had been entirely lost sight of in the drunken dissolute habits of the head of the family. Perhaps it was because of this bad conduct on the part of Mr. Taylor that the virtues of the good wife had not been taken into account; and the fact remained, that it was not until after Mr. Taylor's death — the manner of which was disgraceful, and left a blot upon the family name — that any strong affection was mingled with the pity with which Dan and Ellen were regarded. There were so many singular circumstances connected with the family history. First, there was Susan letting Dan fall out of the window when he was a baby and breaking his legs. Many of the neighbors, with young families of their own, remembered the time when they were boys and girls, and when Susan was twitted and jeered at for being Dan's murderer. Then Susan's strange manner and slovenly dress — not it must be admitted, that her slovenliness had very much to do with the feeling — had not rendered her a favorite; and she was often spoken of as being soft and not quite right in her mind.

Then came that part of Mr. Taylor's career when (it having been whispered about that he had been the death of his wife he fell into deeper and deeper dissipation, and when he was to be seen regularly every night tumbling out of the public-house, and reeling home in a state of intoxication. It is surprising how hard many wives, whose husbands were not quite free from the reproach of over-indulgence, were upon the failings of Mr. Taylor. He was a "drunken beast," a "disgrace to the street," and so forth. And yet, as you have seen, they were proud of the beautiful friendship that existed between Dan and Joshua, and appreciated the good conduct of Ellen from the time that she was big enough — she was young enough, Heaven knows, when her duties commenced — to assist in the cleaning and washing. But the father's drunken habits stained the family reputation, and not all the washing and wringing could wash it clean at that time. Then came the shameful death of the drunkard. From the date of that occurrence, the position of the family began to improve, and the engagement of Ellen and Joshua lifted them up still further in the estimation of their neighbors.

Lastly, there were Basil Kindred and Minnie. Neither of them had ever been favorites out of their own small circle. Basil Kindred had held his head above them, and Minnie was too much of a lady for "such poor folks as us." All the grown-up girls disliked her because she was superior to them, and because she did not associate with them. Therefore neither father nor daughter obtained sympathy, and there was very little pity expressed for Basil's death. As for Minnie, she was generally condemned. The neighbors in speaking of her and her flight said, " she was always a forward thing;" and some even went so far as to call her a "stuck-up slut." They never expected any thing better of her, not they.

The mystery was, how it all became known; for it was known, every detail of it, the day following that on which Basil Kindred had died. Every person, for about a dozen streets round about, knew all the particulars almost as soon as Mr. and Mrs. Marvel were made acquainted with them — knew that Minnie had run away, knew that she was in Joshua Marvel's ship, knew that the intelligence of the flight had caused her father's death. Then they began to be wise in their generation, after the usual manner of human herds, and before nightfall of the second day it was recognized as an established fact, that it had been a cunningly-planned plot from first to last, and that Joshua and Minnie had run away together.

There is no accounting for these revulsions of feeling, and it is perhaps best not to attempt to analyze them. So much small malice and miserable uncharitableness would be brought to light, that we should be ashamed of the exposure — being liable to such influences ourselves. Joshua's character had hitherto been irreproachable; he had been almost loved by many, and liked and admired by all. Suddenly he is tainted by suspicion, and by suspicion only. There is not a tittle of direct evidence against him. But the suspicion is enough; directly it is whispered, it swells and grows, like the cloud which is at first "no bigger than a man's hand," and Joshua's good name is wrecked in the storm that follows.

The additional grief that this general verdict inflicted upon Joshua's parents may easily be imagined. They had to learn that "slander's edge is sharper than the sword," and that though their dear son were "chaste as ice and pure as snow, he should not escape calumny." But they did not receive these lessons meekly. They fought and protested against them with all the strength of their loving souls. They might as well have tried to stop a fierce wind with the palms of their hands.

One of their bitterest experiences was the knowledge that there was a difference of sentiment between them. They did not all believe alike. All of them, except Susan, believed alike in the innocence and purity of Joshua; but not so with respect to Minnie. The mercy that Dan and Ellen accorded to her was denied to her by Mr. and Mrs. Marvel. Neither of them thought well of her; and although Mrs. Marvel's verdict was less harsh than that of her husband, she too, gentle and forgiving as was her nature, could not forgive and hold dear the unhappy girl who had brought this great misery upon them. What Minnie had done was nothing less than a crime in the eyes of the good mother and good woman.

But Minnie had one champion — Susan. It was generally reported, a few days after the tragic occurrence, that Susan had gone mad because of Basil Kindred's death; and a whisper went about, that, mad as she was, she was fixed to the one idea of bringing Joshua to justice. Susan's madness, if madness it was, took a very mild form. She did not speak upon the subject, but she believed thoroughly in Minnie's innocence and Joshua's guilt; and she was ever on the watch to bring that false friend to justice. She was always peering about her and hunting for Joshua. She contracted a strange habit of suspecting that he was hiding in the place she last left, and when she went out of the house, returned, after going a few paces, to see if the man she was waiting for was in the passage. If she opened a gate and shut it behind her, she walked back to it and looked about her, expectant. Never a night passed but she rose from her bed and went into the street, waiting for Joshua; in the dead of night, when all others were asleep, she would sit at her window and look into the street, waiting patiently. When they discovered this habit at home, they tried to break her of it; but their efforts were unavailing. By and by, this proceeding began to be exceedingly popular in the neighborhood, and popular opinion veered round to Susan's view; Minnie was not so thoroughly condemned, and the blame was entirely laid on Joshua's shoulders. And when the neighbors openly expressed their sympathy to Mr. Marvel because Joshua had "turned out bad," he resented it angrily in his dogmatic obstinate way, until he began to quarrel with them. He was so indignant, so hurt, so unhappy, that he refused to speak to his old acquaintances, and gradually they fell off from him, and a coldness sprang up which made his life a misery. Still, he and all that were bound to him cherished the hope that when Joshua came home all would be cleared up. But Mr. Marvel made up his mind that he would never forgive his neighbors for their suspicions. Months passed, and the estrangement between him and his acquaintances grew stronger; his home, too, was not a happy one. He grew morose and ill-tempered, and would not speak to his wife upon the subject of Joshua and Minnie; and when she found that he was determined upon this point, she wisely forbore to press him, knowing his nature.

Before the advent of another spring, Ellen became a mother. Her situation had been concealed from all but Dan and Mrs. Marvel; even Mr. Marvel did not know it until the child was born. It was a girl; and when the news was buzzed about the neighborhood, Joshua and Minnie started again into a notoriety which had been on the wane. Again the busybodies were at work, and again the busy tongues wagged more volubly than before. It was a matter for resentment with the neighbors that they had not been made acquainted with Ellen's situation; it was depriving them of a legitimate privilege. But Ellen and her two confidants had kept the secret well; and now the young mother nursed her child in privacy, and seemed only anxious to keep it from prying and unsympathizing eyes. No news had been received of Joshua or of his ship; and although Mr. Marvel went every other day to the London agents of the "Merry Andrew," they had nothing to tell him. Now that the child was born, their anxiety for news of Joshua increased. But still they received none. Weeks passed, months passed, until the suspense became almost maddening. Ellen nursed the baby, and rejoiced that the pretty little thing had Joshua's eyes, and yearned for Joshua to see them. Mr. Marvel looked more angrily upon his old acquaintances, who were ready to quarrel with him afresh for his sour looks. Mrs. Marvel suffered in patience, and strove by assumed cheerfulness to lighten the loads the others had to bear. Susan waited and watched. And Dan waited and hoped — When there came a time ! —

Ellen was in Mrs. Marvel's kitchen; her baby was in her lap, and she was gazing at and worshipping, for the thousandth thousandth time, the baby's beautiful eyes, and beautiful fingers and nails, and the round cheeks, and the pretty mouth and chin, so like Joshua's. It was evening, and Mr. Marvel was expected home every minute, with news from the agents about Joshua's ship. Ellen began singing this to baby — singing in a low soft voice how father would soon come from over the seas to see his own little darling — his dear darling precious; and she was in the midst of this, enriching the theme with twenty different forms of endearing expression, when Mr. Marvel staggered into the kitchen. There was a wild look in his face, and his hands were trembling. He was drunk.

"O father!" cried Ellen.

"Where's mother?" he asked in a husky voice. "Where's mother?" he repeated in a louder tone.

His wife answered the question by coming into the kitchen. She had seen him reel into the house, and had followed him at once. She knew he had been drinking, but she did not reproach him. He saw in her face the knowledge and the forbearance, and he said, —

"Yes, I've been drinking; I was bound to. O mother, mother! how shall I tell you?"

Her lips framed some words, but she could not utter them. She sank into a chair and gazed at him with blanched cheek, with quivering lips, with blurred eyes.

Hush, baby, hush! you have never seen your father's face, and you do not understand now what one day will be told you — what George Marvel has had to drink brandy to give him courage to tell his faithful wife —

That the good ship, the "Merry Andrew," has foundered, and that every soul on board, Joshua and Minnie included, has gone down to the bottom of the sea. Not one saved — not one.

CHAPTER XXVIII.

ON BOARD THE "MERRY ANDREW."

WHILE the "Merry Andrew" was lying at Blackwall taking in cargo, Capt. Liddle, like the shrewd captain he was, had caused it to be notified that he would be happy to take a certain number of passengers to the New World at fifty pounds per head. It happened, as it usually happens in such like cases, that just at that time the exact number of persons that the ship could accommodate found either that Great Britain was too crowded for them to move freely in, or that at length the hour had arrived for them to make a fresh start in life. The captain of the "Merry Andrew" offered them the necessary opportunity. His ship would take them to a country where they would be able to turn without being elbowed. And there was no doubt that the start they contemplated would be a fresh one, inasmuch as in the new land their heads would be where their feet were now, and night was day and day night, and cherries grew with their stones outside, and many other wonders were commonplaces of every-day life. Accordingly, these enterprising souls, much to Capt. Liddle's satisfaction, paid their fifty pounds per head for four months of quiet misery on the sea. By that stroke of business Capt. Liddle served two purposes. He put money in his pocket as chief owner of the vessel, and he provided society for his wife, who was to accompany him on the voyage. Mrs. Liddle was a cheerful little body, who, although she was thirty years of age, had as much sentiment as a tender-hearted miss of eighteen. Her engagement with Capt. Liddle had been a long one. It was now more than twelve years since she first saw him and fell in love with him, as he did with her; but she happened to be blessed in a father who entertained not uncommon ideas as to the value of money, and as to the difference it made in a man, especially in a man who presumed to fall in love with his daughter. At that time Capt. Liddle was only second mate, and his matrimonial overtures were pooh-poohed by Capt. Prue, which was the name and title of his wife's father; Bessie Prue was hers. Capt. Prue (retired from the service) declared that he loved sailors and loved the sea, and that nothing would please him better than that his Bessie should marry a sailor. But then, that sailor must be a captain, he declared, and that captain must be absolute owner of the ship he commanded. Having passed the principal part of his life on sea, in a position where his word was law, he was, as most old sea-captains are, intolerant of opposition. Having given the word, he would not depart from it. Consequently, second-mate Liddle found that all his arguments and rhapsodies were as wind — a fluid which is much more useful at sea than on land, however it is produced. Bessie, as it proved, possessed a goodly share of her old father's determination of character. Having fallen in love with second-mate Liddle, and having determined to marry him or die an old maid, she informed her lover that if he would be faithful to her, she would be faithful to him — a form of declaration which has been very popular from time immemorial. The pledge being sealed by the infatuated ones in the usual manner — that is, with much protestation, with much unnecessary solemnity, (as if they were doomed to execution, and were to be beheaded within a few hours,) with many kisses and tender embracings — Bessie went to her father and apprised him, melodramatically, of her determination.

"You wouldn't marry without my consent?" was the obstinate old captain's question, after a little consideration. They were absurdly happy, these two determined persons. Bessie was the apple of his eye, the pride of his heart; she had not a wish, except the wish matrimonial, that he would not have made any sacrifice to satisfy. "You wouldn't marry without my consent, my pretty?" he repeated anxiously, for she did not answer his question immediately.

"I won't, on one condition," replied Bessie categorically; "and that is, that you won't ask me or wish me, or try to persuade me to marry anybody but John Liddle; for I love him with all my heart, and I wouldn't give him up — no, not to be made Lord High Admiral."

"I give you my promise, my pretty," said Capt. Prue, secretly admiring his daughter's determination, and loving her the more for it; "I'll never ask you, nor wish you, nor try to persuade you to marry anybody but John Liddle."

It may be guessed how willingly the old sea-captain gave the pledge, when it is known that he looked forward with absolute dread to the time when Bessie might be taken from him to another home. He would give her any thing, help her to any thing but a husband. What right had any body else to her? Why, the ship would go on the rocks without her! "And when John Liddle is skipper and owns a ship," he added, "I'll give my consent free and willing." In which last words Capt. Prue was not quite ingenuous. But the compact was made and adhered to. Second-mate Liddle was informed of it, and was compelled to abide by it. He trusted to chance, as many other men, not lovers, have done before him; and he derived consolation from the thought, that when Capt. Prue and Bessie pledged their word, it would need something very extraordinary and unlooked-for to induce them to break it. He rose from second mate to first mate, from first mate to skipper; and when he returned from his voyages, he found Bessie faithful and true, and received a hearty welcome from her father. And during these long and many years of probation, he learned to love his true-hearted little woman more deeply than he had done at first; she taught him to understand what love really was; she taught him the true beauty of it, the holiness of it — that it was something more than a sentiment, something higher than a passion; she taught him to understand that it was a sacrament.

It seems fated for this story, that its narration should necessitate, for the most part, the depicting of the higher virtues, and what is most noble and self-sacrificing in our natures. But it should be none the less acceptable because of that.

A short time after Bessie's lover became skipper, a relative of his died, and left him some money. Directly he came into possession of it, he bought a share in the "Merry Andrew." Bessie was then twenty-six years of age, as pretty as ever, and as fresh at heart as ever. One would have thought that her father would have spoken to her of his own accord, there and then, and that he would have given her the reward of her faithfulness and devotion. But the truth must be told; he was a selfish old curmudgeon, and he trembled at the thought of losing her. So once more Capt. Liddle sailed away from his lady-love on the voyage in which our Joshua commenced his apprenticeship at sea. The "Merry Andrew" was away, as you know, for more than four years; and when it returned, and Capt. Liddle went to see his Bessie, he found her in mourning. Her father was dead. Before he died he had made her the only reparation in his power. The last codicil to his will, written a few weeks before his death, contained expressions of his love for her, his admiration of her lover, his consent to their marriage, and his regret that he had not consented to it years ago. But it is so easy to regret *after* a thing has occurred which we might have prevented or remedied. I have not yet made up my mind as to the value of death-bed repentance. Neither am I satisfied that we may sin properly for six days in the week, in a comfortable knowledge that we can evade the penalty by crying, "I have sinned!" on the sabbath.

However, the departed Captain Prue had been in all other respects a kind and tender father, and no word of reproach passed the lips of Bessie and John Liddle. They were not too old for the enjoyment of life's blessings. Two months before the present sailing of the "Merry Andrew" they were married; and it is not to be doubted that the circumstances of their engagement promised them a lasting happiness.

Mrs. Liddle had a maid, a beautiful brown-complexioned girl, whose appearance might have suggested some suspicion of a gypsy breed, had it not been for her manners, which showed a refinement no gypsy-girl could have acquired in her vagrant life, and for her eyes, which were gray despite their brightness. The circumstances of her becoming Mrs. Liddle's maid were somewhat peculiar. She had presented herself to that lady a few days before the "Merry Andrew" sailed, and stating that she had heard by accident that Mrs. Liddle wanted a maid to accompany her on the voyage, asked to be engaged in that capacity. There was something so winsome about the girl, that Mrs. Liddle — who had not succeeded in engaging a maid willing to brave the terrors of a sea-voyage — was at once attracted to her, and lent a sympathizing ear to her story of being alone in the world and without friends. Perhaps it was Mrs. Liddle's romantic happiness that caused her to be less prudent than usual; but certain it is that the girl was engaged, and, setting about her duties at once, proved so apt and attentive, that Mrs. Liddle congratulated herself upon her decision. Captain Liddle did not interfere in the matter; but when he first saw the girl her face seemed familiar to him, and he glanced at her more than once, wondering where he had met her. But he could not settle the doubt, and the matter was not of sufficient importance to permanently engage his attention. Thus it was that Minnie succeeded in obtaining a passage in the "Merry Andrew," and in being near to the man who was dearer to her than all other earthly considerations. She was not influenced by any dishonoring passion; she simply desired not to be parted from the man she loved. She did not want him to see her or speak to her — at least, so she thought at that time; it was sufficient for her to know that she was in the same ship with him, and that she would perhaps now and again catch a glimpse of her hero, without his knowing that she was by. When she first made up her mind to leave her home, she did not pause to consider what would be the consequences of her rash act. She was unhappy there and utterly miserable; everybody was against her; and when she discovered, as she did discover, that Susan was playing the spy upon her, she became defiant and more resolved. She loved her father and honored him; but she loved Joshua with all the passion of her passionate nature, and in her mistaken sense of right and wrong, the stronger love usurped the place of duty, and made her oblivious of all else. She was blinded by love, and by love in which there was not a shade of impure passion.

She had had at first a wild idea of dressing herself in sailor's clothes, and had saved a few shillings towards the purchasing of them; but her success with Mrs. Liddle set that aside. When she went on to the ship with her mistress, she was careful that Joshua should not see her; but indeed, if they had met face to face at that time, it is not likely that he would have recognized her in her disguise; for his thoughts were with Ellen, and his heart was too full as yet to be curious about the passengers. But the Lascar saw her, and was puzzled about her directly he set eyes upon her face. He watched her like a cat, and yet he could not make up his mind about her. He had seen her often in Stepney, but he could scarcely believe that the fair girl with the beautiful hair and this dark gypsy with the short curls were one and the same. He knew her name and all about her from Solomon Fewster, and he was quite ready to believe in the villany of Joshua. Resolved to make sure of the value of his suspicions, he contrived to pass close by her as she was taking some bandboxes down stairs to the saloon, and as he passed her, he muttered the name of "Minnie Kindred." A start, a frightened look over her shoulders, and the dropping of the bandboxes down the stairs, were sufficient confirmation of his doubts; and before the pilot left the ship he gave him a scrawl for Solomon Fewster to the effect that Joshua and Minnie had run away together. He was cautious enough also to send upon another piece of paper a private scrawl to Solomon Fewster, saying he was not quite sure, but that Fewster would know how to act if Minnie were missing from home.

But when the Lascar next saw Minnie's face, which was not until the "Merry Andrew" was a thousand miles the other side of the Bay of Biscay, his doubts returned, and he thought that, after all, he must have been mistaken. He did not know the cunning of Minnie. In the startled glance she had thrown over her shoulder when her name was pronounced, she had marked the Lascar's face, so that she was sure she would know it again; and when, after the lapse of weeks, she detected him gazing at her, she looked at him so boldly and contemptuously that he drooped his eyes before her. What added to his perplexity was, that he never saw Joshua speak to her, never saw him look at her. When she came on deck, which she did very rarely, and never unless her duty to her mistress called her there, she was careful not to give Joshua an opportunity of speaking to her or of looking closely at her; and he, detecting in her manner a wish to avoid any little attention he might have it in his mind to offer her, did not trouble himself even by giving her a thought. She was as distant and reserved to all the officers; and in a little while it began to be understood, that the handsome gypsy-maid did not wish to be spoken to by any one on board but her mistress; and her wish was scrupulously respected.

To readers who are not well acquainted with ship-life, it may seem strange that Minnie should have been able to keep herself so free from observation; but there really can be—and there often is—as much exclusiveness on board a passenger-ship as there is in society on land. You may live in a ship for months, and travel for thousands upon thousands of miles over the seemingly interminable waste of waters, without having any more personal knowledge of those who sleep within a few yards of you than you would have of them if you and they were living at the extreme ends of a great city. When the long, long voyage is at an end, and the ship is being piloted into the bay that skirts the land of Pisgah, men and women whom you do not remember ever to have seen before appear magically on deck; and you wonder where they come from, and how it is you have not set eyes on them during all the time that you and they have been living in the wonderful house of wood and iron that has brought you safely over the raging seas.

Joshua knew the Lascar directly he saw him on board, and was not pleased to find that he was one of the crew. But the man did his duty, and worked as well and apparently as willingly as the other sailors; and as he was uniformly respectful, Joshua could not, even if he had been so inclined, treat him harshly with any sense of justice.

And so the "Merry Andrew," containing within its wooden walls its load of human love and hate, cleaves through the ocean onward to its goal steadily and patiently, while before it, with every new rising of the sun, a monotonous hill of waters, never varying, never changing, lies in the gray distance mocking its progress. Through cold weather, through hot weather, burnt up in the torrid zone, and chilled by winds which rush from ice-bound waters; through days when scarce a ripple can be seen on the grand ocean's breast, and others when the waves leap at its throat furiously, as an enemy might do; through nights when the moon rises threateningly in the heavens, like a blazing ball of lurid fire, suggesting thoughts of a dreadful to-morrow; and through dark nights, solemnly beautiful, when the track of the vessel is marked by the brilliant Medusæ (the sailor's girdle of Venus) which gleam and shine — a line of living light — in the wondrous sea: through all these, with unerring faith, the ship pursues its way steadily and patiently to the garden of the world. Now the captain smells the breeze, and hoarse cries, unintelligible to all but the initiated, travel about the ship to clap on sail and make good use of the breath of Boreas. Then the ship dashes on like a god drunk with joy, dives into awful depths, and climbs water-mountains that a moment ago threatened to fall in upon it and dash it to pieces. The curling seas break over the deck, and the toilers that are battling with wind and wave cling fast for dear life to ropes and spars; while ever and anon a water-titan, more angry than his fellows, breaks against the side with such tremendous force that the vessel reels and quivers beneath the mighty shock. So! the breeze slackens and dies away; the anger of the sea subsides, and after many days the ship is becalmed. Then the passengers lie about the white deck in happy indolence, and muse and dream of the great whale they saw a while ago, hung round with sea-weed and barnacles; of the cloudless night, star-gemmed above and below; of the beautiful Southern Cross and the strange Magellan clouds; and while they muse and dream, the white sky stares down lazily into blue peaceful waters. Every one on board is contented with the change, excepting the skipper, who paces the deck restlessly and prays for the breeze to spring up — taking advantage of the calm, however, like the good skipper he is, to splice ropes, and make new sails and mend old ones. Soon wind and water wake into life again, and the waves sparkle, and the fresh breeze blows merrily, when a sudden cry rings through the ship that a man is overboard. The next moment every soul on board is bending over the bulwarks, watching the retreating form of the sailor, who is floating on his back, gazing with agonizing dread at the cruel beaks of the swan-white albatrosses, which are already hovering above him. Quickly the ship is put about; a boat, with rowers in it, is lowered into the sea; and after the lapse of many anxious moments a wild cheer rings through the air, as the man saved from death, is dragged into the boat. He tells afterwards to eager listeners — he is a notable man on board from that day forth — how it seemed to him that he was floating on his back for full a day, and how the only fear he felt was that the albatrosses would pick out his eyes. Then the following week a young man died who was in a consumption when he was first brought on to the ship, and who had hoped that the warm breezes of the South would give him a new lease of life; but he was never to breathe the balmy southern air. The little colony of human beings is very sad when the funeral service is read over the body, and the canvas coffin slips with a dull thud into the sea; and a fear arises that some calamity is near. And surely that night there is a fearful storm. The wind howls and roars; heavy seas dash down the two men at the wheel; the sails split into a thousand shreds; masts and spars crack like reeds. The sobs and lamentations of the passengers are dreadful to hear. Minnie, creeping from her cabin into the saloon, sees a dozen men and women, half-dressed, on their knees, praying for mercy and forgiveness, making vows of reformation, and indulging in all the fear-impelled evidences of a suddenly awakened contrition. Pursued by the conviction that in a few minutes she and all in the ship will meet their doom, she yearns with all her soul to see Joshua, to touch him, to whisper in his ear that Minnie is by his side. Then, if he will but take her hand, she will be content to go down with him into the solemn depths of the awful sea. She creeps to the wet stairs leading to the deck, only to find that the hatches are fastened down, and that she is a prisoner. She tears at the cruel door that separates her from Joshua, until her fingers bleed and her strength gives way. She calls aloud to him, but she cannot hear her own voice, so weak is it and so overwhelming is the roar of the storm. She sinks, despairing, at the foot of the stairs, and in the agony of her mind and the terror of the time so entirely loses consciousness, that the cold waters which steal down the hatchway are powerless to arouse her. But with the next rising of the sun the storm has passed away, and the captain looks joyful, and the sailors sing blithely at their work, and the passengers forget their vows of reformation. So the ship sails on and on, until land is sighted, and the passengers begin to prepare their best clothes to go on shore in. Then comes a quiet evening when the "Merry

Andrew" drops quietly down the beautiful bay, and as evening deepens into night, a thousand twinkling lights from distant hills welcome the wanderers and gladden their hearts. How peaceful, how lovely, is the night! The balmy air, the restful sound of dipping oars, the floating strains of music that come from a neighboring ship, the beautiful star-lit waters— all these bring grateful feelings to weary travellers, and silent prayers of thankfulness arise to Heaven for the mercy that has brought them safely through the perils of the mighty sea.

CHAPTER XXIX.

THE WRECK OF THE "MERRY ANDREW."

BUILT in the bed of a beautiful valley and on gardened slopes rising from the waters which run to the sea, lies Sydney, the fair city of the South. It is spring although the month is October. The heavens are bright with bright clouds, the air is sweet with perfume from tree and flower, the bay is gemmed with gardened isles and promontories. Outside the heads which protect the bay and make it a safe refuge for mighty fleets, the sea dashes against hoary rocks which stand defiant of its wrath; but to-day, swayed by the influence of smiling sun and cloud, the grim old walls sport with the huge waves, splinter them into silver spray, and send them, laughing, back into the sea. In the fair land girt by the blue waters of the South Pacific are orange-groves, the fragrance of whose snow-white blossoms is in harmony with the time and place, and coral-trees with bright scarlet flower, and trees of peach, loquat, and bread, and hill-slopes where the vines grow, and myriad other evidences of Nature's beneficence. All things that see the light contribute to the beauty of spring.

"'Tis the garden of the world," said Captain Liddle to his wife, as they stood apart from the others on board the "Merry Andrew;" "'tis the garden of the world," he repeated, gazing at the lovely hills and gloriously-tinted sky with that sense of gratitude which it is so good for a man to experience.

Her thoughts were in harmony with his, but she did not answer him immediately. She, too, was sensible of the beautiful scene around them, and stood by his side in silent thankfulness. To-morrow, the "Merry Andrew," having discharged her cargo, and taken in another (chiefly hard wood), was to set sail for China, where she had a charter for London. It was of London — of home — that the captain's wife was thinking, and presently her thoughts found simple expression.

"Yes, John," she said; "it is indeed a garden — a beautiful garden; but it is not home."

"Why now, Bessie," said the captain, looking down smilingly upon the wife he had waited and worked for as anxiously as Jacob did for Rachel, "could you not content yourself here?"

"All my life, John?"

"All your life, my dear."

"No," she said without hesitation; "I should always be pining for home. Even if we were poor, and it were a necessity that we should live here, I don't think I could manage to quite content myself. But as it is"—

"As it is, Bessie"— repeated her husband, in secret delight at his wife's enthusiasm.

"As it is, John," she responded softly, "'there's no place like home.'"

Captain Liddle hummed a few bars of the Englishman's household hymn; and then, looking to that part of the ship where Joshua was busy, said : "There is some one on board, Bessie, who is even more anxious to get home than you are."

"Who can that be, John?"

"My handsome mate, as you call him, Joshua Marvel. He was expressing his delight to me yesterday that we should be not away longer than we thought we should when we started. And when I asked him what made him so impatient to get home, he told me that he was married three days before we left Gravesend. How would you have liked that?"

"I wouldn't have allowed you to go," said Mrs. Liddle, with a very positive shake of the head.

"Easily said, little woman; not so easily managed, though, if I had been third mate instead of captain. Thank your stars that you married a captain."

"So I do, John," said Mrs. Liddle tenderly — so tenderly, that her husband would have stooped and kissed her, if they had been alone. "Was it a love-match?"

"Marvel's? Certainly, I should say. When I went to his house in London to see him, I saw a very beautiful girl in his room. Perhaps it is to her that he is married."

"Very beautiful, sir?" exclaimed Mrs. Liddle, with a toss of her head. "I am almost inclined to take you to task for that; but I'll ask you, instead, to describe her."

"I can't, Bess; 'tis not in my line. I tell you what, though : your maid would be like her, if she was fair instead of brown, and if she had long hair."

"Making eyes at my maid, sir!" cried Mrs. Liddle, with a pretty wilfulness. "When I get you home, I shall lock you up."

Captain Liddle laughed, and pinched his wife's cheek.

"I am glad it was a love-match," she said; "I like Mr. Marvel all the better for that. You ought to do something for him."

"I shouldn't be surprised, Bessie, if Marvel was second mate on our next voyage," was the captain's reply. "Now go and see to the stowing away of your curiosities."

During the time that the "Merry Andrew" had been lying in Sydney Harbor, Mrs. Liddle and her gypsy maid had been living on shore, and had only come on board to-day. Her husband's last remark referred to a number of parcels which were scattered about the poop, containing curiosities she had collected in that strange new world — such as feathers and skins, and curious weapons and plants — designed to astonish her friends at home.

Captain Liddle's intention to promote Joshua had been quietly whispered by the sailors to one another for some weeks past, although the captain, from motives of prudence and a proper regard for discipline, had made no mention of his intention, even to his wife, until now. Captain Liddle respected Joshua, and often engaged him in familiar conversation. He saw much to admire in the young sailor, and recognized in him qualities, both intellectual and professional, of a far higher standard than those exhibited by his other officers. A sailor more deeply impressed than Joshua was with the highest qualification a sailor can possess, duty, never walked the deck of a ship; and this merit, added to a quick natural intelligence, made him a great favorite with Captain Liddle. He was much liked, also, by the sailors; for while his sense of duty made him firm, his kindliness of heart made him gentle. Sailors resemble women in one particular: the more they respect a man, the better they like him. Joshua, however, had two bitter enemies on board: one was the Lascar, who was compelled to conceal his hate; the other was the second mate, Scadbolt by name, who made no secret of his animosity. Scadbolt, being both an inefficient officer and one who liked to shirk his work, had been sharply spoken to by Captain Liddle on several occasions. From this may have sprung the rumor of his intended deposition; and when it reached his ears, it made him venomous. Between Scadbolt and the Lascar about this time there sprang up a kind of intelligence with regard to Joshua, which boded him no good if he should chance to get into their power. No conversation passed between them on the subject; but each knew instinctively that the other hated the upstart third mate of the "Merry Andrew."

With his usual foresight and shrewdness, Captain Liddle had announced his readiness to take a small number of passengers to China, or to London by way of China — rather a roundabout route home, it must be confessed, but one which recommended itself to certain colonists from its novelty, and from the opportunity it afforded them of seeing something of the wonderful land where so many Sons of the Moon lived and had their being. Captain Liddle knew what he was about by stating that he could provide accommodation for only a few passengers, for only a few took passage. Here is the way-bill: —

Mr. and Mrs. Pigeon and daughter, the latter five years of age.
Mr. Bracegirdle.
Stephen and Rachel Homebush, brother and sister.
James Heartsease. }
Harry Wall. }
Rough-and-Ready.

So that there were nine passengers in all, including little Emma Pigeon.

The crew numbered twenty-eight persons, all told; and these, with the passengers and the captain's wife and her maid, made the total number of souls on board thirty-nine.

Mr. Pigeon was the son of a wealthy squatter, who had lately died. Desirous of giving his wife and child better advantages than could be obtained in the colony, he had sold out his property, and was now on his way home, for the purpose of settling in the "old country." He was a rough kind of a gentleman at the best, as might be expected of one who had been brought up in the bush; but he had a tender heart, and was passionately devoted to his wife and child. Mrs. Pigeon was a sparkling little creature, full of life and bustle, never still, and with a laugh so merry and contagious, that every soul on board felt glad when it was first heard on the ship. Little Emma, as the child was called, was a small edition of her mother, with precisely the same natural gayety of disposition. The family were in high glee at the prospect of going "home" (even Little Emma, born in the bush, had been taught so to call it), and found in the pleasures of imagination some compensation for the natural sorrow they felt in leaving the bright and beautiful land of the South.

Mr. Bracegirdle was a mystery. No one knew any thing about him; and as no one inquired, and he was not communicative, his antecedents could only be guessed at.

Stephen and Rachel Homebush were a hard-featured morose-looking couple, whose piety was generally recognized as unimpeachable, but whose good-nature was certainly open to question. And this induces the reflection, that it is singular how often piety and sourness go hand in hand. It almost seems as if, with the majority of so-called pious people, religious contemplation chills the generous impulse, and hardens the heart instead of softening it. The light of truth falls on them not like dew, but like a miasma.

James Heartsease and Harry Wall are bracketed in the way-bill, as they were bracketed in heart. They were friends who had travelled together all over the world. They were enthusiastic sketchers; and it was whispered that they were writing a book, which caused them to be looked up to with a kind of veneration.

Rough-and-Ready was as great a mystery as Mr. Bracegirdle, but whereas nothing was known of Mr. Bracegirdle's antecedents, so many stories were current concerning Rough-and-Ready, that the difficulty was to hit upon the right one. None of them were at all creditable to him. One story was, that he was a bushranger; another, that he was a stockman, who had shot down any number of blacks; another, that he was a runaway convict. The name he chose to go by fitted any one or all of these stories. He engaged his passage in the name of Mr. Rough; but before he had been on board half an hour, every sailor knew him as Rough-and-Ready. The lady passengers cast cold looks upon him; but the sailors adored him; and he, taking the aversion of the women and the admiration of the men very philosophically, was as much at home on board the "Merry Andrew" as the captain himself. Captain Liddle saw nothing objectionable in Rough-and-Ready. He was prone, as you know, to form his own judgments of people, and was one of the small minority of men in the world who decline to be led by the nose. There was nothing very smooth or polished about Rough-and-Ready, as was implied by his name; but he had a bright eye, a free manner, and a civil tongue — sufficient recommendations to Captain Liddle's good favor.

At the appointed time the "Merry Andrew" weighed anchor, and started for China. Joshua rubbed his hands, and thought with a light heart of his pretty Ellen and his friend Dan, and his old mother and father, and that good friend the Old Sailor. He saw himself walking along the familiar street in Stepney, and saw all the neighbors running out to greet him, and saw Ellen, his own dear little wife, fluttering into his arms, and nestling there as prettily as could be. What wonder that his face grew bright, and that he went about his work with a cheerfulness that brought a darker scowl into the face of the Lascar! This worthy had not advanced a single step towards the furtherance of the scheme to which he had in a sort of measure pledged himself to Solomon Fewster before he left Gravesend. True, he had gone on board the "Merry Andrew" with the vaguest of ideas as to the manner in which he should be able to carry out his intentions regarding Joshua. The fact was, that he had been only anxious to get away from England for a time; the brawl in which he had been engaged and had used his knife was a serious one, and he was frightened for his own safety. But he had played his cards cunningly with Solomon Fewster, and had succeeded in extracting money and valuables from his cowardly master; thus providing for his safety, and putting money in his purse at the same time. Joshua had kept a sharp eye upon him during the whole of the voyage, and he was compelled to be careful and wary; for he knew that Joshua was a favorite with the captain, and that he would be clapped in irons upon the first sign of insubordination. Then he was disappointed in finding that not another sailor on board but himself owed Joshua a grudge, or was envious of him; so that he was alone in his hate until that instinctive understanding took place between him and the second mate Seadbolt, which made Joshua a mark for their mutual animosity. The Lascar would have dearly liked to do Joshua an ill turn; but he could not see his way to the accomplishment of his wish. But even from this thwarting of his desire he derived a kind of malicious satisfaction; for he could not help thinking with pleasure of the dismay and disappointment Solomon Fewster would experience when Joshua came home safe and sound. He could not help chuckling to himself as he thought, "What a way he'll be in when the 'Merry Andrew' gets into Blackwall, and how he'll storm and swear! But he'd better mind what he's about with me. I owe him one for that threat of giving me into custody for stealing the things he gave me." Certainly no such sentiment as "Honor among thieves" found place in the breast of the Lascar.

And Minnie? She had not calculated the effect of living within herself, as she had been compelled to do. Loving Joshua as she did with all her heart and soul, she had deceived herself by believing that she would be happy if she were only in the ship with him. Happy she would have been, had he known her and spoken kindly to her; but the gulf that divided them seemed to her to be wider than it would have been had thousands of miles of ocean been between them. She had time for reflection on board ship; and reflection, although it did not turn the current of her love, nor lessen it, added to her misery. At one time during the voyage she had been so unhappy that she was almost on the point of throwing herself overboard; and indeed had she known of the marriage between Joshua and Ellen she might really have done so. Happily for her she was not aware of the marriage, and was spared the contemplated sin. But she was on a rack of love and doubt, and was truly unhappy in the present, and despairing in the future. She went about her work in a dull mechanical way, keeping aloof from every one, and never going on deck unless her duties called her there. Mrs. Liddle saw that the poor girl was miserable, and questioned her. But here Minnie's rebellious nature came into play; she shut her heart against the proffered sympathy, and returned cold answers to her mistress's kind questions. Mrs. Liddle was sorry, but not offended; she saw that the girl was struggling with a great grief. "A love affair, depend upon it John," she said to her husband; and she respected Minnie's desire not to have her confidence openly intruded upon. Minnie's behavior on board inspired Mrs. Liddle with the conviction that her maid was a thoroughly good girl, and she could overlook a great deal in a girl who behaved so well. And notwithstanding Minnie's retired behavior, she was an object of interest to all. The officers and sailors called her "the shy beauty," "the pretty gypsy-maid." "the brown-faced little beauty;" and, when she came towards them with her eyes downcast, made way for her with almost as much deference as they did for the captain's wife. But she spoke no word to any one of them, and lived her life of self-imposed isolation in grief and silence.

The wind was fair, and a favorable voyage was anticipated. Sail after sail was clapped on, and Captain Liddle walked up and down the deck with a beaming face and in a state of high satisfaction. Five of the passengers were below in the first agonies of sea-sickness. Four were on deck — the two friends, James Heartsease and Harry Wall, Stephen Homebush, and Rough-and-Ready. The friends had travelled too many thousands of miles upon the ocean to be troubled by sea-sickness now; they had struggled with and vanquished that fell enemy years ago. Rough-and-Ready was not the sort of man to give in; he treated sea-sickness as he treated everything else that came to him in a threatening shape — he laughed in its face. Perhaps previous experience enabled him to do so with impunity. Stephen Homebush was not so fortunate. He had a large stock of bile, and (speaking after the manner of a well-known great man) when he had got rid of a great deal, he would have a great deal left. He certainly got rid of a great deal upon this occasion; and accustomed as he was to wrestle against yearnings of the flesh and terribles foes, this foe was too powerful for him, and this yearning of the flesh sent him into a deep pit of tribulation from which he saw no chance of escape. Some kind friend had advised him not to go below when he was attacked; and in accordance with that advice he remained on deck, possessed by a spirit so fiendish as not only to set at naught the pious exhortations of the worthy Stephen, but even to change words of piety into utterances that sounded very like anathemas. Even in the midst of his agony, he looked round for some one, as was his wont in his happier moods, upon whom to pour the vials of his spleen; for Stephen Homebush had this peculiar conviction with respect to himself. His invariable verdict when tribulation visited other persons was, that it was a just punishment — it was a visitation of the Lord. But there was no such acknowledgment regarding any vexation by which he was afflicted. In that case his opinion was, that he was suffering for the sins of others, and the conviction was to him a sufficient proof of his own worthiness and of the wickedness and unworthiness of every other person. He looked round for some one on whom to vent his spleen; but no person met his eye but Rough-and-Ready, whose merry face and cheerful manner were an additional sting to the miserable Stephen. Rough-and-Ready nodded encouragingly to the pale-faced Stephen, who was leaning against the bulwarks, and said cheerfully, and really from no ill-natured motive,—

"You will be better by and by, Mr. Homebush. Besides, it will do you good."

These last words were unfortunately chosen; for the afflicted Stephen — who had heard the discreditable stories attached to Rough-and-Ready, and who had already judged him as a sinner of the first magnitude — glared at the speaker, and said with difficulty, " Scoffer, sinner ! "

He intended to add, " Repent ! " but a sudden paroxysm compelled him to confide that exhortation to the waves.

Rough-and-Ready laughed gayly, and turning on his heel, met the captain, and fell into step with him.

" Some of the sailors are grumbling," observed Rough-and-Ready, "because we have set sail on a Friday."

"Grumble!" exclaimed Captain Liddle, pettishly. "Ay, and they'll grumble till the end of the voyage. I have had that sort of thing occur to me before. This is the fifth time I have started on a Friday, and nothing more unusual ever occurred than occurred at any other time. But the men wouldn't believe it, and won't believe it now. If a head-wind comes, it is because we set sail on a Friday; if we're becalmed, because we set sail on a Friday; if there's a squall, because we set sail on a Friday; if a man tumbles overboard, because we set sail on a Friday; if we lose a spar, if a sail is split, because we set sail on a Friday. I do believe, if one of them cuts his finger, he thinks, 'Curse the skipper! What the something unmentionable did he set sail on a Friday for?'"

"I have no doubt, skipper," said Rough-and-Ready, smiling and pointing to Stephen Homebush, whose head was hanging over the bulwarks, as if its owner were curiously interested in the swelling of the waves, "that Mr. Homebush is quite ready to side with the men, and to declare that he is sea-sick because you set sail on a Friday."

Captain Liddle smiled at the pious sufferer, and shrugged his shoulders. It was evident, although he said nothing upon the subject, that he had already formed a not too favorable opinion of Stephen Homebush.

For the first three days the prognostications of the sailors, that "something" was sure to happen because the voyage was commenced upon a Friday, did not seem likely to be realized. The weather was fine, the wind was fair, and every stitch of canvas was set. But the grumbling did not cease, and for a very good reason. Scadbolt and the Lascar did their best to keep the subject warm, and between them managed to foment and increase the dissatisfaction. Captain Liddle, cognizant of this, became stern and strict, and took but little rest. He did not know who it was that was encouraging the men; he suspected Scadbolt, and, estimating his second mate at his proper worth, he wanted but the slightest confirmation of his suspicions to take prompt action against the offender. By this time the passengers had recovered from their sea-sickness, and begun to assemble on the deck. Stephen and Rachel Homebush set to work vigorously in their task of reclaiming the sinners, in which category every person but themselves on board was included; but though they prayed (for others), and groaned (for others), and "wrestled" (for others), their efforts were not crowned with success. Indeed, the only person who tolerated them at all was the man who had the worst character, and whom nearly everybody avoided. Rough-and-Ready was a treasure to the pious couple. To him, as the most illustrious sinner within their reach, they imparted the knowledge of their own goodness and of everybody else's wickedness; him they informed that their special mission (out of heaven) was to lead him to the waters of grace, and that his special mission was to be led thereto by them. They prayed for him wrathfully, in stony voices, and would have wept over him, had he allowed them to do so. And when they found that they made no impression upon him (for it was only his good-nature that induced him to listen to them), they groaned the louder, and prayed the longer, and wrestled the more, because of the hardness of man's heart. It was a curious thing, seeing how good they were and how bad he was, to observe the conduct of Little Emma, Mrs. Pigeon's five-year-old daughter, towards the saints and the sinner. The little child ran away from the saints, and cried and struggled when Rachel Homebush took her hand; but when she saw the sinner, she ran into his arms with perfect confidence, and submitted to be tossed in the air and to be kissed by him very much as if she liked it. But then children have no judgment.

Towards the close of the third day the wea her became threatening, and the sails were taken in. This set the grumblers at work more busily than ever. Some time before midnight, the watch being in charge of the second mate, Captain Liddle came unaware upon two of the men who were grumbling, and sternly asked them what they were grumbling at. The Lascar was one of the twain, and of course he did not reply; but the other man, being pressed by the captain, pulled at his forelock, and said that the sailors weren't pleased because the voyage had been commenced on their unlucky day.

"And that's the cause of this rough weather, eh?" questioned Captain Liddle sarcastically.

"Yes, your honor," was the reply. "Why, even the second mate says so."

"Does he?" cried Captain Liddle, turning wrathfully upon Scadbolt, who at that moment approached them. "What do you mean, Mr. Scadbolt, by spreading disatisfaction among the crew?"

Brought face to face with the man to whom he had spoken, Scadbolt, who was no coward, gave him a threatening look, and said, —

"Well, sir, I've an objection to setting sail on Friday; and, as you see, the men have the same objection."

"I see quite enough to warn you to be careful," said Captain Liddle in a determined tone; "I have warned you before, and I warn you now for the last time. Keep your objections to yourself, sir, and trouble yourself only with your duty. — And you, men, attend to yours, and let me hear no more of this nonsense. You know me well enough to know that I will not be trifled with."

The men slouched away, and Scadbolt was obliged to suppress his passion for the time: but it burned the fiercer for that.

The next day the weather became worse, and circumstances thus gave a color to the dissatisfaction, which grew stronger every hour. But the captain was equal to both emergencies; like a good sailor and a stout captain he grappled with the storm that raged without, and with that scarcely less dangerous one that raged within. He was seldom off the deck, and when he did go down to snatch an hour's rest, he left Joshua on board to watch in his place. For Captain Liddle was not slow to discover that Joshua was the man of all the other men on the ship upon whose faithfulness he could best depend. He said this many times to his wife, and often spoke to her in praise of Joshua. Minnie heard this, and heard also of the dissatisfaction among the sailors, and how Scadbolt, the second mate, had fomented the dissatisfaction. About this time a whisper spread among the passengers that there were three or four sailors in the crew who only wanted a favorable opportunity to break into open mutiny. Confirmation of this was given by the captain, on the third day of the bad weather, when the ship was scudding along under bare poles. He, coming down hastily into the saloon, went into his cabin, and made his appearance in a few minutes with a belt buckled round his waist and two pistols in it. The passengers, looking at each other in astonishment, received another shock presently by the surprising appearance of Rough-and-Ready. His dress hitherto had been of a respectable character — black coat and waistcoat and tweed trousers; but now he had on a red-serge shirt, and a rough billycock-hat, and buckskin riding-trousers, and boots that reached half-way up his thighs, and a red-silk sash round his waist, with knife and pistol stuck therein. You may guess the alarm he caused among the ladies; the only passenger who seemed pleased at the change in his appearance was little Emma Pigeon, who skipped round him delightedly, and clapped her hands in approval of his bright-colored shirt and sash. Rough-and-Ready caught the child in his arms and gave her a hearty kiss, and nodded cordially to the fellow-passengers who had so studiously avoided him. They were so frightened at his desperate appearance, that they forgot to frown upon him as they were wont to do. Rough-and-Ready then going on deck, walked up to Captain Liddle, and said, —

"You can depend upon me, skipper. I've seen this sort of thing before."

Captain Liddle gave him a look of grateful acknowledgment, and they made their way into the midst of a knot of sailors who were standing irresolutely about Scadbolt and Joshua. Joshua was cool but perplexed, and Scadbolt was in a furious rage.

"Whose watch is this?" asked Captain Liddle. He knew well enough, but he had a motive for asking.

"Mine, sir," answered Joshua.

"What are the men hanging about for?"

"I gave an order, sir, and Mr. Scadbolt countermanded it."

"Give your order again, Mr. Marvel."

Joshua did so; and as Scadbolt, in a voice thick with passion, was desiring the men not to obey it, Captain Liddle very promptly knocked him down. Calling two of the sailors by name, Captain Liddle ordered them to put the second mate in irons. After the confusion which followed the execution of this order had partially subsided, Captain Liddle cried out, —

"Now, then, what have you to complain of? Speak out like men."

At this one of the sailors stepped forward, and said respectfully, —

"Well, your honor, some of us think it would have been better if we had stopped in port another day."

"That's a matter of opinion," said the captain. "You have a right to yours, but I have a right to mine also, and I am master of this ship. Now I ask you as sensible men and good sailors, is it right that you should forget your duty because we don't agree upon a certain point? Do you know what this means, my men?" pointing to Scadbolt. "It means mutiny. What would any one of you do if you were skipper in my place? You would put a stop to it at once, as I have done, and as I intend to do. I'll do it by reason, if you'll let me, and I'll say nothing of any other means, for I don't want to use them. I speak you fair, men, and I mean you fair. What do you say, now, to treating me as I treat you?"

Acquiescent murmurs ran round the crew, most of whom had gathered together during the scene. "And at such a time as this too," continued Captain Liddle, "though it would be all the same in fair weather or foul. I'll tell you something that many of you, as good mariners, suspect already. We are near a dangerous coast — how near I do not know, for I have not been able to take a sight for two days. And it's at such a time as this that this bad sailor — I found out before we got into the Bay of Biscay that he wasn't as good as he ought to be — it's at such a time as this that he tries to get you into trouble. Come, now, have I spoke you fair?"

"Yes, you have; spoke like a man!" a dozen voices said.

"That's well said. Whoever is on my side step over to me."

Every man — even the Lascar, too much of a coward to stand aloof — stepped to the captain's side and saluted him.

"I'm proud of my crew," was the captain's simple remark after this. "Now go to your duty."

As the captain walked on to the poop, Rough-and-Ready said,

"That was well done, skipper; but there are two or three black sheep among 'em, for all that."

"I know it," replied Captain Liddle, with a significant look. "I shall keep a sharp look-out on them. I've got a man on board that's a match for a dozen black sheep, or I'm very much mistaken."

Rough-and-Ready laughed and turned on his heel, and Captain Liddle went down to say an encouraging word to his wife.

On the eighth day the captain, suspecting that they were in the vicinity of the Minerva Shoal, near which there were some dangerous rocks, ordered a sharp lookout to be kept for broken water. All the passengers were by this time in a state of great alarm, and although Captain Liddle tried to cheer them by encouraging words, his anxious face belied his speech. Perhaps the one who suffered the most from terror was Stephen Homebush. His terror was so great that he forgot his mission, and flew to others for consolation, instead of imparting it. Such men as he are most true to their calling when the weather is fine. It was a miserably dark night. The captain, completely tired out, had gone down to his cabin for a little rest. All the passengers, with the exception of Rough-and-Ready, who never seemed to sleep, and yet was the freshest man of them all, had retired to their beds with hearts filled by gloomy forebodings of what the morrow might bring; and there they lay, tossing about, listening to the raging wind that was driving them perhaps to certain death. In the captain's cabin were Mrs. Liddle and her maid. There was something in the present danger that was to Minnie almost a relief from the horrible monotony of her life. Her self-imposed silence had become unbearable, and she fretted under it until her health was in danger of giving way. So that this change, with all its terrors and uncertainties, was an absolute relief to her. She was too sad and unhappy to be frightened at the prospect of death. Had the future held out to her any hope of happiness, she would have prayed to live; but as it was — "Better to die," she thought, "and so end all." There is no doubt that this miserable state of her mind was due to the want of proper moral training in her childhood. Thrown completely upon herself; with no mother's love to teach her what is often taught by love's instinct alone, that such and such impulses and thoughts are weeds that destroy, and such and such are flowers that beautify: doomed to the almost sole companionship of a father whose misfortunes had rendered him an unfit teacher, it is scarcely to be wondered at that she should have been oblivious of the true duty of life.

"Bessie," said Captain Liddle to his wife, "I have come down for an hour's sleep. I can rest with confidence, for Marvel is keeping the watch."

Mrs. Liddle nodded, and gave him a sweet little smile that was like wine to him; and Minnie heard him say, in answer to a whisper from his wife, "We are in God's hands, Bessie, and must trust to His mercy."

"We are in God's hands, and must trust to His mercy," thought Minnie as she left the cabin; "and Joshua is keeping the watch. Death may be very near. Will it be wrong to speak to him?" Mechanically she made her way to the deck, stumbling two or three times and bruising herself. But she felt no pain. "I should like to die near him," she thought; "if he would take my hand in his, I should be content and happy."

Nothing but darkness surrounded her on deck. She clung to a rope, appalled by the mournfulness of the scene. Not a star was to be seen in the heavens, and the sky and water were as black as the night. So solemn, so mournful was every thing around, that the ship seemed to be rushing into a pit of death, where no light was. She could not see her hand before her, but all at once her heart beat wildly at the sound of Joshua's voice. He was speaking to Rough-and-Ready, and they were quite near her, although she had not seen them. Even now she could but barely discern their forms in the gloom. Joshua had just made a remark that Rough-and-Ready must have been a great traveller.

"Yes," answered Rough-and-Ready, "I've been about a pretty great deal. I've led a wild life; but then, you see, I never had any one to care for but myself."

"Never?" questioned Joshua, in a tone that had a dash of pity in it.

"Never but once, and that was only for a little while. But what matters? It will be all one by and by."

"I should be sorry to think you meant that," continued Joshua; "it would be a sad belief that, at such a time as this."

"You speak as if you didn't believe it, at all events," said Rough-and-Ready, in tones as soft as a girl's; "but then your circumstances are different to mine. You are young; I am" —

"Not old."

"Old enough for twice your years. Then you have friends at home, mayhap?"

"Ay, dear ones."

"Mother and father?"

"Ay; God bless them!"

"Wife perhaps?"

Joshua gave a gasp that sounded almost like a cry of pain.

"Ah, well," continued Rough-and-Ready, "if we were to go down this minute, I don't know the man or woman who would say 'Poor fellow!' when my fate was known. I leave no one behind me, and my death would bring no grief to a single soul. Perhaps my condition is the happier of the two."

"Not so," said Joshua sadly; "and I hope—indeed I believe—that you don't mean what you say. I have a friend at home—Dan, his name—to whom the news of my death would be the bitterest grief. I have dear ones at home, whose lives would be lives of mourning if I were not to return. I know this, and feel the pain that they would experience should it be God's will that we are not to escape this peril. But, strange as it may sound, I would not spare them the pain if it were in my power. Could I, by a wish, destroy the memories that make my life dear to me and them—dearer than you imagine—and so pluck from their hearts and minds the sting that my death would bring to them, I would not do so. For after death, there is life!"

"You believe in the immortality of the soul, mate?"

"Surely; and you?"

Rough-and-Ready made no reply.

"'Tis often difficult to believe in what we don't understand. On such a night as this—bleak, dreary, awfully solemn—with death waiting for us within a few yards perhaps—it is difficult to believe that there are spots on the earth where the sun is shining and where the flowers are blooming."

"That's true, mate; you speak more like a scholar than a sailor. Shake hands."

"I learned a great deal from the friend of whom I have spoken," said Joshua, grasping Rough-and-Ready's hand. "What is that ahead of us?"

A dark cloud. Impossible to see whether it belonged to earth, or air, or water. A moment after he uttered the words, the man who was keeping the look-out cried that there was land ahead. Joshua hastily gave some orders, and was making his way to the saloon to arouse the captain, when he was almost thrown off his legs by a terrible shock. Involuntarily he threw his arms around Minnie, who was clinging to the rope. She held him fast for a moment, and he cried,—

"Who is this?"

"It is me," she said; "cling to me."

"Don't stir," he whispered rapidly, filled with a wild amazement at the familiar tones of Minnie's voice; "if it were not that I know I am not dreaming, I could believe a spirit spoke, and not a woman. But keep you here; do not move for your life."

The next instant all was confusion, and cries and lamentations filled the air. Captain Liddle was on deck barefooted, and all the passengers were there in their night-dresses, clinging to ropes and spars, praying and crying and wringing their hands. Great seas washed over the ship, drowning the cries for a brief time; the night was so dark that their true situation could not be discovered, and imagination added to their terrors and magnified them. The captain could do literally nothing; for the ship appeared to have been lifted on to the rocks, and kept bumping against them in its endeavors to get free. And yet there was sea all around them. Some of the passengers had sought shelter under the lee of the cuddy, among them the captain's wife, Mr. and Mrs. Pigeon and Little Emma, and Steven and Rachel Homebush. Many times during the night was the voice of Stephen Homebush heard, calling upon the Lord to save *him*; while his sister Rachel, braver than he, stood by his side, with a stern set face, in silence. The cheery laugh of Mrs. Pigeon was stilled, but she was not so overcome by terror as not to be a comfort to her husband and child; during the dark night those three clung together and comforted each other as well as they were able; while the captain, making his way from one group to another, bade them not lose heart; for the ship seemed to be keeping together, and when daylight came their condition might be found to be less desperate than it appeared.

"Besides," he whispered to the male passengers, "we have three or four rascals among the sailors, and for the sake of the women we must keep ourselves cool and self-possessed."

To his wife he said simply,—

"Well, Bessie, this is a bad job. I ought not to have allowed you to come with me."

"I would sooner be here with you, John," she said, kissing him, "than I would be at home in safety."

"Brave little heart," he whispered to himself as he walked away from her. "Yet I could bear it better if I were alone."

James Heartsease and Harry Wall kept together, as friends should, all through the night. They felt not a particle of fear; they thought it was very grand and very awful, and spoke in calm tones of what the morrow might bring.

"Don't think we shall see China, Jim," said Harry.

"Perhaps not. Hope no body will be hurt" was the reply. "What a grand painting this would make!"

A few minutes after Joshua had left Minnie, he came to the cuddy, where Mrs. Liddle had sought protection.

"Mr. Marvel," she called to him, " have you seen my maid ?"

Then it came upon him that the woman to whom he had clung when the ship struck was the gypsy-maid who had kept herself so reserved, and he said, "Yes my lady; do you want her?"

All the officers called the captain's wife "my lady," and she was proud of the title.

"Yes," she answered; "I wish you could bring her to me, poor girl; she is friendless and unhappy, poor child!"

"Has she no friends at home, my lady?" Joshua could not help asking.

"None, I believe."

The word "home" reached little Emma Pigeon's ears, and as she nestled in her mother's arms, the child cried, " Mother, are we going home?"

"Yes, yes, my dear," sobbed Mrs. Pigeon; " try to go to sleep, there's a darling." And she rocked the child, and sang a little song about birds and angels.

Joshua, steadying himself as he walked cautiously to where Minnie was standing, wondered to himself whether it was fancy that had made the gypsy-maid's voice sound so familiar to him; a sea washing over the deck, drenched him to the skin, and as he stood upright and shook the water from his clothes, the memories that were stirred within him brought to him a picture of the dear old kitchen at Stepney, with himself half-naked, barefooted, and with the water streaming from him, standing at the door. The vision may have occupied but a moment, but the picture was complete; father, mother, Ellen, Dan and the birds, the Old Sailor, all were there. But where was Minnie? Why, by his side, with short curly hair and brown gypsy-face. "Am I mad?" he exclaimed, as he dashed the waters from his eyes. But when he reached the spot where Minnie stood, and she clasped his hand and said, "Thank God, you are safe!" his amazement grew.

"I cannot see your face." he whispered, with his arm round her, for the better protection of both; " but your voice is strangely familiar to me. Do I know you?"

"Yes. But do not press me farther. Wait till the light comes. Shall we live till then?"

"I hope so."

"Will you promise me to keep near me till daylight comes? It is my dearest wish — my only one."

"I promise," he said, strangely agitated, "until my duty calls me away."

"And even then, you will come back when you have done your task, and stand by my side?"

"I will, my poor girl. I have come now to bring you to the captain's lady."

"She sent you for me?"

"Yes."

"She is a good lady. But wait a little; I have something to say first." Many moments passed before she spoke again. and in the pause a grateful prayer went up from the girl's heart even for the small blessing of gentle speech from her hero's lips. "You have made me very, very happy. Until tonight — for many, many months past — I have been most unhappy." She bent her lips to his hand and kissed it. "Now answer me. We are in great peril ?"

"The greatest, I fear."

"But a danger threatens you of which you are not aware. Listen. The second mate, he who was put in irons the other day" —

"Seadbolt — go on."

"Is loosed."

"By whom?"

"I don't know. But he is loosed, and but five minutes since was near me with a sailor whom I think I know, although I could not see him. Listen. I must whisper, for he may be near us now. They were talking of you, and they swore — O my God! — they swore to have your life."

"They spoke of me by name?"

"By name — Joshua Marvel."

"You think you know the sailor who was talking to Seadbolt. Is he a dark man?"

"Yes; a Lascar I think."

"You are right. He owes me an old grudge."

"Seadbolt said that this coast is one of the most dangerous upon which a ship could strike. He believes he knows pretty well where we are, and that it will be a fight for the boats" —

"We have only two, the jolly-boat and the long-boat; he may be right."

"Be on your guard; tell the captain; be prepared."

"We will; and you" —

"I can protect myself. Feel this."
"A knife!"
"I picked it up. Let them beware."
Another lurch of the vessel made them cling closer to each other. During all the horror of the scene, Joshua had not dared to ask whether it really was Minnie to whom he was speaking; he feared to know the truth. Minnie on the ship with him! and Ellen at home — and Dan — he dared not think of it.
"Come he said; "I will take you to the captain's lady. Cling fast to me."
"Say a few words to me."
"What are they?"
"God bless and forgive you."
"God bless and forgive you! From my heart."
"He will, I think," said the girl, as if communing with herself. "I have not felt so happy for a long time past. Death has no terror for me if you are kind!"

CHAPTER XXX.

JOSHUA IS PROMOTED.

WHEN daylight came — and oh, how they watched for it, and prayed for it! — they saw clearly their great peril. The ship was rolling amongst a mass of sharp rocks jutting upwards from the sea. They saw the points of these rocks on all sides of them; but no friendly land was in view.
"The ship is lost," said Captain Liddle to Joshua, whom he looked upon as his right-hand; "she is breaking up fast. Our next chance is the boats."
It was a wonder indeed how the "Merry Andrew" had kept together during the night, with the tremendous beating she had received from the rocks; if she had been in deep water, she must inevitably have sunk.
Joshua had told Captain Liddle of the understanding between Seadbolt and the Lascar, as overhead by Minnie; and now the captain walked to where the two conspirators were standing in conversation with other sailors. Seadbolt was endeavoring to persuade them to sieze the jolly boat, and leave the passengers to shift for themselves.
"What is that you are saying?" cried the captain breaking in amongst them, and grasping Seadbolt by the shoulder with a grasp of iron. "More incitings to mutiny! Take heed, sir! Give me but a little stronger cause — nay, dare to lay a finger upon boats or provisions without leave — and, by God, I'll throw you into the sea!"

"Will you stand this, men?" shouted Seadbolt, writhing in the captain's grasp.
The Lascar made a movement towards the captain, and the glitter of a knife flashed in the light; but a blow from Joshua sent him reeling, and in an instant the knife was torn from his hand.
"Remember!" said Joshua in a low voice. "You had a lesson from me years ago. What the captain does to Seadbolt, I do to you, you treacherous cur."
"I remember," muttered the Lascar, presenting the singular aspect of a man cowed by fear and raging with furious passion at the same time, "I swore to have your heart's blood, and I'll have it! Look you! the end has not yet come. Give me my knife."
Joshua looked at the knife; it was one-bladed, with a clasp — one of the articles, indeed, which the Lascar had wrested from Solomon Fewster's fears.
"You asked me once before for a knife I took from you," he said; "then I broke it before I gave it back. But this — this I mean to keep."
"Now then my men," cried the captain, in a cheery voice, "this is the second time that this damned rascal has tried to step between you and me. What I feared then has happened now. The ship is breaking up, and can't hold together for many days, and if the weather gets worse, may break up in a day. There are certain chances in our favor, every one of which will be destroyed unless we act in friendly concert and like men. This scoundrel has tried to make you believe that your interests and the interests of the passengers are in opposition. He lies! I declare to you, as a captain and a man" (if he had said a gentleman, all would have been ruined). "that your lives and your safety are as dear to me, as those of anybody else on board — except my wife," he said softly yet stoutly, and murmurs of "Bravo, skipper! Bravo! you're a man!" broke even from the lips of those sailors who were most disposed to be won over by Seadbolt. "Well then, you hear me declare now, as I have declared before, that I mean you fair. And I declare moreover, that our only chance of safety is in union. Once again — With me, — or Against me?"
"With you! with you, skipper!"
During this scene, Joshua did not know that Minnie was standing near him. Now, releasing the Lascar with warning words, he turned and saw her. She met his gaze unflinchingly, and a hot blush mantled over her neck and face. He gazed at her for so long a time, that she drooped her head before him, and stood in an attitude of pleading. But he could not doubt the

evidence of his senses. Her manner, no less than her appearance, convinced him. It was Minnie, indeed, who stood before him.

He covered his eyes with his hand, and staggered to the saloon. If a thousand despairing and undeserved deaths had stared him in the face, he could not have been more shocked and bewildered. He sat down and tried to think. What was the meaning of it? What did they know at home? What did they know? What might they suspect? He saw himself and the Old Sailor together in the boat at Gravesend, and heard that faithful old friend tell him of Minnie's love for him, and what it was his duty to do. He had seen his duty clearly then: love for Ellen no less than duty — affection for his friend and brother, no less than love and duty — impelled him to the right and honorable course of making Ellen his wife. And then! Why, within three days of that consummation of his dearest hope, he and Minnie were together on board the "Merry Andrew." If they at home knew it, suspected it even, must they not believe that his whole life was a monstrous lie? that he had planned, plotted, deceived, schemed, to prove how utterly false he was to the woman who adored him, to the man who believed in him, to the kind mother and father who loved him better than Benjamin was loved? For a few moments he lost all consciousness of present peril. The ship beat amongst the rocks; the seas dashed over the deck: he heard them not, felt them not. He took from his breast Ellen's picture and the lock of hair she had given him at their parting, and kissed them again and again while his tears ran on them. Strangely enough, there came to his ears then, in the midst of his agony, his father's hearty exultant voice, saying, "This is better than being a wood-turner all one's life, isn't it, Josh?" He shivered and sobbed and cried, "O Dan, Dan, do not forsake me!" and stretched forth his hands as if his friend were near. A hand upon his shoulder aroused him. He looked up, and saw the captain's wife. She was a brave woman, and had done much during the night to sustain the courage of the others.

"There is a man's work to do on deck," she said to him gravely and sweetly. "You are not growing faint-hearted?"

"No, my lady," he answered, "not faint-hearted at the prospect of death; but I have received a shock worse than death."

She did not stop to ask for an explanation of his meaning — time was too precious; but she took the picture of Ellen and looked at it.

"My wife, my lady," he said, with a sob.

A troubled expression crossed her features, and she said encouragingly, —

"Nay, all hope is not gone; we may succeed in reaching land, or some ship may see us and pick us up. But all private grief must give way now for the general good. There are not too many faithful men on board; the lives of others depend on them. If they lose heart, and yield to the selfishness of their grief, we are lost."

Joshua jumped to his feet and wiped his tears.

"They are not unmanly tears, my lady," he said bravely; "I can justify them to you when there is no pressing work to do. Thank you for calling me to my duty."

She smiled brightly on him and shook hands with him. When he got on deck, the captain was giving orders to lower the jolly-boat; but as the boat was being lowered, the broken water caught her and splintered her to pieces. The sailors and passengers looked with dismay at the fragments of the boat drifting away and dashing against the jagged rocks. "What next?" they all thought.

"Try the long-boat, men," cried the captain. And in accordance with his instructions, the long boat — the only one left — was launched over the vessel's side; but as she hung in the tackle, a huge wave dashed up and filled her. It was imperative that the water should be bailed out of her.

"Who will do it?" asked the captain, loath to give an order in which there was almost certain death. Joshua was about to start forward, when Minnie's hand upon his arm restrained him. Before he could shake off the grasp, the first mate, crying, "I'm a single man; I've no wife and children waiting for me at home!" jumped into the boat up to his waist in water, and began to bail it out. But he had not bailed out a dozen gallons when the stern-post was jerked out of the boat, which was left hanging in the tackle. The shouts of the men and the screams of the women apprised him of his danger; and as he looked about to see how he could remedy the disaster, the fore-tackle got adrift, and the boat was battling with cruel rocks and water. The force of the current was too powerful for her. The captain threw out lines to the unfortunate man, but he could not catch them. But if he had, he would have been bruised to death by the sharp rocks. The moment before he went down, he waved a good-by to those on board. A long silence followed. The women looked anxiously at the captain, but saw no hope in his face. Then with a gesture to all to follow him, he went down to the saloon, and there read prayers, and commended them to God. He was not what is understood as a religious man; but knowing the danger in which they stood, he conceived this to be a duty. That done, he said, "Men and passengers, we have one chance left, and only one. Out of our masts and spars we can make a raft sufficiently large to hold all of us. Then we may be able to reach some friendly land. To stay on board and wait, and not work, is certain death. Even as it is, a raft will take us some days to make, and the ship may break to pieces before it is done. But we must trust to God for that. What we're got to do is to work like men, for our own sakes, for the sake of the women, and for the sake of wives and children at home. Some of you have these, I know. It is not for me, now that we are in such a strait, to say, do this, or do that; although under any circumstances I shall insist upon discipline and order. I can't make you work, and therefore I submit for your approval the plan I think best for general safety. Have any of you a better one to propose?"

"No, no!" was the unanimous cry.

"Very well; then we'll determine upon this. And for the better carrying out of our design, I appoint Mr. Marvel second in command. He is first mate now. If any thing happens to me, you will look to him. When the raft is made, and safely launched — if it please God that it shall be so — we will set down necessary rules for all on board. Until that time there is but one rule — to work. Every man on board must work — passengers and all; and every man must aid me in preserving order."

The captain's manly speech infused hope into every heart; and exclamations of "Good!" "Bravo skipper!" "Well said, sir!" followed his last words.

"One other thing," he said, in a more determined voice: " to my certain knowledge, we have unfortunately among us two men who have endeavored to spread dissatisfaction and add to our confusion. I will not point out these men; they are known to me and all of you. They are men, though, as we are, so far as the value of life to each of us goes; and it is only fair that they should have equal chances with us. But this I declare, by my dear wife's life! If these men do not work, and if they attempt any thing that is not for the general good, I will shoot them with my own hand! Now then, to the deck!"

Not a man among them who did not take off his coat and set to work with a will. There were a great many loose spars on board, which, with the mizenmast, were found to be sufficient for their purpose. They tried to cut down the mainmast; but there was so much danger in the attempt that it was relinquished. For three days they worked like slaves. The rocks served as a resting-place for the ends of the largest spars, which were firmly lashed together and nailed; the light and short spars were used for the centre of the raft, upon which a kind of platform was raised on which many of the shipwrecked persons could lie out of the water; a mast to carry sails was also rigged up. The raft was not finished too soon; they could not have stopped another day on the ship. While the work was going on, three of the sailors lost their lives, so that already their number was lessened by four. The raft being ready, it was launched with great difficulty. The next anxious question was provisions; and the result of their inquiry blanched many a cheek. All the bread was spoiled by the salt water, and most of the preserved meat had been lost, in consequence of having been brought on deck when they tried to launch the boats. They also made another disheartening discovery. They could only find two small kegs to hold water. Still, when the first shock of these discoveries was over, they were borne bravely, almost cheerfully. The women, excepting Rachel Homebush, were the cause of this; they smiled upon the workers, encouraged them, and made them hopeful in spite of themselves. Even Mrs. Pigeon recovered some of her good spirits; and knowing that her merry laugh was a comfort to the men, she laughed often when she was not inclined for mirth. The little child, Emma, was the only truly happy one of the party, and her presence drove away many a hard thought. Rough-and-Ready had his anxious intervals, but he worked with a will. Between him and Joshua a strong attachment sprung up; each admired the manliness of the other. He was also particularly kind to Minnie, and she grew accustomed to look upon him with confidence, and to trust in him. The night before the raft was launched, Joshua persuaded Captain Liddle to take a night's rest.

"It will be all the better for you and all of us, sir," said Joshua.

"But you too, Marvel," said Captain Liddle, "you want rest as much as I. I don't believe you have had two hours' sleep since we struck." This was really true: both Joshua and the captain had been in defatigable.

"Never mind me, sir," said Joshua, with a sad sweet smile. " You have your wife to attend to. Besides, I promise that I will rest to-morrow night, if you will give me leave."

"You are a noble fellow, Marvel;" and Captain Liddle gazed admiringly at the young sailor. "I have often wondered how you acquired certain qualities that are not common to the ordinary sailor."

"I don't know, sir; I doubt if they were ever in me. They must have been put there by my friend Dan, who is nobleness itself."

"Dan? Ah! the lame boy with the wonderful birds, that I saw at your house. I liked his face."

"He is the dearest fellow"—Joshua turned away his head.

The next day the provisions and the charts and instruments, and many things that would be useful, such as blankets, tools, and writing materials, were stowed safely on the raft. Of the provisions there was a very small store: twenty tins of preserved meat, a small quantity of sugar, about a gallon of rum, and two kegs of water. By the time every thing useful was stowed away and secured, and the passengers were safely on the raft, it was evening, and within three hours the "Merry Andrew" broke completely up. The raft, having parted its moorings, forced by the strong current, was carried to sea, and the passengers watched the last of the ship with unmixed feelings of sadness. The women shed tears, and all of them, men and women, felt as if they had lost a friend. When the vessel was out of sight a stronger feeling of desolation stole upon the unhappy group, and Rough-and-Ready had many looks of astonishment cast upon him as he rubbed his hands and said in a cheerful voice, "This is splendid. Now we can be comfortable." But it was well for them that they had some stout hearts on board.

The direct allusion made by Captain Liddle to Scadbolt and the Lascar had had its effect upon those worthies; they knew that their lives depended upon their conduct. But they found means to exchange confidences, and they resolved to revenge themselves on both Joshua and the captain when opportunity served. "Wait till we make land," said Scadbolt; "they shall smart then the pair of them. I'll teach both of them the meaning of 'general good!'" The Lascar's old feeling of hate for Joshua had been revived in all its intensity by the late scene between them.

"I'll have my knife back," he muttered to himself as he lay on the raft the first night, at a little distance from Joshua, watching him with venomous looks, "and his heart's blood with it."

Not a movement, not a glance, escaped Minnie's notice. Aware of the feelings of hate entertained by the Lascar for Joshua, she set herself the task of watching over Joshua's safety. He, overpowered by fatigue, had been persuaded by the captain to take some sleep, and when he lay down Minnie crept to his side and remained there during the night. He slept long and peacefully through the solemn night and after the gray morning had dawned, dreaming of home, of Dan and Ellen, and murmuring their names with a smile upon his lips.

CHAPTER XXXI.

ON THE RAFT.

JOSHUA, opening his eyes, saw Minnie sitting by his side. She, seeing that he was awake, moved quietly away without a word, and went to where the other women were lying. He had been so fatigued when he lay down to rest, that his sleep had been very profound; and when he awoke, the full sense of his situation did not come upon him. Minnie, sitting by his side with her brown face and short curls, was the first thing he saw; and it seemed to him for a brief space that he was dreaming. But when she moved away and joined the other women, he remembered the perils they had encountered, and the terrible position in which they were placed. He would have called to her, but that some feeling restrained him; and although he thought much of her during the day, he was glad that he had not spoken to her. Besides, his attention was diverted for a time to another circumstance. Some of the men were clamoring for breakfast. Neither Scadbolt nor the Lascar was among the murmurers; these last consisted of the weakest of the party, who were less able than the others to bear hunger, and to whom the fear of starvation made it appear as if they had been already fasting a day.

"Breakfast! breakfast!" they cried.

"Wait till ten o'clock," said the captain, in a stern determined voice; "you can't be hungry already. If you don't cease murmuring, I will put off breakfast until twelve."

This threat silenced them.

In the mean time the captain called his council together, and consulted with them. There were four in the council: himself, Joshua, Rough-and-Ready, and an old sailor named Standish, who had been wrecked twice before, and who consequently was looked upon as a distinguished personage. At eight o'clock the captain read prayers. Then the men, with the exception of the council, sat idly watching the water, and looking out for a fish. The morning was fine; one of the sailors noted for quaint sayings remarked that the weather had no business to be fine; it was a mockery. At ten o'clock the captain piped all hands; the call was answered readily, but there were no signs of breakfast.

"Be seated," said the captain.

They all sat down, with the exception of the captain and his three counsellors. The captain stood in front, his supporters behind.

"We who stand," said the captain, "have been constituted by me, commander of this ship, into a council for the discussion and deliberation of all matters relating to the general welfare. The fairness of the selection will recommend itself to the crew, for the council is composed of three sailors and one passenger. Are you content?"

"Yes, yes!" cried a large number.

Up rose Scadbolt.

"Let us hear first what you have to say about the provisions," he said. "I am not one who says yes without consideration."

"That's fair too," broke from half a dozen throats.

Captain Liddle eyed Scadbolt steadily. Scadbolt returned his gaze. He knew that in the position he had assumed, he could command the sympathies of a certain number, and the knowledge gave him confidence.

"Well, it *is* fair," said the captain; "and a reasonable suggestion is always reasonable, never mind who makes it. The council have drawn out a set of rules this morning, which I have here writ down on paper. If you approve of them, you will approve of the council; do I understand that?"

"Yes, yes!"

The captain produced his paper and commenced.

"Rule 1. All questions in dispute, with the exception of such as are properly within the province of the duties of Captain Liddle —' whose orders as Captain of the 'Merry Andrew,' we promise to obey and uphold to the death — shall be decided by the majority."

"Agreed!" some cried.

"Stop!" exclaimed Scadbolt; "how about the women? We are not going to let them vote."

Thought Captain Liddle, "This is no common scoundrel; he puts in speech what many a malcontent would only dare to think." Said Captain Liddle aloud, "That was not mentioned by the council. I don't suppose the women would wish to vote; a proper man would not have mentioned it. Decided, however, that the women do not vote."

In arguing with Scadbolt, Captain Liddle committed a grave mistake; it put them upon a kind of equality, and from that moment Scadbolt could boast of being the leader of a party, small as it might be.

"Rule 2." continued Captain Liddle. "The small stock of provisions shall be equally divided between every soul on board"—

A little faint cheering here broke out.

"But, in consequence of the smallness of the supply, the quantity to be measured out to each person shall be regulated, as occasion demands, by the Captain and his council."

No demur was made to this.

"Rule 3. That all fish, birds, or food of any kind which may be found in air or water shall be added to the general stock, and shall be fairly and equally divided."

"Unfair!" exclaimed Scadbolt; "each man is entitled to what he can catch in air or water."

"Not so," replied the captain; "for what then would become of the women? — Men, I appeal to you: does this man, who speaks while you are silent, represent your views?"

Two or three voices answered, "Yes;" a score answered, "No."

"Good," said the captain; "he represents but one in a dozen; and even the two or three of you who seem to side with him may be brought to see the selfishness of what he advocates. If he had his way, the weak would be left to die; the strong alone should live, and have a chance of being saved. Is this fair? is it manly? is it honest?"

"Every man for himself, and God for us all," muttered Scadbolt trying to fan the flame.

"Then the strongest man would crush the rest, and might would take the place of right," continued the captain, beginning to see that he had made a mistake in listening so patiently to Scadbolt. "We were never nearer to death than we are this day; but shall that make us forget that we are men? Shall that turn us into brutes? We have helpless women depending upon us, and upon our manliness. They shall be shown no favor in the way of provisions; they shall divide equally with us, share and share alike. But, by God, the one who seeks to deny them their fair chance of life, dies by my hand!"

"I am with you, captain," cried Rough-and-Ready.

"And I," said Joshua.

"And I," said the sailor who had been twice wrecked.

"And I," "And I," from most of the rest.

"Decided, then, that all food that may be found in air or water shall be added to the general stock, and shall be fairly and equally divided."

Seadbolt did not dare demur.

"Rule 4. That, recognizing the full extent of our dread peril, and knowing that death stares us in the face, we resolve to die like men, if it be God's will; and thus resolving, we solemnly declare that, supposing all our food to be gone, we will not eat human flesh"—

A shudder ran round the attentive group, and Mrs. Pigeon fainted; but Captain Liddle proceeded firmly,—

"Nor draw lots as to who shall be killed to feed the rest. This we solemnly resolve, in fear of the Lord, out of common humanity, and out of respect for ourselves as Christian men."

Assented to in silence; not one of them could realize the horrible craving, born of raging thirst and hunger, that had come upon men in such a strait as theirs.

"That is all," concluded the captain after a long pause. "You approve, then, of the council and these rules?"

"Yes."

"Now to breakfast. Water, for the first week, will be served out twice a day—a quarter of a pint in the morning, and a quarter of a pint in the evening—half a pint a day to each person. Of food we have only preserved meat and sugar, and very little of either. One table-spoonful of preserved meat will be served out to each person at eleven o'clock every morning, and at five o'clock one ounce of sugar. Of rum we have about a gallon: a teaspoonful will be served out to each person once in every other day, in the morning or in the evening, as he may choose. The general stock of provisions will not be touched by any one on board, except in presence of all, and it will be guarded by two of the council; the penalty of tampering with the stock, or of attempting to steal any portion of it, will be death. And God give us strength, and send us happy deliverance!"

When breakfast was served, the men lay about the raft idly, watching the water for fish, which they were not successful in catching, and rising every now and then to scan the horizon for a sail. Some slept or tried to sleep; some talked over the chances of deliverance; some spoke in whispers of what they had heard from men who had been wrecked. While the provisions were being measured by the captain, the other three of the council stood by with cocked pistols, ready to fire should a rush be made. Most of the men took their spoonful of preserved meat, and ate it quickly and greedily, some of them at one gulp; but a few, wiser than their fellows, retired with their portion, and sitting down, ate it very slowly. These last were the best satisfied. The council were busy enough all the day; assisted by Mr. Pigeon and the two friends, Wall and Heartsease, they were employed in re-arranging every thing on the raft, and in making things more comfortable for the women. A kind of low tent was built, under cover of which the women could lie down and rest, screened from the men; but it was only used at night; for at first the women mixed with the men during the day, and made themselves useful. Mrs. Pigeon, of her own accord, crept to where the sailors were lying about, and asked if they wanted any thing mended. At first they were too surprised to reply; but presently a dozen voices answered her. One wanted a pair of socks darned; another had half a dozen rents in his shirt; and in a very little while Mrs. Pigeon's hands were full. She made her way back to her female companions, and throwing a heap of clothes in the midst of them, proposed that they should set to work at once. Soon all of them, with the exception of Rachel Homebush, were busily and cheerfully at work; and while their fingers were plying, Mrs. Pigeon sang snatches of songs. It was as little like a picture of shipwrecked persons as one could imagine. But it was a picture that did an immense amount of good. The men looked at the women admiringly, and Rough-and-Ready's eyes glistened every time they wandered that way.

"A pretty bunch!" he observed to Joshua.

Joshua nodded hopefully, for the sight cheered him.

"That's a good little woman of yours," said Rough-and-Ready, turning to Mr. Pigeon. Rough-and-Ready held a very different position now from what he did when he first stepped aboard the "Merry Andrew;" he was a general favorite with men and women. Even Rachel Homebush cast glances of approval at him.

"I tell you what," answered Mr. Pigeon in a confidential tone; "I've not seen much of women—you know out there in the bush they're rather scarce—and we had some hope of getting home"—

"*Had* some hope!" interrupted Rough-and-Ready. "Say *have* some hope. If there's one thing in the world that makes me certain of it, it is that picture there," pointing to the women.

"I am heartily glad to hear you say so. *Have* some hope, then, of getting home, where the streets are crowded with women they say. But there isn't one among 'em to come up to her. Although there were not half a dozen lasses to choose from when I first made up to her, I'd choose her now out of a million."

Having delivered himself of these, his articles of faith in his wife, he sat down by her side, and held her cotton for her as she stitched and sewed.

Meantime the current and their one sail carried them along at the rate of about two miles an hour. No land was in sight, and there was no sign of a ship, although during the day many 'a false alarm was given. The weather remained fine. The light wind died away in the evening, when the thin crescent of a new moon came out in the sky. It was welcomed as a good omen; and the women looked at it, and smiled at one another, the foolish things! as if the silver crescent were a messenger of good tidings. Then the stars came out brightly — another good omen. Many a one on the raft thought, "This is better than being jammed on the rocks in the 'Merry Andrew;' we are moving towards safety. If we do not see a ship, we may see land, and may manage to get ashore." References were made to Robinson Crusoe and the Swiss Family Robinson; not in a gloomy, but in a cheerful spirit. It was the admirable bearing of the men in command, no less than the virtues of the women, that contributed to this state of hopeful feeling. The sailors were also comparatively contented; most of them had a little stock of tobacco — some more, some less — the chewing of which gave them comfort. Each man hoarded his store more jealously than a miser hoards his gold; but some were greedier than others, or craved for it more, and could not withstand the temptation of chewing it almost wastefully, certainly not prudently. But then sailors are not a prudent class of men.

To Joshua, who was sitting musing of home, came Rough-and-Ready, and sat beside him.

"You don't smoke?" asked Rough-and-Ready.

"No."

"That's not sailor-like."

Joshua shrugged his shoulders, and smiled.

"Nor chew?"

"No."

"Here is a little piece of tobacco. Chew it."

Joshua put it in his mouth and chewed it, because he thought it was, after all a certain kind of food, and night make him less hungry. But it made him sick.

Rough-and-Ready laughed a little when he saw the effect of it, and presently said, so that no one else should hear, "You must learn to chew."

"Why?"

"It will help to keep you alive when the provisions run out. I have a dozen pounds of tobacco strapped round me; it was my own, so I thought I had a right to it. By and by it will come in handy. I wish I could teach the women to chew."

"If the men knew you had so much," said Joshua, "your life would not be safe."

"I know that. I had an idea at first of handing it to the skipper for general use; but I thought better of it. There are a few on board to whom I don't think I'd give an ounce to save their lives. What is that in your handkerchief?"

"My accordion."

"Do you play? Of course, though, or you wouldn't have it. I should like to hear some music."

Joshua untied his handkerchief and took out his accordion. The night was very still, and the soft tones floated in the air, and seemed to linger about the raft as it glided through the sea. The quiet bubbling of the water as it stole through the openings between the spars, as if in sport, was in consonance with the melody and the still night and the beautiful peaceful heavens. Men who were lying at full length sat up when the music commenced, and were the better for it. The women crept from out their shelter, and listened and shed tears, not entirely unhappy. Surely it was a night of good omens. As Joshua played, his thoughts wandered back to his boyish life, and to the tender conversations that had taken place between him and Dan. Often he stopped as he mused and thought; but presently his fingers would be on the keys again, playing a few bars of "Poor Tom Bowling," and other more cheerful songs of Dibdin, which the Old Sailor loved so well. They came back to him, the memories of that happy time. Their anxiety about their birds, when they first commenced to train them; the death of Golden Cloud, and the after conversation which he had never forgotten, in the course of which they had read together of the wreck of Robinson Crusoe. Why, it seemed all to have come true! Here he was, wrecked, certainly not alone, and therefore better off than Crusoe was, but wrecked for all that. But under what circumstances, and with what a dreadful web of suspicion surrounding him! Oh, if he could see the end of it! It was horrible to think that he might die — he and all of them on the raft; and that Dan might believe him false because of Minnie. It would not bear thinking of. He ceased playing, and bathed his fevered head and face. Often and often had he said to himself, in former storms and former scenes, the words that Dan had impressed upon him; and now he tried to fancy that Dan could see him, and knew that he was true.

Rough-and-Ready, seeing that Joshua was engrossed in thought, did not disturb him, and presently dozed off. How long he had been asleep he did not know; but he woke up with a curious impression upon him. He must have slept long, for the night was far advanced, and no sound was heard but the plashing of the water against and through the spars. The impression was this: that he and Joshua were lying side by side (as, in fact they were) asleep, and that a woman suddenly came between them. Her back was to him, her face turned to Joshua; that she sat down so, and so remained, for an hour and more, making no movement, uttering no sound; but he could tell that all the while she was watching Joshua's sleeping form. That then she inclined herself gently to Joshua, and pressed her lips to his hand: and that rising to go, she turned her face to Rough-and-Ready, and he saw that it was Mrs. Liddle's gypsy-maid. So far his fancies went. Starting into a sitting position, he saw Minnie a few paces from him, making her way to where the women were lying.

Now this set Rough-and-Ready thinking —for more reasons than one. Had he been dreaming, or had it really occurred? If it had occurred, it must have been love that prompted her. He had observed her the previous night sitting near Joshua; but then it had not been so noticeable, for there was no kind of order on the raft. How long had she known Joshua? He was the more perplexed because he had never seen the two in conversation, and because of the mystery surrounding the acquaintance. He was troubled, too; for, rough as he was, and old enough to be Minnie's father, he had taken a tender interest in her, and the discovery he had just made came upon him like a shock.

Every person on the raft was asleep with the exception of the men in the watch and himself. He did not feel inclined to lie down again, so he sat and thought of things. In such a solemn scene, and at such solemn moments the spirit of nature works wonders in the minds of the roughest men — quickens the sympathies, and stirs into life the tenderest memories. It was so with Rough-and-Ready at the present time. Incidents in his life which had been so long unremembered that he wondered how he thought of them now, came vividly before him. His home — his mother — small domestic joys and griefs — a brother who died when they were both children, with whom he used to play and pelt with daisies — Good God! what kind of a bridge was that in his life that spanned that time and this? By what strange steps had he walked from then to now? The stars grew less bright and paled out of the skies; the water grew grayer in the brief space before the morning's dawn. Soon in the east a thin line of water at the edge of the horizon quickened into life, and Nature's grandest wonder began to work in the dawning of a new day. The water-line, a mere thread at first, but broadening with every second that marked the flight of gray shadows, was rosy with blushing light. Purple clouds, fringed with wondrous colors, surrounded the clear space, in which presently the glorious sun rose grandly from the golden bed of waters; and as it rose, sky and sea rejoiced. At one time, for a few moments, the sea was like a field of golden corn waving in the sun's eye; but soon it deepened, till it and the heavens, that looked down into its mighty depths, were filled with flaming restless light, which in their turn gave way to softer shadows. Many a sunrise had Rough-and-Ready seen, but never one that he had watched so steadily as this; but it seemed as if his thoughts were in harmony with it.

Late in the day, Rough-and-Ready asked Joshua how long he had known Mrs. Liddle's maid. Joshua looked at him curiously, but did not reply. He had not spoken to Minnie since they had been on the raft, and had, indeed, taken pains to avoid her. She did not intrude herself upon him; she submitted in patience to the silence he imposed upon her by his manner. But a strange phenomenon took place in her. While the others grew weaker and paler and more unhappy, she seemed to gather fresh strength, and actually grew rosier and more hardy. The dark color, too, was dying out of her face.

"I have a reason for asking," said Rough-and-Ready, as an excuse for his question.

Joshua nodded, not unkindly, but with a troubled face.

"There is a strange story connected with your question," he said; "so strange and so painful, that I cannot give you an answer."

"I thought there was some mystery in the affair," observed Rough-and-Ready; "but I will not press upon your confidence. Do you know that the night before last she watched by you the whole time you were asleep?"

"Watched by me?"

"Ay. And last night, too, for some time — I don't know for how long."

Joshua gave Rough-and-Ready an amazed look, and turned away to where Minnie was sitting. She saw him coming towards her, and her heart beat fast.

"Why have you watched near me for two nights?" he asked, without looking at her.

"You have enemies on the raft," was the answer, very quietly given.

"I know: Scadbolt and the Lascar. But I can take care of myself."

"Not when you are asleep," she said, almost in a whisper.

What could he do? What could he say? Together on the raft in the presence of Death, from which only something very like a miracle could save them, could he be stern and harsh to her? And his great misery was, that he knew and felt his power. He knew that an unkind word from him to this young girl was as bitter as death could be.

"You are like the rest of us, I suppose," he said, gently; "growing very weak."

"I do not think so," she answered, trembling at the gentleness of his voice; "I feel strong as yet. Shall we be saved?"

"We are in God's hands," he said. "I think there is but little chance of being picked up, or even of making friendly land."

Neither addressed the other by name.

"If the end comes, and you know it, and I am not near you, will you try and find me, and say a kind word to me before I die?"

He gave her the promise, and hurried suddenly from her, for his heart was fit to break, and he dared not trust himself to say more.

The third day passed, and the fourth. No sign of succor near. Hope began to die.

On the sixth morning, when the roll was called, one of the passengers did not answer to his name. It was Mr. Bracegirdle.

"He is asleep," said one.

They shook him, but he did not move. He was dead. This was the first death, and it affected them deeply. Before he was sewn in the canvas, he was searched, in the anticipation of finding something useful. A surprising discovery was then made. He had in his pocket-book and round his waist bank-notes and bills for more than ten thousand pounds. But nobody knew any thing about him; he died, as he had lived among them, a mystery. After his body was slipped into the sea, a whisper went about that the money found on him had not been honestly come by.

That same night two sailors were washed into the sea. When it became known, there were some among them who secretly rejoiced in the thought that there would not be so many mouths to feed. Nearly a third of the provisions was eaten, and the women were very weak. Little Emma Pigeon held out the best; but that was because her mother, from even her small portion, gave some to her child between the times of serving out the provisions; the child also was petted and nourished by the other women. Rough-and-Ready was especially considerate to the females. Joshua saw him chewing something, and wondered what it was. Noticing the look of inquiry on Joshua's face, Rough-and-Ready enlightened him.

"I am eating leather," he said.

Joshua stared at him. Then Rough-and-Ready took from his pocket a dozen very thin strips of leather which he had cut out of his boot, and told Joshua that he had found a new food. He gave Joshua a couple of strips — very thin they were, almost like a wafer — and Joshua set to work on them, and after some difficulty, chewed them to a pulp and swallowed them.

"There's nothing like leather," said Rough-and-Ready with a quiet laugh. "It wants strong teeth, but it fills up an empty place in the stomach."

The next day Joshua noticed that Rough-and-Ready received his tablespoonful of preserved meat in his handkerchief, and later on he saw Rough-and-Ready slyly feeding little Emma with a portion of the meat, and then go to her mother and slip what remained into her hand.

Now and then a few small fish were caught. There being no means of cooking them, the women refused their share with horror, but the men ate them raw. They also snared some birds, and ate them in the same manner.

On the twelfth night Scadbolt and the Lascar lay side by side awake. Nearer than they to the edge of the raft lay a shipmate, chewing tobacco.

"All mine is gone," said Scadbolt enviously.

"And mine," said the Lascar, with a horrible look at the man who was chewing.

"I think he must have a good lot left. I heard him boast of it last week."

"Two men are better than one."

"Wait till that black cloud touches the moon; then stop his mouth; I'll do the rest!"

The black cloud travelled on and on, crept before the moon, and soon shut out its light. When the moon shone again upon the waters there was one man less on the raft, and Scadbolt and the Lascar were chewing tobacco greedily!

These two men had a line out in the water, with a small hook at the end of it. The Lascar felt it jerk. He pulled in the line; there was a fish at the end of the line, weighing more than a pound. He took from his pocket a six-bladed knife, opened the largest blade, and cut the fish in two equal parts. He gave one to Scadbolt, and ate the other himself. So that they should not be observed, they lay down on their faces while they ate.

"That was a good bit of luck," said Scadbolt; "I feel stronger."

"If the skipper caught us, he would throw us overboard," whispered the Lascar.

"He'd try to; but one man is as good as another now. Let us do this and take care of ourselves; we shall outlast the others. I wish they were all dead — all but two."

"Ay, Joshua's Marvel's one. I know what you mean. You'd like to have the doing of him. So would I. Who's the other?"

"The gypsy-maid. She's a rare beauty."

The Lascar did not say any thing to this. He had seen enough since they had been on the raft to convince him that his first suspicions were right, and that the gypsy-looking girl really was Minnie. Notwithstanding their desperate condition, he had cast many admiring glances at her.

"How fine," he thought, "to strike at Joshua Marvel through her!"

CHAPTER XXXII.

SAVED FROM THE SEA.

THE first among the passengers to completely give way was Stephen Homebush. He had observed no manner of discretion in eating his food, and had always swallowed it hastily, so that it did him but little good. Contrary to what might have been expected of him as a man of pious parts, he was the most selfish of all the passengers. Instead of praying for mercy, he rebelled in thought and speech against the misfortune which had overtaken him. He did not think of the others. It was *his* fate that was so hard. The prayers that he had so liberally offered up for other lost men were not for him now that he was lost. All other men were sinners, — so he had preached. There was no grace in any of them. He came to impart it to them. Let them open their rebellious hearts, and receive it, while there was yet time. To all kinds of men had he preached this, striking at them hard, trying to frighten them with threatened penalties if they refused to believe as he believed. He came to give them grace; did he himself require none?

What kind of faith is that which believes all other faiths wrong and sinful? What is the test of faith? Sincerity? Ay, for me; but not for you. *I* am sincere; *I* am born in the grace of God. But you! Fall down and repent!

Such had been the preaching of Stephen Homebush. But now that the earth was crumbling from beneath his feet, and the New Life was before him, he prayed neither for others nor for himself. He maintained a sullen rebellious silence, faithful to his nature for the first time in his life. His mood, no less than the scanty supply of food and his manner of eating it, drove him mad; and within a fortnight of his sojourn on the raft, he was crawling and staggering about, uttering a dreadful jumble of prayers and blasphemies. His sister Rachel attended to him as well as her strength allowed her; but he struck at her often, and often cursed her and himself. It was terrible to see and hear. He did not suffer long. One day he ran from one part of the raft to another, raving that a sail was in sight. At first they thought that he might be right, but they soon discovered that he was raving. But *he* saw the ship coming nearer and nearer. His sister was the only one who had patience to bear with him. He described the ship to her, and described the men and women that were on the deck; and she shuddered as she recognized in his descriptions acquaintances and relatives every one of whom was dead.

"Here it comes," he said, standing up in his eagerness, "nearer — nearer! I shall be able to jump on board presently." She strove to restrain him; but he broke from her wildly, and gave a leap on to the imaginary ship. He sank at once, and was seen no more.

The forlorn woman sat stupefied, and never moved. Hours afterwards, Rough-and-Ready, taking pity upon her condition, spoke to her, and bade her take comfort. The sense of what he said was lost to her, but she understood the sympathy that was expressed in his voice, and she looked at him gratefully while the tears rolled down her face. He placed his hand upon her shoulder, and said gently, "Poor woman! poor woman!" She took his hand in hers, and clung to it, as if her only hope of life was there. He could not disengage his hand except by force; so he sat by her for an hour and more, until she released him. Then he crept to where the women were lying; there was comfort in being close to them.

One of their most frightful experiences was the sight of the sharks snapping at the bodies as they were thrown into the sea. A great number of these creatures followed the raft day and night, scenting their prey. Each of the unfortunates thought, as he saw the sharks tearing at the body of his fellow creature, "Perhaps it is my turn next." About the twentieth day they caught at least a dozen rock cod, but after that they caught no fish for many days. Soon their fresh water was nearly gone; for some time past they had only half a pint a day; now the quantity was reduced to a quarter of a pint. Some tins of the preserved meat were also found to be putrid: the women could not touch it; but a few of the sailors Seadbolt and the Lascar among them, devoured it greedily. When another new moon rose, the courage of nearly every one of them was gone; hope had fled too. They looked upon themselves as doomed.

A curious conversation took place between the two friends, Harry Wall and James Heartsease. In the morning they had refused their portion of food.

"Save it for the women, sir," they said to the captain.

He expostulated with them, and tried to prevail upon them to take it, but he did not succeed.

"Sir," said James Heartsease, "we are going to lie down to die. We both of us feel that our time has come. To rob the poor women of any more food would be simple barbarity. I should like to shake hands with you."

Captain Liddle shook hands with them; and after that they crawled to the women, and shook hands with them, and kissed little Emma Pigeon. Then they crawled away, and lay down side by side.

"The end has come, Jim," said Harry.

"All right, Hal," said James; "it is only a matter of a few years — perhaps not so long as that. If we had had plenty to eat, it might have come just the same. After all, what is time? Draw a breath, and it is gone. It isn't so hard to give up a few years when you think of that. Besides "— But here he paused.

"Besides what, Jim?"

"We are alone; we have no womenties — no wives, no sweethearts. If we had, I think we should both try to live as long as we could."

"I think so too. 'Tis a good job we are alone in the world."

"Did you notice the women, Hal? I don't think they'll last long."

"One of them won't," said Harry. "Mrs. Pigeon will soon go. Well, you know the reason of that."

"Yes; she gives all her food to her little girl. Women are good creatures, Hal."

"Such as she are. Jim, old boy, a sudden weakness has come over me. Put your face closer to mine — I want to kiss you. Good old boy — good old boy!"

They did not speak for some time after that. Heartsease was the first to break silence.

"Hal, old fellow," he said, "we shall meet somewhere by and by."

"Sure to," said Harry; "somewhere, somehow. It is awfully grand to think of — it is good to believe. I am glad I never did any great wrong to sting me now. Jim, depend upon it, there is only one true religion; that is, the religion of being kind and tender and unselfish — the religion of doing unto others as you would others should do unto you, and of living a good life. Give me the man who does that, and who believes in the goodness and greatness of God. All the rest is mummery. We have agreed upon that, haven't we old boy?"

"Ay, times out of mind."

"Now, I tell you what I am going to do. I don't want to quite starve to death — it would be too painful; it's frightful to bear even now. I don't want to commit suicide, although to throw one's self into the water just now would be, in a certain measure, justifiable. I am going to draw myself close to the edge of the raft; then I am going to sleep. If the waves should chance to wash me over in the night — good! Let them; then I shall know something."

"All right, Hal; I'll lie by your side. Good-night, old fellow."

"Good-night."

When the sun rose again, those two good friends had gone to their rest, to meet again Somewhere — Somehow!

So day after day passed, and their numbers continued to grow fewer, until there were no more than eighteen on the raft. In the first quarter of the second new moon — that is, when they had been on the raft for more than thirty days — Mrs. Pigeon died. When the news went round, there were few dry eyes among the poor creatures. Every one loved her, even to Seadbolt and the Lascar, whose clothes she had mended. It was a wonder how she had lasted so long, for it was with the greatest difficulty she could be prevailed upon to take food; she gave it all to her little daughter. When, almost by force, a small portion had been put into her mouth, Joshua had seen her take it out to feed Little Emma. That is why the child lived while the mother starved to death. Between Mrs. Pigeon and Minnie a strong affection had sprung up. Minnie scarcely ever left the side of the dying woman, and what little she could do to ease her last hours — it was but little, God knows! — she did tenderly and cheerfully. Minnie knew that Mrs. Pigeon was starving herself, so that her little girl might live. The beauty of that sacrifice Minnie was well able to comprehend. She would have done the same. But she was terribly unhappy. She knew by Joshua's manner, and by the few words that he spoke to her — kind one day, constrained the next — that her conduct had added to his unhappiness. She had seen him look at her with such a look of fear and wild amazement in his eyes, as to convey to her the impression that she had done him a great wrong. But so blinded was she by her love, that she could not quite understand the meaning of this; indeed, she did not pause to consider. The night before Mrs. Pigeon died, Minnie lay by her side, talking in whispers. But few words were spoken at a time; Mrs. Pigeon was too weak. The mother lay with her child in her arms, and her husband sitting close to her, his hands clasping his knees, and with an expression of stony despair in his face. So he had sat for three or four days, answering his wife vacantly, and with the air of one whose mind was a blank. Little by little, Minnie had told Mrs. Pigeon her story; and the dying woman, notwithstanding her own great trouble, had wept with Minnie, and sympathized with her. But Mrs. Pigeon, as well as expressing her sympathy, had striven to make Minnie aware of the fault she had committed.

"You see, my dear," she gasped in her weak voice, "he has left a sweetheart at home, and he fears that if it were known that you were in the ship with him, she and his other friends might believe that he had played false with them."

"I never thought of that before," sobbed Minnie. "I only thought of one thing: I loved him, and I wanted to be near him. I didn't want him even to know; and those at home had no idea of what I was going to do — they can't even suspect."

"But Mr. Marvel *fears* they may. Then think, my dear, was it not wrong to leave your father?"

"It was — I see it now; but I did not think of it then. But O Mrs. Pigeon, if he would only forgive me! If I ask him, he will; but the answer would come out of the goodness of his heart, and while he forgave he would still condemn me. I know it, I know it, for he has never once called me by my name."

Soon after that, Mrs. Pigeon fell into a doze; and waking when it was near midnight, whispered, "Minnie!"

"Yes," answered Minnie. She had been sleeping too, but so lightly that a whisper was sufficient to awake her.

"I have not long to live, my dear," said Mrs. Pigeon; "and I should like to pass my last minutes alone with my husband and child, and to speak to no one but them — to think of no one but them. But before I go, I should be glad to say good-by to Joshua Marvel. Can you bring him to me? Say that I am dying."

Repressing her sobs, Minnie crept to where Joshua was standing on the lookout. He had grown thin and gaunt like the others; his feet were bare, the only pair of shoes he had possessed having been rotted by the salt water; his clothes hung about him in tatters; and his face was covered with hair, which, having not yet grown to a decent length, added to the wretchedness of his appearance. The moon had gone down, and Joshua, shading his eyes with his hand, was looking out to sea, possessed with the fancy that he saw a sail many miles away. This had now become a very common illusion; scarcely a man on board who did not see imaginary sails and ships a dozen times a day. With a weary sigh Joshua dropped his hand.

"It is folly," he muttered; "there's no hope."

Minnie timidly touched his sleeve, but did not succeed in attracting his attention. Then she called softly, "Joshua!" And he gave a gasp, and turned and saw her; but there was not light enough for him to see the tears upon her face.

"Mrs. Pigeon has sent me for you," said Minnie. "She is dying, and wants to wish you good-by."

He followed her in silence to where Mrs. Pigeon was lying.

"Is it so bad?" he asked gently, as he leaned over her close enough to see her poor thin face.

"Yes," she murmured. "Sit by me for a few minutes."

He sat down, and took her wasted hand in his: it was like the hand of a skeleton, thin and cold — a hand already dead, though it closed on Joshua's fingers.

"Every one speaks well of you," said Mrs. Pigeon in broken tones: "I have heard the captain speak many times of your courage and goodness and constancy."

"I have been glad to hear it, and am glad to hear it again," replied Joshua; "it is my best reward as a sailor."

"You have a kind heart, I am sure,"

continued the dying woman. "If it were in your power to lessen the bitter grief that even a mere acquaintance might suffer, you would do so."

"I think I would."

"I am sure you would; if only for the sake of those you love at home, and to whom you would wish that others might be kind when grief comes to them. You will forgive me for speaking thus; but I am dying, and I am a woman. I cannot say much more; I am too weak. If I could see you do one little thing, I should be glad."

"I will do any thing you ask."

"Because a dying woman asks you; but do it from your own kind impulse as well. That is what I wish. You know who it is that is sitting by us now."

"Yes," he answered with a troubled glance at Minnie.

"She has been very good to me, very kind, very, very patient. And she is so young! Soon you and she may follow me. Think of that."

"What is it you would have me to do?"

"I would have you be kind to this poor child; I would have you, at this awful time, show to her the love that a brother might show to a sister. She has committed a fault; forgive her for it; let her atone for it. Be not you the one to cast the stone at her. And when you speak to her, speak from your heart; for she can read and understand, as all loving women can, the music of the voice."

"Minnie," said Joshua, turning to her. Mrs. Pigeon had loosed his hand; and now he held out his two hands to Minnie. It was the first time he had called her by her name.

"Joshua," she said, with deep sobs, her hands in his, and bowing her head upon his shoulder until her lips almost touched his face.

Was it treasonable to Ellen that he should permit it? Surely not, surely not, at such a time.

"You have made me glad," said Mrs. Pigeon. "Now go. Good-by. Heaven send you peace!"

"And you!" they both said.

Mrs. Pigeon nestled her face close to that of her little daughter, and soon afterwards died peacefully.

Then, for the first time, Mr. Pigeon seemed to awake to the reality of things. Kneeling by the side of his wife, he called softly, "Emma! Emma!" And receiving no answer, shook her gently, and smoothed the hair from her white face.

"Be comforted," said Joshua to him.

"Comforted!" he repeated with a pondering look, as if he were considering what meaning there was in the word. He kissed her passionately, and whispered something in her ear, and waited for the answer that could not come. "My God!" he cried suddenly, "she is dead!"

Minnie placed Little Emma before him, thinking that the sight of his little girl might lessen his grief; but he took no notice of the child, and sat the whole day nursing the dead body of his wife in his lap. One tin of preserved meat was all that remained now of their stock of provisions. They brought his small share to him; but he motioned them away impatiently and fretfully. They went to him, and endeavored to make him understand that, for the sake of the others, he should allow the remains of his wife to be placed in their poor shroud of sacking; but he met them savagely, and threatened to bite at them and strangle them if they did not let him alone.

"For the sharks to eat," he whispered to the inanimate form; "they want to throw you into the sea for the sharks to eat, my darling. But I'll tear their hearts out before they part us."

When the silver crescent looked down again upon the despairing group, Joshua tried once more to comfort the man, and said, with a heavy heart, that perhaps at the last moment a ship might pick them up. But though he uttered the words, he did not believe in them.

"And if it does," muttered Mr. Pigeon hoarsely, "what do I care now? You don't know what it is to lose the woman you love." He staggered to his feet with the beloved form in his arm. "You want to take her from me; that is why you speak the lying words. But nothing shall part us — nothing."

Her face was lying upon his shoulder, and her fair hair was hanging loosely down over his breast. He took some of the hair in his mouth; and as Joshua saw him standing thus in the moon's light, he thought he had never seen a picture so utterly despairing. Thus the man stood, motionless, for a time, until the captain's lady crept to his side, and tried to console him. Poor thing! she was terribly weak, and the words came from her lips slowly and wearily. He gazed at her vacantly while she spoke, then turned his eyes to his dead wife.

"Emma," he said, "don't fear; nothing that they say shall make me give you up. We will go together — we will go together."

He cast one last look at the peaceful heavens, and whispering, "Lord, receive us!" clasped his wife more closely to him, and jumped into the sea. Two or three heads turned at the plash; but no other notice was taken of the event. They were all too weak and despairing. The captain's wife gasped, with heart-broken sobs,—

"Poor dears! poor dears! Their troubles are over; they are happier than we are."

"Yes, my lady," said Joshua; "but I would not end my life like that. We are in the hands of the Lord; our lives belong to Him."

He stretched himself at full length upon the raft, and took Ellen's picture and the lock of hair from his breast, and kissed them again and again. They, and the Bible that Dan had given him, were his most precious possessions. When he looked up, Minnie and Little Emma were close to him. He took the child's hand; and they remained together during the long, long night.

A dreadful announcement was made the next day. The water that was served out was the last—one tablespoonful each exhausted the store; all the provisions were used up also. It seemed, indeed, as if the best thing they could do would be to die at once by their own hands. The rules made by the council were no longer thought of. Something to eat, something to drink: these were the only laws now. When the next man died, the sailors looked longingly at the body. The Lascar had his knife open, and was about to use it, when Captain Liddle called to him to stop.

"Why?" asked the Lascar, with a savage flourish of his knife.

"Why?" echoed the other men: there were only six of them left altogether.

"Because fish is better to eat than human flesh," said the captain.

"So it is," said one; "but we haven't any more fishing-line."

"Come now," said the captain, "even without that we can manage to catch a shark perhaps. Wait a few minutes. I'll think of a way."

And sure enough, very soon he devised a snare. First a running-bowling knot was made; then they cut a leg off the man that was dead (terrible to write, but true), and lashed it to the end of an oar; while on the end of another oar they hung the snare in such a way that the fish, to get at the bait, was compelled to come through it. There were plenty of sharks; and it was not long before one fell into the trap. It was dragged on to the raft; and a few blows from an axe soon killed it. After that, the man was sewed in sacking, and the funeral-service was read over him, as it had been over all the others who had been buried in the sea.

During all this time it was evident that they were near the coast, and yet they never saw it. The captain said that they were in the vicinity of the north-east coast of Australia—a part of the continent which had been very little explored. Here came in Rough-and-Ready's experience. He knew something of the country, he said. It was inhabited by the most savage of the Australian natives, and no white man had as yet had the courage to penetrate far into the country.

"Yet we might make the coast," said Rough-and-Ready, "and not see a native for a long time, if we could manage to live; for I don't believe there are a great many of them. Cannibals they are; but, for all that, I should be glad to get among them. We might succeed in working our way down to a cattle-station."

"Would there be really a chance of that?" asked one or two.

"About a hundred to one against us," replied Rough-and-Ready carelessly; "but that would be better than nothing."

Rough-and-Ready gave them a description of some natives that he had seen, and told of their manner of living, their treachery and wildness. It was not very comforting to hear; the prospect of reaching land, and finding themselves in the midst of such savages, was very dismal.

The suffering that they had now to bear—that of thirst—was the most awful experience of all. Some of them grew delirious, and saw gardens and pools of fresh water. "My lady" was one of these. She whispered to her husband that a beautiful garden was within a few yards of them, and that they should reach it presently. She described the flowers and trees, and the cool fruit waiting to be plucked. And as the vision faded, she clutched him by the hand, and cried, "John, John! What are they doing? We are going the wrong way. O my God! we have passed it—it is gone!" and lay exhausted. The words came from her parched throat with difficulty; and Joshua shuddered as he touched her face: it seemed to be on fire. Soon, however, the gardens dotted with clear-water fountains, and with trees laden with refreshing fruit, grew again for the delirious woman. She saw them in the water, in the air, in the heavens—so bright, so deliciously cool, that her heart almost burst in the vain attempt she made to reach them with her hand. A little rain fell mercifully, and yet mockingly; for nearly every thing on board was so impregnated with salt as to render the pieces of rags and canvas that were held out to catch heaven's tears no better when they were soaked than if they had been dipped into the sea. Rough-and-Ready took the lining out of his wide-awake hat; and he and

Joshua held it out until it was soaked with the blessed drops. The first use they made of the piece of wet rag was to moisten the women's lips with it, and then the little girl's and their own. Little Emma lived still; and Minnie had taken charge of her. As Joshua moistened Mrs. Liddle's lips, the captain, who was lying beside her, motioned him.

"It is all over with me, Marvel," he gasped; "I haven't long to live. If by God's mercy you are rescued, report me at home, and say I did all in my power to save the ship." Joshua pressed the dying captain's hand. "Mind, you are first in command now. In a few hours you will be captain. You have risen quickly," he said with a faint smile. "Beware of Scadbolt and that Lascar dog. When I am dead, take my boots — you have none — and what of my clothes may be useful to you; take the log-book too, and keep it safe. There is a record in it of Scadbolt's conduct, and your promotion. It will be necessary in case a ship picks you up. Scadbolt was your superior officer when we left the port of Sydney; and he might bring a charge against you, which, without the log-book, you would not be able to refute.

Joshua thanked the captain for his thoughtfulness, and expressed a hope that it was not so bad with him as he feared. Then the captain told Joshua how, a few days before, he had struck his head against a piece of iron, and how he had lost a quantity of blood. Joshua put his hand to the back of the captain's head, round which a piece of canvas was tied, and felt a great gash there.

"I did not tell any one; but it so weakened me, that I thought I was about to die then. This is a piteous sight!" pointing to his wife. She lay, pale as death, with her eyes wide open, gazing at the gardens in the air. The tears rolled down Joshua's face. "Bury us together," continued the captain. "There are two or three pieces of iron you might put into the canvas with us, so we may sink at once. You will do this?'"

"Yes."

Captain Liddle pressed Joshua's hand, and creeping close to his wife clasped her in his arms. In the mean time Rough-and-Ready was busy squeezing drops of fresh water into a bottle. He saved nearly a pint.

Shortly after that, Joshua was the first to see land. He went to tell the Captain, but could not arouse him; his heart still beat, but very faintly. Night came on soon; and when day dawned again the land was gone. Rough-and-Ready came to Joshua with a grave face. He said nothing; but Joshua understood him. They went to where the lifeless bodies of the captain and his wife lay, and sewed them in canvas, and placed inside the pieces of iron, as Joshua had promised. Joshua read the burial-service as the bodies were thrown into the sea. They sank at once.

"Not many of us left," observed Rough-and-Ready. "I should like to see land again. If we don't sight it soon, we may find that the worst has not yet come. It is as Scadbolt said when the rules were being read, 'Every man for himself now, and God for us all.' But come what may we'll stick to each other and to the women."

"It does my heart good to hear you speak so," said Joshua. "I know what you mean: the worst men are left against us; but we are a match for them, I think. See, here's the log-book, with the poor skipper's last words: "I appoint Joshua Marvel captain of this raft, made out of the spars of the 'Merry Andrew,' and intrust to him the charge of the surviving passengers and crew.— John Liddle, Master of the 'Merry Andrew.'"

Rough-and-Ready touched his hat in sailor fashion.

"While we are at sea, captain," he said, "I will obey your orders."

A thrill ran through Joshua as he heard himself called captain. Captain! But of what a crew! The promotion had come all too soon.

Before long he had to exercise his authority. They were being driven on to a reef by a strong current. It was necessary to get the raft into deep water before dark. He gave his orders; and although both Scadbolt and the Lascar saw the wisdom of them, they refused to obey.

"I am captain," said Scadbolt. "You will obey my orders now."

Then Rough-and-Ready took a double-barrelled pistol from his belt, and gave its fellow to Joshua. They covered Scadbolt and the Lascar with them.

"Obey orders!" cried Rough-and-Ready in as loud a voice as he could command. "Obey orders! Speak another word of disobedience, and you are dead men!"

The rebellious men were cowed. With scowling faces they worked as Joshua directed; and with some trouble they got the raft clear over the reef, and floated it into deeper water. The night that followed was a night of great anxiety. Joshua knew that they were near land; and he and Rough-and-Ready kept watches of two hours' duration in turn. The reason of this was, that they did not deem it safe to sleep both at the same time; for they suspected that Scadbolt and the Lascar were only waiting for the opportunity to fall upon them and kill them.

"We have all the fire-arms, thank goodness," said Rough-and-Ready, "and all the powder and shot. We are masters while we can keep these."

He had kept a sharp guard over the fire-arms, and had indeed secretly dropped three guns into the sea. "Better there than in those rascals' hands," he wisely thought; "we mustn't cumber ourselves with too much lumber."

In the night Joshua whispered to Rachel Homebush and Minnie that to-morrow probably would decide their fate. They revived somewhat at the news, and Minnie directed Joshua's attention to little Emma Pigeon.

"She has not spoken all day," said Minnie anxiously.

Joshua placed his hand on the little girl's heart: it beat, but very faintly.

"She will live, Minnie," said Joshua, "if we can reach land; we are certain to find food then."

While they spoke, Minnie kept Joshua's hand in hers; it was her only comfort, poor child. He was kneeling by her side, and she saw in his face that he had no harsh thoughts for her. They had not exchanged a word about their friends at home, but Minnie said to-night,—

"Joshua, when you first came to our little room — do you remember? — what should we have thought if a wizard had told us this?"

"What, indeed!" replied Joshua; and then, after a pause, "Do you suffer much, Minnie?"

"Not now. Ah, Joshua, if I can only live to repay you!"

"Keep up your courage, Minnie, and pray that we may reach friendly land — any land — to-morrow," was his answer.

She did pray fervently, and when daylight came they saw land. It did not look very friendly. A long line of dark savage-looking rocks was what they saw; towering gloomily and threateningly for the most part, but with many a little inlet, which offered them a favorable chance of landing, as Joshua's seaman's eye discerned. There were only eight living persons now on the raft out of the thirty-five who first took shelter there. Five men — to wit, Joshua, Rough-and-Ready, Scadbolt, the Lascar, and the sailmaker; two women — Rachel Homebush and Minnie, and the little girl Emma. The men worked and watched with a will. Private animosities were for the time forgotten; but for all that, Rough-and-Ready was never off his guard. Every thing looked fair, when suddenly up sprang a land breeze, and they were driven to sea again; the hope that had been kindled died away. They caught a cod, but the women turned from it with loathing. Then Joshua thought of a fine thing. The sun was high in the heavens. He took a piece of rag and washed it and dried it; then he took a magnifying glass out of a telescope, and caught the sun's fire on to the rag. He had wood ready, and they made a fire on the raft. The sailors ate their portion of the fish raw; but Joshua put his and the women's and Rough-and-Ready's on the wood, and roasted it. Before they gave this delicious food to the women, they moistened their lips with a little of the water that was still left in Rough-and-Ready's bottle; the moistening and the food were new life to them all. Minnie chewed a little of the fish and placed it in the child's mouth; the child swallowed it, with difficulty at first, and seemed to grow stronger soon afterwards; she had been better nourished than the others. As if in reward for this good thought of Joshua's, the wind shifted to a sea breeze, and a couple of hours before mid-night they were driven on to land. It required the greatest care and the most delicate handling to steer the raft safely through the rocks; but it was done. Scadbolt and the Lascar were about to scramble on to the rocks, when Rough-and-Ready, in a voice of thunder — he seemed suddenly to have recovered his full strength — commanded them to stand. Not his voice, but his pistol, enforced obedience.

"Why?" demanded Scadbolt.

"Because you are treacherous dogs," roared Rough-and-Ready; "because you are not men, but savages; because I know how such scum are to be treated. Ah! scowl as you will! but I have shot better men than you down before to-night, and I'll shoot *you* down if you dare to stir, as I would a brace of treacherous dingos or Blacks — they're much the same. The women and child are to be saved first. Why, if we allowed you to get ashore, you'd strike us from the rocks before we got a footing! I know you, you see, you skunks. Marvel, take the women and little girl ashore first, one by one. I'll keep guard here the while. Sailmaker, assist Mr. Marvel."

By this last masterly stroke Rough-and-Ready enlisted the sailmaker on his side, for a time at least. For the sailmaker and Joshua were man to man, and Joshua had fire-arms. So, with difficulty, the women and child were conveyed on to the rocks in safety; then Rough-and-Ready bade Joshua take ashore what things would be useful from the raft. Among other things, Joshua took ashore two axes, all the nails he could find, and some iron pots. The women also had some things they were anxious to preserve — needles and thread and such like.

All this occupied nearly two hours, and was not accomplished without difficulty. Scadbolt and the Lascar stood sullenly by, the while. Rough-and-Ready was in his element; he absolutely revelled in the task he had set himself. It was as good as meat and drink to him to watch those two rascals and beat them through their fears. When Joshua and the sailmaker had completed their task, Rough-and-Ready joined them on the rocks. After him Scadbolt and the Lascar scrambled on to land, and began to look hungrily about them. It was a fine night; the moon was nearly at its full. The first thing Rough-and-Ready did was to cast a glance at the women lying helpless on the rocks; the next thing he did was to smooth his mustache with his hand in a thoughtful manner; the next, to send a dark look at Scadbolt and the Lascar, who were prowling about on the rocks in search of shell-fish; the next, to lay his hand in a familiar manner upon the sailmaker's shoulder.

"I say, mate," said Rough-and-Ready, "have you a wife at home?"

"Two."

Rough-and-Ready whistled loud and long, and followed up the whistle with a laugh.

"It's no joke," said the sailmaker.

"One isn't, much less two," replied Rough-and-Ready, with a wink; "but never mind them now."

"I'm content."

"You seem a good-hearted fellow, sailmaker, and as you have two wives, you must think a great deal of womankind."

"I love 'em,"—looking at the two poor creatures lying near them.

"I'm a bushman myself," said Rough-and-Ready, with assumed carelessness; "I'd as soon be where I am as in any part of the world. I am at home here. What do you say, mate? Shall we be friends?"

"Glad to be." And the two men shook hands, Rough-and-Ready hugging himself for his successful diplomacy.

"You're a man after my own heart," said Rough-and-Ready, really appreciating the crisp utterances of the sailmaker, who evidently was not a word-waster. "Seems to me that the first thing we've got to do is to bring the women round; mustn't let them die, eh?"

"Certainly not."

"There's a split in the camp," continued Rough-and-Ready. "Those two rascals prowling about in search of something to eat, would be glad of an opportunity to get rid of us; and then God help the women! At all events let us three stick together — you and me and Captain Marvel. Agreed?"

"Agreed."

"Good. What I want to do is to get fresh water for us and the women; I know how to look for it. Will you keep guard over the women with Captain Marvel till I return?"

"Yes."

Rough-and-Ready placed a loaded pistol in the sailmaker's hand — he did it without hesitation — and that act completed the conquest. Joshua, standing by, had heard the conversation, and now shook hands with the sailmaker. Scadbolt and the Lascar had also seen the conference.

"They've bought him over," said the Lascar.

"Never mind," replied Scadbolt, "there will be plenty of opportunities."

In less than an hour Rough-and-Ready returned. He had taken two bottles with him, and brought them back filled with bright, clear, fresh water. He had his wide-awake hat in his hand; it evidently contained something good, he was so careful in carrying it. Joshua put his hand in, and started back with a cry; he had grasped a nettle.

"Careful, careful," said Rough-and-Ready, laughing at Joshua's grimaces; "don't be too eager to take hold of things. A great deal of the wood-growth round about here is covered with thorns, and some of them are poisonous to the blood. This isn't, though; 'tis an old friend."

He took out of his hat two small branches with long spines upon them; the branches were covered with fruit resembling a small apple.

"Good to eat?" asked the sailmaker.

"Shouldn't have brought them otherwise," answered Rough-and-Ready, in unconscious imitation of the sailmaker's manner of speaking.

The sailmaker took some of the fruit and ate it, and would have taken more, but that Rough-and-Ready's hand restrained him.

"That's not the way for a man to eat who has been nearly starved for six weeks," he said, "unless he wants to kill himself right out. Here, make yourself useful; but take a little water to drink first."

Rough-and-Ready measured a small quantity of water, and gave the sailmaker and Joshua to drink. He had thrown down a couple of pieces of wood when he said "Make yourself useful," and the sailmaker, after drinking, asked him what the wood was for.

"A good job for you two that you have me for your mate," said Rough-and-Ready good-humoredly; "you might stand a chance of starving else. The enemy"— with a nod of his head in the direction of Scadbolt and the Lascar — "won't be half as well off as we shall be. Just watch me."

He took his knife and cut from the wood two pieces, in one of which he made a kind of groove, which he placed upon the ground. "This is off the black fig-tree, and is the best wood there is for making fire. Now rub away into the groove, steadily, like this, and keep rubbing. It's hard work; but never mind; it's worth the labor."

He disappeared again, leaving the sail-maker at work, and returned with an armful of dry sticks and leaves. Soon fire came into the wood. the sparks dropped on to the dry leaves, and a blaze was kindled, that brought astonishment into the eyes of Seadbolt and the Lascar. Before the fire was made, the indefatigable bushman had gone *down* the rocks this time, and had returned with a hat full of mussels. These he put on the fire to cook; and then sat down and rubbed his hands in a high state of satisfaction. Joshua had not been idle; he had attended to the women and child, and had given them a little water, which was like nectar to them. They were too weak to exert themselves; so the men sat by them and ate supper, and gave them to eat, sparingly, under the direction of Rough-and-Ready, who was regarded by the others with unbounded admiration. The warmth of the fire was very comforting to them, for although summer was coming, their long sojourn on the raft had chilled their blood.

"Well now," said Rough-and-Ready, when supper was over, "I think we ought to be very grateful for our escape. It was touch-and-go with us. We sha'n't be very strong for a few days; and that's what we've got to do first: to get strong. Then we can look about us."

"Where are we?" whispered Minnie.

"As well as I can make out, my dear, we are somewhere on the north-east coast of the continent of Australia; where I don't believe a white man ever trod foot before. That's something, isn't it? We're the first bits of civilization that these rocks have ever seen."

"Is there any chance of a ship seeing us?"

"I doubt it; but for my part I don't want a ship to see me; I've had enough of ships. I feel at home here, or I shall feel so in a little while. I don't doubt but what we shall be able to get plenty to eat and drink, and that's our first great need. Try and sleep for an hour now. Strength is what we want, remember."

Rachel Homebush turned to him and held out her hand. She was grateful for being saved, but she did not speak. The three men arranged to get a little rest also, watch and watch in turn. It was Rough-and-Ready's watch first. Before Joshua lay down, he went to see if Minnie was asleep. Her eyes were closed, but she was aware of his approach.

"That is you, Joshua?"

"Yes, Minnie. Do you think you can sleep?"

"I don't know; I am strangely excited. I thank God that you are saved. Joshua," rising to a sitting posture and taking his hand, "you will not be unkind to me now that we are out of danger?"

"Surely not, Minnie. What makes you ask?"

"I was afraid, that was all."

Here the little child murmured something. Minnie placed her ear to the girl's lips.

"She asked who was talking to me, and I told her you," said Minnie, taking Little Emma upon her lap. "She wants you to kiss her."

Joshua stooped and kissed the little girl, and she put her arms round his neck, and asked where papa had gone to. Joshua turned away, and pressing Minnie's hand, was soon afterwards in the land of dreams. So, during the night, they slept and watched, and in their troubled dreams felt the rocks moving and swaying beneath them. Every now and then they started in terror, and clutched what was nearest to them, as if life was slipping away; they suffered over again the agonies of thirst, and moved their parched lips entreatingly. When it was Joshua's watch, he observed the sufferings of his sleeping companions; he guessed the cause, for he had suffered himself in like manner. With merciful thoughtfulness he moistened their lips with fresh water; the women smiled and grew more composed; perhaps at that moment they dreamed that an angel was bringing them life and health. Minnie's head was lying on her hand, and her face was exposed to the light. It was sun-burnt, but the gypsy stain was dying out of it. Her hair too was growing lighter and longer. Joshua looked up at the sky and round about him at the strange scene. Over his head the light of day was just breaking, but the dusky shadows still lay upon the waters. Behind him a faint light, heralding the sun, was quivering on distant wood and upland.

"Dan made me promise," he said softly to himself, as the wonderful strangeness of his position came upon him, "when I was seeing strange sights in strange places, to think, "Dan is here with me, although I cannot see him." *Is* Dan here with me now? Is it possible that he can have the vaguest idea of me as I stand, heart-wrecked, in this wild country? I will try to believe so; I will try to believe that he and Ellen see me as I am, know me as I am, and pity me. I could die here now contentedly, if that were a conviction. Ellen, dear wife! Dan, dear friend! dear mother and father! stand fast to me, and believe that I never wavered in my love and my truth!"

This was his theme that he thought of and mused upon, while all the others were asleep. The rocks were burnished with golden light before they awoke.

CHAPTER XXXIII.

ON THE ROCKS.

As the sailmaker was stretching himself, Rough-and-Ready, who was already stirring, said, —

"I say, mate what name shall we call you by?"

"Isn't Sailmaker good enough?" was the Irish answer.

"It's good enough; but it's no name."

"Tom, for short, then."

"That'll do, Tom; it's like your talk, short, and to the point."

From that time they talked of him as Tom the Sailmaker.

"We're going to look for something for breakfast, Marvel," said Rough-and-Ready. "Don't wake the women — let them have their sleep out. And keep your eye on those two rascals yonder. If they come to close quarters, have no mercy. They'd have none on you. Come along, Tom."

They returned some two hours afterwards, with smiling faces. The women gathered hope from their cheerful countenances. The sailmaker was loaded with wood to replenish the fire, which had not been allowed to go out during the night.

"We're going to have a fine breakfast," said Rough-and-Ready, flourishing half a dozen plump pigeons. He chuckled as he exhibited them; but he had no time for trifling. There was more serious business to attend to — the cooking of the pigeons.

With those and a few mussels they made a breakfast fit for kings and queens. The two malcontents in the distance had no fire and no pigeons; they made their breakfast off cold shell-fish, and looked with envious eyes at the cooking going on among the other party.

"Ah, ah, my fine fellows!" cried Rough-and-Ready, waving half a roasted pigeon in the air; "what d'ye think of mutineering now?"

They could not hear him, but they understood his taunting action.

Said Rough-and-Ready to the women, when breakfast was finished, —

"Can you handle a pistol? Could you pull the trigger of one straight in the face of man or beast, if danger threatened?"

They looked at him inquiringly.

"You might have to do it," continued Rough-and-Ready; "so you had better learn, and be prepared."

"But why?" they asked.

"You see, my dears, there are two parties of us. Here we are. one party. Yonder are two rascals, another party. We are not the best of friends, we two parties. If they could get rid of us, they would. By fair means they can't; but they might try foul. Now I take it that we men have to look after you and protect you — and you may depend upon us for doing our best, my dears. We must see to every thing — food, lodging, protection from storms and from savage Blacks. That may take us away from you sometimes, and those rascals might steal upon you unaware. Or another thing might happen: we might fall sick. Then who will protect you? Or another thing — But, pshaw! there are a dozen other reasons why you should learn to use fire-arms."

Without more ado he showed them how to load a pistol and fire it, and indeed was not content until they did it to his satisfaction. Minnie was the more expert of the two; she soon learned. Then said Rough-and-Ready, —

"Now, we are going to take a walk. A mile, I dare say. We shall be followed, you'll see; the enemy will want to know where we are going."

Rough-and-Ready took Little Emma in his arms, the sailmaker assisted Rachel Homebush, and Joshua attended to Minnie. As Rough-and-Ready expected, Scadbolt and the Lascar followed them at a distance. Rough-and-Ready led the way over the rocks, on to sand, into forest. They were nearly an hour before they came to the end of their journey, for the women were very weak and could walk but slowly. Without any forewarning, Rough-and-Ready stopped.

"Here is another thing I have to teach you. A native call."

And to their astonishment, he put his hands to his mouth and emitted a shrill cry, that rang through the woods and seemed to linger there. The word he uttered was "Coo-ēē!" and the sound was composed of two notes, the second an octave higher than the first. He made them all repeat the cry after him many times, and made them dwell on the notes as long as their breath lasted.

"If we miss each other, and lose our way,

that cry will be a signal. You have no idea how far it will travel, if you dwell long enough on the notes. Now, you" (to the men) "stop here for a little while. You, (to the women) "follow me."

They obeyed him unhesitatingly. He led the women over a rise in the woodland, where the trees were thickly grouped; and when they were on the declivity on the other side, they saw at the base of the rise a lovely creek of fresh water sparkling in the sun.

"You will not be disturbed for an hour," he said, and darted away.

They divined the meaning of this delicate thoughtfulness, and with full confidence in him and his party they made their way to the creek, and bathed and combed their hair. (I vouch for the comb, but am not prepared to say where it came from, for the cunning of woman is beyond me.) The men looked at them with astonishment when they came back, sleek and trim. They appeared to have grown a dozen years younger. They blushed and smiled as the men gazed at them, and Little Emma lisped, "It was so nice!" Even Rachel looked brighter and more womanly.

After them, the men went in turns and bathed, and by that time they were hungry enough for their dinner. Rough-and-Ready had already provided it, having shot a sufficient number of birds for three or four meals. Nothing could satisfy them after dinner but to go to the rocks, and look seaward for the sight of a ship. Rough-and-Ready declared it was useless. "Time thrown away," he said. "If we see a ship, we have no means of signalling it; and even if we had, 'tis a thousand to one that they would not see the signal." But all-potent as his authority and advice were in every other matter, he could not prevail upon them to cast away the hope of being rescued by that means. Before night came they made their way back to the woods, and constructed some rough tents with branches of trees, to sleep in. As they were collecting suitable timber, Rough-and-Ready, who never omitted an opportunity to instruct his companions in the resources of the country, called their attention to a group of curiously-twisted trees, which he said were apple-trees, although there was no fruit on them. On nearly every one of them, three or four feet from the ground, was a large knob, bulging out like a tumor.

"See how bountiful Nature is," said Rough-and-Ready. "You need seldom be in want of water or food, if you know the secrets of the bush."

He dug his knife into one of the knobs, and fresh water ran out of the wood. They tasted it, and found it very sweet.

It was a beautiful night, and they sat talking for some time before they retired to rest. Their strength was recruited by the nourishing food they had eaten, and by the bath they had had. They had not seen the Lascar or Scadbolt since the morning, and they deemed it prudent to keep watch during the night. Now that the first excitement of being saved was over, their thoughts turned to their unfortunate companions who had found a grave in the cruel sea, and they shed pitiful tears over the memory of the dead.

Rough-and-Ready's experience of the Australian natives was largely drawn upon during the night. Although he said nothing of his past career, it was evident that he was well acquainted with every thing appertaining to Australian bush-life. His descriptions of the natives were not comforting; he described them as treacherous, mean, and cruel. As to their chances of escape, he declared that there was no hope from the sea. Their best plan would be to try and work their way southward, but not for some time, until they were quite strong.

"We will camp here," he said, "for two or three weeks at least, and try and learn something about the country."

But he told Joshua, when they two were alone, that he only said that to console the women.

"We can manage to live here; but to get south we should have to cross country, where we should almost certainly be starved to death or butchered by the Blacks."

The prospect was dismal indeed; they seemed to be cut off from the world.

Notwithstanding that the women shuddered and trembled as they listened to Rough-and-Ready's account of the natives, with whom they were almost certain to come in contact soon, the subject was too fascinating to be avoided. So, being compelled to talk about them, he spoke of many strange things concerning them. The conversation turning upon their superstitions, he told his hearers of the savage beliefs in water-spirits and land-spirits, who are all females, and walk about without heads; of the Oorundoo, who comes out of the water to drown bad wives; of the Balumbal, a gentle race of spirits who live upon the sweet leaves of flowers; of the Bunyip, a monster who lives in the large lakes, and who issues therefrom to seize women and children; of Potoyan, a spirit of darkness, whose Whisper strikes terror; and of many other singular beliefs.

Said Rough-and-Ready, "There is no surer way to frighten the blacks than through their superstitious fears. Their 'doctors' can work upon them as they please."

Joshua had taken care of his accordion, and had preserved it almost uninjured. He played, and they all listened wonderingly to the soft notes of "Home, sweet home," floating through the woods. It was like a dream; they could scarcely believe they were awake. When he ceased playing, a melancholy cuckoo-note came from the distant woods.

"'Tis the more-pork, a night-bird," said Rough-and-Ready. "I never heard it sing in the day."

They retired to their beds of dry leaves soon after that, and dreamed of the strange things they had heard. But Joshua could not sleep. Some time before midnight — it might have been an hour — he rose and wandered away from the camp, through the solemn woods. He took no notice of the groups of majestic trees through which he walked — here masses of the silver-leaved iron-bark; there thick clusters of the gigantic palm, woven together, as it were, by luxuriant vines trailing through their topmost branches. Strange effects of light and shade were produced by this natural network; but Joshua took no heed of them, nor of the other wonders of the woods by which he was encompassed. A sense of awful desolation was upon him; tremblingly he retraced his steps till he came to the camp, where he sank upon the ground exhausted by emotion. The full moon rose and shed its light upon him. He took from his breast the Bible which Dan had given him, and read upon its first page, "From Dan, with undying love and confidence." Those words did much to calm him; he kissed them, and pressed the book to his heart, and gradually fell into a deep sleep.

CHAPTER XXXIV.

BITTER REVELATIONS.

HERE in the grand Australian woods are two tents — gunyahs, Rough-and-Ready calls them — built of tea-tree bark, bound round by vine creepers. They are in the form of a hive, and are wonderfully picturesque and comfortable. Up to this time, the castaway dwellers in these gunyahs have been undisturbed by savages, and this has been a matter of surprise to all but Rough-and-Ready. "Wait till after the rainy season," he has said a dozen times; "we shall have plenty of them then." Rough-and-Ready has made this "rainy season" a pretext for lingering near the spot where they first camped after their rescue. It would be suicide, he told them, to attempt to move at present; they would not be able to make their way through the country. But indeed all of them, with the exception of Joshua, were content to remain where they were; they dreaded to encounter the horrors of the wild country through which they would have to pass. Joshua was the only one who fretted at their life of inaction. It seemed to him the cruellest thing to remain passive while Ellen and Dan and his parents were waiting for him at home. But what could he do? Without the assistance of Rough-and-Ready he was powerless; and that wise man of the woods declared emphatically that it would be madness to start upon such an expedition. So Joshua was compelled to wait for events to shape his destiny, and fretted and worried because he could take no hand in the direction of them. It was a good thing for him that he had plenty to do; he might else have lost his reason. Rough-and-Ready was the best of physicians; he would not allow any of his companions to be idle, and he took care to supply them with more work than they could conveniently accomplish. He derived a huge pleasure from this cunning proceeding, and had many a sly laugh to himself because of it. The building of the gunyahs was a matter in which he took especial delight, and he and his mates labored at them for many days; when they were finished, Rough-and-Ready declared that they were better than the finest stone houses that ever were built. The women took delight in them also, and decorated them with the prettiest creepers they could find. During all this time they were not molested by Scadbolt and the Lascar. In their rambles through the woods they occasionally came upon traces of the two rascals and caught distant glimpses of them, but they never came to close quarters. Once Scadbolt had attempted to make overtures; but he was warned off with small ceremony by Rough-and-Ready, who declined to parley with him.

On a certain moonlight night, not many nights ago, Rough-and-Ready invited Joshua to accompany him on an expedition. Coming to a place where the moon was shining over the tops of the gum-trees, Rough-and-Ready motioned Joshua to be still, and in a few minutes they heard a call, half scream, half chatter. Presently Rough-and-Ready raised his gun, pulled the trigger, and down came two animals shaped like cats, with long brushy tails, sharp claws, and something like thumbs on their hind feet.

"'Possums," said Rough-and-Ready in explanation.

He had found out a haunt of these animals, and that night they brought back more than a dozen, some ring-tailed, some silver. They could only be shot on moonlight nights, said Rough-and-Ready, and are chiefly found where the gum or peppermint-tree abounds. They had a splendid harvest, and in a week they collected nearly a hundred. Rough-and-Ready was mighty particular about the skinning of them, and about rubbing the fleshy parts of the skins with fine wood-ashes before fixing them on the trees to dry. They also caught a score or so of the sugar-squirrel, whose fur is real chinchilla. Upon these skins Minnie and Rachel are busy now with needle and thread, making caps for the men. It is a strange sight to see such evidences of civilization in the wild woods. The women had begged Rough-and-Ready to spare the lives of two young opossums which were found alive in their mothers' pouches, and he, knowing that they could be easily tamed, had readily consented. They were the most docile and harmless little things, and soon became domesticated, if such a word may properly be used in the life I am describing. At the present time, one of them is hanging head downwards, with its tail curled round the branch of a tree, in a state of serene happiness and content. The other is with Little Emma, who is sitting not far from the women, playing with it in the midst of a great heap of wild flowers she has collected.

The females are not alone. Two of the men are away, but Joshua is in sight, busy with his axe cutting up a tree for slabs. To tell truth, Rough-and-Ready is not desirous of moving from the woods where they are now camped, unless they are compelled to do so by the savages or by unforeseen circumstances. They are camped upon high land, where they are comparatively safe from floods; the country round about is fairly stocked with game; and there is water in abundance — somewhat of a rare circumstance, and, rarer still, the water is sweet. As for the life itself, none could be more attractive to him. The slabs that Joshua is cutting now are designed for a fence round their homestead. "Even if Blacks come," thought Rough-and-Ready "and they are not inclined to be friendly, we may frighten them away with our guns." He is very sparing of their powder and shot, of which they have not too large a store, and has taught his companions to make and lay many kinds of cunning snares for game. He is a thorough bushman, and in his present circumstances is certainly the right man in the right place.

The character of Rachel Homebush appears to have completely changed. The trials she has gone through have softened her hitherto hard nature. No stony-voiced exhortations to repent drop from her lips; she is humanized and humbled. But a short time since she was intolerant, arrogant, harsh, and proudly-insolent in her armor of sanctity; but now she has doffed that armor, and has inward doubts of herself. She believes in the goodness of others. She is less sanctified and more godly. Said Rough-and-Ready to Joshua, when they were talking of the women, —
"Rachel Homebush is a different creature to what she was. She is not so good as she was, and I think she's all the better for it."

Joshua smiled at this paradox, and said,—
"At all events she has a different opinion of you."

"Think so, mate?" asked Rough-and-Ready, a little anxiously. "I'm sorry for it, in one way. There's only one woman "—

But he paused unaccountably in the middle of his speech, looked at Minnie, who was a few yards away, looked at Joshua, and walked off whistling.

Here is the picture. Two hives, bright with flowering creepers; Rachel and Minnie sitting in the shadow of the hives, on stumps of trees, making fur caps; a 'possum hanging by its tail, studying gravitation; the little child, not far away, lying on the ground, surrounded by wild flowers, playing with her pet; in the distance, Joshua busy with his axe; surrounding and encompassing all, bright sky and lovely forest. Rachel, raising her eyes from her work, looks at the child in the midst of her garden, and a soft expression rests upon her face. The child sees the look, and thrusting the 'possum in the bosom of her frock, runs towards Rachel with a handful of flowers. Rachel kisses the child, strokes the silky coat of the 'possum, and selecting a piece of wild jasmine, places it in her breast. Then Little Emma goes to the back of Minnie, and twines some of the brightest flowers in Minnie's beautiful hair; and after falling back and admiring the effect of her handiwork, whispers to Minnie to get up, for she wants to show her something. Minnie smiles and rises, and they walk hand in hand to where Emma's wild flowers are, but the child leads her farther on, in the direction of Joshua. Made aware of the child's intention, Minnie falters, and tries to release her hand gently; but Little Emma clings to her, and laughingly strives to pull her along. Joshua's attention is attracted to the gentle struggle, and, coming forward, he asks the meaning of it. The child explains that she wanted Joshua to see how pretty the flowers looked in Minnie's hair, and that Minnie tried to run away. Joshua looks at Minnie, who stands trembling before him, as if she were guilty of some deep offence. Her bosom is heaving, her eyes are luminous with tears, her face is bright with blushes, and the tell-tale blood dyes her fair neck. Surely he has never looked upon a more beautiful picture! He says some kind words to her, and she goes back to her place near Rachel, and he to his work. But, within a few minutes afterwards, he swings his axe over his shoulder, and walks away in deep thought. The bees are humming about him, many-colored locusts and golden-green grasshoppers flit among the tangled brushwood, gorgeous butterflies skim through the air; the gaudy beetle creeps lazily along; the praying mantis, with its leaf-like wings, darts before him; the tree-frog utters its strange cry; a great lizard, with a frill round its neck, disappears at the sound of his step. He walks past these and myriad other wonders of the woods, until the character of the country changes, and he finds himself among rocky gullies, with many a fissure in the stony ranges that lead down to them. The buzz of woodland life has ceased; unfathomable silence seems to dwell in these rocky hills and valleys. But suddenly a sharp shrill note sounds upon the air. It is a bird's note, but no mate's voice replies. It is like himself, solitary in the midst of this ungracious scene, which frowningly proclaims, "Love finds here no dwelling-place." Again the note sounds, and as he makes his way toward it, curious to see what kind of bird haunts so desolate a place, he hears a faint echo answer — a voice with no soul in it, he thinks in his then melancholy mood. He comes to the opening of a small cave, the walls of which assume fantastic shapes in the dim light. And there, uttering its wail, to which only mocking echoes make response, he sees the Solitary Warbler standing alone in the centre of the cave, like the Cain of its race. He sighs and walks on — over the rocky range, into woodland again, where the ground dips, and where the rich soil is teeming with new wonders; and coming to a great pool, he sits down by its side. He has been to this spot before. Chancing upon it by accident in one of his rambles, he was attracted by its beauty, and by the singular effect of the shifting shadows upon the bosom of the pool, whose surface is almost covered by lovely pink-and-white water-lilies. He looks now into the water, and sees his haggard face reflected between the beautifully-colored lilies. And singularly enough he sees at the same time, with the eyes of his mind, the picture of Minnie as she stood before him, with eyes downcast and the flowers in her hair. It is because he was disturbed by thought of her that he left his work. He knows her secret but too well. She loves him with all her soul. She tells it in every look, in every word; every little act of hers towards him is imbued with dangerous tenderness, and yet she is unconscious of wrong. Every day she grows more devoted — every day grows more beautiful. And it is a part of his great misery to feel that her society gives him pleasure as well as pain. He is storm-tossed by a conflict of feeling. In this conflict no miserable vanity finds place, although it might be well excused in most men in such a position; nor is he by a thought false to Ellen. But Minnie is dependent upon him, lives upon his kindness, asks nothing from him but gentle speech. Shall he deny her this? Shall he be false to his nature, and be harsh where harshness would be brutality? He is strong; she is weak. Her power is in her weakness; his weakness is in his strength. She leans upon him for support, and rules by submission.

Something stirs behind him. A sound so light that it might have been produced by the fall of a leaf or by the swaying of a bough from which a bird has flown. Joshua, whose senses have been quickened by his late experience, turns rapidly, and meets the Lascar face to face. In the woods thought and action are twin-like. Quick as lightning Joshua's pistol is in his hand, and the muzzle is pointed straight at the Lascar's breast.

"Stand!" cries Joshua, "if you value your life."

The Lascar stands motionless, his hands behind him.

"Show your hands and what is in them, or I fire."

The Lascar shows his hands — a large piece of rock in one. He had seen Joshua sitting by the pool, and had intended to brain him with the stone. At Joshua's command, he drops the stone. A bitter smile wreathes Joshua's lips, and something like a savage instinct whispers to him to shoot his enemy dead upon the spot. But the thought that it would be nothing less than murder restrains him. The Lascar sees the struggle in Joshua's face, and trembles; miserable wretch as he is, he has not conquered the fear of death. He is re-assured when Joshua drops his hand and moves away, still facing him. At this, fear being subdued, the venom in his nature begins to work. Shall he let his enemy depart without a sting? He commences with a piece of bravado.

"Ah," he exclaimed, "you have robbed me, but you can't make up your mind to murder me."

"Robbed you!" exclaims Joshua, forgetting for a moment. "Of what?" "Of my knife. Give it me back. I can't hurt you with it. You are more than a match for me with your pistols. How do you think I can live without a knife?"

Joshua makes no reply to this appeal to his humanity, and moves off a few steps, warily.

"I suppose you think yourself a manly sort of fellow," continues the Lascar, moving step for step with Joshua, but keeping at a safe distance nevertheless, "robbing people of their knives, threatening to murder them, and running away with an innocent girl, and ruining her!"

"You villain!" exclaims Joshua, quivering at this reference to Minnie, "do not make me forget myself!"

"So far as to shoot a man in cold blood!" sneers the Lascar. "But don't forget that the first time you struck me it was for running after a woman. What better are you than me? I ran after a woman, not an innocent girl. Perhaps you'll say you didn't trick her from her father's house, and make love to another girl, her friend, all the while, and that girl the sister of the man you pretended such fondness for! Going to be married to her too, I heard. But I can tell you something you don't know. You were precious sly with your sweetheart, Ellen Taylor, in Gravesend; she wouldn't suspect you, I dare say you thought, if you had her down at Gravesend until the ship sailed — she wouldn't have an idea then that your other sweetheart, Minnie Kindred, with her face stained brown, was waiting for you on board the 'Merry Andrew.' Ah! you played a cunning game, you pink of perfection, you sailor-hero; but I outwitted you, I think, in a way you're not aware of."

"How?" asks Joshua, constrained to listen.

"How? I watched you, and was paid for it. You little thought that, did you? I'll tell you something more. The man who paid me for watching had a fancy for your sweetheart Ellen: you've no need to ask me who he is, for you'll not find out through me. I did my duty to him, and he paid me for it. Why, directly I set eyes on that brown-faced gypsy-maid aboard the 'Merry Andrew,' I says, 'Minnie Kindred, by God!' and I set a trap for her, and she fell into it. Then what did I do? I sent a letter to my master by the pilot, and told him to go to Minnie Kindred's father, and to Dan, and to your mother and father, and to your other sweetheart, Ellen, and let them know that you had run away with the girl, and that you parted from Ellen Taylor one minute, and was courting Minnie Kindred aboard ship the next. Was that a good game to play? Was I as cunning as you? Was that paying you for what you first did to me? Do you remember what I said, when you called me a dog of a Lascar? I told you that the Lascar dog never forgets — never, never! Why, now I look into your face, I could hug myself to think that we're wrecked, and that we shall die and rot here, every one of us, and that your sweetheart (who's my master's sweetheart now, I'll be sworn) and your friends know you for what you are — a mean false hound! I put a cross against you once, and I swore to have your heart's blood. Have I had as good? Think of it, and tell me if I have had my revenge."

But he does not wait to be told. There is so dangerous a look in Joshua's face, that he darts away and disappears in the bush. It is well for him that he has escaped, for Joshua is maddened by what he has heard. Truly the Lascar has struck at him with a cunning hand. The agony of his soul is shown in the convulsive twitching of his features, in his white lips, and in the veins of his strong hand, which swell almost to bursting as he grasps a stout branch for support. So he remains fighting with his agony with a bleeding heart, for full half an hour. This knowledge that he has gained is more bitter than all the rest. He knows the worst now. The evidence against him is awful in its completeness. "Even the Old Sailor will believe me guilty," he thinks, and groans aloud at the thought. But there is one duty before him to do. He must tell Minnie. This last resolve comes upon him when the force of his first passion is somewhat spent. Between him and Minnie no word has ever passed of those at home; their very names have been avoided. But Joshua now makes up his mind that silence on this subject must be broken. It *must;* both for Minnie's sake and his own.

It is past sundown. The day has been very hot, and the shadows of night bring cooler breezes, grateful to the senses of the castaways. Joshua has drawn Minnie a little apart from the others; she, yielding to his slightest wish, accompanies him to a part of the forest where they can talk unobserved. His first impulse is to ask her why she came on board the "Merry Andrew" unknown to him, and why she had disguised herself from him; but he spares her this pain, and takes from his breast Ellen's portrait and her lock of hair, and Dan's Bible. He hands Minnie the Bible.

"Do you know what this is?" he asks.

"Yes," she answers; "it is the Bible that Dan gave you."

"Read what is on the first page."

She reads the inscription: "From Dan to

his dearest friend and brother, Joshua. With undying love and confidence."

"You know the love that existed between Dan and me, Minnie?"

"I know. It is perfect. Why do you say existed? Surely it exists!"

"I don't know; I'm afraid to think. Your words are in some sort comforting to me; for they prove you have acted in ignorance, and that you have not wilfully wronged me."

She looks at him imploringly.

"You will understand presently," he says.

He takes Ellen's lock of hair, and presses it to his lips, and kisses Ellen's portrait also. The hot blood flushes into Minnie's face, then suddenly deserts it, and she clasps her hands convulsively. She is but woman, after all. Yet she controls her agitation sufficiently to ask in an unsteady voice, —

"Is it necessary to speak further of this, Joshua?"

"It is more than necessary," he replies; "it is imperative. My duty and my honor demand it."

She bows her head; he pauses a while, and when he speaks again, it is in a softer tone.

"Minnie, do you know that Dan loved you?"

"Loved me!"

"Ay, with all the strength of his constant heart."

"I did not know it. I thought he liked me, but I had no idea it was as you say."

"He told me in confidence some time before I left. My heart bleeds as I recall that conversation. No girl could hope to be more fondly, more faithfully loved. When the 'Merry Andrew' left Gravesend, I said to myself, 'When I return, Minnie will be Dan's wife,' for I could not but believe that you would have learned to appreciate the worth of such a love as his. But it was not to be."

"No, it was not to be," says Minnie sadly. "If I had known, it could not have been; if I had remained at home, it could not have been. You, who knew Dan so well, do you not know something of me also? I understand the motive that impels you to speak to me of these things, and I honor you the more for it. It is another proof of your goodness and generosity"—

"Minnie, Minnie!" he cries, "do not speak to me like that!"

"I must; I cannot help myself. Have you so poor an opinion of me — do you know so little of me — as to think I would marry a man I did not love? Rather than that, I would choose for him I loved the bitterest lot that life can offer — misery, shame, humiliation — and be content. Dan is all that you say; but I did not love him, did not deceive him. If he told you so, he told you what is false."

"He did not tell me so, but said that from your manner to him sometimes, he hoped to win your love."

"Must I shame myself to justify myself?" she cries recklessly. "I was happy in his company because he was your friend, and because he loved you. I was happy in his company because he spoke of you, and because — Joshua, have pity on me and forgive me! O my heart, my heart!"

He catches her fainting form, for she is falling. Weeping, she turns her face from him and hides it in her hair. Soft breezes play among the branches of the trees, stirring them into worshipping motion, and the more-pork, with its sad-colored plumage, flits by on noiseless wings, uttering his melancholy note. Joshua waits until Minnie is more composed; presently her sobs grow fainter and she leaves the shelter of his arm, and stands a little apart from him, with her face still averted.

"I do pity you," he then says, "and forgive you. What I have said and what I have done springs from no feeling of unkindness to you, Minnie. God knows, in such a strait as ours, such a feeling would be worse than cruel. But there are certain things of which I am afraid you are ignorant, that I must speak of and that you must hear. Do you know that, before I left home, I was suspected of playing with your feelings — of making love to you clandestinely, and so betraying the friend whom I would have laid down my life to serve?"

"No, no, Joshua, do not tell me that!"

"It is the truth; but I did not know it until after I had bidden good-by to mother and father and Dan, in Stepney. Where were you on that day?"

"I — I was not at home," she falters.

"You had left, then. I went to your father's room to wish you and him good-by. He refused to see me. I asked to see you, and Susan told me you were asleep. I was deeply grieved; and I can understand now what caused Susan to beg me imploringly to be true to Ellen. What a cowardly villain they must believe me to be! Your father suspected me; Susan suspected me. If I had died that Christmas night at mother's door, it would have been happier for me! Minnie I thanked you once for saving my life; but I cannot thank you now, for you have made me the unhappiest of men."

She does not answer him, but stands before him trembling and suffering, as before a judge, enduring her punishment and admitting the justice of it.

"It is part of my unhappiness," he continues, "that I have to speak thus to you; it is part of my unhappiness that I have to show you the consequences of your rash conduct. Listen: To-day I saw the Lascar; he came behind me stealthily, to kill me, I believe; but I turned and saw him in time. I could have shot him dead where he stood; indeed, some savage prompting urged me to do so, but I held my hand and was spared the crime. This man hates me, Minnie. In an encounter I had with him before I first went to sea, I struck him and hurt him. He has had a bitter revenge upon me. He saw you on board the 'Merry Andrew' before the pilot left the ship, and recognized you, despite your disguise."

Minnie holds her breath. She remembers how the Lascar whispered her name in her ear the first day she went aboard.

"He did a devilish thing then. He wrote a letter home, saying that I had run away with you, and that we were together on board the 'Merry Andrew.'"

She falls on her knees before him, and raises her hands supplicatingly, and begs him again to forgive her, and to believe that she knew nothing of this, and that if she had known—

"If you had known, Minnie," he says, gently raising her, "you would not have done what you have. But you did not stop to consider, poor child! You see the consequences of that letter, do you not? Suspecting me, your father told me the story of his life, to warn me not to betray you. Suspecting me, Susan implored me to be true to Ellen. Dan confided to me his love for you, and I listened to and sympathized with him. Well, what must he and all of them think, when they have learned that you and I are together on board the 'Merry Andrew'? And I have something to tell you more painful than all the rest."

He puts Ellen's portrait into her hand.

"Do you know who this is?"

Her eyes are blurred by tears, and she sees Ellen's sweet face through the sorrowful mist.

"It is Ellen's," she says.

"It is my wife!"

As Joshua utters these words, earth and heaven fade in Minnie's sight; nothing is visible, nothing is palpable to her senses, but the knowledge that flashes upon her, that her love, instead of being her glory, is now her shame. "There is no earthly sacrifice that love will not sanctify," her father had said. Could love sanctify such a sacrifice as she had made—a sacrifice that had brought disgrace and dishonor upon the man she loved? For the first time some slight consciousness of her error breaks upon her, and she looks upon herself as a shameful thing. As Joshua, witnessing her agony, moves a step nearer to her, she cries, "No, no, do not touch me!"

and with a wild shudder sinks upon the ground. He, animated by sincerest compassion, throws himself by her side, lays his hand upon her head, and raises her face to his. She bows her head upon his shoulder, and sobs her grief out there. By every means in his power—by gentle speech, by tender act—he strives to soothe her, and succeeds. And then, true to his purpose, he finishes his story—tells her what occurred between him and the Old Sailor at Gravesend; how surprised he was to find that the good old man, and even his own mother, had seen Minnie's fancy for him, and had devised the cure for it; and how, prompted by duty and by his love for Ellen (he dwelt much on that), he had married her quietly at Gravesend, and had spent there the three happiest days of his life. And when his story is finished, and she has learned all, they sit hand in hand, very quiet and sore-smitten, until Minnie, in a singularly-subdued voice, asks what she shall do: as if, having committed this fault, and brought such terrible suspicion upon him, he has only to tell her how to atone for it, and she will straightway do it. Sadly he replies, "What *can* you do, Minnie? Nothing—nothing but wait. There is, to my mind, not the barest chance of escape. We shall make our graves in this wild forest; but we must live so—you and I, my dear—that upon my death-bed I shall be able to think that I have been true to my wife, true to my friend. Life is not the end of all things."

Meekly she assents. He calls her "Sister," and kisses her; and then they rejoin their companions, who are seated by the gunyahs, cooking turtles' eggs found by Rough-and-Ready, the discoverer.

CHAPTER XXXV.

SURPRISED BY SAVAGES.

THE wisdom of Rough-and-Ready's plan of action was soon proved. One night, thunder awoke them from sleep. The thunder that breaks over the housetops, and the lightning that flashes in at the window-panes of a populous city, are very different from what are heard and seen in mountain ranges and great wastes of forests. Nature seems to be toned down in the city; in the forests and mountains she is grandly beautiful in repose, terrifically beautiful in travail. The thunder-peals were so loud and awful, that the women and child lay clasping each other in speechless fear. Like savage Titans the sound swept down upon them, and rushed through the forests and over the mountains and into them in search of echoes. The lightning darted upon the trees, and ran along the branches, and leaped through the woods into the bowels of the earth. Every thing that lived in stream and woodland, in rocky range and dark lagoon, sought shelter from the storm, of which Sound was but the herald. Presently it came, the swift rush of waters, like a second deluge, filling the creeks and rivers, and flooding all the land. Great torrents rushed down the mountainside into the low land, sweeping all before them. The storm raged the whole night through, abating slightly when morning dawned. It was well for the castaways that they had a little food stored by, for they could not go out in search of any. The second night the women begged the men to stay with them; so they all occupied the women's gunyah, lying side by side in the dark, and whispering to each other little words of comfort. All but Rachel Homebush, who was struck dumb by fear. The second night's storm was more terrific than the first, and about midnight so tremendous a peal of thunder broke over them, that they started up in dread.

"Who screamed?" asked Rough-and-Ready. But his voice was not heard; and swift upon the heels of the thunder another vivid lightning-flash, instantly followed by a terrific burst of thunder, darted through the gunyah, and struck them blind for many moments. Then, during a slight lull, Rough-and-Ready asked again, —

"Who screamed?"

"Not I," said Joshua.

"Nor I," said the sailmaker.

The women did not speak. Joshua's heart beat with a new fear as he whispered, —

"Minnie! Minnie! speak to me. You are not hurt?"

And tears of thankfulness came into his eyes as Minnie answered in a trembling voice, —

"No, Joshua; I am only frightened. Let me hold your hand."

"Where's the child?" he asked.

"Rachel has her. Rachel! Rachel!"

No voice replied. Thoroughly alarmed, they called to her again and again, and to the child, but could not rouse them. They were in the deepest darkness.

Presently Rough-and-Ready said, "Hush! we must wait for the light."

They waited for the light, and by the first faint glimmer they saw Rachel and the child lying down peacefully, the woman with the child folded in her arms. Light had come to them before the others!

Rough-and-Ready, who was the first to discover it, turned to his companions, with the tears streaming down his face and beard.

"Comfort her," he said to Joshua, pointing to Minnie.

Joshua put his arm round Minnie and turned her face from where the woman and child lay.

"Poor Rachel! Poor Little Emma!" he said. "Be brave, Minnie, my dear. Do not give way, for my sake."

He knew what words to utter to give her strength to bear the shock, and he made use of his power with a wise compassion.

Her poor white lips trembled as she said to him, —

"Pray for one thing for me, Joshua. Pray that I may not die before I have made atonement."

"Hush, hush, my dear!" he replied; "there is none to make. It is I who rather should have to make it, for my hardness to you. Be comforted, my dear."

The words came from his heart. He would have been unfeeling indeed if he had not learned to appreciate the beautiful unselfishness of Minnie's love; her meekness, her faithfulness, her devotion, her unmurmuring submission, could not fail to have a powerful effect upon such a nature as his.

The men went into their gunyah, and before night came again had made a rough coffin of bark. The next morning they dug a grave, and stood round it bareheaded, while the rain was falling. They kissed the child's face and poor Rachel's also before the cover was put on the rude coffin. Amid deep sobs — the men were not ashamed of their tears — Joshua read prayers; some vine-creepers were thrown into the grave; the earth was piled up into a mound: and they went back sadly to their tent. The loss of some one very near and dear to them could not have been more severely felt. From that time forth it became a practice for Joshua to read a chapter out of the Bible every morning and evening.

The rainy season lasted for three weeks, and during this time they lived very miserably. Minnie thrived, however — perhaps because Joshua was tender to her. The hot weather came, and they were able to go in search of food. But Minnie was never left alone. Joshua and she were waiting one evening for the return of Rough-and-Ready and the sailmaker, but Rough-and-Ready came back without his companion. He looked round in some anxiety.

"Hasn't the sailmaker returned?"

"No," said Joshua; "you went out together."

"I know; but I missed him a couple of hours ago, and although I have searched for him and coo-ēēd for him everywhere, I haven't been able to find him."

The sailmaker did not make his appearance. To the surprise of his companions, Rough-and-Ready, after dark, fired half a dozen shots from his pistol into the air.

"You look surprised," he said; "well, now" (to Minnie), "can you bear a shock? Will you promise to be brave if I tell you something?"

She nodded.

"It is only something that I have been expecting. I think that the sailmaker is with the natives."

"Why do you think so?" asked Joshua.

"For good reasons. I saw some tracks of them when I was hunting for Tom. Perhaps they have captured him."

"He had his pistols."

"Frightened to use them, perhaps; or perhaps there were a lot of the Blacks, and he thought it would be foolish and useless. Besides he is new to them. He's all right, though; they won't hurt him, for he's a plucky fellow. Now, mind. When you first see the natives, and indeed always after that, show no fear of them. What I am going to say is to my mind a most foolish thing; but there's the faintest chance in the world that, making friends with them, you might make your way down south, from one tribe to another, in a few months, and come upon some cattle station. But, lord! there's one chance for you, and a hundred against you."

"Why do you say 'you'?" asked Minnie. "'We,' rather."

"No, my dear," said Rough-and-Ready with a blush. "I have two reasons for saying you and not we. The first reason is not a reason — it is a presentiment. I shall die in the bush. The second reason is a plainer one. It wouldn't be pleasant for me to get into civilized company in New South Wales."

"Why?"

Rough-and-Ready looked at her with admiration, and said, very inappropriately, as she thought, —

"Do you know that you have made me a better man?"

"A better man!" she exclaimed. "Why, you are a good man, and a brave man, too."

"You think so. So let it be," he said, half seriously, half gayly. "I'm not going to spoil your delusion just yet."

They saw no signs of the savages that night. They did not retire until late, and Rough-and-Ready went many times short distances in different directions to look for the natives, but they did not appear. Joshua took out his accordion and played. Rough-and-Ready listened thoughtfully, and when Joshua had finished an air, he said, —

"I told you, when we first came ashore here, that there is no surer way to frighten the blacks than through their superstitious fears. Your playing to-night, connected with the near presence of the savages, brings that remark back to me; and I'll tell you why. That music of yours may possibly be a great power with them. They have never heard any thing like it. If you don't lose your self-possession when you get among them — and you must take care not to, for Minnie's sake; her life may depend upon your courage — you may obtain an influence over them by means of your accordion. Sound for which they cannot account has a wonderful effect upon them. Here you have it. Don't forget what I say. Come, now, I can hear no sign of the black devils. You take some rest. I'll wake you in a couple of hours.

So they watched in turns during the night.

"What is the best thing to do," asked Joshua the following evening, "when the savages come? — to make friends with them, or try to frighten them?"

"There are too few of us to fight," answered Rough-and-Ready. "We might frighten them for a time, but they would be sure to come back in larger numbers. Then we haven't too much powder and shot left. No; the best and wisest course will be to be friendly with them, if possible. I *have* heard of white men living with them for many years. I saw an Englishman myself once who had been with them for five years. He was glad enough to get away from them; but they treated him kindly, he said. One man, whom I never saw, lived with them for thirty years. His name is Buckley, and he is living now."

"Do you know any thing of his story?"

"I'll tell you what little I know. He was a bricklayer in Cheshire — came from Macclesfield, I've heard. A great big hulking lazy fellow he was — brick-making was too hard work for him, so he enlisted as a grenadier. A fine grenadier he must have looked — he was six feet six inches in his stockings. But grenadiering didn't satisfy his wants. He was a natural vagabond like myself, and he got into trouble, and was sentenced to transportation. So he and three or four hundred other natural and unnatural vagabonds, being deemed fine material for the purpose, were sent out to form a colony. Buckley and his mates were put ashore at Port Phillip; but the governor, whose name was Collins, liked the place as little as the convicts, and he moved them off to Van Dieman's Land. Then they began to talk of escaping. They didn't know any thing of the interior of the country; but they thought, perhaps, that any thing was better than the devil's life they led as convicts. Buckley got away with two mates, of whom nothing more was ever heard. About twelve months after he escaped, he fell in with the natives, and lived with them for more than thirty years. During the whole of that time he never saw a white man. At length he heard from the tribe he was living with, that some men with skins the same color as his had been seen within a few miles of the native camp. They belonged to a band of explorers headed by a man named Batman. Buckley went in search of them, and presented himself to them. You can imagine what a sensation he created; a white giant, who had forgotten how to speak English, with native weapons hung round his body, and a kangaroo-skin rug his only clothing. He soon picked up a bit of English, and was taken to a white settlement, where he was made a pet and a wonder of. He might have done good service for the white people with the natives, for they say he has great influence with them. But my opinion of him is, that he is a lazy, skulking thief, and that living with the savages, where he hadn't to work for his food, just suited him. I expect that some part of his influence over them was produced by his tremendous height and big limbs. However, he is among the whites again, with a free pardon granted him, I've heard, and earning his living as he has earned it all his life — by doing nothing."

During the recital of this story, which Rough-and-Ready declared was veracious, every word of it, he was busy baking a fresh-water turtle, which he had caught that day while he was fishing in a lagoon. The turtle was baked in its shell, and they made a delicious supper off it. They had arranged to fish for eels that night, and Rough-and-Ready said, —

"Come along; it's of no use being frightened by thinking of the natives; we must get accustomed to them. We shall soon see them, and Tom with them."

They took all their fire-arms. Minnie had two pistols in her belt, and Joshua and Rough-and-Ready, besides pistols, had guns slung across their shoulders. Each of them wore a cap made of the beautiful fur of the sugar-squirrel. They walked through the quiet wood, looking sharply about them as they went along, but neither heard nor saw any signs of the natives. When they came to the lagoon, Rough-and-Ready told them he was going to show them a fine way of catching eels without trouble. He had his fire-sticks with him, and in half an hour he had a great fire blazing by the side of the lagoon. Attracted by the light, the eels came swarming towards them; and in a very short time they caught as many as they desired. Loaded with their spoil, they made their way back to their gunyahs; and as they got near them, they saw a dark figure glide swiftly away from the spot into the bush.

"A native," said Rough-and-Ready. "We must look out to-night."

"Or Scadbolt, or the Lascar, do you think?" suggested Joshua, supporting Minnie, who was clinging to him in alarm.

"No; a white man couldn't move away with such a cat-like motion. I fancy I saw his dark skin."

Thereupon Rough-and-Ready, for the purpose of familiarizing Minnie with the idea of living with the savages, and so lessening her fears, commenced talking of them, and continued talking for a couple of hours. By which time Minnie's fears really were lessened.

"What a number of stars have fallen the last few nights remarked Joshua.

"Ah, you have noticed that!" said Rough-and-Ready. "And if you observe, they have fallen immediately over this spot, in the direction of the sea. Well, those shooting-stars may have brought the natives here; for although some tribes believe that danger lies where stars fall, or that they indicate the direction of hostile tribes, others have a kind of belief that a great and good spirit may be seen where they fall. They believe that there is a new sun every day and a new moon every night, One tribe throws up the sun at daybreak, and another tribe catches it at sunset."

Here they were interrupted by cries of fear, and by the running towards them of some person who fell at their feet trembling and grovelling. It was the Lascar, who was evidently in a state of horrible fright. He looked more like a wild beast than a man. What few clothes he had on were torn and tattered, his nails were long, and his disordered hair and grovelling fears deprived his features of any likeness to humanity.

"The savages, the savages," he cried.

He had chosen what he considered the lesser of two evils; his white foes were preferable to black cannibals. Rough-and-Ready looked down upon him contemptuously, and touched him with his foot.

"The cowardly ruffian!" he said. "I'd sooner trust the Blacks than such as he.

Where's his rascally mate, I wonder — Get up!" he cried, and administered so smart a kick to the prostrate wretch that he jumped up on the instant, imploring mercy.

"Be silent, you chattering imp of darkness!" roared Rough-and-Ready; "be silent, and answer me. You've seen the Blacks, I suppose?"

The Lascar muttered an affirmative.

"Well, what are you frightened at? Why don't you go and make friends with them? They haven't much the advantage of you in color, and you are more of a wild beast than they are. Frightened of being eaten, eh? Faugh! they'd spear you and throw you away; you're not good enough even for them." The Lascar trembled the more at this; he was a true coward. "What d'ye think of mutineering now, eh? Answer me, you copper-colored devil, or I'll make an end of you — where's your mate, Scadbolt?"

"I don't know; I haven't seen him for days."

"Ah, two of a trade never agree. I thought you'd be cutting each other's throats. Captain Marvel, here's one of your crew who tried to raise a mutiny. As if that was not enough, he has murdered his mate." (It is a fact that Scadbolt was never heard of again, nor was any thing ever known of his fate.) "Now then, you, as captain of the 'Merry Andrew,' pronounce judgment — death, nothing less — and I'll take him away and execute it, as truly as I'm a living man!"

There was something so determined in Rough-and-Ready's speech, and something so threatening in his action, that the Lascar leaped away in mortal fear. Whereat Rough-and-Ready laughed loud and long, and fired a shot in the air to frighten the Lascar the more.

In the morning, while they were at breakfast, two savages suddenly made their appearance, about twenty yards from where they were sitting. They appeared so suddenly, that they seemed to have started out of the ground.

"Now, Minnie," said Rough-and-Ready quietly, "don't scream out, and don't show any alarm. By the look of those fellows they are friendly, and do not mean to harm us."

Minnie conquered her fears bravely, although her heart was beating fast, and by the direction of Rough-and-Ready they went on with their breakfast, to all appearance quite unconcerned, and as if the presence of the savages was the most natural thing in the world. The two men who stood gazing at them were naked, with the exception of a girdle of emeu-feathers round their waists; their color was pale black; they were tall, with thin limbs and fine chests, and their hair was thick and curly. They had spears in their hands, about seven feet long, made from the stem of the tea-tree.

Seeing that they stood quite quiet, Rough-and-Ready held up part of an eel towards them, and smiled, and nodded his head gently. Whereupon the two savages looked at each other, said a few words, and disappeared. Both Joshua and Minnie drew a long breath of relief, for which Rough-and-Ready was inclined to be cross with them.

"They will be back presently," he said, "in company."

They had not long to wait. In less than half an hour the two who had first presented themselves returned with nearly a score of others. To the joy of the castaways, they saw Tom the sailmaker in the rear, and they nodded and smiled at him. Seeing that the savages, who had been jabbering among themselves, made signs to the sailmaker; and after the display of much pantomime, he came towards his mates. They shook hands with him, and Rough-and-Ready asked him how he was.

"Jolly," he replied. He told them in crisp sentences, all of them in answer to Rough-and-Ready's questions, that the natives seemed disposed to be friendly, and that they were not half so bad as they looked.

Rough-and-Ready, accompanied by Tom, then walked half a dozen yards in the direction of the savages, and held out his hands to them. Tom looked at the savages, touched Rough-and-Ready on the breast, and then himself, with sufficiently expressive pantomime, to denote, "We two are one." Minnie and Joshua stood in the background, side by side, with linked arms. The savages, coming a little nearer, pointed to them, and jabbered unintelligibly, as much as to say, "What do you do here? Who are you?" Joshua, observing the success of Rough-and-Ready's pantomime, touched Minnie on the breast, and then himself, conveying the same meaning, "We two are one."

Here it must be told that Minnie had regained her naturally fair complexion, and that her hair, also fair, had grown to a great length. Tall and well-formed, with bare arms beautifully shaped, with pure complexion, with dreamy eyes, with long hair hanging loosely down, and with the charm and grace of youth upon her, she stood before them in her strange dress of civilized cotton and woodland fur; and her singularly-beautiful appearance had a powerful effect on the savages. They approached Rough-and-Ready, and felt his clothes, and made friends with him in their primitive fashion; but they kept some distance from Joshua and Minnie, regarding her with looks of reverence and astonishment. Presently, after much grimacing and flashing of hands and fingers, Rough-and-Ready came towards Minnie, and, to her surprise, bowed low before her, and stood in an attitude of respectful worship. The savages, who were watching him attentively, saw only his back; but if they had seen the merry twinkle in his eyes, they would have been as puzzled as Minnie was.

"I've heard say that every woman is an actress," he said, smiling. "Prove yourself one now, for all our sakes, by not moving, and by listening to me attentively. Your conduct may decide our fate. I have told you what significance the natives attach to shooting-stars, and how they either avoid the direction in which they fall or are impelled there by some powerful superstition. Fortune has favored us. I don't understand a single word these savages utter; but I understand from their actions that they are so amazed at your appearance as to entertain a belief that you are not quite mortal — that, in fact, you are a superior spirit. If they can be kept in this belief (supposing they entertain it), it will be of immense service to us. If you are brave enough not to show fear, they will almost be certain not to attempt to harm us."

No better speech could have been spoken to Minnie to inspire her with confidence and courage. But she turned to Joshua first, and asked, "Shall I do this?"

"Yes," he answered; "I think it will be well, if you can nerve yourself to it."

Smiling at the "if," she said softly, "For your sake, Joshua," and then, with queenly motion, walked towards the savages, conquering her disgust at their appearance. They awaited her approach; and when she was within a few steps of them, an old graybeard came forward, and held out his hands, saying some words expressive of respectful welcome. Minnie understood as much by his expressive action. She touched his hands, and waved hers, bidding them welcome, and beckoning to Joshua, touched him on the breast, and placed her hand upon his shoulder. Then, smiling placidly upon the dusky group, she walked away with Joshua, and sat down in the shade of the gunyah. Whatever meaning her pantomime had conveyed, it evidently excited great interest among the savages. They conversed earnestly and excitedly, and pointed to the sky and to the earth, describing by their motions the action of a star falling gently to the ground.

"Bravely done," said Rough-and-Ready to Minnie. "Whatever notion they have in their heads, it is one that will do us no harm. See, they are moving off, taking the sailmaker with them."

And, indeed, the natives went away in a body, leaving behind them four of their party, however, who squatted upon the ground, with their eyes fixed upon the castaways.

"They are left to watch us," said Rough-and-Ready; "but I think we may make ourselves easy about their being disposed to be friendly."

He and Joshua went about their pursuits as usual; but to keep up the fiction concerning Minnie with the natives who were watching them, they would not allow her to work, and treated her with such marks of deference as could not fail to impress the savages. During the day, Rough-and-Ready offered food to the savages, who accepted it. To show their gratitude, two of them went away into the forest, and returned with a quantity of honey in a reed basket, which they placed at Minnie's feet, and which she partook of to their evident satisfaction.

"There isn't the slightest mistake," said Rough-and-Ready merrily, "that the devil isn't half so black as he is painted."

They were left apparently undisturbed for two days, when the natives returned, with different descriptions of food — sweet roots many of them, pleasant and good to eat. "They have some plan in their heads," said Rough-and-Ready. He was right. Early the next morning the natives gave them to understand that they were going farther inland, and that the white people were to accompany them. "Now we shall see something," observed Rough-and-Ready as they plunged into the forest. They walked for three days before they came to the native camp. They made short stages to accommodate Minnie. During this time, Minnie kept close to Joshua, as if to protect him; but Rough-and-Ready mixed freely with the natives, and made some snares for game, which he gave to them, and with which they were much pleased. When they were within a few miles of the camp a number of the tribe, chiefly women and children, came out to meet them. Soon they arrived at the camp, and were surprised at its picturesqueness. It consisted of about a dozen roomy huts, roofed and thatched with bark and reeds. At a short distance from the huts was a large pool, the vegetation around which was singularly beautiful. Among the strange trees which attracted the notice of the castaways, the umbrella-tree, with its dark leaves and crimson flowers, seemed to them the most remarkable.

There were also a large number of great fig-trees, and magnificent palms with feathery leaves. The air was sweet with the perfume of lily and jasmine and the golden-flowered thorn. There was one hut which appeared but newly built; it was prettier than the others, and its sides were decorated with wild flowers and flowering vines. Towards this the natives led Minnie, upon whom the women and children looked in awe and wonder. She, clasping Joshua's hand, entered this hut, and sank upon the bed of dry leaves, wondering what was next to come. She begged Joshua to stop with her, for she was frightened of being left alone. So, after partaking of the food which the natives brought to them, he lay down near the mouth of the hut, and she at the farther end on her bed of leaves. Joshua could see the glories of the sunset from where he lay; and he saw the fire die out of the sky, and saw the stars come out. But he was tired with his day's walk, and sleep overpowered him, although he tried to keep awake. Early in the morning they rose, and walked towards the banks of the pool, —

" To where the weed of green and red
  Its floating carpet gayly spread,
  Whereon the emerald frog reclined,
  Fanned by the fragrance of the wind;
  And all was darkened by the shade
  The water-weeping branches made —
  Save where a paler, tenderer green
  Made bright the beauty of the scene.
  The birds flashed down, to drink or lave,
  With varied note and joyous stave,
  And plunging sidelong from the reeds,
  That wavered mid the water-weeds.
  Flashed in the stream so cool and calm,
  O'erhung by many a fern-tree palm;
  And bell-bird peals, whose silvery chimes
  Found in the rippled water rhymes.
  Throughout the perfumed thicket rang,
  Whence the tall-headed bulrush sprang."

CHAPTER XXXVI.

THE POWER OF MUSIC.

THE natives were busy preparing for a grand Corroboree, which, being interpreted, means a grand gathering and celebration in honor of some imposing event. Scouts were sent out in every direction, and every hour brought fresh comers, who evinced the greatest possible curiosity in the white people. At one time nearly sixty members of a different tribe arrived in a body, and a fierce jabbering took place between the old men of the tribes. Rough-and-Ready, who had by this time picked up a few native words, came to Minnie and Joshua with a look of concern on his face.

" They are quarrelling about us," he said. " As far as I can understand, this new tribe lay claim to us for having been found in a country which they say is theirs. I think I know how they will settle it, if they settle it at all peaceably."

" How ? " asked Joshua anxiously.

" They will separate us — two for each of the two strongest tribes." Minnie caught Joshua's hand convulsively. " I know what you mean, my dear," said Rough-and-Ready, a little sadly; " you and Joshua must not be parted. And indeed, it would not be right; you belong to one another. Well, the sailmaker and I will go our way and you will go yours. Only you must be cunning and keep together. Joshua, to-night, before the natives go to sleep, play a few soft airs upon your accordion. You and Minnie must be in your hut together while you play. And don't let them see the accordion. The music will fill them with wonder, and it will be a strong reason with them why you should not be parted. But indeed, my dear, if you continue to act your part well there will be no fear of that."

" You are a good man," said Minnie gratefully, holding out her hand to Rough-and-Ready.

He took it and pressed it to his lips, and held it in his with infinite tenderness.

" No, my dear," he said, " I am not a good man. You have seen me at my best. I am a convict, and when I came on board the 'Merry Andrew,' I was trying to escape from the colony. There's many a black mark against me which I doubt will never be wiped out in this world. I was a little sinned against at first, it is true, but I had my revenge afterwards; I couldn't be meek and humble under undeserved punishment. There! that's all I shall tell you about myself. Your imagination must fill in the outlines. And, mind you ! you can't make me out worse than I am. I am glad I have made this confession, lame and bald as it is; it has relieved my mind." He turned his back to them, with a motion which said, " You see what a vagabond I am ; I am not fit company for such as you."

But Minnie laid one hand upon his shoulder, and with the other turned his face towards hers.

" You are a good man," she repeated earnestly, looking into his eyes, which were filled with tears, " and I honor and respect you."

" And I, too," said Joshua, grasping his hand heartily. " If it should be our good fortune to meet under happier circumstances than these, I will show my gratitude to you."

" There, there, there ! " exclaimed

Rough-and-Ready, half roughly, half tenderly; "enough said about the past. We sha'n't be together much longer, as I've told you, and as you'll soon find. We must take things as they come, and make the best of them. Do you know the natives have a curious fancy about you?" he said to Minnie. "There was once in their tribe a young woman of rare beauty and virtues, who was idolized by all. I don't know how long ago this was, and it is only by piecing stray words and actions together that I have been able to understand it. Well, this young woman, by some means or other, was transformed into a star. They believe you to be her, having taken mortal form again to visit them. 'Tis a pretty fancy, isn't it?"

"But I am white, and"—

"She was black," interrupted Rough-and-Ready gayly. "That is easily accounted for; they believe that when they die they jump up white. If you were of their color, they would not have the fancy about you."

By the evening there were not less than a hundred and fifty savages collected together. Although the weather was warm, they were lying down before their camp-fires, with the exception of one group of about twenty old men and doctors of the principal tribes, who were earnestly engaged in discussing matters relating to the white people. An old chief of the tribe who had first discovered the castaways was on his feet, declaiming violently, with extravagant action, in which, nevertheless, there was much dignity. Opara was his name. His hair and beard were white, and his face and body were scored with ugly seams gained in battle, or in the exercise of the strange rites and ceremonies of his tribe. On his neck and breast, and from his shoulders to his hips, were still to be seen, old as he now was, the gashes made in his youth to entitle him to the dignity of manhood. A great chief was Opara — wise in council, fearless in battle, and had been the most skilful of all his tribe with boomerang and spear, and middla, and in throwing the wirra.

"The strangers are ours," he said; "the sacred crow, Karakorok, witnesseth that they are ours by right. The heavens were filled with light, and great voices thundered. We listened in awe. Fire rent the mountains, and made new caverns sacred. Light dived into raging waterfalls, cutting the earth. We waited full a moon. The storm ceased; the spirits spoke no more. We waited another moon. The stars fell near the sea — into it. We went there, wanting to know. We brought the strangers back. They are ours."

Up rose Wealberrin, chief of the other tribe. No less famous he than Opara. White-bearded, too, and tattooed from top to toe, and no less cunning with war and hunting weapons. Around his waist was a belt made of the hair of the enemies he had slain in battle.

"Not so," he said. "The land is ours. There, in Pandarri Kurto (heaven's cavern), lie our miutapas — our doctors. There are our hunting-grounds — our fishing-lands. There we make men of our sons. Shall I take Opara's food, and call it mine by right? He would reply as becomes a warrior. If I ask, he would give. But I ask not now. The land is ours. What is found on the land is ours."

"Once lived Mirgabeen," said Opara. "Bright-eyed, fleet-footed, hollow-backed. Her tongue spoke the music of the birds. Her dark hair hung down to her arched feet. She could shroud her glory in it — as night the day. She was beloved by all. Too bright for earth, she lives in the heavens now, a star. She looks down on me. She hears me speak. So dwelt with us a maid, whose supple limbs cleaved the water, who sang the music of the woods. The trees bent to her as she walked. The branches bowed before her, and whispered to her, and she replied. She left us for the grand vault where moons are made. What was ours is ours. She has come back to us. She is ours."

"So be it," said Wealberrin. "The others then are ours. Opara has spoken."

"She has with her a mate," said Opara, "whom she has touched upon the breast. Let Wealberrin take two — we two. Then we shall have peace."

Wealberrin would have replied, but as he rose to his feet a wondering expression stole into his face, and into the faces of all assembled there. For from Minnie's gunyah issued sounds so soft and sweet that the night-birds hushed their voices to listen. The breeze was so light that the melodious notes hung upon the air, and lingered long before they died away. The savages clutched each other, and stood transfixed with fear and wonder. What voices were these that were speaking? In their dreams they had never heard any thing so sweet. Opara had said it. Minnie had come from the vault where the moons are made, and was speaking to the spirits of another world. Motionless, with bended heads or with forms inclined towards the sound, they stood like figures of stone, in reverential attitude. And did not move a limb when the music ceased; for a shadow fell upon the moonlit space, and Minnie came to the opening of the gunyah and looked in dumb amazement at the strange scene before her.

And now the day has come upon which the grand ceremony of the Corroboree is to be celebrated. The rival tribes have settled their dispute. Rough-and-Ready, who is the Chorus of the party, tells his friends that Joshua and Minnie are to remain with Opara's tribe, and that he and the sailmaker are to be attached to Wealberrin's. Joshua hints at resistance, but Rough-and-Ready declares it would be madness.

"If there was no woman in the case," he says, "I might counsel differently; but for Minnie's sake we must have no fighting. We might kill a score or two of the natives, but you must bear in mind there are half a thousand of them here now. Then their spears are poisoned. Suppose one should strike Minnie. No, no; submission is our best course." So, with much grief, they are compelled to make up their minds to submit.

All day long, there is great feasting. An emeu has been hunted down, and the fat carefully distributed among the natives; honey and sweet roots have been brought in in abundance, and the bushes have been stripped of their fruit. Rude seats of vines, decorated with flowers, have been placed for Minnie and Joshua in front of their gunyah, and in front of the seats a kind of arched screen of leaves and branches has been erected, through the network of which they can see and be seen. When night comes, fires are lighted, the flickering flames of which give birth to monstrous shadows that flit about the trees, and fill the woods with grotesque shapes. Minnie and Joshua watch with a kind of wonder the shadows created by the fire nearest to them. Now the light goes down, and the black shapes dart through the woods, or run swiftly along the branches, ravenously, and with cruel intent, as it appears; anon, the flame leaps up, and the shadows fly and shift restlessly about, with lightning speed, as if suddenly surprised by an enemy. Their attention, however, is soon diverted from these inanimate creations. The natives are assembling. Men, women, and children troop in from all quarters, and seat themselves round and about the fires in somewhat orderly fashion. There cannot be less than five or six hundred of them. All being seated, a long silence ensues, broken at length by a circle of singers, who chant a monotonous song, narrating how they had journeyed towards the sea into which stars were falling, and how they had found the strangers, and brought them to their camp. As they sing this song over and over again, they beat time with their clubs. A brave then chants a tradition of one of their ancient chiefs, who was compelled to fly before a hostile tribe; all his young warriors were slain, and he alone escaped; but his enemies determined to put an end to him, set fire to the bush around him, and he was encircled by a net of flame. Suddenly the earth opened, and water stole up from the caverns and extinguished the fire, and so the chief was saved, and a great river was made, in which fish was plentiful. In the midst of the silence which follows this song, a man springs from out the shadows. His face is crossed with lines of red and yellow, and his body is painted white. In his hand is a branch of green leaves, and a great tuft of emeu-feathers is on his head. He stands perfectly still for full a quarter of an hour, looking into the sky for the spirits of dead men. What inspiration falls upon him at the end of that time it would probably be difficult to explain; but he waves his branch of green leaves to and fro, and the singers strike up another song, and the musicians beat time as before with their war-clubs, while the chief actor in the scene rushes about, and flourishes his arms in a gradually-worked-up state of the wildest excitement. He vanishes in the shade as suddenly as he had appeared, and in his place leap a dozen men, presenting so startling an appearance that Minnie clasps Joshua's hand in sudden alarm. Flowers are twined round their ankles and above their knees. Some have tails of dingoes wound about their heads, others wreaths of down from the white cockatoo; some have tails of wallabies attached to their peaked beards, and all have feathers in their hair. White rings are round their eyes, their noses are striped, and lines of red, yellow, and black are painted from their shoulders and breasts down to their waists, where a white ring encircles them. The singers burst into song again, and the hideously-decorated figures begin to dance, advancing towards the singers and retreating from them; their motions at first are slow and tremulous, but soon they are leaping and jumping frantically from side to side, each trying to out-tire the others, with such violent exertion as to cause them presently to fall upon the ground in a state of exhaustion. As soon as each recovers, he rises, and dances by himself, and the women utter cries of commendation, and beat the ground in ecstasy. These performers are followed by others, who dance in a serpentine line, until they present the appearance of a serpent coiling and uncoiling itself; as they dance, they make a hissing sound with their tongues, to imitate the hissing of a serpent. And so through the night the Corroboree continues, until, thoroughly worn out, the savages retire to their rest, and the woods that a while ago were filled with such strange life and sound, are lying quiet and solemn in the peaceful light of the stars.

Wealberrin and his tribe are ready to start, and Rough-and-Ready and the sail-maker have come to wish Minnie and Joshua good-by. They go into the woods, out of sight of the natives, and sit sadly upon trunks of trees that have been blown down by storms.

"I have heard say, or have read somewhere," says Rough-and-Ready, striving to speak gayly, "that life is made up of meetings and partings, so that this is quite a natural thing, and not to be repined at. What we've got to do is to make the best of things."

"It might be worse," says Tom the sail-maker, good-naturedly assisting Rough-and-Ready to cheer Minnie's spirits.

"Bravo, Tom!" exclaims Rough-and-Ready. "It might be a good deal worse. We have escaped greater dangers than the present one, and if we act wisely and bravely we shall escape this. But it all depends upon ourselves, and if we lose courage, we lose all. You must bear that in mind, my dear. Why, this day twelve months we may be talking together, and smiling at these experiences which now seem so hard to bear!"

But Minnie only smiles sadly in reply, and Joshua asks Rough-and-Ready if there is any thing they can give him to enable him to bear them in remembrance.

"Nothing is needed," replies Rough-and-Ready. "We have not been together for a very long time, but our acquaintanceship has been sufficiently eventful to cause us never to be able to forget each other. Yet I should like one thing," with a tender glance at Minnie.

"What?" she asks, learning by his look that it is something in her power to give.

"A piece of your hair, Minnie," he says.

Minnie desires Joshua to cut off a lock with his knife, and he cuts a thick tress and gives it to Rough-and-Ready, who winds it round his finger and puts it into his pocket.

"Now," says he, "for a little sensible talk. Your sole aim must be to endeavor to work your way near to the settled districts, where you may have the chance of falling in with white people. Southward lies your chance of being rescued. Every day the squatters are coming farther inland in search of new ground for cattle-stations, and every day this fresh opening up of the country adds to the chances of escape. Whosesoever lot it is to first fall in with our countrymen must tell them that there are two white people living with one of the native tribes who are desirous of getting into civilized company again. That will make them look out for us perhaps. You will find that stockmen and bushmen are as fine and manly a set of fellows as you would desire to meet. I think you have the best chance of first hearing the crack of a stockman's whip, for your tribe is more of a southern one than ours." Then Rough-and-Ready told them, as much for the purpose of diverting Minnie's attention from the sad parting near at hand as for any other, of the wonderful enterprise of the Australian pioneers of progress, of the dangers they cheerfully encounter, of the unknown country they bravely plunge into, of the hardships they bear and make light of, and of the grand future that awaits the beautiful Australian continent.

"To my thinking," he says with enthusiasm, "there is no life that contains so much pure enjoyment as the life of a backwoodsman. I would not change it for any other — only I would prefer, for occasional mates and companions, white people instead of savages. I don't believe man was intended to live in close cities."

"But even such a life as you describe," says Joshua, "leads to the making of great cities. The pioneers go first, and the masses follow."

"That's the worst of it," says Rough-and-Ready; "they follow, and are not content to live naturally. They make streets and cramp them up with just room enough for a score of men to walk abreast in. Down in Sydney there are streets, as you know, where not a half a dozen men could walk abreast through; but that's the way of all cities, large or small. Directly new land is opened up, in troop the masses, as you call them, who make their streets and build their houses as if there wasn't an inch of ground to spare; while all around them are thousands and thousands of miles of lovely country, with trees and flowers, and fruit, and fish, and game, inviting them to come and enjoy life as it ought to be enjoyed!"

"Well," says Joshua, "'tis the way of the world. You were never intended to live in cities, that's clear."

"I don't know. I dare say, once upon a time, I should have thought I was mad if such ideas as I have now had entered my head. I wasn't always so rough as I am now. But cities are necessary, I suppose; and it's folly to talk as I do. Why, I don't doubt that in less than fifty years a city will be built even here in these wild woods; and perhaps on this very spot where we now sit they'll build a prison." He speaks these last words with a dash of bitterness; but he soon shakes of his cynical humor, and proceeds to speak of more important matters concerning the present. "Be especially careful of one thing," he concludes, " never by any chance let them see your accordion." (Joshua had it slung round his shoulders, wrapped in a bag of fur which Minnie had made for it.) "When you play, let the natives *hear* the music, not *see* where it comes from. By that means you will best preserve your influence and Minnie's over them. And bear in mind — work southward."

Here two natives make their appearance, and after looking attentively at the white people, glide away quietly.

"'Tis time to go," says Rough-and-Ready, jumping to his feet; "that is their delicate way of telling us that they are waiting." Minnie, with streaming eyes, raises her face to his. He stoops and kisses her, and says tenderly, "God bless and protect you, my dear!" The four of them shake hands sorrowfully, and part — never again to meet on earth. So Rough-and-Ready and Tom the sailmaker disappear from the yearning gaze of their friends, and from this story; and Joshua and Minnie are left thus strangely alone.

CHAPTER XXXVII.

HARSH JUDGMENTS.

THE foundering of the "Merry Andrew" and the loss of every soul on board were duly recorded in the newspapers, and utterly shattered the happiness of that humble home in Stepney wherein love and content had dwelt for so many years. If Mrs. Marvel's daughter Sarah, who has played an insignificant part in this history, had been at home, unmarried, her parents might have derived relief and consolation in watching the progress of her fortunes; but Sarah had had the rare good fortune to be quickly wooed and quickly won by a country mechanic, and her subsequent career has nothing in common with these pages. So that Mr. and Mrs. Marvel were left alone in their unhappy position. They could not bear to live longer in the house in which Joshua had been born and reared, and they agreed to Dan's proposition, that they should move, and live with him and his sisters. What added to their unhappiness was, that they were at war with every one of their neighbors. When the news of the loss of the "Merry Andrew" reached Stepney, the neighbors one and all decided that Joshua was guilty, and many of them declared that the punishment which had overtaken him was a just visitation. To listen to this in silence seemed to Joshua's family to be nothing less than flat treason; they fought stoutly and earnestly against the calumny, and defended the character of their lost son with all the strength of their loving hearts. But vainly. The neighbors persisted in their belief until George Marvel gave out that if he caught any man speaking against the dead, he would thrash him. He had not long to wait to give effect to his words. He came home one day with a black eye and a bruised face. "I've been fighting Bob Turner," he said in explanation, "for taking away our Josh's good name." Now Bob Turner was a favorite in the neighborhood, and the cause in which he received a drubbing was not his alone, but all his neighbors' as well. Was free and fair speech to be burked by such an obstinate and opinionated old fellow as George Marvel? Were they to be deprived of their legitimate privilege of gossiping and tittle-tattling? Things had come to a pretty pass, when a man was to be allowed to bully all his neighbors because they wouldn't agree with him. The fight between Bob Turner and George Marvel was an exciting topic of conversation in every house for a dozen streets round; and a unanimous verdict was given in favor of Bob Turner, who was looked upon in some sort of way as the general champion of the important privilege of Tittle-tattle. Much sympathy was expressed for him, inasmuch as he had been taken home after the fight with a battered nose and bunged-up eyes, and could not go to his work for a week afterwards. During that week George Marvel thrashed another man, and called a woman unpleasant names; and when the woman's husband demanded an explanation, he received one of such a nature as to convert him instantly into an active enemy. Then Bob Turner, convalescent, made his appearance in the streets again, with traces of disfigurement in his face; and burning with animosity and shame, armed himself with a stone tied in the corner of his pocket-handkerchief, and, swinging his sling defiantly, expressed his regret that Joshua had been drowned, for thereby the gallows had been cheated. George Marvel, hearing this, went in search of his enemy Bob, and came away again with his hand so disabled by a blow from the sling, that he also could not work for a week. At which Bob Turner rejoiced, and all the neighbors rejoiced with him. After that George Marvel refused to speak to any of his work-mates, and they, in retaliation, passed a resolution sending him to " Coventry" for six months; which sending to "Coventry" may, to the uninitiated, be described as the very refinement of cruelty, inasmuch as it ignores the offender's existence, and condemns him not to be spoken to by any of his fellow-workmen. This enforced silence was a dreadful punishment to George Marvel. He bore it patiently enough for two or three weeks; but then it became a horrible torture. To sit at his work day after day, and week after week, uttering no word, and with his work-mates avoiding his very look, was almost maddening. It drove him to something which I am sorry to have to record; it drove him to drink. And the habit that began to grow upon him was of the worst kind. Having no one to drink with him, he drank by himself, and soon began to carry a flat bottle in his pocket, liberally supplied with that national curse — Gin.

Although it may be objected of George Marvel that in his behavior towards his neighbors he carried things with too high a hand, he acted only in strict accordance with his nature; and indeed, if he had been less dictatorial and more conciliatory it is likely that the same result would have been produced. It was not to be expected of him to be gentle and self-suffering under the dreadful accusation that was brought against his son, when Mrs. Marvel's conduct was taken into consideration. She could not listen patiently to the revilings of the neighbors; to remonstrate with them, to speak gently to them, to beg of them to be more merciful in their speech, would have been an injustice to the memory of her son. Every tender remembrance connected with him — and ah, how many there were, and how she cherished them! — urged her to defend him. And she did defend him, with all her mother's love, and with flaming eyes and agitated breast; told the revilers that they ought to be ashamed of themselves, and that they must be bad and wicked themselves, else they could not set their tongues to such bad and wicked accusations of the best son that ever blessed a mother's eyes. Poor thing! it was a sad sight to see her make her indignant defence in public, and then to see her in her room — pale, powerless, trembling — sink into a chair, overcome by the agony of her grief. It was not long before white hairs began to multiply, and before the cheerful look quite died out of her face. And Dan and Ellen worked on, and never lost their faith in the dear one who was lost to them; and Susan, notwithstanding what had befallen, still watched and rose in the night, and went into the street, awaiting the return of Basil Kindred's murderer. But no word

of him passed her lips; she worked at her dressmaking in silence, and never uttered a cheerful word. A blight had fallen upon those once happy homes.

They had, however, two friends and constant visitors, Praiseworthy Meddler and Solomon Fewster. Through good and evil report, these two friends remained faithful to them, although from widely-different motives. Considering all the circumstances, every thing had turned out very fortunate for Solomon Fewster. He confessed as much to himself exultantly, and curiously enough, gave himself some credit for having brought it about. Every tittle of evidence against him had been destroyed; no suspicion rested against him. Joshua was drowned; and Ellen remained, looking prettier in her black dress than he had ever seen her. He was sure of her now. He had only to wait. She had an encumbrance, certainly, which he would gladly have dispensed with — her baby-girl, born in sorrow. But he made up his mind that he would be kind to her, if she lived; and this resolve, to his own thinking, atoned for any hand he may have had in Joshua's misfortunes. When he saw Ellen with her baby in her lap, he thought, and thought rightly, that he had never seen a more beautiful sight. "One day," he said to himself, "I shall see her with a child of mine upon her breast;" and he dreamed with tender pleasure, and with no pangs of conscience, of the happy time to come.

So time passed on, and no ray of sunshine illumined the darkness of that unhappy home. Things were going from bad to worse. George Marvel was not a confirmed drunkard, but he drank more than was good for him; and his reputation as a cunning workman was on the wane. He did not work regularly either; he was often absent, and earned less money. His wife expostulated with him many times, and begged him not to drink. He listened without impatience, and said, " It's of no use, Maggie; if I didn't drink I should go mad. I'm an altered man to what I was, and I've brought it all on myself."

"Nay, George," she said, " you cannot say that and mean it."

(It is to be noticed as a singular thing that now she never called her husband "father," and indeed had not done so since the news of Joshua's death had reached them. The delicacy and thoughtfulness of a faithful wife's love are not to be excelled.)

"I can say that and mean it, Maggie," he replied; "I have been the cause of all this. I wasn't content that my son should be a wood-turner; no, I drove him to sea and away from all of us. We might have been as happy as the day is long if he had remained at home. And he would have remained but for me. I remember what you said, Maggie, as well as if you'd said it last night: 'If Joshua is shipwrecked, don't forget that I warned you beforehand."

"O George!" cried Mrs Marvel, in an agony of remorse, "how can you bring my wicked words up against me now?"

"I do not bring them up against you, wife; I bring them up against myself. And they were wise and good words — not wicked ones. I ought to have listened to them; but I was obstinate and pig-headed, and thought, like a fool, that I knew better than you. Ah! but it's too late to alter what is past; and I've brought death to our son and misery to you, and shame on all of us."

Then he refused to listen to her longer, and walked away to chew the cud of his remorse, and to drink more gin. To her and to the others in the house he was gentle: but to everybody else he was a bear. One night he came home in a condition which may be described as neither drunk nor sober. Dan and Ellen were sitting together, and the baby — to whom they had given Mrs. Marvel's name of Maggie — was lying in the cradle, when he came into the house. It belonged to his humor not to show himself ashamed of his new bad habit: when he was drunk he did not slink away and hide himself, but exhibited a kind of reckless defiance, for which it would have been as hard for him as for others to account. So upon this occasion he came into the room, quickly followed by his wife, who never watched him out of doors, but who attended to him in the house as if he were a child. He took his seat in the chair which Ellen placed for him, and sat moody and silent while Mrs. Marvel quickly set his supper before him. But he could not eat it. He pushed the food from him fretfully, and took his wife's hand and patted it, and then said suddenly, —

"Maggie, we must go away from here."

"Go away, George!" she exclaimed. "Where to?"

"I don't know; but I can't stop here much longer. If I do, I shall bring fresh disgrace upon you. I can't live this life any longer; it is killing me. We have already lost our good name and our good character in the neighborhood, and where I used to get respect I now get contempt. And, Maggie, I am afraid of myself! A new workman came into the shop to-day, and I heard Bob Turner tell him about us and about our poor lost boy, and speaking of him in such a way — Dan! Ellen!" he cried, appealing to them in justification of himself "*could* you stand by quietly and listen to shameful words spoken of our Joshua? Could you restrain yourself if you heard him spoken of as a—Oh, but I cannot say it!"

Ellen rose, with flashing eyes and cheeks burning with honest indignation.

"No," she exclaimed; "I could not, father. I should tell the wretch he was a coward and a villain."

"I told him so—your very words: I called him a coward and a villain; and I almost had my hand on his throat, when the other men interfered. But there was a row in the place for an hour: for I was almost mad. And then the master called me into his room, and told me— what do you think? Why, that he was very sorry to see the change that had taken place in me lately; that he was very sorry to see that I had taken to drink; that I was a good workman, and that I had worked well for him for a many years; but that if I couldn't behave myself as I used to do, I must find another shop. That was a pretty thing to say to me! — the best workman he ever had, and the steadiest too — no, I can't say that now; but I could up to a little time ago. I had a mind to take off my apron, and fling it in his face, but thought of all of you stopped me. Instead of that, I asked him what he would have done in my place supposing he had had a son; but he stopped me there, and said that he was talking business, and not sentiment. With that I flung myself out of the room, and swore I'd join the Chartists, and teach the masters one day that workmen have hearts" — But Mr. Marvel broke down here and glared about him in violent agitation.

They let him be, and waited till he was calmer; they had studied how best to humor him. Then Mrs. Marvel said: —

"What do you think we had best do, George?"

"I don't know," he answered somewhat roughly; "I'm not fit to give advice. I was dead against you when you didn't want our poor boy to go to sea, and I'm rightly served for it; but I'll never advise again. I'll be led now, not lead."

At this point, Dan, purposely, but without attracting observation, pushed the cradle so as to awake baby, and thus caused a diversion. After that, he quietly gave Ellen and Mrs. Marvel to understand that he wanted to speak to Mr. Marvel alone, and the women presently glided out of the room. George Marvel took no notice of their departure, and indeed did not notice it until Dan aroused his attention. Then he said, —

"Where's Ellen and the wife?"

"Gone to bed, sir," replied Dan; "and

I'm glad of it, because I wanted to speak to you."

George Marvel gave Dan a disturbed look, and said, —

"Won't another time do, Dan?"

"No, sir; I want to say what I have to say now, particularly."

George Marvel nodded, and somehow or other, the flat bottle in which he carried his gin obtruded itself unpleasantly upon his notice. It made a bulge in his pocket, and he tried to hide it from Dan, but did not succeed.

"Will you give me leave to speak of certain things in the past, sir, and not consider it a liberty?" asked Dan.

"Say what you like, Dan; I can't consider any thing you say a liberty."

"Ah — then I may speak of another thing presently, which makes us all very unhappy." (George Marvel shifted uneasily upon his chair, and wished he could get rid of the flat bottle which made itself so conspicuous in his breast-pocket.) "We have gone through many changes in our humble life; but for the most part we have been very happy. Do you remember, sir, when father died, how perplexed I was as to how we should live, and how, when every thing seemed to be a failure, and there didn't seem to be a ray of hope, you came to me with twelve pounds four shillings, in a bag, which you had collected for us among the neighbors?" (George Marvel groaned, and thought, "What would the neighbors say to me now if I went to them on such an errand? But I was respected then.") "Well, sir, from that time fortune smiled upon us, and we got on, until the unhappy day came. You know, sir, what father died of; it causes me shame and sorrow to think of, although it is a long time ago. I remember how Ellen and I used to sit here, in this very room, and tremble when we heard his step in the passage — she was frightened, but I was more ashamed than frightened. There was the day poor mother was buried — I shall never forget that night when we sat here in the dark; Mrs. Marvel was very kind to us that day, but indeed she was always that. Jo's mother couldn't be otherwise." (George Marvel gave a gasp, and lowered his head.) "It cuts, sir, to speak of Jo in this way; I feel it as well as you. But it may do good. Now I'll tell you what I thought that night of poor mother's funeral, when I heard father stumbling in the passage. I thought it was cruel and unkind to mother; I thought that even if he had the right to bring shame on himself (which I am certain he hadn't, for no man has), he had no right to bring it on us; I thought that perhaps poor mother died sooner than

17

she might have done if father had been a steady and sober man. For father earned very little money, and mother had to work very hard to make both ends meet. I have known her get up in the winter mornings at five o'clock, and work and slave till near midnight, and all because of father's idleness. Now tell me, sir, you whom I have always looked up to because you are a just man, could any thing justify father in leading the life he did?"

"Nothing, Dan," replied George Marvel, in a low voice.

"He did not even have the excuse of a great grief," said Dan courageously and tenderly. "Why, when he died that dreadful death, shamed and shocked as I was, I looked upon it as a mercy to him and to us that he was taken away. Yet, going a long way back, to the time when I was very young, I remember that father was not so very bad; he used to drink a little, but was not always drunk. It grew upon him, I suppose, until it mastered him, and made him what he became." Certainly, Dan proved himself the cunningest of physicians; he had brought home to George Marvel a consciousness of the abyss towards which he was walking, and had executed his task tenderly, wisely, and without giving offence. "Now, come, sir," continued Dan boldly; "let us look things straight in the face. You said you must go away from here — you mean all of us, of course. Have you any idea where we should move to?"

"None, Dan. Only one thing is plain to me — ay, much plainer to me after what you have said — and that is that I must go from this neighborhood, where once I held up my head and was respected, but where now every man and woman is my enemy. I never will be friends with them again — never! If they held out their hands to me now, I should refuse them, after what they have said of our poor dead boy."

"Dead boy!" mused Dan. "Are you certain, sir, that Jo is dead?" So startled was Mr. Marvel by the question, that he gazed at Dan in speechless astonishment. "I haven't spoken of it to anybody else, but something tells me that our Joe is alive. Yes, sir, you may well stare at me, for every other person but you and Ellen and Mrs. Marvel would call me mad for saying such a thing. I can give you no reason for the belief — for it is a belief, not a fancy. Haven't you heard, sir, of men being wrecked on strange lands, and living there for many years after they were supposed to be dead? Haven't you heard of men living amongst savages, and suddenly appearing among their friends years and years after they were lost? Some such thing, happily, may have occurred to Jo."

"But it's two years now since Josh went away," gasped Mr. Marvel; and then added, "Don't tell mother, Dan; it would drive her out of her senses."

"I shall wait before I tell her, but I shall tell Ellen when the proper time comes. Hope isn't a bad thing, sir."

"But hope without reason," suggested Mr. Marvel.

"Except the reason that exists and the comfort that exists in thinking of the cases that we have read of in stories of shipwrecked men who have been preserved from death. But hope is a good thing always, whether it comes from reason or fancy. And if you can believe as I believe, it will be the better and not the worse for you. Indeed, indeed, sir, you don't know how earnest I am in this. Think of the friendship that exists between me and Jo; I believe it to be something better and higher than ordinary friendships among boys and men. It has grown up with us, until it has become almost a part of our very being. We are never out of each other's thoughts; when he was away on his first voyage he was always thinking of me, and I of him. And that Christmas night that he came home — do you know what happened then, sir? Ellen can tell you that during the whole of that day I was uneasy about Jo; I had dreamed of him the night before, and my dream made me unhappy, for I was convinced that he was in danger. I had no reason for that, nor had I any reason for telling Ellen that Jo was very near us an hour before he came to the door. But unhappily, it all came true as I feared. Now, sir, I have thought often that if Jo was dead, I should feel it and know it — and I don't feel it and don't know it. Something keeps whispering to me, 'You will see him again, be with him again.' And I believe that I shall. For last night, sir, I dreamed of Jo, and Jo was alive; and as surely as we're sitting here talking, we shall see Jo one day, and all the dreadful mystery that looks so black against him will be cleared up."

Mr. Marvel jumped to his feet, and walked excitedly about the room. There was something contagious in Dan's enthusiasm. So earnest, so thrilling was Dan's voice, that Mr. Marvel's heart beat high with the hope in which there was no reason.

"I have not done yet, sir. When you said to-night that you must go away from here, I was amazed, for it seemed to belong to part of my dream. Jo seemed to say to me, 'I can't come to you, Dan; come to me.' And I want to go to him" —

Mr. Marvel stopped suddenly in his walk, and stood before Dan with a startled look on his face.

"I want to go to him, or as near to him as I can. The last place Jo was heard of was at Sydney, and the ship is supposed to have foundered somewhere near the Australian coast. Well, sir, if by any means it can be managed, we ought to go to Australia."

"All of us!" exclaimed Mr. Marvel.

"All of us," repeated Dan. "Why not? We are miserable here — unhappy here. We haven't, as you say, a friend in the place. Everybody is against Jo, and believe him to be bad, while we *know* him to good. I agree with you, sir, that if those we thought were our friends and who have spoken against Jo were to hold out their hands to me, I would not take them. It would be treasonable to Jo. To live on here in this way would only be adding to our unhappiness. I dare say we could manage to get along out there. Mr. Meddler says it is a rising place, and a splendid country for a poor man to get along in. You could take your tools, and could get work. I could take my birds, and should be able to get plenty there that I could train. Why, sir, it would be a splendid thing, and the best for all of us."

"I believe it would — I believe it would," said Mr. Marvel, his voice trembled with eagerness; "but where is the money to come from?"

"We have forty pounds of Jo's, sir, that he left for you and me; I wouldn't mind it being spent that way. That wouldn't be any thing like enough, I know; but I think I have a friend. However, sir, let us think over it for a little while. I am glad that we've had this talk. You'll forgive me, sir, won't you, for what I said in the first part of it?"

George Marvel made no reply, but, standing by Dan, put his arm affectionately round the neck of his son's friend; then left the room, and comforted his wife by a very simple act. He took the flat bottle out of his pocket, and said, "Maggie, I have done with this; I shall never fill it again." And, happily for him and all of them, he kept his word.

CHAPTER XXVIII.

MR. MARVEL SHAKES THE DUST FROM HIS FEET.

DAN took the Old Sailor into his confidence, and the impracticable old fellow excitedly proposed that they should leave

Stepney and come and live with him in his barge. But as Dan declared that that was impossible, the Old Sailor's hopes fell down to zero.

"We can't live in this neighborhood much longer," said Dan; "it wouldn't so much matter to me, for I'm always indoors, but it does to Jo's father. I know what he must suffer. You see, what we want is a friend."

"Ah!" said the Old Sailor, "what you want is a friend. Well, we'll talk of this again by and by."

He went down stairs to see Ellen, and found her crying over her baby.

"Come, come, my dear," he said; "this won't do; you'll be making an old woman of yourself in no time." And he dried her eyes with his handkerchief.

"You're the only friend we've got now," said Ellen sadly.

The Old Sailor thought: "Says Dan, 'What we want is a friend.' Says Ellen, 'You're the only friend we've got.'" And he put this and that together, as he had done once before in the memorable conversation he had had with Joshua at Gravesend, when he set all matters straight.

"What were you crying for, my lass?" he said aloud.

"Ah, sir!" replied Ellen, "I don't mind telling you. I was looking down at baby, and thinking that when she is old enough to understand things — and baby is very quick, and almost understands already, don't you, my pet? — she will hear such stories from ill-natured people about father, as will make her as unhappy as her poor mother is. When I thought that, sir, I began to cry, and was almost wicked enough to believe that it would be better for both of us to die than to live amongst such bad-hearted people."

The Old Sailor did not stop long, but walked away in profound thought.

Soon after that, another misfortune occurred. George Marvel told them that he had left his situation. "I gave it up of my own accord, Maggie," he said to his wife, to whom he first spoke upon the subject; "If I hadn't, I should have done something that would have made the master give me warning, and I should have been disgraced. I can't make sure of myself now; my blood boils up so when I hear a word dropped about Josh, that every thing swims before my eyes. I can't help it, my dear. Don't blame me."

She did not blame him, but said she was sure he had done what he thought was for the best.

"I've worked in the shop, man and boy, for more than thirty years," he said huskily, "and I doubt if I shall get another. Trade's overdone. A good many men are out, and I'm not as young as I was. I don't quite see the end of it, Maggie."

She cheered him and comforted him, and he went out the next morning in search of work, feeling very much ashamed of himself. It was like begging. He came home disheartened and footsore, and hadn't a cheerful word or look for any one. "A nice ending this is!" he said bitterly. "But I brought it all on myself. I shouldn't have driven our boy to sea." He seemed to think it was nothing but strict justice that he should take all the blame upon himself. He earned so little money, that presently he had to break into Joshua's legacy to him and Dan, and it began to melt like magic. Things were getting very bad. The dress-making work, too, was slackening, and Susan and Ellen had many idle days.

Solomon Fewster observed all this with inward satisfaction, although outwardly he sympathized with them, and was profuse in his offers of assistance. But they would not accept any thing from him; and very soon the proceeds of the birds he continued to purchase from Dan became their most dependable source of revenue. Notwithstanding that he was careful never to say a word of the past that would be distasteful to them, he did not make much way in their good graces. They did not show this, however; he was consistent in his offers of assistance, and in his friendly behavior, and they could not show ingratitude; but their instincts were against him. He allowed a year to pass before he spoke to Ellen of his love for her, and even then he thought it best first to make sure of the co-operation of her friends. He addressed himself in the first place to George Marvel, who opened his eyes very wide, and was indeed very much astonished at Mr. Fewster's declaration. He had never suspected that Mr. Fewster had an attachment for Ellen.

"I loved her before she was married," said Mr. Fewster to him; "but then I saw that she loved your poor son, and I was too honorable to interpose. So I did not distress her by telling her of my love."

Mr. Marvel thought that that was manly and straightforward, but asked Mr. Fewster why he spoke to him upon the subject.

"You are in a sort of way Ellen's father," replied Mr. Fewster, "and it is due to you that I should speak to you first. I should not be justified otherwise in offering myself to Ellen. I have something to say also, if you will excuse me for taking the liberty" —

Seeing that Mr. Fewster hesitated, Mr.

Marvel bade him proceed, and then the wooer cunningly placed before Mr. Marvel certain advantages that would accrue to him if Ellen consented.

"I should feel it my duty," said Mr. Fewster, "to see that the man I look upon as Ellen's father is properly cared for."

"Never mind that," said Mr. Marvel; he had recovered from his astonishment, and felt a sort of displeasure at Mr. Fewster's proposal. "Never mind that," he repeated dryly, "but tell me what it is you want me to do."

"I want you to give your consent, Mr. Marvel, and to assist me."

"Assist you in making a woman love you, Mr. Fewster!" exclaimed Mr. Marvel. "No, no; the matter rests with you and Ellen. It is none of mine, and any feeling I may have in the matter it is but right I should keep to myself."

"But you won't say any thing in my disfavor," urged Mr. Fewster, alarmed at Mr. Marvel's coldness of manner, and thinking to himself that when Ellen was his wife, he would have as little as possible to do with the Marvels.

"I shall say nothing to Ellen one way or the other," replied Mr. Marvel moodily. "I have no doubt Ellen knows what is due to herself. And to Joshua," he was about to add, but he only thought the words; they did not pass his lips. When Mr. Fewster went away, Mr. Marvel was very despondent, and thought with some bitterness that he would have spoken to Ellen's lover very differently, if he hadn't been so low down in the world. So discouraged was Mr. Fewster by his interview with Mr. Marvel, that he did not speak to any other members of the family, not even to Dan, but came straight to the point at once with Ellen. After all, whom else did it concern but Ellen and himself? She was sitting in the kitchen, working; baby was in the cradle, and upon Ellen's face were traces of tears. When she and baby were alone, her tears flowed too readily now. Solomon Fewster had prepared himself carefully for the occasion. He was attired in his best, and presented quite a holiday appearance. He bought a bunch of flowers for Ellen, of which he begged her acceptance. With a little hesitancy of manner, she took them from his hand and placed them on the table. There is something in the air of a wooer that betrays his purpose to the woman he loves, and when Ellen looked into Mr. Fewster's face and saw this, she rose hurriedly and stooped to take baby out of the cradle, intending to leave the room. But Mr. Fewster's hand upon her arm restrained her.

"Nay, Ellen," he said awkwardly, "baby alone for a little; don't disturb her — she looks so pretty in her sleep." And calling up a look of admiration in his face, he contemplated baby with an appearance of affectionate interest, which would have won its way to the heart of most mothers at once. But not to Ellen's. Mr. Fewster's tender manner brought back to her the memory of all his disagreeable attentions when they were first acquainted, and she waited in silent apprehension for what she dreaded was to come. But round about the bush went Mr. Fewster.

"Things are very much changed, Ellen," he observed. She would have resented his calling her by her Christian name on the present occasion, although he had often done so before; but he was Dan's patron and their chief dependence, and she did not dare to object. "Very much changed," he repeated. "Mr. Marvel, poor fellow, looks quite shabby. He has a difficulty in getting work, I believe. Very sad — very sad. But it's the way of the world. One man up, another man down, Lucky man that who can always keep up."

"He is indeed, Mr. Fewster," said Ellen, constrained to say something in reply. "But we can't help misfortunes coming."

"No; but we can often turn bad fortune into good. Now, looking lately at Mr. and Mrs. Marvel, who are far from happy, poor things! far from happy, I have been thinking what a beautiful thing it would be to make them easier in their mind as regards their worldly circumstances, for there is no doubt that that constitutes the greatest part of their unhappiness. As for the other part of their unhappiness — family grief — time will soften that. But time doesn't soften poverty if it is always with you. It is a sad thing, a very sad thing, but it is so unfortunately. There is no harder misfortune in the world than poverty."

"Yes, there is, Mr. Fewster," said Ellen, who had taken baby on her lap as a kind of protection. "There are griefs of the heart which are bitterer to bear than poverty."

"I stand corrected. But then that will be the case with the few, not with the many — with the few who are superior to most people, and who are the more to be admired for the possession of such excellent virtues. I know one woman who is far above all others in this respect, and whom I therefore love and admire far above all other women." Ellen trembled and turned very pale, but Mr. Fewster proceeded rapidly, fearful lest he had been too precipitate, "Coming back to Mrs. Marvel — would it not be a good thing to make her comfortable in her mind about her worldly circumstances?"

"It would be — a very good thing," answered Ellen, in a low tone.

"And it can be done. There is one person who has it in her power to do this for Mrs. Marvel." Again Mr. Fewster paused until Ellen asked, "Who is that person, Mr. Fewster?"

"You," he said eagerly. "You can do this, and at the same time you can make a man who has loved you from the first day he saw you the happiest man in the world."

"Stop, sir!" cried Ellen, in a firm voice. "You must not say what you were about to say. It would be folly — worse than folly — it would be wicked for me to pretend not to understand you. It would be merciful to me, and best for both of us, that you should not say any thing more now. I have no heart for any thing but my grief and my child.

So earnestly did she speak, that Fewster was fain to desist. The only words he said were, "You shall see how I respect and love you: your word is my law;" and straightway left her. But he did not leave her despairingly. One little word that Ellen had unconsciously uttered filled him with hopeful anticipation. She had said, "It will be merciful to me, and best for both of us, that you should not say any thing more *now*." She had put no impression upon the word; but the wish that "keeps the word of promise to the ear" imbued it with a distinct utterance to Solomon Fewster's sense. "I must not say any thing more *now*," he thought; "that opens the way for the future. I must be content for a little while." He thought he had made a good move, and that he was sure to win the game.

When he was gone, Ellen caught her baby to her bosom, and ran to Dan's room for consolation — almost, as it seemed to her, for protection. There she found George Marvel sitting in an attitude of sadness. He had not had an hour's work for the last fortnight, and half of Joshua's savings was spent: but barely twenty pounds remained. When that was gone! Well, that was what was fermenting in George Marvel's mind now. When that was gone, what was he to do? Sit down and starve? Without doubt, they could not all live upon Dan's earnings; for Dan and his sisters earned barely enough to keep themselves. He groaned in bitterness of spirit to think that he, the only man in the house who could work, was doomed to idleness. He had striven hard, and still strove, to obtain employment — with what success has been narrated. He felt at times as if he would be justified in demanding work, instead of begging for it. Indeed, on one occasion he had asked for work in some-what defiant tones, and, being refused, had spoken out of the bitterness of his heart, of the injustice and hardship that stood in his way of earning food, being willing to work for it honestly. The only answer he received was an order to quit the shop immediately, if he did not wish to be given in custody. The sentiments to which he had given utterance were soon made known to many masters in the trade, some of whom afterwards, in reply to his applications, said they did not want any Chartists in their workrooms. His case was a desperate one indeed. The problem which he was trying to solve as Ellen entered the room after her interview with Solomon Fewster was a common one enough, more's the pity. He would have expressed it in very simple words: "I must work to live. I am able to work, and willing. I cannot get work. How am I to live?" Ellen saw the trouble in his face, and sat down by his side. He gave her just one glance, and learned what had occurred; for he had seen Solomon Fewster go out of the house.

"I know what has occurred, my dear," he said anxiously. "Mr. Fewster has been speaking to you. And your answer?"

"I have no need to tell you, father," said Ellen, raising her eyes to his. She said nothing of the bribe Fewster had offered for her love.

George Marvel saw that Ellen had refused Mr. Fewster, and he nodded grave approval; yet, from a sense of justice, was compelled to ask, —

"Have you considered all the circumstances, Ellen? Have you considered the future?"

"I don't know," she answered; "I only know that I have done what is right, and what is due to my dear Joshua's memory."

All this was Greek to Dan, and it had to be explained to him. He listened in silence, and was very thoughtful afterwards. He let the matter drop, however, until he and Ellen were alone; and then he told her, gently and by degrees, of his belief that Joshua was not lost, and of his earnest desire to go over the seas and commence a new life. She, listening eagerly, almost breathlessly, pressed his hand to her lips and kissed him again and again, and was absolutely so simple as to share his belief. Hope revived within her; and when Dan said, "You are not widowed yet, dear; of that I feel assured," she blessed him for the words in which there was no reason.

Other troubles came. Solomon Fewster, strong in cunning, made a new move in the game. His orders began to fall off, and in a short time he bought one bird where formerly he had bought three. Perhaps he thought, "If love won't drive Ellen into my arms, necessity may." It was a cruel device, mean and merciless, and it struck fresh terror to their hearts. They could do nothing but wait and watch the tide come up. And things grew so bad for them that they had to content themselves with two meals a day, and those but poor and scanty ones. Their condition was a strange parallel to that of the unfortunate passengers of the "Merry Andrew" on the raft. There are wrecks on land as sad as any in the records of the sea.

Solomon Fewster, of course, was profuse in his regrets at the falling-off of the business, and offered to lend Dan and Ellen money, which they refused. He renewed his offer many times, not offended at the refusal. "He wants to buy Ellen," thought Dan; "but he doesn't know her. Jo said once that Ellen was not the kind of a girl for a heroine. Would he say so now, if he could see her, I wonder?"

It was in this way that he often thought of Joshua as of one who would be restored to them some day. He had fixed the belief firmly in his mind, and nothing could shake it. He had no hope of ever seeing Minnie again. She was as one who had passed out of his life forever. But she lived in his mind and in his heart, and came to him in his dreams. And in the light, often and often, he would muse upon her tenderly and lovingly.

So they lived on, and the tide of adversity rose higher and higher, until they were compelled to begin to pawn things. But a better time was coming. The Old Sailor passing a pawn-shop one day in Dan's neighborhood — he was on his way to Dan's house — saw Ellen hurry out of the shamefaced door. He was so staggered that he allowed her to escape his sight. He had had no idea that things were so hard with them as that. When he recovered himself, he gave his chest a great thump, called himself "a blind old swab," and made his way to Dan's house. He went straight down to the kitchen, prying old interloper as he was, and caught Ellen, in the act of counting a few — very few — small pieces of silver and copper in Mrs. Marvel's hand. He was so distressed, that the blood rushed into his face. He only desired to see Ellen alone and speak to her, and here he was shaming them in their poverty. The tender-hearted old fellow was fit to sink into the ground, he was so remorseful. He stammered out a few words of apology, said he thought Ellen was alone, but that Dan would do as well. He went up to Dan, and to Dan's astonishment locked the door. Then he inclined his head melodramatically, to be sure that no one was listening, and, being satisfied, drew a chair close to Dan's.

"Hark ye, my lad," he said: "can you and I speak to the point, and without beating about the bush?"

"I think we can, sir," replied Dan, smiling; the Old Sailor's voice always did him good.

"Frankly, then," said the Old Sailor, "do you find it a hard matter to live?"

"Very hard, sir."

"No money in the house, eh?"

"None, sir."

"And business falling off?"

"Fallen off would be more correct, sir. My earnings for the last month not more than ten shillings."

"And Mr. Marvel?"

"About a day's work in the week, sir."

"And the money that poor Josh left?"

"All gone, sir."

"O Dan!" groaned the Old Sailor, "why wasn't I told of this?"

Dan gave him a sad look, but made no other reply.

"And the poor mother," continued the Old Sailor, "how must she have suffered! And Ellen, poor lass! and the little one! Dan, Dan! if I don't feel to you as if you were my son, I could find it in my heart to be angry with you!"

"Nay, sir," urged Dan gently, "you are not to blame. We are unfortunate, that is all. We are not the only ones, I dare say."

"Come, now, open your mind to me. Look things in the face. What do you see before you this time twelve months?"

The practical question was like a blow, and Dan trembled. The answer came from his reason in which there was no hope.

"What do I see before me this time twelve months? Worse poverty than this — and this is hard enough, God knows! We are growing poorer every day, and every day it is a puzzle where to-morrow's food will come from. All our friends have fallen off from us; when Ellen and Jo's mother go into the streets, not one pleasant face greets them. They come back, sad and suffering. And they must bear it while they remain in this neighborhood, if they are to be true to Jo. I can understand now how some good people are made bad by the world's injustice. It won't make them bad, I can answer for that; but I'm not so sure of Mr. Marvel. I haven't seen a smile on his face for months; his nature seems to be completely changed. I am almost afraid to think what remorse might drive him to, for he is continually reproaching himself with being the cause of all our misfortunes. He says he drove Jo to sea, when his influence would have kept him at home; and this thought stings him day and night. As for me, I earn very little money now. And I am so stupid," he added, with an odd smile, yet thoughtful withal, "as to repine sometimes that we can't live without silver and copper."

The Old Sailor dabbed his face with his handkerchief in a state of great excitement during this recital, and was compelled to wait until he was cool before he said, "So, taking them altogether, things are very bad."

"Taking them altogether, sir," said Dan, "I don't see how they could be worse. We have only one consolation."

"What is that, Dan?" asked the Old Sailor eagerly, with a faint hope that it was something tangible.

"Our faith in Jo, and our knowledge that he is good and true, as we have always known him to be. Poor Jo!"

The Old Sailor groaned.

"You can't live on that, Dan," he said.

"No, sir," replied Dan with rare simplicity; "but it is a great comfort, nevertheless."

The Old Sailor pressed Dan's hand.

"'Tisn't so bad a world," he murmured more to himself than to Dan, "despite its injustice." Then aloud: "What would be the best thing for all of you to do, Dan, under the circumstances?"

"There is but one thing, sir; and I might as well wish for cheese from the moon as wish for that."

"Perhaps not, Dan, perhaps not. Tell your wish."

"I want some money."

"Ah! how much?"

"Enough to take us to Australia, where we could commence a new life."

"You hinted at that some time ago, Dan."

"Yes, sir."

"That's what you meant when you said you wanted a friend?"

"Yes, sir."

"And I took no notice of it, like a hard-hearted old hunks as I am. Do you know why I took no notice of it, Dan?"

"No, sir."

"Because I didn't want to part from you — because I didn't want to lose the only friends I have in the world — because I thought only of myself, and how lonely I should feel when you and my little Ellen and the good mother were thousands of miles away. Well, well! Old as I am, I'm not too old to learn from younger heads. Look you, my lad! But stop — we'll have the women up."

The Old Sailor went down into the kitchen where Ellen and Mrs. Marvel were, and took a hand of each, and led them gravely up stairs into Dan's room.

"This is a family council, my dears," he said, kissing them, "where we are to speak our minds without hesitation. Dan has been making things clear to me, and I see a good deal to which I've been blind, selfishly blind, more shame to me. When the storm came on, I had an idea that you might be able to weather it; but you were not strong enough, and human hearts have not been so kind to you as winds and waves are. The winds howl to-day, but a calm comes to-morrow; the waves dash over you for a time, but presently the sea grows smooth. That's at sea; 'tis different on land sometimes. You have found it so, my dears, eh?"

They sighed assent, and waited in a state of painful expectancy for what was to come.

"And here you are with every sail split, with every spar broken, with bulwarks dashed in, and every thing adrift. And around you cruel tongues and unjust hearts. What! with all this craft in view, won't one come forward, and ask, What cheer? Not one? And yet you've held out a helping hand many a time, my dear" (to Mrs. Marvel), "as I well know, and spared a spar here and a bit of canvas there, with a willing heart and a free hand. But you are pearls, you women, and teach us goodness. The Lord love you, and send you happier days!"

He almost broke down here; but he recovered himself by a great effort, and continued, somewhat huskily at first: —

"Ah, my dears, I've been in storms, but never a worse than this has been to you. Look up, my lass!" he cried to Ellen, and pointing upwards to the dingy paper ceiling in so earnest a tone that he found all of them followed the direction of his finger, while a new-born hope entered their hearts. "Look up! D'ye see the clouds a-breaking? D'ye see the sun tipping the edges with white light? If you don't, take my word for it, the storm's over, and a friendly craft is bearing down upon you." He paused awhile before he spoke again. "'You see,' says Dan to me, 'what we want is a friend.' Says Ellen to me, the very same day, 'You're the only friend we've got.' What did I do? Clap on sail and bear down upon you? Not I!"

"Nay, sir," interposed Dan.

"Hold your tongue, Dan; I deserve to have the cat for my behavior. Now, hark ye. Before my poor lass here was married to Josh — don't cry, my dear — I made over my little bit of money to them jointly, for better or worse. I dare say it will come to a matter of two hundred pounds. Will that be enough, Dan?"

Dan's sobs prevented a reply, and the women sat silently thankful.

"So look upon that as settled," said the Old Sailor, rising; "and make your arrangements. I'll see what ships are going out, and 'll let you know to-morrow."

He left the room abruptly, unable to bear the thankful looks and tears of his friends. Besides which, he was almost unmanned at the thought of parting from them. They were the only friends he had in the world, as he had said; and when they were gone, he would be left lonely in his old age. The thought flashed across him to go with them, but he dismissed it at once. Not only was he too old to cross the seas, but he felt he could not leave his barge near the old Tower Stairs.

"I should be like a fish out of water," he thought; "and besides, I should only be an encumbrance to the poor souls. I shall be in my dotage soon, and they have troubles enough of their own. No; I'll stop and lay my bones in Old England."

So the faithful old soul set to work at once, and left himself with the very barest pittance to live on, in order to get together sufficient money for the necessities of his friends.

The news soon spread. Some of the neighbors said it was a good job they were going; some were envious; and a few repented of their harshness. These last went so far as to make slight advances towards Mr. and Mrs. Marvel. Mr. Marvel looked at them angrily, and responded with hard words; but his wife, a true peacemaker, was more conciliatory. When she remonstrated with him, and begged him to consider that they were sorry because they had concurred in the general verdict of condemnation of Joshua, he said, —

"Let be, Maggie; if they're sorry for what the've said about Josh, the more shame for them for hurting us as they did. You can do as you like; I sha'n't mind your shaking hands with them. But for me, I've said I'll never forgive them, and I never will." When Susan was told that they were going to Australia, her dull vacant face suddenly lit up.

"We shall be near *him*," she muttered; "near Minnie too. Poor Minnie! where is she?"

The next moment her old manner was upon her, and she relapsed into vacancy again.

But there was one by whom the news of their intended departure was received with a chill of angry despair. Solomon Fewster could scarcely believe it when he was told. He hurried to the house, blaming himself for his stupidity in trying to starve Ellen into acquiescence.

"This would never have come about," he thought, "if they had not been driven to it by necessity. I ought to have shown myself a greater friend than ever to Dan. Gratitude would have made Ellen love me."

To obtain Ellen's love had become a mania with him. The farther she was removed from him, the stronger grew his desire. "Perhaps it is not yet too late," he thought. He broke into Dan's room in feverish haste, and cried, —

"Good news, Dan! I've got a customer for four birds, and he wants them at once."

"Here are two bullfinches and two canaries," replied Dan with a queer smile; "I thought you would have wanted them earlier. I have others ready, if you want more."

"I'll take them by and by," said Solomon Fewster; and then treated Dan to a long account of the late dulness and the expected revival of trade, and to the certain prospect of there being a great demand for Dan's birds presently. Dan listened in silence, and discomfited Solomon Fewster by charging a higher price than usual for the bullfinches and canaries. Solomon Fewster thought it would be fatal to hesitate, and he paid the money with apparent willingness; and Dan gave another queer little smile as he put the money in his pocket. Then Fewster referred to the rumor, and Dan said it was true.

"We shall sail in about a month," said Dan.

"But why go at all?" asked Fewster.

"We are not able to get a living here, sir," said Dan. He did not tell everybody of his fancy about Joshua.

"If that's your only reason," urged Fewster, "stop, and let me be your friend. I promise that you shall never want, especially if — if"—

But he could not get the intended reference to Ellen gracefully off his tongue.

"I understand you, sir," said Dan; "but nothing that you can say can keep us here."

At this point Mr. Marvel entered, and Fewster left. Between the two men there had been an utter absence of cordiality since Fewster's overtures respecting Ellen. Besides, Mr. Marvel had suspected why Fewster's commissions for birds had fallen off, and had made Dan acquainted with his suspicions; and this, indeed, was the reason why Dan, whose eyes were open to Fewster's meanness, had taken a secret pleasure in charging him a high price for his present purchase.

Solomon Fewster tried by every means to induce them to stay, but his efforts were unavailing. The passages were taken, the day was fixed. The Old Sailor made special arrangements for the accommodation of Dan's birds on board ship, and Dan bought a number of young songsters to train on the voyage out, although the Old Sailor shook his head and expressed grave doubts whether the birds would live. As the day of departure approached, the excitement in the neighborhood grew stronger, and public opinion veered steadily round in favor of the Marvels. The band of the remorseful ones received fresh recruits daily, until, when the day arrived, there were not a dozen of the neighbors who were not sorry for the judgment that had been pronounced against Joshua, and who did not, in one way or another, give expression to their sorrow. Mr. Marvel would not listen to them; the others did, and took pleasure in listening to apologies which were in some sort a vindication of Joshua's character. But Mr. Marvel declared bitterly that he would shake the dust from his shoes the day he left Stepney, and that he was only too thankful to escape from the nest of vipers.

"You women," he said, "are too soft-hearted for justice: if a scoundrel who has wronged you comes crying to you, you look kindly on him, and cry with him, out of the tenderness of your hearts. But for me, when I think of the many years we've lived here, with never a black mark against us — when I think of the good turns we've done for this one and that one, and of the manner in which they have returned our good offices, I'm fit to choke with passion. They tried to disgrace me, and would have seen us starve without offering us bit or sup. But now that we're going, well off as they think, they come whining round us, sorry for the mud they threw at us. The mud didn't stick, that's one comfort. I could dash my fist in their faces when I think of it!"

So matters went on until the morning came when they were to go aboard the ship at Blackwall. They had a few little odds and ends to take with them, and a cart was at the door to convey them to the docks. All the women and children in the neighborhood flocked round the cart to see the last of the emigrants. First Ellen, with her child, got in; the women kissed their hands to her, and murmured to each other that she looked older than her years. Ellen's eyes were blinded with tears as she looked up at the old house and at the familiar faces in the crowd. Susan was the next: she looked vacantly at the throng, and turned her eyes to her lap, taking no further heed of them. Dan followed with his birds, and listened gravely, and not without tenderness, to the farewells which greeted him. After him came Mr. and Mrs. Marvel.

"Good-by, my dear; God bless you! God take you safely over, my dear!"

In twenty different ways were these farewells and good wishes expressed, and Mrs. Marvel pressed her hand upon her heart, and sobbed till she could not distinguish a face in the crowd that surrounded her.

"Get in Maggie," said George Marvel; and then, deliberately and gravely, stooped and took off his shoes. He climbed into the cart in his stockings, and bending over the wheel, shook the dust from his shoes. "I'll take no dust from here with me," he said in a loud tone; " I leave that and your lying words behind me. I loved you once, and loved these streets; but I've hated you and them from the time you turned upon us and made our lives bitterer than misfortune had already made them. By and by, you can tell the men I've worked with and been kind to, that I was glad to go from the place where I was born, and that I shook the dust from my feet before I went away."

Then, amid a dead silence, the cart lumbered away from Stepney on to Blackwall. There they found the Old Sailor waiting for them. "I will keep with you until you are fairly off," he said. They were thankful enough for his company, and as he did what he could to cheer them, and they had plenty of work to do in their cabins, they soon became more cheerful and hopeful than they had been for many a day. Soon the ship was at Gravesend, a place fraught with sad and sweet memories — for Ellen especially. Mrs. Friswell, at whose house the wedding was celebrated, came aboard to see them, and admired the baby, and whispered to all of them, in turns, that if there ever lived a man with a heart tender enough for twenty men, that man was the Old Sailor, and no other. No need to say with what heartiness they all indorsed this sentiment.

A surprise awaited them. On the morning of the ship's sailing, there came climbing up the side Solomon Fewster. He accosted them gayly.

"You were wondering, I dare say, why I hadn't been to wish you good-by."

"We thought you would be sure to come, although at the last moment," answered Dan.

Solomon Fewster first rubbed his hands and then his chin.

"No need to say good-by," he said, with a conscious look at Ellen; "I am going with you."

They were too much astonished to reply.

"Yes," he continued; "when my best friends were going, I didn't like the idea of stopping behind. So I've sold my business upon capital terms — capital terms. A good sum down, and a share in the profits for the next ten years. Shall be able to make plenty of money in Australia, eh, Mr. Meddler?"

"No doubt, no doubt," said the Old Sailor, with a disturbed look.

Solomon Fewster, divining that his absence would be agreeable to them, hurried away to look after his boxes.

"I am sorry he's going," said Dan; "but it can't be helped. We must make the best of every thing, not the worst."

In the tender conversation that ensued, consequent upon their parting from the Old Sailor, Solomon Fewster was forgotten.

"Write to me as often as you can," said the Old Sailor, "and I will do the same to you, though my old joints are getting stiff. You'll soon be settled down somewhere, and you can let me know. 'Tis a sad word — good-by. But I shall soon be saying good-by to all the world, my dears."

He sat among them until the last moment, and first wished Susan good-by.

Then said George Marvel, as he and the Old Sailor stood hand in hand, amidst the confusion of ropes and cases, " If there had been hearts like yours among our neighbors, my poor Josh's name would not have been blackened. Heaven will reward you. I couldn't honor my own father more than I honor you."

The Old Sailor quivered at the stroke; he could better have stood a hard knock. He kissed Ellen tenderly, and she him; and he put a ribbon round baby's neck with a little silver whistle at the end of it.

"In memory of me, my dear," he said.

"I will teach her that it is the symbol of the heart of a good man, dear sir," said Ellen, her eyes full of tears; "and when she is an old woman — if she lives to be such — it may happen that she will show it to her children, and tell them her mother's sad story, and how her life was sweetened by the kindest, dearest, best" — Sobs choked her voice.

The Old Sailor waited a while until she recovered, and then said, with exquisite tenderness, —

"If she will sound the whistle sometimes when she is a young woman, and I am in my grave, I shall hear her perhaps." He smiled thoughtfully at this conceit. And then folded Ellen in his arms, and saying, "God bless you, my lass!" released her and turned to Dan and Mrs. Marvel. She took his hand and kissed it; she could have knelt to him, her heart was so full — too full to speak.

"I know, I know, my dear," he said, and kissed her. "I asked you once if you would like to be a sailor, Dan; do you remember?" His arm was resting on Dan's shoulder, and Dan drew it round his neck and laid his face upon it. The action conveyed such tender meaning, that the tears rolled down the Old Sailor's cheeks.

"When I see Joe," said Dan, "I may tell him that you never doubted him?"

"Ay, Dan," replied the Old Sailor aloud; but thought, "I shall see him before you do, my lad." He would not disturb Dan's faith by uttering the thought.

"Do I remember your asking if I would like to be a sailor?" continued Dan. "Ah, yes! what of that day can I ever forget? You taught me to splice a rope, and I showed you Jo's heart and mine spliced, so that nothing could sever them. And the poor birds shipwrecked, as Jo is. We little thought then, did we, sir?" The Old Sailor grasped Dan's hand, and the next minute was in his boat; and the ship was swinging round, hiding him from the loving gaze of his friends.

Through the river that runs to the sea the ship makes its way slowly and grandly. In the ship's stern, looking with dimmed eyes over the bulwarks, are Dan and Ellen and Mr. and Mrs. Marvel. Good-by, dear friend! Good-by, dear heart! Smaller and smaller grows the ship in his eyes. Can they see him still? he is lost in the whirl of boats. No; he is standing up, cap in hand. Good-by, faithful simple heart, richer in your honest goodness than if you were endowed with all the jewels that lie concealed in earth's depths. He is lost to them now, and they shall see him no more — here!

Lost? No. He is with them every night in their prayers — he dwells in their hearts. To their dying days they think of him tenderly. Blessings on the dear Old Sailor!

CHAPTER XXXIX.

SO NEAR AND YET SO FAR.

"MINNIE!"

"Yes, Joshua."

"That is all; I thought you were asleep."

"You are very kind to me, Joshua. I feel a little better to-day, I think."

"That's a good hearing, Minnie. Get strong, my dear, for my sake."

"Ah! If I could; but I fear — I fear." (This last to herself, under her breath.)

"Sit nearer, Joshua."

Many moons had passed, and with the exception that Minnie had grown very weak, only one event of importance had occurred since the departure of Rough-and-Ready and Tom the sailmaker. That event was the death of the Lascar; and the discovery made a deep impression on Joshua. It occurred within a few weeks of the parting of the tribes. The tribe of which Opara was the chief, observing that Minnie was drooping, resolved to return to the spot where they had found her. By easy stages they travelled near to the rocks where the castaways had landed, and rested there some days, in the belief that Minnie would regain her health. The mysterious influence she had over them was never weakened, and as she and Joshua were inseparable, he shared in the favor which was shown to her. She saw this, and would not allow him to quit her side, fearful lest harm should befall him. One evening she and Joshua had wandered from the native camp to the pool where the Lascar had stolen upon him, with the intention of killing him; and they talked together of the villain, and wondered what had become of him. They saw a wonderful sight as they sat and talked. From the distant woods rose an immense army of flying foxes, not less than four or five thousand in number, flying in a straight line to a distant pool. When they arrived over the water, they dipped down to drink in regular order, keeping their ranks, so that presently they presented the shape of a perfect curve. Joshua and Minnie watched the singular flight until the last of the animals had satisfied its thirst; shortly afterwards the entire flock disappeared. As they retraced their steps to the native camp, Joshua observed something unusual lying on the ground. It looked like a crouching animal, and Joshua drew Minnie aside fearing that it might be a dangerous creature; but it remained perfectly still, and Joshua, drawn thereto by an irresistible impulse, slowly approached the spot. To his horror he found that it was a human creature — dead; and turning the face recognized the Lascar. So! his enemy was dead, and this was the end of his animosity. The circumstances of the eventful meeting when he had rescued Susan from the Lascar's pursuit came to Joshua's mind as he looked upon the dead form. "His hate of me would not have lived so long," thought Joshua, "if it had not been fed by other means. Whom did he refer to when he spoke of his master the day he stole upon me with the stone? But that is past discovery now!" The dead man's face was distorted by agony, as if he had died in torture, and Joshua looked around for the cause of death. There were a variety of trees near the spot — among them some stinging trees. Joshua knew the fatal effect of the deadly tree, and divined that the Lascar had fallen from one of the higher trees, which he must have climbed in search of food, into the poisonous nettles, and so been stung to death. He could not have been dead above a few hours. Joshua turned away, and told Minnie.

"You will not leave him there unburied, Joshua?" said Minnie.

"No, Minnie, it would not be right. He was our enemy, but there is an end to all that now. Sit down on this trunk, my dear, and I will be kinder to him in death than he was to me in life." With his knife and a stout stick he removed sufficient soil to lay the dead man in; as he moved the body, a silver watch fell from a pocket. Joshua picked it up, and involuntarily opened it. There was an inscription on the case, roughly scratched in, and Joshua read, "From Solomon Fewster to his Lascar friend." Joshua's heart beat loudly as he read these words. He felt that he was on the eve of a discovery. "They knew each other," he thought in amazement; and then, like a flash, it came upon him that Solomon Fewster was the master for whom the Lascar said he was working. Eagerly he searched the Lascar's pockets for more evidence; and found it in the shape of the following document: "To my Lascar friend: I give you twenty-five pounds in gold, and a silver watch and two knives for services you have rendered me in connection with J. M. And I promise you twenty-five pounds more in gold, if, when you return in the 'Merry Andrew,' you have accomplished what has been agreed upon between us. — S. F."

Joshua read this document twice, and then looked round, as if in expectation of meeting Solomon Fewster face to face.

"Let me fix the villain's features in my mind," he thought; "I will raise him before me, so that when we meet, in this world or the next, I may bring his treachery home to him." With the eyes of his mind he saw Solomon Fewster's false face, and he dashed his fist into the air with a loud cry. "Fool!" he muttered, recovering himself; "am I growing as much a savage as those amongst whom I live? Was it Fewster or this villain who stabbed me when I came home?" He looked down, and seemed to find his answer. "It was your hand that struck the blow, and he employed you. He was too much of a coward to do it himself, and he paid you for your services as you have told me. And he wanted to get me out of the way, so that he might win the love of my Ellen." A bitter smile came to his lips, passed away, and a sweeter expression took its place. "To win the love of my Ellen! No, he can never do that; she is mine till death, and after it, and is as true to me as I am to her. Ellen, dear wife! hear me, and be comforted."

Concealed beneath his covering of fur, was a small bag, made of stout skin, well dried, containing Ellen's portrait, her lock of hair, Dan's Bible, and the page from Captain Liddle's log-book, appointing him captain. Into this bag he put the silver watch and Fewster's document.

"Rest there," he muttered. "When I am dead, chance may direct these relics into the hands of my friends. I will write a statement myself of certain things, and place it with these. Be merciful, O God! and keep firm the faith of my friends."

The appeal was like a prayer, and its utterance soothed him. He laid the Lascar's body in the shallow grave, and covered it as well as he could with earth and leaves and branches. Then he returned to Minnie, and they walked to the camp. He did not tell her of his discovery. It would have made her more unhappy.

On another occasion they were sitting together in the woods, in silence and resignation. They had sat so for full half an hour, and not a word had passed between them; their thoughts were with their friends, thousands of miles away. Suddenly there came to their ears the tinkle of a bell. They started, and looked at each other in wonder. A wild hope entered Joshua's heart. The sound was faint but distinct. It was like an evidence of approaching civilization. Presently it sounded again, and was followed by other bells of different tones, but each note being clearly uttered. Tinkle, tinkle, tinkle! till the woods were filled with music. Creeping slowly and softly in the direction of the sounds, they discovered the cause. The sounds were not produced, as they had hoped, by bells on the necks of cattle, but by a congregation of small birds of a greenish-yellow color, who, perched upon the branches of trees, in a spot where the trees formed a circle, were singing to each other their sweetest songs. Disturbed by the approach of footsteps, the birds hid themselves among the leaves, and were silent; but Minnie and Joshua remained perfectly still, and soon the sweet sounds were heard again, and the concert was resumed, to the delight of the hearers.

For many evenings after this Joshua and Minnie came to the spot to listen to the melody of the bell-birds. It was on one of these evenings that an idea in association with the birds presented itself to Joshua. Why should he not employ a little of his idle time in training some of the birds with which the beautiful woods abounded, as Dan and he used to do in their boyish days? He trembled with delight at the thought, and was eager to begin. It seemed to bring him nearer to Dan and the beloved ones at home. He told Minnie of his fancy, and she encouraged it. He would set about it at once; but first he must make a cage. He made one of wickerwork, sufficiently large to hold a score of birds; and in a very little while his cage was inhabited by birds as beautiful and almost as docile as any he had taught at home.

All this while they were allowed by the natives to do pretty well what they pleased. Food was supplied to them regularly, and they were not expected to work or hunt for it. Scarcely a night passed without Joshua played his accordion in the shade of their hut, and the singular fancy which the natives entertained respecting Minnie was strengthened by these mysterious melodious sounds. From time to time the natives shifted their camp, according to the seasons, and they invariably regulated their day's walking by Minnie's strength. Uncultured and savage as these ignorant creatures were, they were tender and kind to Minnie and Joshua, and showed them a thousand little attentions which could only have been prompted by the most delicate consideration. Joshua's fancy about the birds was quite a natural thing in their eyes. Minnie wanted the birds to talk to; she understood the mysterious voices of birds and trees. Their reverence for her was increased when they saw her one day with a golden-crowned honey-sucker upon her finger. This was one of the first birds which Joshua had tamed; he was careful to give it its favorite food, — the blossoms of the blue gum-tree when it was in flower, and at all times honey and sweet leaves, and had anticipated the effect it would produce upon the natives, when they saw it perching contentedly upon Minnie's bosom.

"See!" said Opara, "the birds know our Star; she talks to them the language of the trees. From us they fly, and hide themselves in clouds; but she bids them come, and they rest upon her bosom."

Soon other birds were tamed and trained; and the wonder spread to distant tribes, who made long journeys to see the Star of Opara's tribe, who understood the voice of Nature, and talked with all the children of the Great Mother; for so the simple savages interpreted it.

But Minnie grew weaker and weaker. She concealed her weakness as much as possible from Joshua, who was very tender to her, very, very kind. He had quite forgiven her; no cloud disturbed the harmony of their strange lives. Bearing always in mind the advice which Rough-and-Ready had given them to endeavor to make their way southward, and knowing the one great wish of Joshua's heart, she had used all her influence with the tribe to induce them every time they shifted their camp to move in that direction, and had succeeded so far, that every season found them nearer to the settled districts. But, although three years had passed, they had not seen the slightest signs of civilization.

Once Joshua was in a terrible state of agitation. He was gathering sweet leaves for his birds, when "Crack!" went the sound of a whip. He uttered a joyful cry, and threw himself upon the ground with all his heart in his ears, for he had not caught the direction of the sound. "Crack!" went the whip again. He ran swiftly towards it, and listened again. Rough-and-Ready had told him many times to keep his ears sharp open for the crack of a whip, and here it was, at last, after weary, weary waiting.

"You will find most likely," Rough-and-Ready had said, "that it is a stockman looking after some stray cattle. Then you will be all right."

The thoughts that crowded upon Joshua's mind in the few moments that elapsed between the cracking of the whip would occupy an hour to describe; they may be summarized thus: "That is a stockman's whip. Thank God for it! I shall see him presently, and he will wait while I fetch Minnie. Then we will go to where his companions are, and I will get some presents for our kind friends the natives. Minnie will soon grow strong; thank God! We will go down to Sydney, and get passage home in the first ship. Then — then — O Ellen, Ellen! O Dan, dear friend! dear mother and father! All will come right — all will be set right. Thank God!"

"Crack, crack!" Nearer — nearer. He was close to it, but saw nothing. He looked round carefully, watchfully. "Crack!" Over his head. He turned his eyes to the clouds, and saw a bird — the whip-bird — flying over the trees, uttering its "crack!" as it flew, taking his hopes with it, and bearing them away to where perhaps he would never meet with them again.

And Dan is sitting in a wooden hut built near the banks of a beautiful river. Seas do not divide him from his friend. They both live on the same bit of land, ignorant of each other's whereabouts. The same continent holds those two faithful hearts. What is Dan doing? who are with him? what kind of a place is this where he and they reside? A village in which dwell not more than a few hundred inhabitants. Not free from care, for care is human; but happier than inhabitants of great cities are. There is plenty of work for hands to do; more than there are hands to do it. What luxury there is, is the luxury of nature — rich fruits, bright flowers, clear atmosphere, sweet air, lovely skies, grand sunrises and sunsets, and sparkling watercourses whose banks teem with graceful shapes and lovely color. Here a city is to be formed, and they who live in it and are content shall see it grow up to strength — ay, to manhood — and shall have a share in its increasing wealth. First, tents of canvas to live in; now huts of wood; by and by houses of stone. But these last, though they be stronger, will not bring more enduring happiness. And here is Dan, with his birds, as usual. He earns money enough now. Not a hundred miles away, in the capital of the colony of which this little village is a speck, lives a dealer who comes regularly to Dan's wooden house, and buys such birds as he has trained, and pays handsomely for them. Not Solomon Fewster. He also is in that rising capital, and Dan will not sell him a bird. Not that Solomon Fewster needs them; for he is making money fast, and the miserly passion of accumulation is growing very strong in him. His business carries him often to Dan's village, — twice a month, perhaps; and regularly every two or three months he makes some kind of overture to Ellen, who shakes her head, and sometimes answers him, and sometimes evades the subject. Dan has remonstrated with him, and has begged him never to refer to the subject again. But he answers, —

"I cannot help it, Dan. If you knew what love was, you would know that a man can no more help loving than he can help feeling. It was love that first brought me to your house in Stepney. I didn't want the birds; but so that I might have the privilege of coming to the house — and of doing you and Ellen a good turn at the same time, mind, Dan — I took a deal of trouble to find dealers in birds who would buy them of me at the same price I paid you for them; and I shouldn't be telling an untruth if I said that I lost money by many of the birds I paid you for. One man I sold to failed, and I had to take a composition. Well, I didn't know then that Ellen loved Joshua; nothing was said between them; and when he first went away he wasn't old enough to know his own mind. He came back, and when he was ill I didn't show a bad spirit to him. After Ellen and he were engaged, I did not desert you; and I didn't annoy Ellen by forcing my attentions upon her. You spoke to me once about that unfortunate canary that died in my hand when I bade Joshua good-by. You can't think that I killed it purposely. But you may be able to form some idea of my feelings (which can't always be suppressed, Dan), and of the restraint I had to put upon myself when in the presence of the man who had taken from me the most precious thing in the world to me — Ellen's love — and you can put down the poor canary's death to that cause. I've no need to say any thing more. I've loved Ellen all along, and I've always treated her with respect and consideration. You mustn't debar me from the chance of being happy; Ellen may change her mind one day. It is many years now since I first saw her, a girl; and that I am content now to wait and hope ought to be sufficient proof of my disinterestedness and sincerity."

To such-like pleading Dan finds no reply, and so they go on as usual.

To Dan, as he sits with his birds, comes Ellen with her peaceful sad face. She has not found happiness, but she has found peace. Solomon Fewster is not her only suitor. Every single man in the village is enamoured of her, and would be glad to make her his wife. But she tells her story to all with a womanly purpose. She is married, and her husband went out as third mate of the "Merry Andrew," and the ship was lost and all hands, as it is supposed. But she cannot believe that her husband is dead; something tells her that he is alive — living upon some uninhabited shore mayhap, and looking forward to the time when, by the mercy of God, they shall be together again. Her story is repeated from one to another; and some kind souls who have been in the colony a few years come to her and Dan with little scraps of information concerning the "Merry Andrew," such as the finding of a piece of a figure-head which belonged to her husband's ship, and other similar evidence, which convince them that the "Merry Andrew" was lost off the Australian coast. "Is it not possible," asks Dan, "that some of the crew may have been saved, and may be dwelling now on some part of the uninhabited Australian coast?" "Quite possible," they answer: and they relate such instances as they know of vessels being wrecked, and of some of the sailors being saved and found years after they were supposed to be lost. Dan and Ellen derive much comfort from these narrations.

Ellen's little child Maggie is the pet of the village. At the present moment she is playing with her goat in the paddock at the back of the house, breathing in health with fresh air. To-night, when she says her prayers, she will pray that God will please send her father home — a prayer joined in by all of them every night.

Who is this? Susan. In no whit changed. With the same strange watchful manner upon her as in the old days in Stepney, but never uttering a word concerning Joshua. Sometimes she will go for days without speaking to a soul, and a smile never crosses her lips.

And this gentle woman, going about the house quietly, doing her work cheerfully, with a sweet smile for every one she comes across, and by whose side the little Maggie is content to sit in silence with her hands folded in her lap? This is Mrs. Marvel. You would know her if you had only seen her once, although her hair is nearly white now; for hers is one of the peaceful faces that dwell in your memory and remind you of your mother. As for her hair being nearly white — for the matter of that, so is Mr. Marvel's. It would not do for him to pay for every white hair that is pulled out of his head, as at the commencement of this story.

They sit together on this evening, as is their wont, and as they used to do in the dear old kitchen in Stepney, and talk of Joshua. And George Marvel smokes his pipe, and his wife darns — more slowly than in the old days, for her sight is not so strong as it was — and Dan trains his birds and reads to his friends. They have been sorely afflicted, but faith and love have banished despair.

On this very evening, hundreds of miles away, Joshua is sitting on the ground in his gunyah, amusing himself and Minnie with his birds. She is reclining on her 'possum-skin rug, looking affectionately and gratefully at Joshua, who has grown very wise in the different habits and natures of the strange birds he has before him. With what care he has collected them! Here is the quaint kingfisher, flitting about as contentedly as it used to flit among the dead trees that lie on the banks of creeks. Joshua, watching it one day, saw it suddenly dart into the water with such eagerness that it was completely submerged; he thought it was drowned, but the next instant it appeared above the surface with a small fish in its mouth, with which it hopped, exultant, into the woodland again. It is a handsome bird, and a singular-looking one too, with its beak about a quarter as long as its body, and its light crimson breast and azure back and shrewd brown eyes. Here is the mountain bee-eater, the wondrous blending of colors in whose plumage suggests the fancy that its feathers must have been dyed in the glorious sunsets of the South, and that it first saw the light when rainbows were shining. Here are the honeysuckers, yellow-eared, blue-cheeked, and golden-crowned; and the crimson-throated manakin, with its pleasant song; and the spotted finch, with red eyes; and the scarlet-backed warbler; and the pretty thrush, black-crowned and orange-breasted, whose piping in the early morning was the cheerfullest of all the birds; and the yellow-rumped fly-catcher, fussing about, and chattering like a magpie. All these are here, and many others: and Joshua often thinks how delighted Dan would be with them. Joshua and Minnie are clothed completely in fur garments; all their civilized clothes are gone. Joshua's hair has grown so, that his face is quite covered with it.

"Would they know me at home, Minnie, if they could see me as I am?" he asks.

"I doubt it," she replies; "but they would know your voice."

"Shall we ever see them again?" he asks, more of himself than of her.

She sighs, and does not answer. He may; she prays that he will. But she! The breeze sighs with her, as she thinks that she will never again look upon the faces of her friends. Well! perhaps it is better so. She desires no happier lot than to die in Joshua's arms, with his eyes looking kindly upon her. She has been growing weaker and weaker every day; she does not complain, but he often regards her with apprehensive looks, and prays that she may not be taken from him. They live together as brother and sister; the love he bears for her is as pure as the love he bears for his mother. He speaks to her often of Dan, and she listens with sweet patience. But he does not understand that her love for him is part of her very nature, and that it cannot be transferred — that it cannot change. He does not understand it, does not know it; he deludes himself with the hope that, if it should mercifully chance that they should reach home, the dear hope of Dan's life may be realized, and that Minnie's love and Dan's belief in her purity may brighten the days of his friend. She knows that Joshua entertains this hope, and does not pain him by telling him how false it is.

So the days pass, and the seasons change. In accordance with Minnie's wish, the tribe moves farther and farther southward, and is rewarded by finding plenty of game in the woods, and fish in the rivers and pools. Summer dies, and the beautiful autumn brings strength to Minnie; but the succeeding winter strikes her down. Her savage friends and worshippers are grieved to the heart at her weakness, and she, true to her purpose and to Joshua, makes them understand that health and strength for her lie southward, and urges them on towards the settled districts.

"If we are saved," says Joshua, "I shall owe all my happiness to you, Minnie. Once you gave me life; now perhaps you will give me what is better than life."

A look of content rests in her eyes as he says this, and she muses upon it for days afterwards, murmuring the words to herself before she falls asleep. Speaking to her of her father at one time, he is surprised to hear her say, "Father is dead, Joshua."

"How do you know?" he asks, startled.

"I feel it — here," pressing her hand to her heart; "I have dreamt that I saw him and mother together. Some things come to us intuitively; we do not need to be told."

"Do you know any thing else about those at home?" he asks, half awed by her solemn tone.

"No; but one other thing I know that I ought not to keep from you."

He waits in silence for what is to come, dreading to speak. She takes his hand; hers is hot with fever.

"Do not think me unkind," she says, "but for many weeks I have felt impelled to tell you, and now that the time is drawing near, I must no longer keep it from you. Can you guess what it is, my dear?"

"O Minnie! Minnie!" he cries, falling on his knees at her feet; "do not tell me that you are going to leave me!"

"I cannot help it, dear," she says, tenderly. "Before the spring dies I shall leave you. I shall spend my summer in another world." She repeats the words, as though they conveyed to her some deeper meaning than they implied. "Yes, I shall spend my summer in another world. My heart has been wintered in this."

He strives to reason her out of her belief, — tells her that it is fancy; but she gently checks him, with "Nay, dear Joshua. 'Tis but a little time to spring. Let us talk of other things."

Soon the buds begin to come, and the leaves grow green. Minnie hides her weakness, says that she feels stronger, and Joshua begins to hope. But he does not know what motive she has in this; he does not know that she puts on an appearance of strength, so that she may not retard their course southward. In many of their marches she sustains her fainting heart by strength, of love. "Nearer, nearer," she whispers to herself; "he shall owe all his happiness to me."

Come there to the camp one day some members of another tribe, who speak of having seen men of the color of Joshua and Minnie a couple of hundred miles to the south, mounted on strange animals. These aboriginal wanderers, indeed, are at variance with one another: some say that men and animals are one; others, that they are distinct creatures. Opara tells Joshua and Minnie, who are able by this time to understand the native tongue, and to make themselves understood.

"What Opara says is good," says Minnie. "We will go towards these men. They are our brothers. They will give me back my strength."

Opara being gone, Minnie asks Joshua what he thinks. Joshua, with eager voice and sparkling eyes, cries that they are stockmen on horses, as Rough-and-Ready had told them.

"All will yet be well," he says, his voice trembling with joyful emotion; "in a few months perhaps we shall be among white people again."

She listens in silence: and presently, in accordance with their nightly custom, he takes his accordion from its bag of fur, and plays the sweetest airs he knows. "Poor Tom Bowling" and "Bread-and-cheese and Kisses" are his principal themes; and as he plays, the newly-inspired hope stirs into life his dearest memories, and brings before him those pictures of his boyish days that he most loves to dwell upon.

CHAPTER XL.

FAITHFUL UNTO DEATH.

The river runs onward like a sparkling stream, now rushing between high banks of forest land, dotted here and there with miniature islands of rocks covered with lichens and shrubs, now settling into a still-looking reach, its surface covered with delicate mauve-colored water-lilies. Near to a great grove of palms upon the river's bank the native camp is fixed; and not far from the spot the channel forms a descent, more steep than abrupt, where it is cut up into hundreds of brawling streams by islands of beautiful shrubs. The natives have pitched their camp here, in accordance with Minnie's wish; they have been marching southward for more than a week, and Minnie has borne up bravely; but her strength has failed her at last, and she is compelled to succumb. It is understood among them that their Star is sick, and the mintapas (doctors) are anxious to practise their healing arts upon her, but their efforts are firmly and gently repulsed by Joshua. For this, they look upon him with no friendly eye, and but for Opara his life among them would not be so pleasant as it has been. He pays no heed to them; his anxiety concerning Minnie engrosses all his thoughts now.

She is sinking fast, and has grown so weak that he is obliged to carry her about. The spot she most loves is where the river is still and quiet; there she will lie for hours, with Joshua by her side, watching the shifting shadows of the clouds in the water's depths. She says but little; but every time her eyes turn to Joshua, they are filled with gratitude and love. Once she expressed a desire to write something, and Joshua makes a little ink with paint and gum-juice, and makes a pen from a duck's quill; but paper he has none.

"Your Bible," says Minnie.

He gives it to her, and she writes a few lines on the blank page at the end. Then she tears out the leaf, and folding it carefully says, "This is for Dan, when you see him" (having a full faith that Joshua and Dan will meet); "do not read it, but place it carefully by."

He puts it with Ellen's lock of hair in the bag he wears round his neck.

That same night a change comes over Minnie. He has been away from the hut for a few minutes, and when he returns he sees her sitting in a listening attitude with her hand to her ear.

"Minnie!" he exclaims; but she holds up a warning finger, and says,—

"Hush, Joshua! I am listening to the singing of the sea. Is it not sweet?"

His heart beats rapidly, and he takes her disengaged hand in his, and asks her what she has in the hand she is holding to her ear.

"It is a shell," she says. She shows it to him, and her face assumes the exact childlike expression of pleasure and simplicity it wore in the farewell interview he had with her before he first went to sea.

"You know me, Minnie?" he says, distressed.

"Yes, dear Joshua! What a question! But you must not be angry with me. I took the shell—but I took it for you."

"Nay but, Minnie," he says, striving to arrest her wandering thoughts; "listen to me"—

"Call me little Minnie," she pleads like a child, in the softest of voices.

"Little Minnie!" he sighs, with an almost broken heart.

"Little Minnie! Little Minnie!" she repeats. "The shell is singing it. Hush!" She remains silent for some time after this, and Joshua deems it best not to disturb her. An hour may have passed when she calls to him.

"Say that again, Joshua," she says.

Wondering, he asks her what it is she wishes him to repeat.

"Nay," she answers, "that is to tease me. But you must say it after me, word for word: 'What you did, you did through love, and there could not be much wrong in it.'" He recognizes his own words to her, and in a troubled voice he repeats, "What you did, you did through love, and there could not be much wrong in it."

"I am satisfied," she says; "you have made me happy. I shall try to sleep now."

He covers her with a rug, and watches by her side during the night.

He has no heart for his birds, and were it not that she takes a childish delight in them, and is glad to have them around her, he would have taken them to the woods and set them free. She does not recover consciousness of her true position; she believes that she and Joshua are children together, and — it may be happily — all the horrors through which she has passed have faded from her mind. Her great delight is to play with the birds and listen to her shell. Sometimes the fancy that he is at sea possesses her, and she talks to him of himself, as she used to talk to Dan, and coaxes him to tell her the story of the death of Golden Cloud and other incidents of his boyish life. In this condition she remains for many days, until the time comes when she awakes from a deep sleep, and says, in her weak voice, "I have been dreaming, Joshua. I thought we were children again." Then opening her hand with the shell in it, looks at it, blushing, and says, "It is the old shell, Joshua. You remember."

"Do you feel stronger, Minnie?"

"No, dear; I shall not grow stronger. It will be as I told you a little while ago. Spring is not gone yet; but it will be soon. Have they asked about me?" meaning the natives.

"Yes, many times every day, Minnie; and have brought their choicest food for you regularly."

"They have been very kind to us. Rough-and-Ready was not quite right about them. I used to tremble with fear when he spoke of them. Poor Rough-and-Ready and poor Tom! What has become of them, I wonder!"

They muse sadly over the memory of those two good friends.

"Some lives are very hard, Joshua," she continues. "His was, I am sure. I suppose it was as he said, and that he has done bad things. Yet how kind and gentle he was to us! It is hard to reconcile; but it seems to me, my dear, that our lots are shaped for us. We can't help our feelings; we don't make them; they come, and we must act as they prompt us to act. Opara and the savages now: they couldn't help being born savages, and they have had no good teaching. Don't think me wicked for what I am going to say, my dear."

"No, Minnie; go on."

"Well, I can't help believing that a good deal of what is called wrong is not wrong, and that bad is not always bad. I can't explain exactly what I mean, but I feel it." She appears to think that she has got out of her depth, and suddenly changes the subject. "Take me out, and let me see Opara. You must carry me; I am not as heavy as I was."

He lifts her in his arms, and carries her, with her arm round his neck, out of the hut towards the savages. They crowd round her, and she speaks a few words to them, and smiles upon them. Then, by easy stages, he carries her to her favorite spot by the river's side, and there they rest.

"All rivers have currents, Joshua?"

"Yes, my dear."

"Even this, that looks so still and quiet?"

"Even this, my dear; the current is running, although you cannot see it. But remember, the river is not so still everywhere. A very few miles away it is full of life; it is rushing over the rocks, and is never still for an instant day and night."

"Strange! So restless there, so quiet here! It has been so with me: so restless there, so quiet here! Look! we can see the fish in the clear depths. How beautifully the wild jasmine smells!"

He gathers a little for her, and a bunch of fringed violets, and she puts them in her breast. Then she encourages him to talk of home, and listens with sincere pleasure to his praises of Dan.

"It is good to be loved by such a heart," she muses.

"Ah, Minnie!" he ventures to say, "it could have been with him as he once hoped it would!"

"About me?" she replies unhesitatingly. "Does not that seem to be a proof that our lots are shaped for us? Tell him that I was very, very sorry, and that I begged him to forgive me."

But it is chiefly about Joshua's mother that she speaks, and wishes that *her* mother had lived. In the midst of the conversation she falls into a light slumber, and opening her eyes half an hour afterwards, resumes from the point where they had left off, as if there had been no interval of silence.

On another occasion they are together on the same spot, and Joshua is telling her of a beautiful part of the river's bank which she had not seen. "The river is narrow there, and even more peaceful than this," he says. "The trees on both sides bend over the water until the topmost branches almost touch, so that the river is in shade. The sun was peeping through the arch of branches, lighting up the water here and there, and the golden light streaked the white leaves of the lilies, over which the pretty lotus-bird was running with so light a step as not to stir the flowers."

"How beautiful!" she says softly. "At night, when the moon is shining on the water and the lily-leaves through the arch of branches, how grand and peaceful it must be! Joshua, bend your head, my dear. When I am gone, let me be buried there. Nay, don't cry; but promise."

In a broken voice he promises her, and she is content. Then she bids him bring Opara to her; and the aged chief comes and sits by her side.

"Opara," she says, taking Joshua's hand and kissing it, "this my brother and I are one. You understand?"

"I understand," he answers; and Joshua wonders what it is she is about to say.

"You see how weak I have grown, Opara. Look at my hand; you can see the light through it."

"Say, my daughter," asks Opara; "you who know the language of birds and flowers, — you who know the mysteries of the Grand Vault, — can you not make yourself strong?"

"No, Opara; I am wanted."

"Cannot our mintapas make you strong?"

"No, Opara; their skill is not for me. Tell them so; and tell them I thank them, and will not forget them. Listen. Many moons ago, I walked in the woods, where the leaves were singing to each other, and where the wind whispered strange things as it travelled through the trees. I heard a voice; I listened; and I was told that when the next summer came, I should be wanted — There!"

Opara gravely followed the motion of her hand, as it pointed upwards.

"The summer is coming, and I must go. Do not disturb me then; my brother will see to me; and tell your young men and women to let me rest."

"I will tell them, and they will obey. Will our daughter return to us?"

Minnie catches at this question eagerly, and clasps Joshua's hand with a firmer clasp.

"I will return, if you will do one thing for me."

"Opara will do it."

"It will take many days to do."

"If it takes many moons to do, it shall be done."

"Opara's name shall be known in the Grand Vault," says Minnie in an earnest tone. "Take heed of my words. Those men of the same color as my brother, of which you were told some time ago, you have not seen them?"

"No."

"They are southward. My brother has a message for them from me. He has promised to deliver it to them; but he does not know the country. If he goes by himself, bad men of other tribes may meet him and take him with them. If you and some of your young men will accompany him south until he sees the strangers, or is near to them, I will return to you by and by, and your tribe shall never want food. The strangers will be kind to you, and will give you good things. Will Opara do this, and protect my brother?"

"Opara will do this, and will protect your brother."

"Good." She gives the old chief her hand, and he places it on his eyes, and departs gravely.

Joshua for a time is too agitated to speak. This last proof of her devotion is the crowning sacrifice of her life. She is the first to break the silence.

"Joshua, my dear, I have made atonement?"

He can only say, "O my dear, my dear, how unworthy I am in my own eyes!"

"Nay, nay," she says soothingly, "you are all that is good and noble. A better heart, a purer, never beat. I have committed a great fault, and have done you a great wrong — unconsciously, my dear, and without thought; and, by the mercy of our Father, I have been able to atone for it. Think of me as a child, my dear, who has loved you with all her heart, despite her wilfulness. Take me in your arms as you would a child, and say that you forgive me."

He takes her in his arms, and, to satisfy her, sobs out the words she wishes to hear. Her face is close to his.

"This kiss for Ellen," she whispers; "this for your dear, kind mother; this for Dan. Tell all of them of my fancy, that I wish to live in their minds, not as a woman, but as a child — as a child who erred through love, and who had not been taught to understand what duty was. Who said this, "There is no earthly sacrifice that love will not sanctify."

"Your father!" he whispers, amazed.

"I heard him; I was in the room when he blessed my mother for devoting her life to him."

Presently she asks him to fetch his birds, and he runs and brings them. He opens the cage, and they hop about her contentedly. He gathers some wild flowers, and places them by her side. Shortly afterwards she directs his attention to the fringed violets, which do not live an hour after they are gathered. "They are withering," she says. "Do not pluck any more of the pretty things; let them live." He supports her in his arms; and she watches the birds with glistening eyes, and whispers that they remind her of dear Dan. Then she falls asleep, with her face turned to Joshua. He does not disturb her. Every thing around is very still and quiet. He thinks of the restless river a few miles away, and of Minnie's words, "So restless there, so quiet here! It has been so with me." The afternoon passes; the sun is going down, and the heavens are filled with wondrous color. Minnie has been asleep for a long while now. Shall he arouse her? Her fair face is perfectly still, and a smile is on her lips. "Minnie!" he whispers. Her hand is on her heart, and in her hand the shell. She does not speak; and a darkness comes upon him, and his heart grows cold as he presses his lips to hers. She has gone to spend the summer of her life in another world.

Opara holds the last words of Minnie sacred. To the expressed desire of the doctors of the tribe to inter Minnie according to their rites, he says, "Our daughter has spoken, and Opara has promised. Her brother will see to her. Let her rest." So, on the following night, Joshua is standing alone by Minnie's grave, which he has strewn with wild flowers. In the rude coffin of bark, which he has cut and made with his own hands, he places also the sweetest-smelling flowers he can find. Her shell he leaves in her hand, and cuts a long tress from her hair. "For Dan," he murmurs.

He buries her in the place he had described to her, and where she had expressed a wish to be laid. It is just such a night as she pictured. The moon is streaming through the interlaced branches on the beautiful lilies and the peaceful water. He reads prayers from Dan's Bible, and falls upon his knees; and, as he sobs there, the words of her father recur to him, and he repeats their sense prayerfully: "She is a wild flower; the impulse of her mind is under the control of the impulse of her heart. She is oblivious of all else, defiant of all else. Those of her friends who have the consciousness of a higher wisdom than she possesses, those of them who can recognize that the promptings of such a heart as hers may possibly lead her into dangerous paths, must guide her gently, tenderly. If any betray her, he will have to answer for it at the Judgment-seat!"

"Judge me," he cries aloud, raising his arms to heaven, "and so deal with me! This dear angel lies in her grave pure as at her birth. But she will speak for me, dear, honored sister!"

In the distance, standing in the shadow of the trees, are the natives, their bodies streaked with white. They do not intrude upon Joshua's sorrow. Slowly he piles the earth upon the faithful heart, and kisses the earth with passionate grief. When he is calmer, he reads his Bible by the moon's light; and, as he reads, peace comes to him.

CHAPTER XLI.

JOSHUA AND THE OLD WIZARD.

FOR two weeks the natives mourned for Minnie. Their grief was sincere, notwithstanding that it was expressed in barbarous fashion — such as painting their bodies white with pipeclay, and inflicting painful gashes upon their breasts and arms with shells and stones. They observed Joshua gathering wild flowers to place upon her grave, and every day after that, the women and children collected the prettiest and rarest flowers they could find, and decorated Minnie's grave with them. During this time a terrible feeling of desolation came upon Joshua. If Opara failed to keep the promise he had given Minnie, what would become of him? He thought of some words Dan had spoken to him in one of their boyish conversations, when they were talking of Robinson Crusoe. Dan had said he thought it strange that Robinson did not forget how to speak his native language, and had wondered that he didn't go mad. This remembrance was terrible to Joshua. At night, when he was alone in his hut, he would speak to himself, and would tremble at his voice; and stopping sometimes with half-uttered words upon his tongue, would be seized with sudden terror as at an unfamiliar sound. But at the end of a fortnight, Opara came to Joshua, and said, "Our days of mourning are over; but the image of our daughter will dwell forever in our hearts. To-night we hold a council. Shall we tarry yet a while, or shall we prepare to depart?"

"I have a message for my brothers and hers," replied Joshua. "They live southward. Is that the direction Opara will take?"

"Opara will do as he has promised," said the old chief with dignity, "and will accompany you to the south."

"My sister will be glad if her message is delivered soon;" and Joshua's heart beat quickly at the prospect of deliverance.

Opara gravely bent his head; and that night it was decided that twenty young men and doctors of the tribe, including Opara, should start in a couple of days, with Joshua, for the south. When Joshua was informed of this, he went to Minnie's grave, and shed tears of joy, and gathered a little of the earth, and placed it in the bag round his neck which contained his most precious possessions. On the appointed morning they started early, accompanied by the entire tribe; but by noon all the stragglers had departed. In a few days their road lay through very rough country, where, although fruits and birds were plentiful (it being summer), Opara said they would not be able to live in the winter. Their great difficulty was to obtain water, for the creeks and water-courses were drying up; and Joshua was filled with admiration at the resources of the natives, who found water in places — digging it out of trees, indeed, very often — where a stranger would never have dreamed of searching for it. When Joshua saw them strike their stone weapons into a tree whence cold bright water flowed, he could not help thinking of Moses striking the rock. A favorite food with them was a species of shrubby plant which they called Karkalla, and which yielded a rich luscious fruit; and they ate, with intense relish, many species of grubs which they cut out of the bark of trees.

Among the party was one famous wizard and doctor, who was not disposed to look upon Joshua with the same friendly eye as the others did. When Minnie was ill, he had been especially desirous of exercising his arts upon her, and of restoring her to health, by which means his reputation with the tribe would have been enormously increased; and when Minnie died, he entertained the belief that he could have saved her if he had been allowed. This doctor's name was Nullaboin, and he had joined Joshua's escort because he thought that he might, by watching Joshua's movements, obtain some kind of knowledge that might be useful to him.

During the latter days of Minnie's illness Joshua had not played his accordion, which, it must be borne in mind, the natives had never seen. Joshua had kept it jealously concealed in its covering of fur, and had never played it in sight of the natives. It was at the end of the second week of their journey, when Joshua was looking out anxiously for traces of white settlers, that a circumstance occurred which boded him great danger. He had wandered, as he had been in the habit of doing every night, a long distance from where the natives pitched their camp. From time to time Opara and his party had met natives of different tribes, with whom they had conversed (though sometimes with difficulty, for their dialects differed) concerning the white men; and on this morning a strange native had given them such information as led Opara to tell Joshua that he believed he would soon be able to deliver Minnie's message to her brothers. Interpreting by this that the stranger they had met had seen something of Englishmen, Joshua, in the night, wandered farther from the camp than usual, in the vague hope that he might come upon traces of his countrymen. He saw none, and yet thought they might be near. An idea struck him. "Why should I not play my accordion?" he thought. "I might be within a short distance of my deliverers, and not know it. The sound of civilized music might reach their ears, and they would come to me." He acted upon the thought without delay. For the first time for many weeks, he took his accordion from its covering (it was slung round his shoulders by a strap of dried skin), and walked through the woods, playing, and swinging the instrument in the air, so that the sound should travel far. He little dreamed of the effect he produced. Nullaboin was tracking him — had tracked him every night in his wanderings. Hitherto Nullaboin had learned nothing; but now directly the music struck upon his ears, he was so amazed as almost to betray himself. The idea that flashed through that cunning savage mind was as singular as it was original. It was neither more nor less than that Joshua held Minnie's spirit imprisoned in the strange instrument from which the melodious sounds proceeded. They were the same as used to proceed from Minnie's hut, when it was imagined she was speaking with invisible shapes. What wonders might he not perform, could he obtain possession of that power! The mysterious spirits of air and heaven would speak to him, and would tell him strange things. But how could he obtain it — how? Joshua was strong — too strong for him. He was an old man — ay, he was an old man, and these spirits, if he could speak to them in their language, might teach him how to become young again. The courses of his blood quickened through the old wizard's veins at the wild hope, and he picked up a stone and cut at his breast in his excitement. He could not hope to wrest the magic power from Joshua singly. He must enlist his companions on his side. His influence was great, but Opara's was greater. He dreaded that aged chief. "If Opara knows," was his cunning thought, "Opara will claim it for himself. No, no; it is mine, Nullaboin's. Here me, Pulyalauna! Strike Opara with your thunder to-night! Strike him dead! He has lived long enough." But as he thought, he started away in terror. Among the trees, some twenty yards away, he saw a crouching figure, which he took to be one of the fabulous Purkabidnies, that roam through the woods at night to slay black men. It was but the charred stump of a tree, but it was sufficient to cause Nullaboin, the wizard, to fly from the spot in direst terror, towards the camp. He lay awake until Joshua returned, and noted with his lynx eyes that Joshua wore the magic instrument strapped round his shoulders. The following day he took occasion to speak to Joshua in a subtle manner, as thus: "Nullaboin dreamt last night of his daughter the Star."

Joshua nodded.

"She spoke to me. Her voice was like the voice of the birds. I shall see her soon."

Joshua gave him a startled look.

"Has her brother seen her?"

"No."

"Has she not spoken to him?"

"No."

"Nullaboin is a great mintapa, and his daughter knows his power."

All this was Greek to Joshua, and he did not encourage the old wizard to continue his revelations. But during that day and the next, Nullaboin was busy working upon the credulous minds of the younger natives, and found but little difficulty in inflaming their curiosity. Joshua's eagerness had become almost painful by this time; and when they were travelling over plains, every speck on the horizon became a horseman in his anxious eyes. Occasionally they had to make their way through dense scrub, where there were but few trees; but for the most part their road lay through the woods, where tall timber was abundant. Under any other circumstances, Joshua would have found the life he was leading wonderfully interesting, fatiguing as it was. Now they were wending their way through a gully, the heights on each side of which were so thickly wooded as almost to shut out the light of heaven; now they were on a plain somewhat thinly dotted with trees, when suddenly a young savage would dart off in pursuit of a bee which his wonderful sight had detected fifty feet high in the air. Away buzzed the bee through the clear air, and, with his eyes fixed upon the tiny insect, after it flew the savage joined by other young men of the party, the older men following more leisurely. With unerring sight the hunters ran until the bee settled upon a tree; and with wondrous speed the bee-hunter, seeing the sugar-bags in the topmost branches, climbed the trunk, cutting notches in the bark with his toes with his stone hatchet, until he reached the sweet store, with which he loaded himself, and then rejoined his companions. Now they caught an enormous guana, more than five feet in length, upon which the natives feasted; and saw strange specimens of the mantis, which looked like rotten pieces of dead twigs until they were touched, when they crawled away by the aid of their abundant misshapen limbs. Now they came to a place where, surrounded by almost impenetrable scrub, in which patches of wild bananas grew, were a number of fresh-water lagoons, filled with reeds and weeds of every description, and abounding in screeching cockatoos and beautifully-colored ducks. While Nullaboin was busy with his scheme for obtaining the magic box in which he imagined Minnie's spirit was imprisoned, some members of a strange tribe came to the party, one of whom, to Joshua's amazement, was singing in imperfect English a verse of the ballad, "He promised to buy me a bunch of blue ribbons." * The singer knew no other words of English: but he contrived to make Joshua understand that he had been among white men, which, indeed, was sufficiently evident from his singing.

"Opara," said Joshua, with sparkling eyes, "my brothers are near."

"It is well," was Opara's simple reply. "Opara will have performed his promise. When his daughter returns to her tribe, she will thank Opara."

But by this time Nullaboin's plans were matured; and that night, when Joshua wandered into the woods, his heart filled with grateful feelings towards the faithful savages, he was followed stealthily by Nullaboin, and a half-a-dozen braves who had joined in his plot.

* A fact.

"At last!" thought Joshua, visions of happiness to come floating before his eyes —"at last! Perhaps to-morrow I shall see the faces of my countrymen, and then, and then"— But he could not think clearly; for as the images of those dearest to him came before him, the false face of Solomon Fewster seemed to cast a shadow upon his happiness. He leaned against a silver-leaved gum-tree, and tried to calm himself, and in a little while succeeded. Ellen was true to him, he was sure. And Dan? "Is he training his birds still?" he thought. "How has he borne his great grief?" He saw before him the dear old kitchen in Stepney, exactly as he had seen it last; every chair and every piece of crockery was in its exact place. Every detail of those last few minutes at home presented itself clearly to him: his yearning look at the old familiar room; his walking up the stairs to the street-door with his face hidden in his mother's neck, and she caressing him, as she had done when he was a little child. Almost unconsciously he had taken out his accordion, and his fingers were wandering over the keys, playing softly those airs most in consonance with his thoughts. He even murmured the words of "Tom Bowling:"

"Here, a sheer hulk, lies poor Tom Bowling,
The darling of our crew."

"Dear Old Sailor! How glad I shall be to see his honest face!" And he saw the Old Sailor take a wedding-ring out of a piece of silver-paper, with a triumphant expression upon his face, as he had done in that memorable interview in Gravesend, when — whiz! Good God! what was this? The sky seemed to come down upon the earth, and he sank through it — down! down! —

Nullaboin, snatching the accordion from the falling man, hugged it to his naked breast, and glided swiftly away, followed by his confederates. They must have traversed full four miles before they paused, and then they looked cautiously around, to assure themselves that they were alone. The old wizard had kept the instrument tightly pressed to his bosom during the flight, so that no sound had proceeded from it; but now, when they paused, his grasp relaxed. His hand was on the keys: and and as the accordion gradually distended itself, a slow wail issued from it, which so terrified him that he let it fall to the ground, so that the weak and plaintive sound was followed by a harsh and sudden jangle of all the notes. Appalled at this angry cry, which was to them full of fearful meaning, the younger savages, with palpitating hearts and dismayed faces, flew from the spot, and left Nullaboin alone with the terrible prize. He stood like a statue for many minutes, although the thick beads of perspiration were rolling down his face and beard, and then cautiously approached the prostrate mystery. Encouraged by its silence, he stooped over it, and, after his savage fashion, entreated it to speak to him. No answer came. What should he do? A sudden light came into his eyes. Minnie's spirit was imprisoned there, and she was angry. He would release her. He lifted the accordion gently from the ground, and timidly pressed his finger upon one of the higher keys. The response was gentle, almost piteous; it was an appeal to him.

"O Star of the tribe!" he whispered, "Nullaboin will set you free. Make him great!"

He took a small green-stone mogo (hatchet) from his girdle, and carefully cut a long hole in the cloth. He held his hand over it to grasp the spirit; but he saw nothing, heard nothing. He waited; nothing came. He took it in his hand, and waved it up and down; no sound issued from it. The spirit had fled, and the old wizard was left despairing.

Joshua felt no pain. A delicious sense of rest was upon him. Of all the memories that came to him in his dreams, the happy holiday he had spent with Dan and Ellen on the Old Sailor's barge was the most vivid. He lived once more through the whole of that happy day — stood in Dan's room in his holiday clothes, with food for the birds which were to be presented to the Old Sailor — went down to breakfast, and saw Ellen's yearning look as they talked of the coming pleasures of the day — saw her run out of the room and run in again, almost mad with delight because Susan had obtained permission for her to accompany the lads — rode in the creaking cart through dingy Whitechapel — saw Dan swinging in the hammock and gazing at him affectionately while he was rowing — heard every word of the Old Sailor's sea-stories over again — sat on the deck in the twilight in a state of delicious happiness by Ellen's side, and went down into the saloon, and heard the Old Sailor sing, and then Ellen, her favorite song of "Bread-and-cheese and Kisses." After that a darkness came upon him, and he opened his eyes, and saw the stars shining in the heavens; but they were shut out immediately afterwards, and he was standing on the deck of the "Merry Andrew" the night the ship struck on the rocks; holding Minnie in his arms; the dead faces of his shipmates crowded upon him, rising from the cruel sea with the exact expression upon their features that they wore when he last saw them; then came his encounter with the Lascar in the woods; and that memory brought to him the face of Solomon Fewster, which lingered long; but it faded in its turn, and gave way to other fancies, the most enduring of which was the river near which Minnie was buried, and the refrain of her words, "So restless there, so quiet here!" dwelt in his mind through the long night.

When he awoke it was daylight. He struggled to his feet, but could scarcely stand for weakness. He had been struck by a boomerang on the temple, and had lost a great deal of blood. He was so weak and bewildered that, even now that he was awake the past incidents of his life were strangely mingled in his mind. It was not until after long mental pondering and sifting of incidents that the true knowledge of his position and of what had occurred to him dawned upon his senses. He looked round for his accordion; it was gone. Then he thought, "Opara has betrayed me at the last moment. They have stolen my accordion, and they have left me here for dead. But they may return at any moment to strip me of what I have about me." Weak and faint as he was, he crawled cautiously towards the most thickly-wooded part of the forest, and there concealed himself. "What now?" he thought. "Must I wait for death?" For indeed he was too weak to walk. His heart almost fainted within him.

"Now, when I was so near to deliverance," he groaned aloud, shedding bitter tears, "to be thus dashed back to misery!" But even as he uttered the words, he heard the crack of a stockman's whip. Crack! It rang through the woods and through his heart. Not the mockery of a whip-bird this time! No, no; it was too near; and it was followed by the sound of horses' hoofs and by the sound of English voices. Thank God! thank God!

CHAPTER XLII.

FAITHFUL HEARTS.

ON a pleasant summer evening Dan and Ellen and George Marvel were sitting in the shade of the veranda which surrounded three sides of their house. The house was built of wood, and was all on one floor, and there was a garden in the front and in the rear. George Marvel was smoking his pipe as usual, and having by this time got used to the short clays, which were the only ones he could now obtain, had just declared that he enjoyed a short pipe as well as a long one; "though I couldn't stomach them at first, Dan, as you know." Dan nodded in acquiescence; he had no time to reply; for at that moment a great shouting was heard, and the mail-cart was seen driving round the corner towards them. The arrival of the mail-cart in the village was an event of the utmost importance, and was always greeted with cheers by the excited population. There was a mail-service once a fortnight, and sometimes it would be a day or two behind, which was most serviceable to the inhabitants of the village, as giving them something to be anxious about and to talk about. The driver (who was contractor for the mail, owner of the mail-cart, and driver of it, all in one) had one invariable excuse when he was late; he had been waiting for the birds. Now, when Dan first heard this, he, without knowing its meaning, felt instantly attracted to the driver of the mail, whose name was Ramsay; and when he had an explanation from the lips of a neighbor to whom Ramsay had given a lift (he was always giving kindly "lifts" to one and another), Dan was disposed to be affectionately familiar with him. This feeling being reciprocated by Ramsay, an intimacy sprung up between them, the consequence of which was, that Ramsay, after delivering his mails to the postmaster (a rheumatic old woman, deaf, and almost blind), came as regularly as a clock to have a smoke and a chat with Dan and the Marvels. A curious character was Ramsay; a man who had seen better days — who had, indeed, once been very wealthy — who had been plundered and deceived from his youth upwards — and who yet retained a kindliness to every living thing with which he came in contact. Thus, his waiting for the birds: it was whimsical, pretty childish, some said; consisting in stopping whichever of his two steady old mares he was driving, immediately he saw a bird on the bush track before him. "Get out of my way, little bird," he would say in a singularly gentle voice, and he would give his whip a flick at the back of his cart, which had not the slightest effect in disturbing the little creature that blocked the road. But Ramsay could no more drive past it than he could drive through a wire fence; and he often found it necessary to descend from his cart, and walk softly towards the bird, which, having probably by that time finished its pecking, would jerk up its cunning head towards the intruder, and leisurely take flight to the nearest tree, where it would watch the lazy old mare trotting along, and would receive perhaps a comical "Good-morning, little bird!" from the gentle-hearted mail-contractor.

When Ramsay had delivered his mail to the rheumatic old female postmaster, he would look over the letters and newspapers (five minutes was long enough to sort the lot of them) to see whether there was anything for Dan and Mr. Marvel. On this evening there was a newspaper; and Ramsay, taking possession of it, walked leisurely to the house of his friends. Ellen's child, Maggie, saw him, and ran to him for a jump in the air, and he stopped to indulge her until he was out of breath, when he was glad to deliver her into her mother's charge, shaking his head laughingly in answer to her cries for "more!"

"Ili, Mrs. Wattles!" he shouted to a woman who was passing. "There's a letter for you at the post-office." Which sent Mrs. Wattles off, in eager haste, to receive her missive.

"You're a day late," said Dan, as Ramsay opened the gate.

"Waiting for the birds, Dan; couldn't get along for the creatures. Here's a newspaper for you."

The newspaper had an English postage-stamp upon it, and there was something marked inside.

"It's from the Old Sailor!" cried Dan, and pressed it to his lips, and so did Ellen, and all those simple foolish people, in turns, one after another. The paragraph that was marked related how a ship, with all hands, was reported lost ten years ago, and there was nothing more heard of her until a week before the newspaper was printed, when into the London Docks came a vessel from China, which had been driven out of her course, luckily, and had in consequence picked up six men off an island, who had been living there for many years; and how that these men belonged to the crew who were supposed to have gone to the bottom ten years before. You may imagine that they read this paragraph half a dozen times at the least, having Joshua in their minds al. the time, and that Ellen and Mrs. Marvel disappeared for a few minutes to have a cry together. While they were away, the men sat silent and grave, Dan reading the newspaper, and George Marvel and Ramsay smoking their pipes.

Now, once in every month — that is, by every other mail — Ramsay had to deliver a mail-bag at a cattle-station known as Bull's Run. The station was between forty and fifty miles distant from the village, and Ramsay took two days for the journey, out of a merciful regard for his old mare. As he had to start for Bull's Run early in the morning, he did not stay late with his friends, but bade them good-night at about nine o'clock. When he was gone, the Old Sailor became the subject of conversation, and every circumstance of their intimacy was recalled and dwelt upon with loving affection. Every night they sat together — Susan as well, although she never joined in the conversation — talking of one thing and another. Time had softened their grief, but it had not made them less constant; their hearts beat as fondly and devotedly for Joshua as ever they had done.

Susan and Mr. and Mrs. Marvel had gone to bed; Ellen and Dan were alone. Between these two an undefinable sympathy existed; they could almost read each other's thoughts; and this night Ellen lingered when the others had retired to rest, because she had read in Dan's face the signs of something more than usually important in his mind. For a long time they were silent, the stillness of every thing around impressed them deeply. The nature of their thoughts, and the stillness of the night, in which there was something solemn, brought to both of them the memory of another night, years ago, when they had sat alone, as they were sitting now, with Basil Kindred's unopened diary before them.

"Ellen," said Dan, playing with her fingers thoughtfully, "I have dreamed of Jo lately more often than usual, and to-night my thoughts dwell upon him so strongly that I shall not go to bed for a while."

"I will sit up with you, my dear."

The windows in the room were folding windows, and reached to the ground. Ellen opened them; and she and Dan were presently sitting beneath the veranda, he upon a chair, she upon the ground, with her head resting in his lap.

"Do you remember that Christmas night, Ellen, when Jo came home?"

"Yes, Dan."

"And the strange impression I had upon me that Jo was near us, although I had no actual knowledge of it?"

"Yes."

"I can see the street as we saw it then, Ellen, with its covering of snow, and that cruel black gash in it which the only man who passed tore with his feet. It was like an ill-omen. You see nothing to disturb the beauty of the scene, Ellen?"

"No; but why do you ask, my dear?"

"Because I have upon me to-night the same feeling that I had then; because, notwithstanding that it is almost madness to say it and believe it, I believe that Jo is near us."

"Dan!"

"To no one else but you would I say this, my dear. ♦ Long dwelling upon one subject fills the mind with singular thought concerning it, and it may be that this feeling that is upon me now is but the creation of the wildest fancy. Yet there are strange influences within us and around us for which we cannot account, and which affect us in mysterious ways. When I first knew that it was Jo's wish to be a sailor, and that we should be parted, I tried with all my mind and soul — it may be that it was a foolish, childish fancy, Ellen, but I had it — to create such a heart sympathy between us that we could never be parted in spirit. I had some wild ideas then of being able to dream of what he was doing and seeing when he was thousands of miles away from our little room in Stepney. Of course they came to nothing; but it would be strange, indeed, if this earnest striving of mine had not produced some feeling within me which time only can test. You remember what poor Minnie's father used to say: 'There are more things in heaven and earth than is dreamed of in our philosophy.'"

So they sat together talking and musing, and it was past midnight before they retired to rest.

Early in the morning, the whimsical mail-contractor was jogging along towards Bull's Run; he had to stop so many times for the little birds in the road, that his progress was slow; but he had reckoned upon these impediments, and he arrived at the station not more than a couple of hours after the usual time. That was the end of his journey; the following day he had to make his way back to Dan's village. The residence of the owner of Bull's-Run station was built of slabs split from the bloodwood-tree; the roof was of shingle; and the interior of the house was lined with rich dark-red cedar, which gave it quite a cosey, comfortable appearance. The workmen's huts were built of palm-tree slabs, and the roofs were thatched with strong sword-grass, which grew in great profusion on the banks of a river within a few miles of the homestead. Ramsay was always welcomed at Bull's Run; the men and women on the station — for, primitive as it was, there were women and children living on it — used to cluster round him, and ask him for news from the villages through which he passed, and the smallest items were received with thankfulness, and eagerly listened to. On this occasion, Ramsay had but little news to tell, and his budget was soon exhausted. In return, they told him theirs: one of the bulls had torn a man's arm open; a child had been lost for a whole night, and all the men were out searching for it miles away, and it was found the next morning within half a mile of the hut; three bushrangers, splendidly mounted, passed the station last week at full gallop; one of the shepherds had come in with a cock-and-a-bull story of gold being found somewhere or other; another shepherd had gone mad; Yellow-hammer Jack and his wife had had a row; and — but Oh! this was the best bit of the lot! — a man had been brought in by two stockmen who were looking for lost cattle, and had found him instead; he was almost dead, and had been living a long time with the Blacks. He seemed a decent kind of fellow, had been a sailor, he said, but was strangely silent about himself — for good reasons, some of the ill-natured ones said. Any ways, the man was better, although still very weak, and intended to start the next morning for Sydney; nothing would stop him.

"A long tramp for a weak man," said kind-hearted Ramsay; "if he's a decent fellow, I'll give him a lift."

As he said this, there came towards the group, walking very slowly, a strange-looking man. with a beard down to his breast, dressed in skins and furs; he had a stick in his hand, and seemed to require its support. They pointed to him, and said that was the man. Ramsay looked at him keenly, and the air of melancholy that rested in the man's eyes impressed the mail-contractor with a feeling of pity.

"A sailor, eh?" he thought; "and living with the savages. Wonder what he lived with them for?" Then he thought of Dan's and Ellen's anxiety concerning strange sailors and castaways, and that perhaps they would be glad to see this man. He said nothing, however, but was up the next morning early, and saw the man start on his road with slow and painful steps. A few minutes afterwards the old mare was harnessed, and its tail was turned to Bull's Run. Soon he came up to the man, and as he did so, two purple-breasted robins pecking at a bit of honeysuckle barred his progress. "Get out of my way, little birds," said the mail-driver, pulling up his mare; and he gave a soft flick with his whip in a direction where the robins were not. The words reached the man's ears, and he turned his head in surprise, and saw the little comedy. A gentle, sweet smile rested on his lips, and he looked at the mail-driver almost gratefully. Ramsay smiled in return, and again bade the little robins get out of his way; and presently they took flight, each with a tiny piece of the sweet flower in its beak. Then the old mare jogged lazily along, and the strange-looking man gazed wistfully after the cart. Ramsay, looking back, saw the wistful expression, and stopped at once. "Hi, mate!"

Joshua came slowly forward.

"Where you bound for?"

"Sydney."

"Going to walk all the way?"

"If I can," sighed Joshua; and could not help adding, "and if I don't die on the road!"

"Jump up, mate; I can give you a lift for forty miles."

"I have no money," and Joshua turned away, with a sob.

"I don't want your money; I want your company. But how were you going to live, if you've no money?"

"I should trust to the Providence that has so wonderfully delivered me," thought Joshua, but made no reply aloud; though it could be seen in his eyes, which were filled with tears.

"Jump in," said Ramsay, imperatively and kindly, "without another word."

And without another word Joshua climbed into the cart.

"I dare say now," said Ramsay in the course of conversation, as the old mare trotted steadily on the road, "that you wonder what made me so anxious for your company. Well, I'll tell you. In the village where I shall put up to-morrow afternoon, and which is forty odd miles on the road to Sydney, live some people I'm very fond of, who had a sailor friend that they've not heard of for a long while."

"Ah!" sighed Joshua; "I know what their feeling must be. Did they love him?"

"Love him! Well, you shall see for yourself; if, in return for the lift I am giving you, you won't mind talking to them a bit."

"I shall be glad to; it may remind me of my own friends."

"Where are your friends? — Now, Dozy!" this to the old mare, who had stopped suddenly short; "what d'ye stop for? The sense of the creature!" he added proudly, pointing to a bird some yards in front of them. "Get out of my way, little bird!"

"When I first heard you say that," said Joshua, "I was sure you had a kind heart."

"Fond of birds yourself, mate?"

"Very, very fond. The tenderest remembrances of my life are connected with them."

Ramsay cast a sharp glance at the half-savage.

"Been long among the Blacks, mate? or isn't the story true?"

"It's true enough. Long among them? Ay — years, but I don't know how long." Joshua, indeed, had lost count of time.

"From choice?"

"No; but I've told my story to no one yet. It would scarcely be believed. But tell me about your friends and the sailor."

"There's a mother there, that lost a son when she lost her sailor" — Joshua pressed his fingers to his face, and sobbed convulsively at the thought of his own dear mother, who had lost a son when she lost her sailor; and the mail-driver felt a choking in his throat, and had to wait a few moments before he could proceed. "And a father that lost a son at the same time. And a wife that lost a husband. And a friend that lost a friend. And a little child that can hardly be said to have lost a father, for she never saw her father's face."

"Merciful God!"

"What's the matter, mate?"

For Joshua was trembling — like a child; and great sobs came from his chest — like a man.

"You remind me — you remind me," sobbed Joshua. "Don't think me unmanly, don't think me mad. I have been sorely, sorely tried!"

Whereat Ramsay stopped the mare, and got out of the cart, and went into the bush to look for birds. He must have had a great difficulty in finding them, he was away so long; and the old mare stood perfectly still and contented the while, twitching her tail to knock off the flies, which was the only spirited action she was ever known to be guilty of. When they were jogging along again, they did not speak a word for a full hour, and then it was Joshua who spoke first, taking up the thread where it had been dropped.

"The child who has never seen her father — a girl then?"

"Yes, mate."

"How was it that she had never seen him?"

"Married her mother; went away to sea, and never heard of since."

"How old is the child?"

"Five years, I should say."

"If you knew," said Joshua in a slow trembling voice, "what a chord you have touched in my heart, you would pity me. Forgive me for my strange manner, and answer me. The mother who has lost a son; describe her."

"An angel. I'm not good at picking faces to pieces; but when I look at her, she reminds me of my own mother, dead and gone this many a year. Never thinks of herself; always putting herself out for other people — bless her old face! And yet she's not so old, although her hair is nearly white — that's from grief."

"The father who lost a son?"

"A fine fellow; a little self-willed and obstinate; a wood-turner."

A long, long silence. The mail-driver did not break it, nor did he intrude upon his companion's thoughts. "Twit-twit-

twit!" came from the throats of some diamond sparrows, which were flitting among the gum-tree branches and a flock of scarlet lowry parrots floated through the bush that lined the road on either side, their wonderfully-gorgeous plumage lighting up the dark trees with brilliant light.

"The wife that lost a husband, and the friend that lost a friend?"

"Treasures both; brother and sister."

"One other question — where do they come from?"

"London. I don't know what part."

A mist floated before Joshua's eyes, and he remained like one in a dream during the afternoon — wondering, hoping, fearing. When they were near to the village the following afternoon, Joshua said, —

"It may be that you have rendered me one of the greatest services that a man can possibly render another. If it be as I scarcely dare to hope, we shall know each other for long after this. Complete the service by doing one little thing more. Drive past the house where your friends live and point it out to me, so that I may descend and walk to it alone when we are at the end of your journey."

Ramsay nodded. It was about five o'clock when the mail-cart rattled into the village. The contractor for the mails always made a great clatter when he came in, as if he had been driving for his life — a fiction which, although no one believed in, he thought it desirable to keep up. "It looks government-like," he said.

Solomon Fewster is in the garden at the rear of the house, pleading his suit to Ellen for the twentieth time. She stands silent until he has finished a rhapsody, in which love and money are strangely commingled.

"Think of the time I have waited, Ellen," he says; "think of the constancy of my affection, and of the position I can offer you. I am making money fast, and only wait for you to say yes, to buy a house for us, which in three years will be worth three times what they ask for it. What is the use of your wasting your life in this out-of-the-way village when all the attractions of a city-life are open to you? Come now, give me your hand, and reward the man who has been your constant friend and lover, and who can make you rich."

But Ellen is insensible to the splendor of the offer; indeed, she is weary of it and him, and she tells him so spiritedly, and yet cannot repulse him. At length she says, —

"Mr. Fewster, there must be an end to this. I shall never, never marry again; and even if I did," she adds, to put a stop to what has become persecution, "I should not choose you;" and leaves him with this arrow in his heart.

He stands amazed. Not choose him! Why, a thousand girls would jump at him. Not here perhaps, for womankind was a scarce commodity; but at home, or anywhere where girls were more plentiful. Not choose him! He follows her into the house, wounded and mortified, and into Dan's room, where Mr. Marvel and Dan are at work. Mr. Marvel has all his tools, and does a great deal of wood-turning — having, indeed, more than he can do — and is putting by money. He scarcely looks up as Solomon Fewster walks in, somewhat defiantly; and as no one speaks to him, an awkward silence ensues upon his entrance; broken by Mr. Marvel, who, noticing Ellen's flushed face, observes, —

"Been teasing Ellen again, Mr. Fewster?"

"Teasing her, indeed!" exclaims Solomon Fewster loftily; "honoring her, I should say."

The flush upon Ellen's face deepens at this, and she casts such a look of aversion at Mr. Fewster that all the blood rushes into *his* face, and he says some injudicious words about ingratitude, and about what one might expect if one condescended to lower himself as he had done.

Upon this George Marvel starts to his feet in a great heat, and exclaims, —

"What do you mean by ingratitude, and by lowering yourself, Mr. Fewster? What gratitude do we owe you?"

"Ask Dan," says Mr. Fewster, — "ask Dan who it was bought his birds to keep you when you were starving, and when no one else would look upon you. But it serves me right for noticing you and helping you, instead of treating you as all your neighbors did. I ought to have known what return I might expect."

"And I dare say you got your return," says George Marvel, "when you sold Dan's birds at a good profit. As for Dan selling his birds to keep us from starving, that was no business of yours, so long as you got value for your money. That is a matter between Dan and me; and Dan's satisfied with the way that account stands, or I'm mistaken in him." Dan presses George Marvel's hand. "Thank you, Dan. Now, as to lowering yourself, Mr. Fewster. Do you mean to tell me that you would be lowering yourself if Ellen here was free to marry you, and would accept you? You mean-spirited dog! I'm a good deal older than you are; but if you were not in my house, I would thrash you for speaking as you have done, as I've thrashed others in Stepney when they let loose their lying tongues at us. Get out of the place, and never set foot in it again!" Attracted by the loud voices, Susan and Mrs. Marvel, with Ellen's child, have come into the room; and Mrs. Marvel now goes to her husband's side and lays her hand upon his arm. "Nay, Maggie — let be; I'm not going to hurt him; I wouldn't lay a finger upon him here; and I don't want to anywhere else; only, don't let him cross me if he says a word against us out of this house. — Dan!" he cries, "do you want to see Mr. Fewster here again?"

"No, sir; I think it will be best if Mr. Fewster will keep away from us."

"And you, Ellen? what do you say?"

"I never wish to see him again. For the sake of what is past, I would have been content to see him, if he would have ceased from persecuting me; but after what he has said to you, I hope he will leave us in peace."

"You hear," exclaims George Marvel; "we are happy enough without you. Go, and never darken this door again!"

Solomon Fewster looks round, almost savagely; his face is white with passion, and all the vindictiveness of his bad nature comes into play.

"You are happy enough without me!" he sneers, with his knuckles to his mouth. "Don't make too sure of that. I have been your friend hitherto. What if I now make myself your enemy? What if, when I go from this house, I spread about *my* version of your reason for leaving London? What if I tell your neighbors here of the real character of your sailor-hero, and how, because of his villany, all your friends turned their backs upon you" —

But he has no time to say more; for the door, which has been partly open, swings on its hinges, and Joshua enters.

Not one of them recognizes him. In his strange garb, with his fur-cap pulled over his eyes, and with his face covered with hair, no trace of Joshua is discernible; and yet they look at him spell-bound, waiting for him to speak. He gazes at the forms of all the dear ones, and grasps the back of a chair to steady himself. He takes them all in at a glance, and sees in one brief moment the changes in them that time has made. His mother's white hair; the deepened wrinkles in his father's face; Ellen more matronly than she was, but fair and pleasant to look at as when she was a girl; Susan, like an old woman; Dan grown a little stouter, and with the same dear boyish light in his eyes and on his face — but the child, clinging to Ellen's apron and looking at him wonderingly, with Ellen's eyes and his! —

He had thought, before he entered, that he would be strong, but he has no more control over himself for a few moments than a straw in a fierce wind. Then muttering, "Justice first!" he turns upon Solomon Fewster a glance of hate and scorn, and grasps him by the shoulder with so powerful a grasp, that Fewster writhes with pain.

"I heard your last words," he says. But directly he speaks, a thrill runs through them, and they are running towards him with outstretched arms, when he cries, —

"Stand off! By what strange chance I find you, I can scarcely imagine. But do not come nearer to me for a little while, or I shall fall dead at your feet!"

Awe-struck and trembling they obey him.

"I would not touch one of your dear hands till you have heard me and judged me, though death were the penalty for depriving myself of the joy! I would not receive one kiss from your honored lips upon my cheek till you have heard me and judged me, though I were sure that my tongue would be paralyzed in the utterance of what I have to say! Some part of your sufferings, some part of your pain, I know from my own suffering and pain, and I will clear myself before your eyes, so help me Thou! or go forever from my sight!"

Susan is running to him with cries of "Justice! justice!" and is about to throw herself upon him, when George Marvel's arm restrains and keeps her back. "Be still, madwoman!" he mutters sternly, and stands by her side, watchful of her, and no less watchful and attentive of every word that falls from his son's lips.

Joshua takes the cap from his head, and lets it fall to the ground, still keeping his strong grasp upon Solomon Fewster, whose cowardly blood grows thin as he writhes and listens.

"Justice!" echoes Joshua. "You shall have it, and so shall this base dog, whose presence pollutes the air I breathe. Listen well. Of another matter that we must speak of presently, and which is near and dear to all our hearts, I will say nothing before him. But in the 'Merry Andrew' in which I sailed from Gravesend, and which is now at the bottom of the sea, with many dear brave souls that were aboard her, was a villanous sailor — a Lascar, from whose hands I once rescued the woman who calls for justice, and who struck me down on that dreadful Christmas-eve when I first came home from sea. He shrinks and trembles beneath my grasp, this false friend, of whose bad heart I warned my brother Dan before the 'Merry Andrew' sailed. At one time during the voyage, when we were in danger, there was an attempt at mutiny, and this Lascar was one of the cowardly wretches who endeavored to spread dissatisfaction. When we were in dread peril, this Lascar sailor and a mutinous mate, whom we had to put in irons, strove hard to injure me and the captain — Heaven rest his soul! — and, happily, failed. The ship was wrecked, and we had to abandon her, and take to a raft which we had made; and on that raft we suffered more than six weeks hunger and thirst, and every species of misery. Out of the entire crew and passengers only seven were saved, among them being myself and this Lascar sailor and his confederate, the mutinous mate. Before the captain died, he appointed me to succeed in the command, and I have the record from the log-book about me now. We got ashore. How we lived, you shall hear from me by and by; but once the Lascar (whom we suspected of having killed his confederate) stole upon me, and but that I turned my head in time, I should not be here now to expose the villany of this cowardly wretch. Foiled in his devilish design, he told me then that he had been set to trap me, and was paid for it. Some time after that, I found the Lascar dead in the forest; and before I buried him — not wishing to leave a human creature, however vile, to be eaten by birds and beasts — I obtained evidence which proved to me that the wretch who writhes now within my grasp was the master who paid him to ruin, and perhaps to murder me."

"A clever lie," Solomon Fewster manages to say, though he is shaking with terror.

"A lie! I have the proofs. Be thankful that I have met you here, among those who are all that the world holds dear for me. If I had met you in the forest, in the midst of such scenes as I have witnessed lately, I would not have answered for your life."

Joshua hurls Solomon Fewster from him with such force that he falls, almost stunned, in the corner of the room. Then Joshua takes from his neck the bag containing his relics, and selects from them the silver watch and the document which Fewster had given the Lascar, and after reading aloud the document and the inscription on the watch, lays them upon the table.

"Here are the proofs of your crime and your villany," he says to Fewster. "Be thankful if you are allowed to escape punishment. Go, and go quickly, and without a word!" He stands aside to let the man pass; and Solomon Fewster, without a word or a look to any one there, passes out of the room, and out of the village. And is never seen in it again.

When they are alone, Joshua turns to Susan, and, in a softer voice, says, —

"Susan, you cried for justice. Upon me!"

"Yes, upon you. Where is Minnie? What have you done with Minnie?"

The big tears roll down Joshua's beard at the mention of her name.

"You think I took her away?"

"You know you did."

"Then truly, if all of you believe as Susan believes, my life is darker than the darkest night." With upraised hand he checks them from speaking; but he sees in their faces what gives him precious comfort. "When I went away from Gravesend," he says in a soft and gentle voice, "I had no knowledge that Minnie was aboard. When we got to Sydney I did not know it. My duties occupied all my time. We sailed from Sydney, and I was still in ignorance. But on the night the 'Merry Andrew' struck on the rocks I heard her voice for the first time. I suppose she thought that we were lost, and in her agony she made herself known to me; but I did not see her — the night was too dark. When I saw her the next day, I saw to my amazement that she had stained her face, and that her hair was not so long as she used to wear it. We were together on the raft. We were together on the shore. She was one of the seven who were saved. We lived together like brother and sister. When the savages discovered us, they had a strange fancy respecting her, and she obtained great influence over them. She used all her influence to protect me, and but for her I should have lived and died where the tribe we fell amongst chiefly wandered — in the north, many hundreds of miles from here." He takes from his bag Ellen's portrait, the lock of her hair he had cut before he left Gravesend, and Dan's Bible. He places these on one side. "What is left, Dan, is yours. This tress, cut not many weeks ago; this paper, which she desired me to give you, and which I have never read; this earth, which I gathered from her grave! Before she died, she sent you all her dearest love, and a kiss for mother, Dan, and Ellen. She died pure as she had lived, dear, faithful, mistaken heart! As I hope for redemption, I speak the truth. If you believe me, take me to your hearts again, and let me live in them as I know I once lived!"

As he once lived! as he had always lived! They cluster round him, and kiss him, and sob over him. Had he not been saved from the deep — ay, and from greater perils — to comfort them? And they put his little daughter in his arms, who asks, hearing that he was her father, "Has God sent my father back? God is very good."

O good faithful mother! can this great bearded man be your son? Not often can such a cluster of loving hearts be seen — faithful to each other, believing in each other's goodness and purity, in face of terrible adverse circumstance. Their faithfulness is a proof of their own worth. To the pure all things are pure. But hush! for Minnie's last words; Dan is reading them aloud.

"I have learned, too late, the consequences of my fault. But I, and I alone, am to blame. No one knew it; no one suspected it; no one aided me in it. I am writing this upon a page of Dan's Bible, and it seems to me like an oath. I cannot live long. I am dying. But a long-life's devotion could not repay Joshua's brotherly care. All good angels guard him and you! If Joshua is preserved to give you this — and I believe he will be — think, while you read it, that my spirit is near; and forgive me, dear Dan and Ellen. My love to you both, and to good Mrs. Marvel and Joshua's father; and to Susan, who must have no bad thoughts of Joshua. God bless you, and send you happiness!

"MINNIE."

Dan and Joshua sit talking together until late in the night. Ellen and Mr. and Mrs. Marvel are sitting up also, but in another part of the house. They know that Dan wants to speak to Joshua of Minnie, and they leave the friends undisturbed.

What is said to each other by the two faithful friends cannot be written here; but it may be easily understood by those who have read these pages. Joshua tells Dan as much as time will allow of his and Minnie's lives, and is tender and indignant in turns, as Dan relates to him the history of the family in Stepney after the sailing of the "Merry Andrew." Be sure that the Old Sailor is not forgotten. If tender speech and loving thought are worth any thing, the Old Sailor is rich indeed.

Their eyes are wet with tears, and their hands are in each other's clasp. Joshua has just finished his relation of Minnie's death, and of her words about the river — "So restless there, so quiet here!" — when a knock comes at the door, and Ellen enters. He takes her in his arms, and they sit, the three of them, and talk in a state of wondering happiness.

Another knock at the door — Mr. and Mrs. Marvel. The magnetism of love has drawn them all together.

"It reminds me of the night before you first went to sea, Jo," says Dan. Do you remember? The knocks at the door one after another."

"Josh," said George Marvel to his son, a fortnight afterwards, "what are you going to do?"

"What do you mean, daddy?" asked Joshua in return.

"What do I mean? Well, you don't want to go to sea again?"

"No, I shouldn't like to leave Ellen and Dan and all of you again."

"Well, then, what are you going to do? You must do something."

Mrs. Marvel sat silent, and smiled a little smile, but very slyly, so that no one should see it.

"You can get plenty of work as a wood-turner, daddy?"

"Yes, Josh, a good deal more than I can do — and well paid for it too."

"Well, daddy, I think " —

"Yes, Josh, you think " —

"I think I'll learn wood-turning, if you'll teach me."

Whereupon George Marvel, after the slightest amount of hesitation, rose and kissed his wife.

www.ingramcontent.com/pod-product-compliance
Lightning Source LLC
Chambersburg PA
CBHW031825230426
43669CB00009B/1223